1981

NEUROBIOLOGICAL BASIS OF LEARNING AND MEMORY

ORGANIZING COMMITTEE

Osamu Hayaishi (Chairman)
Department of Medical Chemistry, Faculty of Medicine, Kyoto University, Kyoto 606, Japan

Yasuji Katsuki
National Center for Biological Sciences, Okazaki, Japan

Yasuzo Tsukada
Department of Physiology, Keio University, School of Medicine, Tokyo, Japan

Hiroshi Yoshida
Department of Pharmacology, Osaka University Medical School, Osaka, Japan

Teruo Nakajima (Secretary General)
Department of Neuropharmacology and Neurochemistry, Institute of Higher Nervous Activity, Osaka University Medical School, Osaka, Japan

PROGRAM COMMITTEE

Yasuzo Tsukada (Chairman)

Yutaka Nagata (Vice-Chairman)

Masao Ito

Hiroaki Niki

Sakutaro Tadokoro

SPONSOR

The Taniguchi Foundation

NEUROBIOLOGICAL BASIS OF LEARNING AND MEMORY

Edited by

Yasuzo Tsukada
Bernard W. Agranoff

A WILEY MEDICAL PUBLICATION
JOHN WILEY & SONS
New York • Chichester • Brisbane • Toronto

THE SECOND TANIGUCHI SYMPOSIUM OF BRAIN SCIENCES

Library of Congress Cataloging in Publication Data

Taniguchi Symposium of Brain Sciences, 2d, Ōtsu, Japan, 1978.
Neurobiological basis of learning and memory.

(A Wiley medical publication)
The symposium, which was held Oct. 24–25, 1978, at Ōtsu, Japan was sponsored by the Taniguchi Foundation.
Includes index.
1. Learning—Physiological aspects—Congresses.
2. Memory—Physiological aspects—Congresses.
3. Neurobiology—Congresses. I. Tsukada, Yasuzō, 1922– II. Agranoff, Bernard W., 1926–
III. Taniguchi kōgyō shōrei kwai. IV. Title.

QP408.T36 1978 ∘ 153.1′5 79-24605
ISBN 0-471-05148-9

Printed in the United States of America

10 9 8 7 6 5 4 3 2 1

Symposium Participants

Bernard W. Agranoff
Department of Biological Chemistry, Neuroscience Laboratory, The University of Michigan, Ann Arbor, Michigan, U.S.A.

Per Andersen
Institute of Neurophysiology, University of Oslo, Oslo, Norway

Horace B. Barlow
Physiological Laboratory, Cambridge University, Cambridge, England

Eberhard E. Fetz
Physiology and Biophysics, University of Washington, School of Medicine, Seattle, Washington, U.S.A.

József Hámori
First Department of Anatomy, Semmelweis University Medical School, Budapest, Hungary

Yoshiki Hotta
Department of Biophysics, Faculty of Science, Tokyo University, Tokyo, Japan

Masao Ito
Department of Physiology, School of Medicine, Tokyo University, Tokyo, Japan

Shin-ichi Kohsaka
Department of Physiology, Keio University, School of Medicine, Tokyo, Japan

Arata Kubota
Laboratory of Physiological Psychology, Faculty of Literature, Waseda University, Tokyo, Japan

Hisashi Kuribara
Division for Behavior Analysis, Behavior Research Institute, School of Medicine, Gunma University, Japan

Yasushi Miyashita
Department of Physiology, School of Medicine, Tokyo University, Tokyo, Japan

Noburo Mizuno
Department of Anatomy, Faculty of Medicine, Kyoto University, Kyoto, Japan

Tetsuhide H. Murakami
Department of Physiology, Okayama University, Medical School, Okayama, Japan

Yutaka Nagata
Department of Physiology, Fujita-Gakuen University, Tokyo, Japan

Teruo Nakajima
Department of Neuropharmacology and Neurochemistry, Institute of Higher Nervous Activity, Osaka University, School of Medicine, Osaka, Japan

Hiroaki Niki
Department of Psychology, Faculty of Letters, Tokyo University, Tokyo, Japan

Alberto Oliverio
Laboratory of Psychobiology and Psychopharmacology, National Research Council, Rome, Italy

Steven P. R. Rose
Biology Department, The Open University, Milton Keynes, England

Sakutaro Tadokoro
Department of Behavioral Analysis, Institute of Behavioral Medicine, Gunma University, Japan

Jun Tanji
Department of Physiology, School of Medicine, Hokkaido University, Sapporo, Japan

Keisuke Toyama
Department of Physiology, School of Medicine, Tokyo University, Tokyo, Japan

Yasuzo Tsukada
Department of Physiology, Keio University, School of Medicine, Tokyo, Japan

Hiroshi Yoshida
Department of Pharmacology, Osaka University School of Medicine, Osaka, Japan

Masataka Watanabe
Department of Psychology, Faculty of Literature, Tokyo University, Tokyo, Japan

Shigeru Watanabe
Department of Psychology, Faculty of Literature, Tokyo University, Tokyo, Japan

Preface

The search for a biological basis of behavioral change remains among the most challenging in science. The pursuit is in no small measure responsible for the recent rise of neurobiology as a discipline. New disciplines borrow heavily from existing ones, and in this case, biochemistry, pharmacology, psychology, physiology, genetics, and morphology, as well as the clinical sciences have served as the sources.

It is timely that the Taniguchi Foundation, having recently made a commitment to extend its goals into the brain sciences, has now turned to questions of learning and memory. This volume is itself a "memory" of such an effort, in the form of a symposium, held October 23–25, 1978 at Ohtsu-shi, Japan. The various aforementioned approaches have been applied to further our understanding of learning and memory and of brain plasticity in general. An important aim of this meeting was to exchange information and to strengthen lines of communication between young Japanese and visiting scientists. As might be predicted, cultural and linguistic barriers are minor compared with those between the scientific disciplines. Hopefully, the meeting served to help bridge the disciplinary gaps and to widen scientific horizons for the participants. To preserve the informality necessary for free exchange, the meeting was a small one. Consequently, this volume should be considered a sampling from a vast field rather than a comprehensive summation. The participants are grateful to Mr. Toyosaburo Taniguchi and the Taniguchi Foundation for sponsoring this meeting. The publication of this book marks the fiftieth year of the Foundation's efforts in the dissemination of knowledge.

Yasuzo Tsukada
Bernard W. Agranoff

Left to right. *Front row:* M. Watanabe, E. E. Fetz, Y. Tsukada, B. W. Agranoff, S. P. R. Rose, A. Oliverio, H. B. Barlow, P. Andersen, J. Hámori, and Y. Nagata. *Back row:* A. Kubota, H. Kuribara, S. Tadokoro, M. Ito, S. Watanabe, H. Niki, T. Murakami, S. Kohsaka, J. Tanji, Y. Hotta, Y. Miyashita, N. Mizuno, K. Toyama, and T. Nakajima.

Contents

NEUROBIOLOGICAL BASIS OF LEARNING AND MEMORY

1
Plasticity During Neuronal Differentiation: An Experimental Morphological Study of Developing Synapses and of Neuronal Networks

József Hámori

The genetically inherited capabilities of nerve cells and of neuronal networks do not automatically materialize during maturation. The proper expression of intrinsic potentialities is made possible by the remarkable developmental plasticity of the differentiating nerve elements. The main source of plasticity during brain development is—as known from the studies of Ramón y Cajal (43–45)—the excess neurons and, especially, neuronal processes. This results in a relative overdevelopment of synaptic connections during synaptogenetic processes. Through a selective process, the use or disuse of the neuronal elements and synapses will then determine which nerve cells, neuronal processes, and synaptic connections can survive. Only properly linked and functioning neurons and networks will be stabilized, whereas numerous "erroneous" or simply "unnecessary" nerve elements will be eliminated (3,6,9,41).

The aim of this chapter is to demonstrate that the same natural selection law, by "trial and error," also operates at the subneuronal level in the development of synaptic junctions.

QUANTITATIVE ELECTRON MICROSCOPY OF DEVELOPING SYNAPTIC JUNCTIONS

In the adult nervous system the chemical synaptic junction is characterized by the presence of an accumulation of synaptic vesicles and of dense projections opposite the presynaptic membrane, as well as of a varying amount of osmiophilic material adhering to the postsynaptic membrane ("thickening") (Fig. 1-5). The synaptic cleft varies from 10 nm to 30 nm in interneuronal synapses.

Considerable differences of opinion exist about the nature of the earliest structural events associated with synaptic development. Glees and Sheppard (11), Hâmori and Dyachkova (18), Larramendi (29), Alley (1), Spira (52), Bunge et al (4), Matthews and Faciane (34), and McArdle et al (35) have suggested that the first signs of impending synaptic development are desmosomoid membrane thickenings of presynaptic and postsynaptic membranes. Occhi (37) and Sheffield and Fischman (47), on the other hand, have observed an accumulation of vesicles in advance of any membrane thickening. In a more recent study of the synaptic differentiation of local interneurons in monkey lateral geniculate nucleus (20), it was found, however, that although synaptic vesicles in the newborn are present in the presynaptic dendritic processes, the profiles are exclusively postsynaptic until the end of the second postnatal week. Only at this time, after the appearance of postsynaptic thickenings, will the synaptic vesicles exhibit the characteristic presynaptic accumulation and will the neuronal process consequently become also presynaptic. Bodian (2) suggested that the two events, that is, the development of synaptic membrane thickenings and the accumulation of presynaptic vesicles, appear simultaneously. Indeed, from recent studies of the differentiation of cerebellar mossy fiber synapses (21), it is apparent that both mature and immature synapses (Figs. 1-13–1-15) can be found at a very early stage of synapse development. (Synaptic contacts exhibiting both presynaptic vesicle accumulation and an enhanced osmiophily of the synaptic membranes are considered "mature" [Fig. 1-5]; those having only postsynaptic membrane thickening [e.g., Figs. 1-1, 1-2], "immature.") Similarly, immature contacts on Purkinje and basket cell bodies (Figs. 1-1, 1-3, 1-4), as well as on Purkinje dendritic spines (Figs. 1-6, 1-7), could be also observed during early differentiation of these synaptic contacts, accompanied by the simultaneous appearance of more mature synaptic contacts (e.g., Fig. 1-4). It was also observed that during the synaptogenetic period, which occurs between one to five weeks postnatally, there was a gradual numerical diminution, and by the sixth week the immature contacts completely disappeared from rat cerebellar mossy terminals (21). This led to the logical assumption that the immature contacts have been transformed during synapse differentiation to mature synaptic junctions. Using quantitative electron microscopy, however, we have gained good evidence, at least for the two synaptic junctions studied, that this is not the case.

1. The *optic terminal* in the newborn monkey's lateral geniculate nucleus is in a relatively advanced developmental stage. Nevertheless, as was shown in an earlier study (40), it exhibits both mature and immature asymmetric (synaptic) as well as symmetric contacts with the dendritic processes of the principal neurons (Figs. 1-8,–1-10).

Figure 1-3. A transient form of immature synaptic contact between a basket terminal (ba) and Purkinje cell soma (P) from 14 dpn rat cerebellum. Early signs of differentiation of presynaptic dense projections (ringed arrows) are seen in addition to the presence of postsynaptic "thickening" (arrows). The synaptic vesicles in the axon terminals are ovoid or polymorphic (×78,300).

Figure 1-4. Mixture of mature (arrows) and immature (thick arrow) axosomatic synapses on basket neuron (*b*) from 14 dpn rat cerebellar cortex (×42,630).

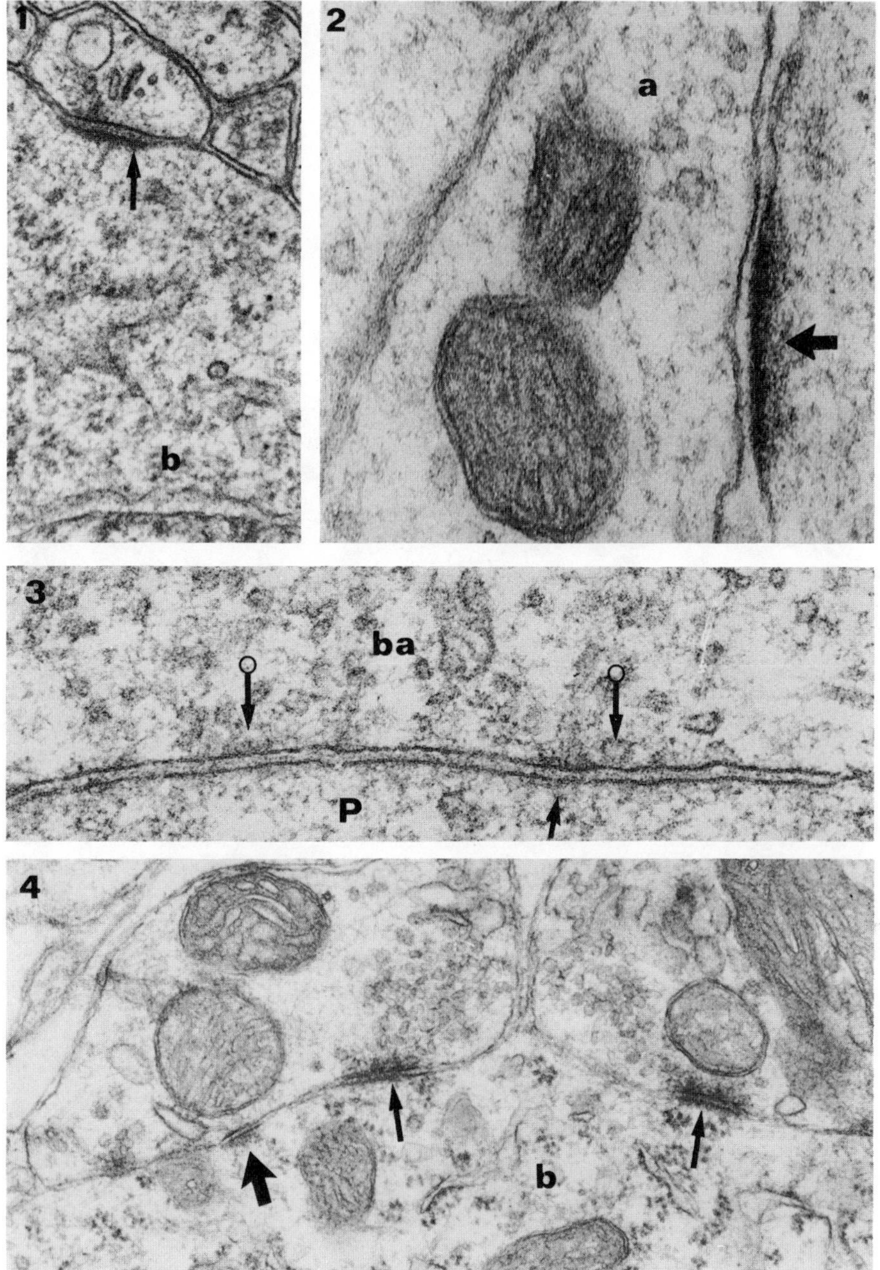

Figure 1-1. Immature axosomatic contact (arrow) on a differentiating basket neuron (b) in a 14 dpn rat cerebellar cortex (×4263).

Figure 1-2. Immature axondendritic synaptic contact from 6 dpn dog lateral geniculate nucleus. Note the presence of scattered synaptic vesicles in the axon terminal (a) but the absence of vesicle accumulation opposite to the well-developed postsynaptic membrane (arrow) (×97,440).

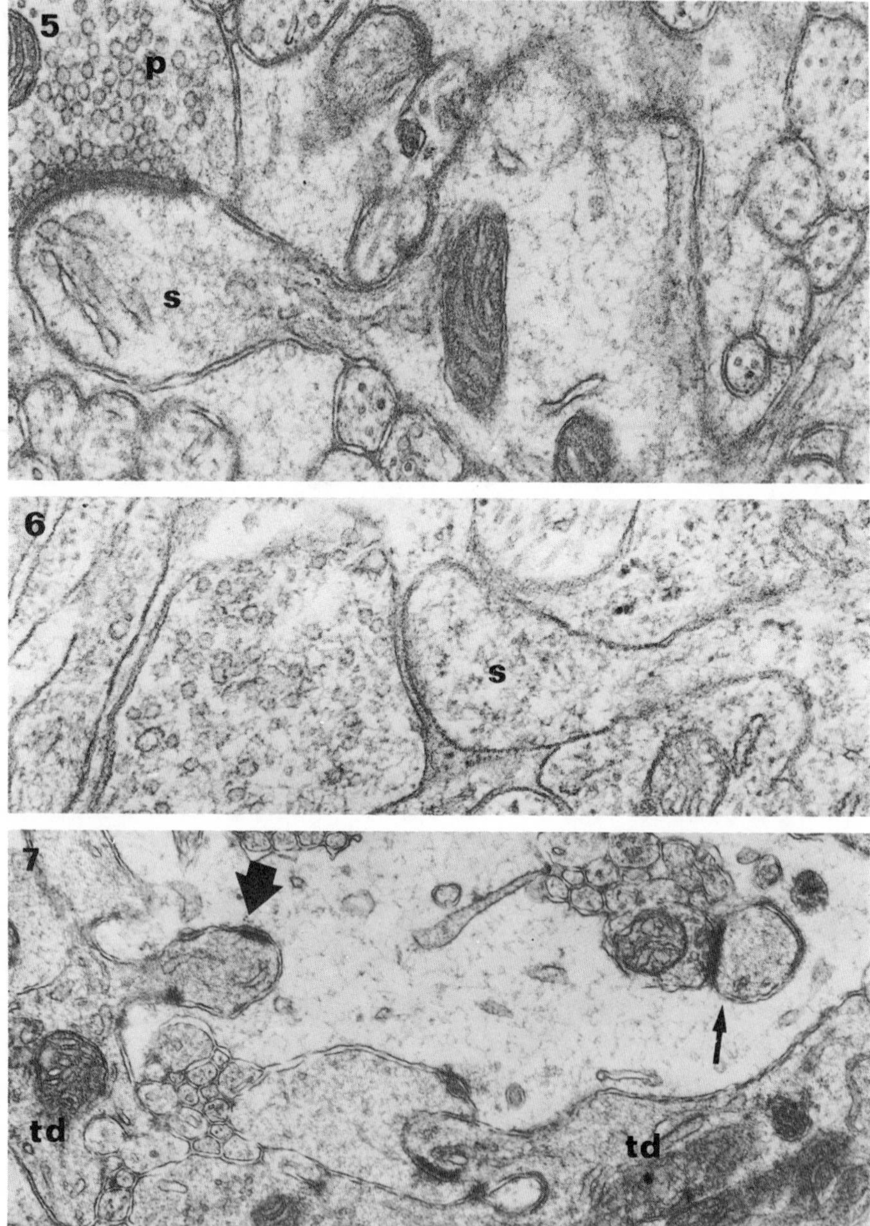

Figure 1-5. A typical axon-spine synapse between a parallel fiber (p) and a tertiary dendritic spine (s) of cerebellar Purkinje cell. Adult rat cerebellar cortex (×49,590).

Figure 1-6. A developing, not fully matured, axon-spine synapse from 15 dpn rat cerebellar cortex for comparison with Figure 1-5. s: dendritic spine (×56,550).

Figure 1-7. Synaptic (arrow) and nonsynaptic (thick arrow) tertiary dendritic spines of Purkinje cell from 11 dpn rat cerebellar cortex. Note the presence of postsynaptic membrane "thickening" on the nonsynaptic spine, which is contacted, however, only by glial process. td: tertiary dendrite (×27,840).

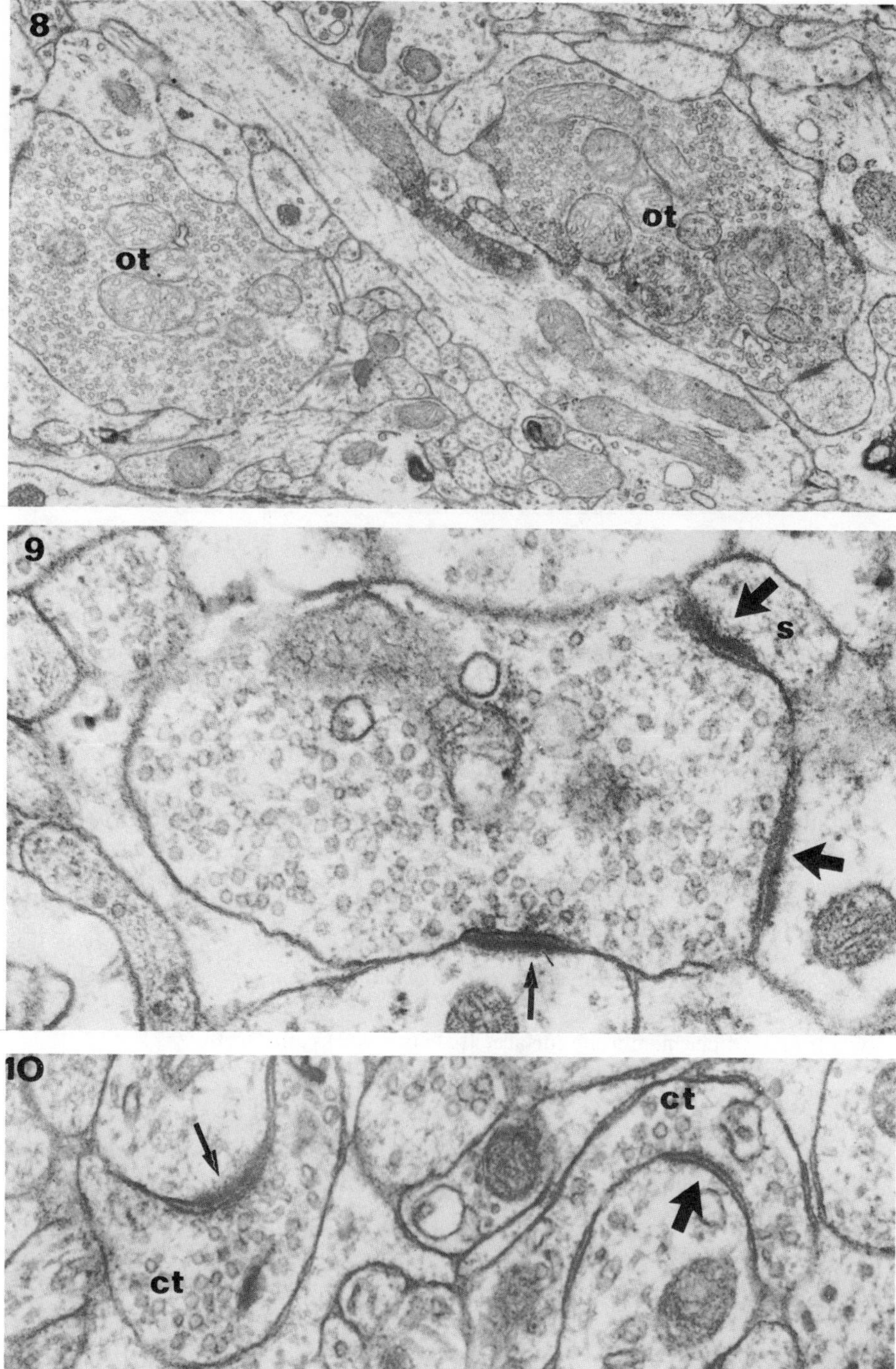

Figure 1-8. Two optic terminals (ot) from lateral geniculate nucleus of newborn monkey. The axon terminals are surrounded by vesicle-bearing presynaptic dendrites and by principal cell dendritic processes (×24,360).

Figure 1-9. Mature (arrow) and immature (thick arrows) synaptic contacts between optic terminal and postsynaptic dendrites and dendritic spines (s). Lateral geniculate nucleus (LGN), newborn monkey (×56,550).

Figure 1-10. Mature (arrow) and immature (thick arrow) axodendritic synaptic contacts between cortical terminals (ct) and postsynaptic dendritic processes in newborn monkey LGN (×56,550).

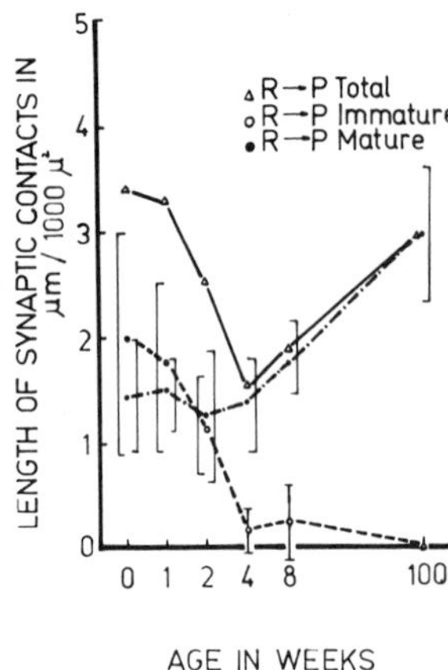

Figure 1-11. Diagram showing the results of quantitative measurements on electron micrographs from developing LGN of monkey. Note that increase in the number of mature retino-principal synapses begins only after the apparent disappearance of immature contacts between the two synapsing elements. R: retinal terminal, P: projective neuronal dendrites.

Between 0 and 28 postnatal days (dpn) there is a definite decrease in asymmetric contacts, which is caused by the gradual disappearance of immature contacts. Contrary to our expectations, however, the decrease in the number of immature contacts is not accompanied by a simultaneous increase in the number of mature synaptic junctions, which will occur only after the almost complete disappearance of the immature contacts (Fig. 1-11).

2. The same trend characteristizes the developing mossy fiber synapse in the cerebellar cortex of the rat. At the beginning of synapse differentiation, that is, 6 dpn, mature and immature synaptic contacts occur simultaneously (Figs. 1-13–1-15). The number of both contact types increases until about the twelfth postnatal day. From the seventeenth postnatal day onward, simultaneously with the pronounced development of the characteristic labyrinthine structure of the synaptic glomerulus (Fig. 1-12), a definite diminution in the number of immature contacts can be observed (Figs. 1-16,1-17). At the same time, however, the number of mature contacts exhibits the same decline and, after a steady decrease, will reach the adult level, that is, 5.5% of the whole mossy fiber membrane surface, at about 8 weeks after birth.

These observations clearly show that during early synaptogenesis there is an excess offer of synaptic contacts, both mature and immature. It is also obvious from both examples (optic and mossy terminals) that most of the immature contacts are not transformed to mature, permanent synaptic contacts but will simply be absorbed, together with many already mature contacts, with progression of the differentiation of the whole synaptic complex. This indicates that elementary synaptogenesis consists of a secondary selection accomplished by the disappearance—possibly as a consequence of disuse—of the excess of immature or otherwise nonfunctioning synapses.

ROLE OF PRESYNAPTIC ELEMENTS IN THE DEVELOPMENT OF POSTSYNAPTIC STRUCTURES

The next logical question to be raised is whether the development (and overdevelopment) of postsynaptic junctional complexes is an autonomous process, independent of the connectivity of the particular neurons, or if this plastic process of synapse differentia-

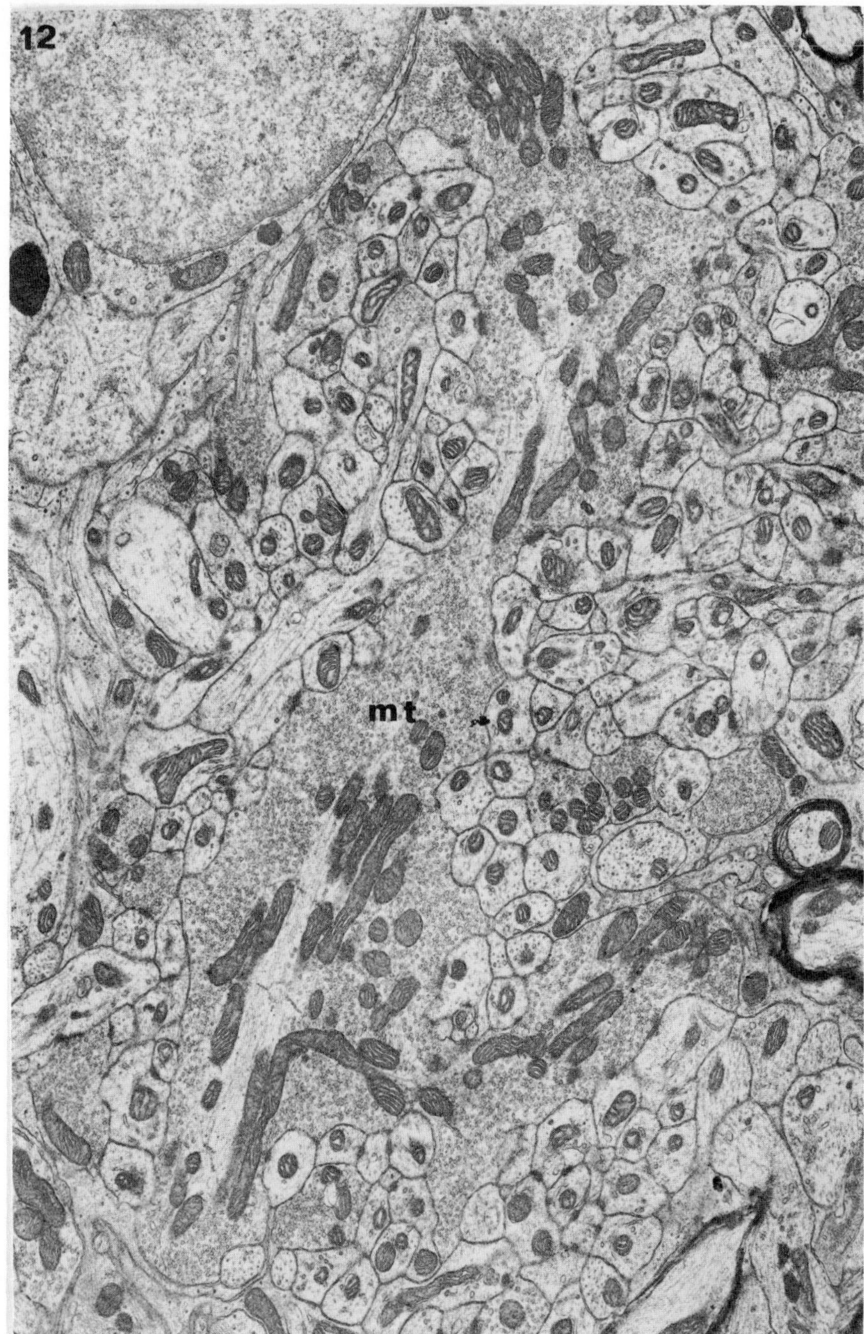

Figure 1-12. Cerebellar glomerulus from adult rat cerebellar cortex. The central big mossy terminal (mt) is surrounded by numerous postsynaptic dendrites and dendritic digits of granule neurons. Synaptic contacts are all mature by morphological criteria (×13,050).

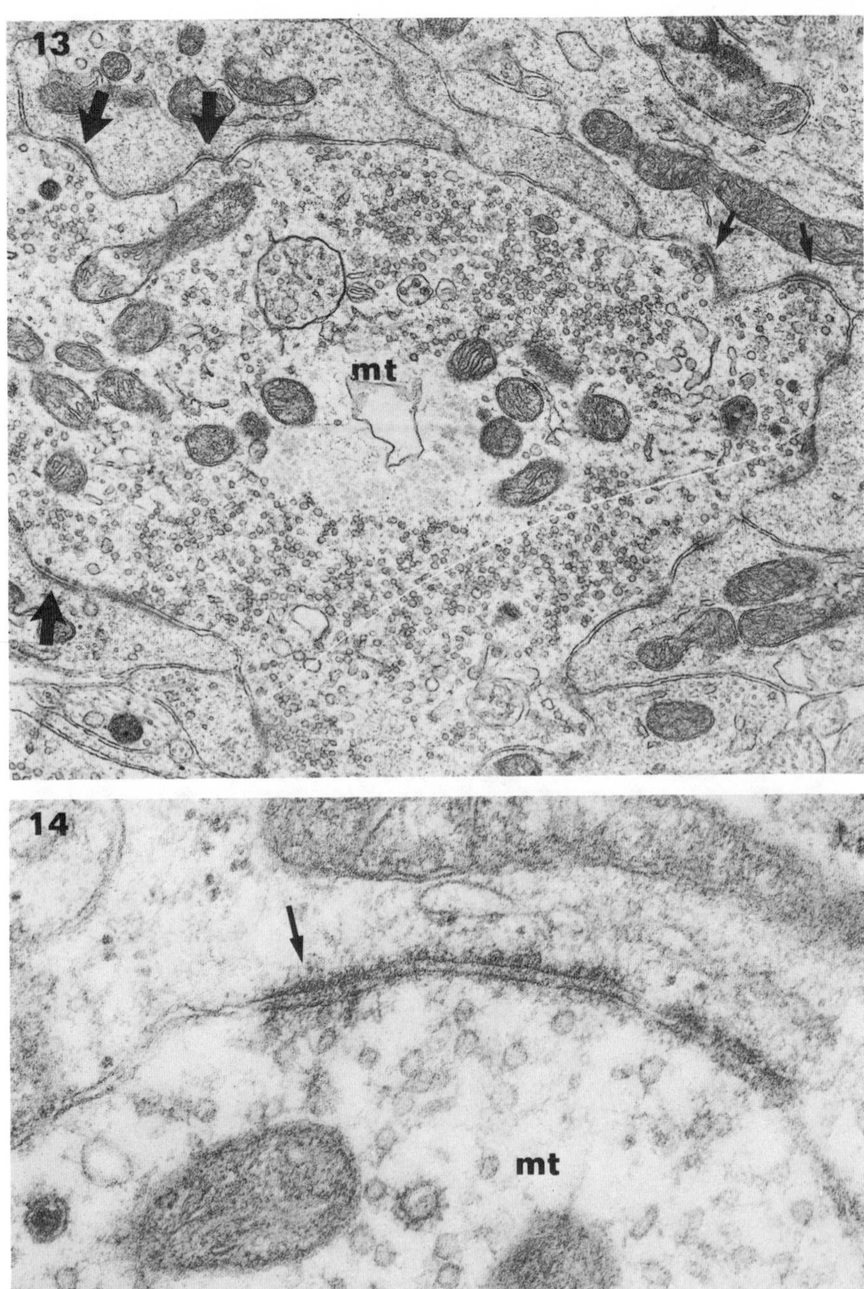

Figure 1-13. Maturing cerebellar glomerulus from 14 dpn rat cerebellar cortex. A few "mature" synaptic contacts (arrows) can be detected with simultaneous appearance of immature or transient type of synaptic contacts (thick arrow) (×24,360.)

Figure 1-14. Mossy fiber (mt) to granule cell dendrite synapse from 14 dpn rat cerebellum: the larger portion of the contact is of immature type lacking synaptic vesicle accumulation at the presynaptic membrane. Only small area (arrow) shows indication of mature synaptic contact (×84,390).

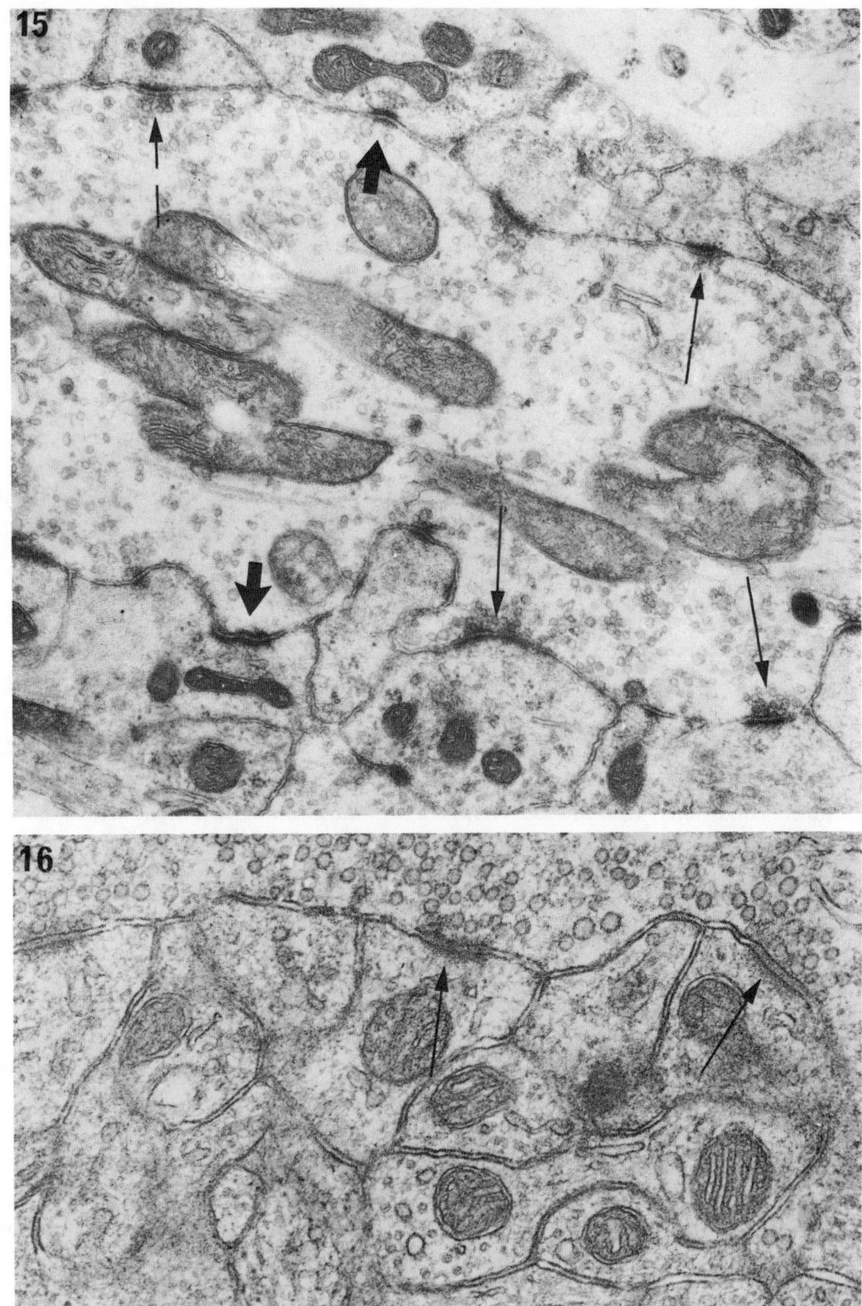

Figure 1-15. Part of a cerebellar glomerulus from 18 dpn rat cerebellum. Arrows point to mature synaptic junctions; thick arrows, to immature and desmosome-like contacts (×28,710).

Figure 1-16. Synaptic contacts (arrows) from 30 dpn rat cerebellum are exclusively "mature" by morphological criteria (×49,590).

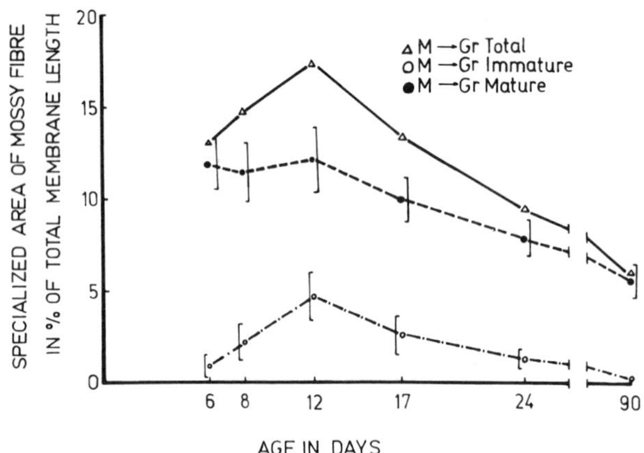

Figure 1-17. Quantitative electron microscope measurements of developing mossy fiber synaptic contacts (mature and immature) in the cerebellar cortex of the rat. M: mossy terminal, Gr: granule cell dendrites.

tion is influenced by the afferents to the differentiating nerve cells. As for the development of the postsynaptic (membrane) specializations, the evidence available so far is not sufficient to give a satisfactory answer. In dissociated nerve cell culture, in which the neurons develop in the absence of extrinsic and intrinsic connections (28), no development of postsynaptic specializations was observed (as long as the nerve cells of the culture did not contact each other). One has to consider in this case, however, the rather unnatural conditions for the surviving neuroblasts and neurons, which make it hazardous to draw any firm conclusion about the validity of such observations.

Another approach that reveals the possible role of connectivity in the development of postsynaptic structures, widely used by the neurobiologist, is the deafferentation or functional deprivation of certain centers during early differentiation in vivo. From most of these experiments and observations it appears that final maturation of dendritic arborization, and especially of the development of dendritic, synaptic spines, is dependent in various degree on the presence (and also on the normal functioning) of the presynaptic afferents (13,49,50,54,58). From these experiments it became clear that the inductive effect by the presynaptic afferents on the developing postsynaptic neuronal structures is time dependent. Prenatal deafferentation of developing cochlear and vestibular centers in which the neurons receive only one or two kinds of synaptic inputs (30,38) (up to day 11 of the developing chick embryo), did not affect the early differentiation of the nerve cells. Later, however, the maturation of the deafferented neurons (including the development of normal dendritic arborizations) was severely affected, demonstrating the decisive role of synaptic connections in the completion of differentiation (and maintenance) of the nerve cells Although deafferentation of nerve centers in a later period, that is, postnatally, severely impairs the differentiation of synaptic connectivity, as seen in studies on visual system differentiation after visual deprivation (7,23,60), it does not result in a similar regression of the dendritic trees or in the dramatic cell loss seen after prenatal deafferentation. In fact, there is now ample evidence to state (50) that the earlier the deafferentation or functional deprivation of a particular nerve center, the more severe the effect on differentiation of neuronal and postsynaptic structures.

Naturally, the critical period, when neuronal differentiation is most sensitive to the presence or absence of extrinsic or intrinsic afferents, differs from cell type to cell type. The degree of sensitivity to deafferentation might also be remarkably different for each cell type. The cerebellar Purkinje cells in tissue culture explant, for example, when taken from newborn animal (42,48), develop primary and secondary dendrites (but not the spiny, tertiary branchlets), but if taken from rat fetus (day 15–16), develop only abortive dendrite-like processes (39,61). Interneurons at the same time in the same tissue explant develop a more mature dendritic tree showing that extrinsic afferents are not as important for their differentiation as they are for the Purkinje neurons.

The mechanism by which presynaptic afferents exert their inductive (trophic?) effect on the development of postsynaptic structures might also be different in the various systems studied so far. Two main types of presynaptic induction (as an inference from deafferentation or deprivation studies) can be recognized: direct and indirect (15,16).

Direct Induction

Dendritic spines of the projective neurons in the lateral geniculate nucleus of the dog or kitten (54) fail to develop if the newborn's eyelids are sutured. The synaptic articulation surface of the projective neuronal dendrites significantly diminishes in spite of the presence and contact of morphologically normal appearing optic terminals. Similarly, visual deprivation by dark raising and enucleation (58,59) or by destruction of the lateral geniculate nucleus (LGN), the main source of specific afferents to the visual cortex, resulted in a significant diminution in the number of spines over the central portion of the apical dendrites of pyramidal cells. Conversely, Schapiro and Vukovich (46) described an increase in the number of dendritic spines of the cortical neurons in rats raised under enriched environmental conditions. Similarly, extensive neocortical ablations in newborn dogs and kittens result in a transneuronal corticopontocerebellar atrophy of the contralateral cerebellar hemisphere caused mostly by an underdevelopment of the postsynaptic dendritic digits, while the presynaptic mossy terminals appear nearly unchanged morphologically (14). It was shown (17,57) that even the next synapse in this neuronal chain, that is, the parallel fiber–Purkinje cell dendritic spine synapse, is affected by this corticopontocerebellar, transneuronal process. Interestingly, the number of spines did not change, but their size was considerably reduced.

Early entorhinal lesions, also in the rat, exhibited a very similar transneuronal effect through the mossy terminals on the differentiation of the dendritic region of hippocampal CA3 neurons (10). Again, the most affected mossy axon terminal appeared morphologically normal. On the other hand, the number of postsynaptic spines, as well as the synaptic articulation surface, was significantly decreased.

On the basis of these experiments it can be suggested that for the normal, full differentiation of postsynaptic structures of certain neurons (LGN projective neurons, cerebellar granule cell dendrites, etc.) the presence of and contact by normally functioning presynaptic afferent is necessary. Using functional deprivation as a tool, the striking observation was made that it is always the postsynaptic dendritic structure that shows remarkable morphological signs of regression or underdifferentiation, whereas the presynaptic axon terminals appear (morphologically) practically unchanged. The reduction of postsynaptic articulation surface after deprivation in all systems studied results in the diminution of established synaptic sites—as described by Cragg (7)—for the visually deprived visual cortex.

Indirect (Heterotopic) Induction

The idea that the development of postsynaptic structures, for example, dendritic spines, are induced during differentiation by an afferent with which the spines do not establish synapse emerged originally from the contradiction between the apparent spine loss of the apical dendrites in the cortex (13,58,59) after visual deprivation and the fact (53) that specific afferents, thought to terminate on apical dendrites, actually synapse only with the basal dendrites of the same pyramidal neurons. The apical dendritic spines, in fact, are supplied by axonal arborizations of a local interneuron, which incidentally also receives synaptic input from the specific afferents. It was theorized, therefore, that the atrophy of apical dendritic spines after visual deprivation might be a transneuronal effect through the local interneurons or the result of a loss in excitatory impulses or some other trophic information reaching the pyramidal cells normally—by the visual afferents—over the basal dendrites, or both. In other words, the specific afferents would induce the host pyramidal cells to develop postsynaptic receptors (spines) for intrinsic axon terminals at a distance from their own termination area.

A similar indirect induction mechanism for the development of the spiny branchlets and their spines in cerebellar Purkinje cells was suggested (15,16), since these spines of the tertiary dendritic branches synapse exclusively with parallel fibers. It was shown, however, in different experimental models that the presynaptic parallel fibers are not necessary for the differentiation of the tertiary spines, which not only develop in the absence of their presynaptic partners but also exhibit the characteristic postsynaptic thickenings (16,22,32,55).

Even in normal development (Fig. 1-7) similar "empty" spines covered by glial processes can occasionally be found accompanied by maturing parallel fiber–spine synapses. Also, as mentioned previously (57), the functional deprivation of the mossy fiber–parallel fiber system does not change the number of contacted tertiary spines. Therefore, the hypothesis was put forward (15,16) that the other extrinsic afferent to the Purkinje cell, the climbing fiber, which otherwise establishes synaptic contact with the primary and secondary dendrites and the dendritic spines, but not with the spines of the tertiary branchlets, would induce heterotropically the differentiation of spines for their natural presynaptic partners, these parallel fibers. In fact, this hypothesis was in agreement with earlier observations (27) and was later also corroborated by other studies (26) demonstrating the importance of climbing fiber input in the formation of Purkinje dendrites. The results of the tissue culture experiments by Privat and Drien (42) showing that in cerebellar explants taken from newborn animals primary and secondary dendrites and their spines developed but no spiny branchlets were differentiated, can be taken also as an indication that climbing fibers are in fact necessary for the development of these tertiary dendritic structures. The appearance of primary and secondary dendritic spines and of synapses contacted by intrinsic axons shows again the critical importance of the age of the cerebellum from which the tissue culture was taken: explants in these experiments (42) were taken from postnatal cerebella. Although the climbing fibers do not make synaptic contact in newborn rats, they are located near or at the Purkinje cell body in an "arrested" position. The observation (39,61) that in explants from prenatal cerebella (i.e., before the ingrowing of the climbing fibers) and other extrinsic afferents, even primary and secondary dendrites, differentiation is very poor, a clear indication of the importance of climbing fibers in the normal maturation of Purkinje dendrites, and especially of tertiary branchlets.

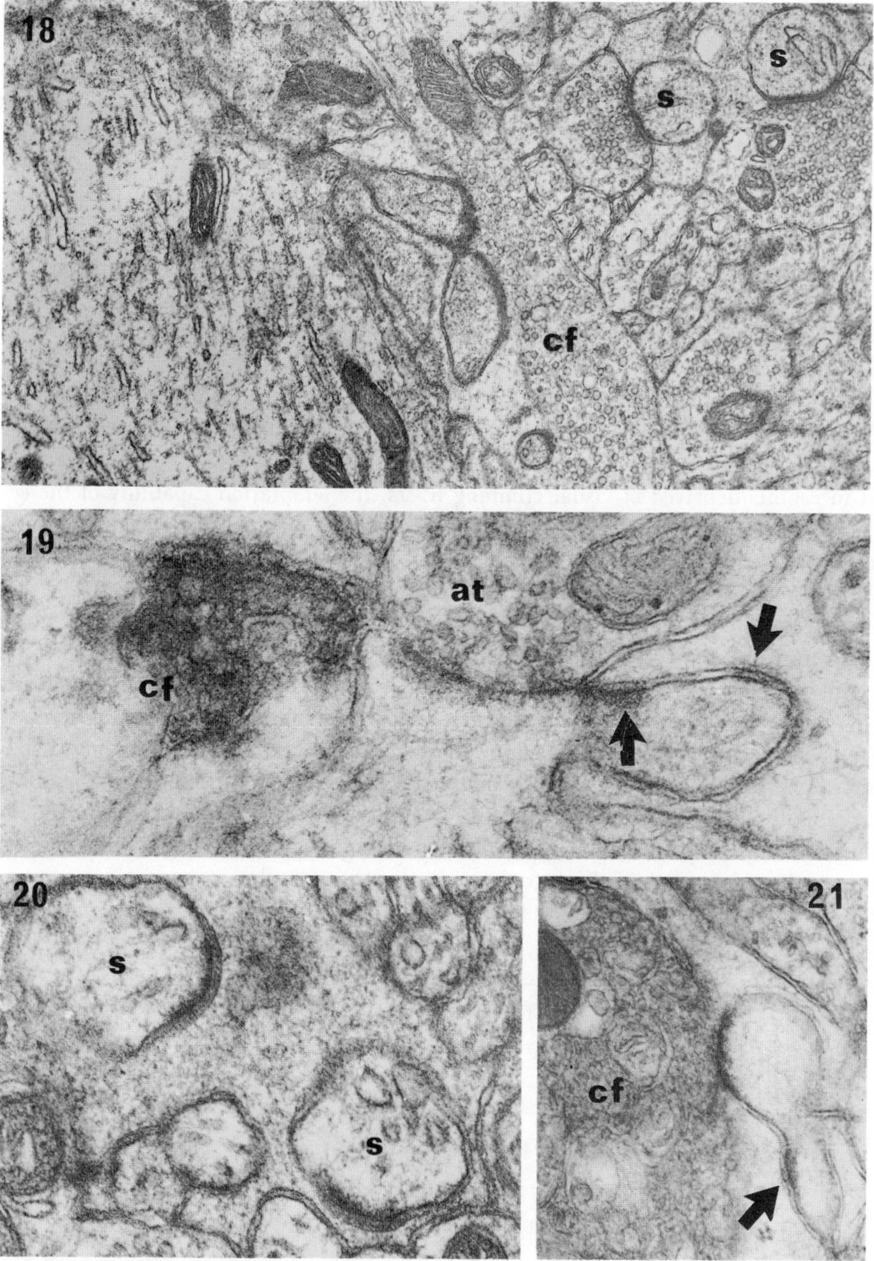

Figure 1-18. Climbing fiber (cf) synapsing with spines of the secondary dendrites. Tertiary dendritic spines (s) contacting parallel fibers are less dense than the secondary dendritic spines. 30 dpn rat (×24,360).

Figure 1-19. Degenerating climbing fiber (cf) 1 day after cutting of the inferior peduncle in 3-week-old rat. Note secondary dendritic spines with synaptic thickening (arrow) after being vacated by climbing fiber. Intact axon terminal (at) exhibiting ovoid vesicles is of local origin (×56,550).

Figure 1-20. Vacant but persisting secondary dendritic spines (*s*) with postsynaptic thickenings; 21 days postnatally, 1 day after climbing fiber destruction (×51,330).

Figure 1-21. Secondary dendritic spine with vacant postsynaptic site (arrow) 1 day after climbing fiber (cf) destruction. Adult rat, cerebellar cortex (×43,500).

In recent experiments in our laboratory, we cut the inferior peduncle (the route for the olivocerebellar climbing fibers to the cerebellum) of different aged young rats and let the animals survive for 1 to 7 days. We observed that there is a different degree of spine loss in the hemispheres, and that there is an especially marked spine atrophy in the paraflocculus (Fig. 1-22). This spine loss can be attributed exclusively to the atrophy of the tertiary dendritic spines; as was shown by Sotelo et al (51), the destruction of climbing fibers in the adult does not result in the disappearance of secondary dendritic spines which the climbing fibers originally contacted. We found similar secondary dendritic spine survival in developing animals after olivocerebellar deafferentation (Figs. 1-18–1-21).

These observations appear to corroborate the hypothesis put forward by Marr (33) about a "teachers" role of the olivocerebellar climbing fibers in supposed cerebellar learning. Relevant to this is the work by Ito and coworkers (24,25), who have shown that in rabbits deprived of visual climbing fibers, the adaptation capability of the cerebellum in horizontal vestibulo-ocular reflex was lost. They also have evidence that, in addition to their role in adaption, climbing fibers from the inferior olive appear to be involved in the maintenance of the normal activities of Purkinje cells.

As the mechanism of induction of postsynaptic structures by presynaptic axons—either direct and indirect—one might assume a specific presynaptically released trophic substance to operate. Nothing certain is known so far about this supposed inductive, trophic material. It is perhaps relevant to mention here that in the developing cerebellar cortex we have found (19) an unusual myelinization of Purkinje dendrites and of the cell bodies of Golgi inhibitory interneurons after the selective destruction of climbing fibers. Interestingly those parts of the Purkinje dendrites and interneuronal cell bodies that originally were in contact with climbing fibers were myelinated. This finding seems to indicate that the trophic effect (or its absence) is not always synaptic-connectivity specific, but other nonspecific effects must also be accounted for.

No. of animals	Postnatal day of operation	Survival time	Cerebellar region investigated	No. of spines on 1000 μ^3			Surface fraction of spines %		Volume of one spine μ^3		Spine density in 1000 μ^3	
				op.	con.	sign. diff.	op.	con.	op.	con.	op.	con
3	8d	7d	haemisph. lob.V.	247,5	429,0	p>0,01	5,61	7,84	0,144	0,091	388	795
3	8d	7d	paraflocc.	61,6	194,0	p>0,001	1,68	4,16	0,195	0,132	88	315
4	11d	7d	haemisph. lob.V.	233,3	301,4	p>0,01	4,59	3,67	0,118	0,102	389	640
4	30d	1d	paraflocc.	325,6	550,0	p>0,001	3,87	6,02	0,057	0,049	680	1206
4	30d	1d	haemisph. lob.V.	477,4	443,6	0	6,26	6,36	0,064	0,073	976,6	866,9

Figure 1-22. Values of quantitative measurements of dendritic spines in the molecular layer of developing rat cerebellar cortex after inferior peduncle destruction.

SUMMARY

From quantitative electron microscopic studies on the development of synaptic contacts during synaptogenesis it can be concluded that in this developmental stage there is a characteristic excess offer of postsynaptic membrane complex. Most of the immature contacts and many of the mature-like synaptic junctions disappear by the end of the synaptogenetic period. This clearly shows that elementary synaptogenesis is characterized by a secondary selection accomplished by the disappearance of possibly unused protosynaptic immature or synaptic structures. By this process, synaptogenesis as a plastic and selective process of differentiation is comparable with the (over)development and excess offer by differentiating dendritic and axonal processes preceding and during synaptogenesis.

Experimental evidence also favors the proposition that the development of postsynaptic structures and the final shaping of postsynaptic dendritic arborizations requires the presence and normal functioning of presynaptic (extrinsic or intrinsic) axons. This presynaptic inductive effect is most pronounced at about the time of synaptic differentiation of the nerve cells, whereas early nerve cell process differentiation is probably directed exclusively or at least primarily by intrinsic factors. Naturally the development of postsynaptic structures is undoubtly a preprogrammed, inherent property of the particular neuron, and the presynaptic induction obviously is only the "push" needed for manifestation of the inherited properties. The degree to which inherent properties are manifested depends, however, on functional parameters brought to the cell by the presynaptic inductive axon terminal(s). It makes the whole process of presynaptic induction a very selective, plastic event, at least for the establishment of neuronal networks and circuitry with different and differentiation-dependent qualities of synaptic organization.

The most common feature of presynaptic induction is the direct induction, which is brought about by direct contact between the inductor axon and the differentiating postsynaptic structures. Another type of (heterotropic) induction is more indirect and is thought to occur with such neurons as cortical pyramidal and cerebellar Purkinje cells, for example (the term *heterotopic* means that the development of a particular postsynaptic structure is induced by an axon that does not terminate on the developing structure but on other regions of the same neuron). This morphological finding coincides with the findings of other functional studies (12,24) and with Marr's hypothesis (33) about the role of climbing fibers in the supposed learning of cerebellar Purkinje neurons.

Finally it is suggested that nerve cells of different centers exhibit very different degrees of developmental plasticity. The more the synaptogenetic period and synaptic differentiation of particular nerve cell depends on presynaptic afferentation, the more plasticity can be expected for the establishment of neuronal networks of high quality. Conversely, those neurons, which develop their synaptic properties relatively independently of presynaptic influences, contribute to the neuronal circuitry in a predetermined, rigid manner. It is interesting, in this respect, that neurons of invertebrates, which maintain and probably also develop their characteristic dendritic arborization patterns independently of extrinsic factors, (56) appear to belong to the second type, whereas pyramidal and Purkinje neurons in vertebrates, who are supposed to have special learning abilities, clearly belong to the class of neurons with more plastic synaptic differentiation.

REFERENCES

1. Alley KE: Quantitative analysis of the synaptogenetic period in the trigeminal mesencephalic nucleus. *Anat Rec* 177:49–60, 1973.
2. Bodian D: Development of fine structure of spinal cord in monkey fetuses. II. Pre-reflex period to period of long intersegmental reflexes. *J Comp Neurol* 133:113–166, 1968.
3. Brown MC, Jansen JKS, Van Essen D: Polyneural innervation of skeletal muscle in new-born rats and its elimination during maturation *J Physiol* 261:387–422, 1976.
4. Bunge MB, Bunge RP, Peterson EP: The onset of synapse formation in spinal cord cultures as studied by electron microscopy. *Brain Res* 6:728–749, 1974.
5. Cowan WM: Anterograde and retrograde transneuronal degeneration in the central and peripheral nervous system, in Nauta WJH, Ebbeson SO (eds): *Contemporary Research Methods in Neuroanatomy.* Berlin, Springer Verlag, 1970; pp 217–251.
6. Cowan WM: Neuronal death as a regulative mechanism in the control of cell number in the nervous system, in: *Development and Aging in the Nervous System.* New York, Academic Press, 1973, pp 19–41.
7. Cragg BT: The development of synapses in kitten visual cortex during visual deprivation. *Exp Neurol* 46:445–451, 1975.
8. Crepel J, Delhaye-Boushaud N, Legrand J: Electrophysiological analysis of the circuitry and of the corticonuclear relationships in the agranular cerebellum of irradiated rats. *Arch Ital Biol* 114:49–74, 1976.
9. Crepel F, Mariani J, Delhay-Boushaud N: Evidence for a multiple innervation of Purkinje cells by climbing fibers in the immature rat cerebellum. *J Neurobiol* 6:567–578, 1976.
10. Frotscher M, Hámori J, Wenzel J: Transneuronal effects of entorhinal lesions in the early postnatal period of synaptogenesis in the hippocampus of the rat. *Exp Brain Res* 30:549–560, 1977.
11. Glees P, Sheppard BL: Electron microscopical studies of the synapses in the developing chick spinal cord. *Z Zellforsch* 62:356–362, 1964.
12. Gilbert PFC, Thach WT: Purkinje cell activity during motor learning. *Brain Res* 128:309–328, 1977.
13. Globus A, Scheibel AB: Loss of dendritic spines as an index of pre-synaptic terminal patterns. *Nature (Lond)* 212:463–465, 1966.
14. Hámori J: Development of synaptic organization in the partially agranular and in the transneuronally atrophied cortex, In Llinás R (ed): Chicago, American Medical Association, 1969, pp 845–858.
15. Hámori J: Developmental morphology of dendritic postsynaptic specializations, in Lissák K (ed): *Recent Development of Neurobiology in Hungary* Vol 4. Budapest, Akadémiai Kiadó, 1973, pp 9–37.
16. Hámori J: The inductive role of presynaptic axons in the development of postsynaptic spines. *Brain Res* 62:337–344, 1973.
17. Hámori J: Plastic changes in the cerebellar cortex. *Exp Brain Res,* suppl 1, 1976, pp 130–132.
18. Hámori J, Dyatshkova LN: Electronmicroscope studies on developmental differentiation of ciliary ganglion synapses in the chick. *Acta Biol Acad Sci Hung* 15:213–230, 1964.
19. Hámori J, Lakos I: Myelinated dendrites in partially deafferented developing cerebellar cortex, in: *Neurosci Letters.* Abstract of the Second European Neuroscience Meeting, Florence, Italy, Neled Suppl. Amsterdam, Elsevier, North-Holland, 1978, p 146.
20. Hámori J, Pasik P, Pasik T: Postnatal differentiation of "presynaptic dendrites" in the lateral geniculate nucleus of the rhesus monkey. *Advances in Neurol* 12:149–161, 1978.
21. Hámori J, Somogyi P: Quantitative aspects of cerebellar mossy fiber synapse differentiation during ontogenesis. *Developmental Neurosci* (in press).
22. Herndon RM, Margolis G, Kilham L: Virus induced cerebellar malformation. An EM study. *J Neuropathol Exp Neurol* 28:164, 1969.
23. Hubel DH, Wiesel TN Binocular interaction in striate cortex kittens reared with artificial squints. *J Neurophysiol* 28:1041–1059, 1964.
24. Ito M: Cerebellar learning control of vestibulo-ocular mechanisms. In Desiraju T (ed): *Mechanisms in Transmission of Signals for Conscious Behavior.* Amsterdam, Elsevier, 1976, pp 376.
25. Ito M, Miyashita Y: The effects of chronic destruction of the inferior olive upon visual modification of the horizontal vestibulo-ocular reflex of rabbit. *Proc Jap Acad* 51:716–720, 1975.

26. Kawaguchi S, Yamamoto T, Mizuno N, Iwahori N: The role of climbing fibers in the development of Purkinje cell dendrites. *Neurosci Letters* 1:301–304, 1975.

27. Kornguth SE, Scott G: The role of climbing fibers in the formation of Purkinje cell dendrites. *J Comp Neurol* 146:61–82, 1972.

28. Kruger L, Hámori J, Miller R, et al: Electron microscopic studies of dissociated cells from chick embryo cerebrum in single layer cultures. *Anat Rec* 166:333, 1970.

29. Larramendi, LMH: Analysis of synaptogenesis in the cerebellum of the mouse. In Llinás R (ed): *Neurobiology of Cerebellar Evolution and Development.* Chicago, American Medical Association, 1969, pp 803–844.

30. Levi-Montalcini R: Regressione sacondaria del ganglio ciliare dopo asportazione della vesicola mesencefalica in embrione di pollo. *R Acad Naz dei Lincei,* 3:144–146, 1947.

31. Levi-Montalcini R: The development of the acoustic-vestibular centers in the chick embryo in the absence of the afferent root fibers and of descending fiber tracts. *J Comp Neurol* 91:209–242, 1949.

32. Llinás R, Hillman DE, Precht W: Neuronal circuit reorganization in mammalian agranular cerebellar cortex. *J Neurobiol* 4:69–94, 1973.

33. Marr D: A theory of cerebellar cortex. *J Physiol* 202:437–470, 1969.

34. Matthews MA, Faciane CL: Electron miscroscopy of the development of synaptic patterns in the ventrobasal complex of the rat. *Brain Res* 135:197–215, 1977.

35. McArdle CB, Dowling JE, Masland RH: Development of outer segments and synapses in the rabbit retina. *J Comp Neurol* 175:253–273, 1977.

36. Morest DK: The growth of dendrites in the mammalian brain. *Z Anat Entwickl-Gesch* 128:290–317, 1969.

37. Ochi J: Electron microscopic study of olfactory bulb in rat during development. *Z Zellforsch* 76:339–349, 1967.

38. Parks TN, Robertson J: The effects of otocyst removal on the development of chick brain stem auditory nuclei. *Anat Rec* 184:479–498, 1976.

39. Palacios-Prü E, Palacios L, Mendoza RV: In vitro vs in situ development of Purkinje cells. *J Neurosci Res* 2:357–362, 1976.

40. Pasik T, Pasik P, Hámori J: Quantitative aspects of synaptogenesis in monkey dorsal lateral geniculate nucleus (LGNd). *Exp Brain Res* 23(suppl):156, 1975.

41. Prestige MC: Differentiation, degeneration and the role of the periphery: quantitative considerations. In Schmitt FO (ed): *The Neurosciences II.* New York, Rockefeller University Press, 1970, pp 73–82.

42. Privat A, Drien MJ: Postnatal maturation of rat Purkinje cells cultivated in the absence of two afferent systems: An ultrastructural study. *J Comp Neurol* 166:201–244, 1976.

43. Ramón y Cajal S: Sur l'origine et les ramifications des fibres nerveuses de la moelle embryonaire. *Anat Anz* 5:111–119; 609–613, 631–639.

44. Ramón y Cajal S: *Degeneration and Regeneration of the Nervous System,* May RM (trans). New York, Hafner, 1928.

45. Ramón y Cajal S: *Studies on Vertebrate Neurogenesis.* Charles C Thomas, Springfield, Ill, 1960. (Revision of a 1929 edition).

46. Schapiro S, Vukovich KR: Early experience upon cortical dendrites: a proposed model for development. *Science* 167:292–294, 1970.

47. Sheffield JB, Fischman DA: Intercellular junctions in the developing neural retina of the chick embryo. *Z Zellforsch* 104:405–418, 1970.

48. Seil FJ, Hendon RM: Cerebellar granular cells in vitro. A light and electron microscope study. *J Cell Biol* 45(2):212–220, 1970.

49. Smith DE: The effect of deafferentation on the postnatal development of Clarke's nucleus in the kitten. A Golgi Study. *Brain Res* 74:119–130, 1974.

50. Smith DE: The effect of deafferentation on the development of brain and spinal nuclei. *Progr Neurobiol* 8:349–367, 1977.

51. Sotelo C, Hillman DE, Zamora AJ, et al: Climbing fiber deafferentation: its action on Purkinje cell dendritic spines. *Brain Res* 98:547–581, 1975.

52. Spira AW: In utero development and maturation of the retina of a nonprimate mammal: A light and electron microscopic study of the guniea pig. *Anat Embryol* 146:279–300, 1975.

53. Szentágothai J: Synaptology of the visual cortex, in Jung R (ed): *Handbook of Sensory Physiology,* VII/3B. Springer Verlag, 1973, pp 269–324.

54. Szentágothai J, Hámori J: Growth and differentiation of synaptic structures under circumstances of deprivation of function and of distant connections, In Barondes SH (ed): *Cellular Dynamics of the Neuron.* New York, Academic Press, 1969, pp 301–320.

55. Thomas H, Hartkop MS, Jones MZ: Methylazoxymethanol-induced aberrant Purkinje cell dendritic development. *J Neuropathol Exp Neurology* 36(3):519–532, 1977.

56. Tweedle CD, Pitman RM, Cohen MJ: Dendritic stability of insect central neurons subjected to axotomy and de-afferentation. *Brain Res* 60:471–476, 1973.

57. Uzunova R, Hámori J: Quantitative electron microscopy of the cerebellar molecular layer in corticopontocerebellar atrophy. *Acta Biol Acad Sci Hung* 25:117–122, 1974.

58. Valverde F: Apical dendritic spines of the visual cortex and light deprivation in the mouse. *Exp Brain Res* 3:337–352, 1967.

59. Valverde F: Structural changes in the area striata of the mouse after enucleation. *Exp Brain Res* 5:247–292, 1968.

60. Wiesel TN, Hubel DH: Effects of visual deprivation on morphology and physiology of cells in the cat's lateral geniculate body. *J Neurophysiol* 26:978–993, 1963.

61. Woodward DJ, Seiger A, Olson L, et al: Intrinsic and extrinsic determinants of dendritic development as revealed by Golgi studies of cerebellar and hippocampal transplants in oculo. *Exp Neurology* 57:984–998, 1977.

2
Influence of Deafferentation on the Synaptic Organization in the Inferior Olivary Nucleus: A Quantitative Electron Microscopic Study in the Cat

Noboru Mizuno
Akira Konishi
Yasuhisa Nakamura
Sakashi Nomura
Kazuo Itoh
Tetsuo Sugimoto

INTRODUCTION

There is considerable morphological evidence for neuroplasticity in the mature mammalian central nervous system (for recent reviews, cf. refs. 1–5). Studies of the responses of neurons to injuries are thought to provide information on the capacity of the neuronal system to change its patterns of connections. Electron microscopic studies have suggested that denervated synaptic sites on neurons in partially deafferented areas in the central nervous system could be reoccupied with axon terminals supplied by collateral sprouting or by the shifting of intact axon terminals existing locally, even in adult animals, in the ventrobasal complex of the thalamus of the mouse (6); in the ventral cochlear nucleus (7), lateral vestibular nucleus (8), superior colliculus (9), septal nuclei (10,11), dentate gyrus (12,13), and pyriform cortex (14) of the rat; in the lateral geniculate nucleus of the rabbit (15); in the nucleus gracilis (16), lateral cuneate nucleus (17), spinal trigeminal nucleus (18), and red nucleus (19) of the cat; and in the spinal cord of the rat and monkey (20–22).

The most convincing evidence of this phenomenon in the mature mammalian brain was presented by Raisman (23). He showed that, in the medial septal nucleus of the rat, afferent fibers from the medial forebrain bundle terminated both on the soma and dendrites, while the fimbrial fibers from hippocampal areas were restricted in termination to the dendrites, and that several weeks after a lesion of the medial forebrain bundle the fimbrial fibers gave rise to terminals occupying somatic sites (10).

Similar findings were reported in the red nucleus of the cat electrophysiologically as well as electron microscopically: The magnocellular red nucleus neurons are known to receive axosomatic and axodendritic afferent fibers, respectively, from the cerebellar interpositus nuclei and the cerebral cortex (24–27). Tsukahara et al (28,29) observed in cats with chronic lesions in the cerebellar nuclei that the rise times of EPSPs evoked in the red nucleus neurons by stimulating the cerebral corticorubral fibers became shorter progressively for 4 to 10 days after destruction of the cerebellar interpositus nuclei. They explained this phenomenon as resulting from the sprouting of corticorubral axodendritic fibers onto "vacated" areas on somatic membranes and proximal portions of dendrites of the red nucleus neurons deafferented from cerebellorubral axosomatic fibers (30–32).

This conclusion was supported by our electron microscopic study (19): In cats allowed to survive for more than 3 weeks after placing lesions first in the interpositus nuclei, electron-dense degenerated axosomatic terminals were found on the red nucleus neurons 2 to 4 days after the second operation in the frontal cortex. Since degenerated axosomatic terminals of cerebellorubral fibers were proved to disappear completely in 3 weeks after the first operation in the interpositus nuclei, the degenerated axosomatic terminals found in the red nucleus after the second operation in the cerebral cortex were considered to be corticorubral axon terminals that sprouted or shifted from dendritic portions to make new synaptic contacts on neuronal somata of red nucleus neurons deafferented chronically from cerebellorubral fibers. There were few axosomatic terminals arising from corticorubral fibers, however, and our quantitative electron microscope study on sequential changes of synaptic organization in the red nucleus deafferented chronically from cerebellorubral fibers provided no unequivocal evidence for reinnervation of vacated synaptic sites by preexisting intact axon terminals in the region (33).

In view of these previous findings the present study was undertaken to analyze quantitatively the changes of axon terminals in the areas of the inferior olivary nuclei of the cat after deafferentation from spinal or mesencephalic fibers.

METHODS

The present study was based on the examination of samples of the inferior olive (IO) obtained from 17 cats ranging in weight from 2.5 to 4.3 kg . Of the 20 cats used, 16 were allowed to survive for 2 to 35 days after hemicordotomy in the second cervical cord segment (10 cats) or after placing rather large electrolytic lesions stereotaxically in the red nuclear regions of the midbrain (6 cats); the remaining 4 cats were served for controls. Of these cats, 3 normal cats, 9 cats with spinal lesions, and 4 cats with midbrain lesions were the same animals used in the previous studies (34,35). Surgical procedures were carried out under deep general anesthesia (sodium pentobarbital, 35–40 mg/kg IP), and all cats were treated postoperatively with antibiotics.

Two to 35 days after the operation the cats were deeply anesthetized with an overdose of pentobarbital and perfused intravitally through the ascending aorta with 1.5–2 liters of a mixture composed of 4% paraformaldehyde, 0.5% glutaraldehyde, and 0.002% calcium chloride in Millonig's phosphate buffer adjusted to pH 7.3. Perfusion was extended over a period of 15 minutes from a height of about 1 m. After perfusion, the caudal portions of the brain stem were removed immediately and sectioned transversely at 150 μm thickness on a Vibratome (Oxford Laboratories, Foster city, California) floated on a bath of perfusion fixative. Subsequently, small tissue slices containing the IO areas were cut with fresh razor blades under a dissecting microscope. Thin tissue slices were then postfixed for 40 to 60 minutes in a chilled 2% solution of osmium tetroxide in the same buffer used for preparing the perfusion fixative. Embedding was performed in an epoxy resin after dehydration in a graded series of ethanol.

The location of the IO areas was again verified in semithin sections, which were cut from each block and stained with 0.5% toluidine blue in 1% borax; caudolateral portions of the medial and dorsal accessory olive and the middle areas of the dorsal lamella of the principal olive were selected. Thin sections for electron microscopy were cut on an LKB Ultratome III 8800, stained on uncoated or collodion-coated copper grid with lead acetate (36) or lead citrate (37), and viewed with a Hitachi HU-12 electron microscope. The location and extent of the lesion in each of the operated cats were verified histologically as described elsewhere (34).

Counting of Axon Terminals

On the basis of the shape of synaptic vesicles, both axosomatic (AS) and axodendritic (AD) axon terminals were categorized into terminals with round vesicles (R-type) and those with pleomorphic ones (P-type: mixture of varying ratios of round and elongated synaptic vesicles).

In the central parts of each grid hole (120–130 μm diameter), 21 rectangular fields ($21 \times 67.4\ \mu m^2$) of the neuropil were photographed serially at an initial magnification of 10,000×, and subsequently enlarged on paper to a final magnification of 25,000×. On these prints, the numbers of axon terminals of each category were counted. From these data, the relative numbers of the two types of axon terminals were calculated. The density of AD terminals (number of AD terminals per 100 μm^2 of the neuropil) was also estimated.

Calculation of the Density of Axosomatic Synaptic Terminals

In the electron microscope, somatic profiles of nerve cells cut through the nuclear plane were sampled randomly, and the number of axon terminals with synaptic active zones on these somatic profiles were counted through direct inspection of the actual section at high magnification (20,000–30,000×). Subsequently these somatic profiles were photographed with a magnification of 2000–5000×. The sheet film (8 × 9 cm) were printed to a final magnification of 5000–20,000×. Some of these prints were taped together to form montages of neuronal somata. On these prints or montages the length of the membrane of the soma was measured with an odometer; dendritic membranes were excluded. From these data, the density of AS terminals with synaptic active zones per 100 μm length of the cell membrane on each somatic profile was calculated. Using the photographs of somatic profiles cut through the nucleolar plane, the longest and shortest diameters of each somatic profile were measured, and the mean of these values was recorded.

Measurement of the Size of Profiles of Axodendritic Axon Terminals

Measurement of the size of each profile of AD terminals was attempted with the aid of an electronic graphic calculator (Imagelyzer HTV-C995, Hamamatsu Television Co., Hamamatsu, Japan). From the electron micrographs of the neuropil taken randomly as described above, contours of AD terminals were traced on transparent tracing papers with black ink; the R-type or P-type terminals were traced on a separate paper. Each of the closed areas thus demarcated with black ink on the tracing papers was measured automatically with the electronic graphic calculator.

Statistical Analysis

Values obtained from the operated cats were compared with those from the unoperated animals by χ^2-test to determine significance. In the case of histograms, statistical significance was tested by the Kolmogorov-Smirnov test.

RESULTS

Of the various subdivisions of the inferior olive, the caudolateral portions of the medial and dorsal accessory olive (MAO and DAO) were selected for the observation in the cats with lesions in the spinal cord, and the middle areas of the dorsal lamella of the principal olive (PO) were chosen in the cats with lesions in the midbrain, because spinal or mesencephalic fibers were reported to terminate most numerously in these portions of the inferior olive (IO) (38–45).

Observations on Unoperated Cats

Most of the ultrastructural characteristics of cat IO neurons reported previously were substantiated in the present study. The frequent occurrence of the intranuclear inclusions (46) and the casual appositions between a soma and a dendrite, between neuronal somata, and between crossing dendrites (46) were confirmed. Of 87 intranuclear inclusions identified in the present study, 8 were of the lattice type (47,48) and 79 were of the rodlet type (48,49). On rare occasions, somatic spines, perikaryal myelin, and the gap junctions between dendrites (46) were also observed.

For each neuronal somatic profile cut through the nucleolar plane, the largest and smallest diameters were measured. The mean of these values ranged from 13.1 to 28.7 μm with an average of 18.1 μm in the MAO (36 profiles), from 13.4 to 27.9 μm with an average of 17.5 μm in the DAO (34 profiles), and from 13.8 to 23.0 μm with an average of 18.3 μm in the PO (30 profiles).

The density of AS synapses (the number of AS terminals with synaptic active zones per 100 μm length of the cell membrane) was calculated on each somatic profile cut through the nuclear plane; the density ranged from 0 to 11.8 with an average of 2.4 in the MAO (61 profiles), from 0 to 8.1 with an average of 3.0 in the DAO (45 profiles), and from 0 to 8.3 with an average of 1.7 in the PO (41 profiles). An analysis made on 100 somatic profiles cut through the nucleolar plane shows that no clear correlations exist between the cell size and the density of AS synapses (Fig. 2-1).

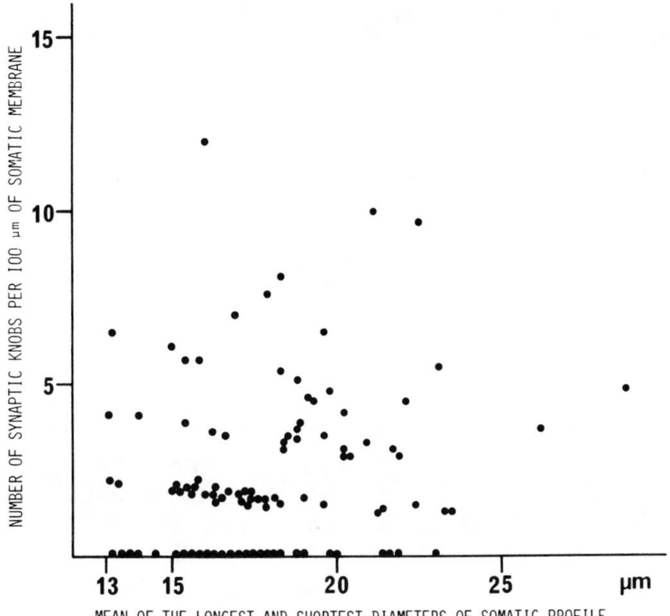

Figure 2-1. The density of AS synapses. Black dots represent IO neurons sampled. The sizes of the cell bodies are represented by the average diameters of somatic profiles through nucleolar plane.

About 70 to 80% of the AS terminals contained pleomorphic synaptic vesicles (P-type), and 20 to 30% were filled with round ones (R-type) (Tables 2-1,2-2). One or more dense-core vesicles of 50 to 100 nm diameter were seen in about 40% of the AS terminals of P-type and in about 50% of the AS terminals of R-type. No consistent association was noted between the shape of the synaptic vesicles and the type of synaptic active zones; the vast majority of the AS synapses were associated with the symmetrical active zones.

Table 2-1. Axosomatic Synaptic Terminals

Subdivision	*Terminals Counted*	*Terminals with Round Vesicles* (± *SEM*)	*Terminals with Pleomorphic Vesicles* (± *SEM*)
Medial accessory olive			
Controls	234	48 (20.5 ± 2.64%)	186 (79.5 ± 2.64%)
7 days' survival	117	26 (22.2 ± 4.50%)	91 (77.8 ± 4.50%)
35 days' survival	148	37 (25.0 ± 3.56%)	111 (75.0 ± 3.56%)
Dorsal accessory olive			
Controls	232	59 (25.4 ± 2.86%)	173 (74.6 ± 2.86%)
7 days' survival	122	34 (27.9 ± 4.06%)	88 (72.1 ± 4.06%)
35 days' survival	137	40 (29.2 ± 3.88%)	97 (70.8 ± 3.88%)

Differences from controls: $P > 0.36$ (χ^2-test).

Table 2-2. Axosomatic Synaptic Terminals

Subdivision	*Terminals Counted*	*Terminals with Round Vesicles* (± *SEM*)	*Terminals with Pleomorphic Vesicles* (± *SEM*)
Principal olive			
Controls	252	73 (29.0 ± 2.86%)	179 (71.0 ± 2.86%)
7 days' survival	131	33 (25.2 ± 3.79%)	98 (74.8 ± 3.79%)
35 days' survival	162	44 (27.2 ± 3.50%)	118 (72.8 ± 3.50%)

Differences from controls: $P > 0.43$ (χ^2-test).

Of 6097 AD terminals counted randomly in the IO areas (1476 in the MAO; 1266 in the DAO; 3355 in the PO), 3728 (61.1%) were filled with round synaptic vesicles (R-type) and 2369 (38.9%) contained pleomorphic ones (P-type). The ratio of the two types of the AD terminals was essentially the same in the MAO, DAO, and PO (R-type: 58.2% in the MAO, 61.2% in the DAO, and 62.4% in the PO) (Tables 2-3,2-4). One or more round dense-core vesicles of 50–100 nm diameter were seen in about 35% of the AD terminals of R-type and in about 25% of the AD terminals of P-type.

The density of AD terminals (the number of AD terminals per 100 μm^2 of the IO areas) was 14.5 in the MAO, 11.6 in the DAO, and 11.3 in the PO (Tables 2-5,2-6). The ratio of area occupied by AD terminals to the total IO area was also estimated; the area occupied by R-type terminals was 13.7% in the MAO, 16.8% in the DAO, and 12.4% in the PO, whereas the area occupied by P-type terminals was 7.2% in the MAO, 7.1% in the DAO, and 5.2% in the PO (Tables 2-7,2-8).

Although the association between the shape of the synaptic vesicles and the type of the synaptic active zone was not consistent, the AD terminals of R-type were associated usually with the asymmetrical active zones of the synapses. Several AD terminals were often arranged in a glomerular manner (46,50). On rare occasions, synapses of the en passant type, and synaptic terminals protruding directly from a myelinated portion of axon or a node of Ranvier were observed. No axo-axonal synapses were found.

Table 2-3. Axodendritic Axon Terminals

Subdivision	*Terminals Counted*	*Terminals with Round Vesicles* (± *SEM*)	*Terminals with Pleomorphic Vesicles* (± *SEM*)
Medial accessory olive			
Controls	1476	859 (58.2 ± 1.28%)	617 (41.8 ± 1.28%)
7 days' survival[a]	1513	974 (64.4 ± 1.23%)	539 (35.6 ± 1.23%)
35 days' survival[a]	1375	561 (40.8 ± 1.33%)	814 (59.2 ± 1.33%)
Dorsal accessory olive			
Controls	1266	775 (61.2 ± 1.37%)	491 (38.8 ± 1.37%)
7 days' survival	1671	1069 (64.0 ± 1.17%)	602 (36.0 ± 1.17%)
35 days' survival[a]	811	355 (43.8 ± 1.74%)	456 (56.2 ± 1.74%)

[a] $P < 0.01$ when compared with controls by χ^2-test.

Table 2-4. Axodendritic Axon Terminals

Subdivision	*Terminals Counted*	*Terminals with Round Vesicles (± SEM)*	*Terminals with Pleomorphic Vesicles (± SEM)*
Principal olive			
Controls	3355	2094 (62.4 ± 0.84%)	1261 (37.6 ± 0.84%)
7 days' survival	1546	923 (59.7 ± 1.25%)	623 (40.3 ± 1.25%)
35 days' survival[a]	1428	463 (32.4 ± 1.24%)	965 (67.6 ± 1.24%)

[a] $P < 0.01$ when compared with controls by χ^2-test.

Observations on Operated Cats

In all of the nine cats allowed to survive for 2 to 7 days after hemicordotomy in the second cervical cord segment, degenerated changes of axon terminals were observed in the caudolateral portions of the MAO and DAO ipsilateral to the lesions. Electron-dense degenerated axon terminals with discernible active zones were observed most frequently in the cats with a survival period of 3 to 4 days. Electron-dense axon terminals and dense bodies engulfed by glial profiles were seen even in a cat with a survival period of 2 days, but these were found most numerously in the cats with a survival period of 5 to 7 days. In a total of 274 electron-dense axon terminals found in the MAO and DAO, 269 were seen on dendritic profiles and 5 on somatic membranes; the synaptic active zones were identified in 43 of the former and in 2 of the latter.

Within a DAO area of about 12,500 μm^2 in a cat with a survival period of 4 days, of 355 axon terminals on dendritic profiles 19 (5.4%) were electron dense; 1 electron-dense axon terminal was in contact with a somatic profile, and 30 dense bodies enveloped by glial profiles were also seen. Within a MAO area of the same cat, of 273 synaptic terminals on dendritic profiles 13 (4.8%) were electron dense.

Degeneration features of axon terminals within the dorsal lamella of the PO in the five cats with lesions in the red nuclear regions of the midbrain were essentially the same as those observed in the MAO and DAO of the cats with lesions in the spinal

Table 2-5. Density of Axodendritic Axon Terminals (Number of Axodendritic Axon Terminals per 100 μm^2 of the Nuclear Area)

Subdivision	*Number of Unit Areas Examined*	*Total Area Examined (μm^2)*	*Number of Axon Terminals Counted*	*Density of Axon Terminals*		
				Total	*R-type*	*P-type*
Medial accessory olive						
Controls	63	4246	1476	34.8	20.2	14.5
7 days' survival	69	4651	1513	32.5	20.9	11.6
35 days' survival	94	6336	1375	21.7	8.9	12.8
Dorsal accessory olive						
Controls	63	4246	1266	29.8	18.3	11.6
7 days' survival	91	6133	1671	27.2	17.4	9.8
35 days' survival	68	4583	811	17.7	7.7	9.9

Table 2-6. Density of Axodendritic Axon Terminals (Number of Axodendritic Axon Terminals per 100 μm^2 of the Nuclear Area)

Subdivision	*Number of Unit Areas Examined*	*Total Area Examined (μm^2)*	*Number of Axon Terminals Counted*	*Density of Axon Terminals*		
				Total	*R-type*	*P-type*
Principal olive						
Controls	165	11121	3355	30.2	18.8	11.3
7 days' survival	84	5662	1546	27.3	16.3	11.0
35 days' survival	126	8492	1428	16.8	5.5	11.3

cord. The extent of the lesions in the red nuclear regions varied from animal to animal. Electron-dense degenerated axon terminals were most numerous in a cat with large lesion that involved the red nucleus and its surroundings, including the medial longitudinal fascicle and the central gray. Within a PO area of about 14,000 μm^2 in this cat, of 420 axon terminals in contact with dendritic profiles 29 (6.9%) were electron-dense; 1 electron-dense axon terminal on a somatic profile and 59 dense bodies were also found. Of 96 electron-dense degenerated axon terminals so far found in the PO, 94 were in contact with dendritic profiles and 2 were on somatic profiles; the synaptic active zones were recognized in 18 of the former and in 1 of the latter.

Thus, degenerated axon terminals constituted only a small fraction of the total axon terminals in the IO areas deafferented from spinal and mesencephalic fibers. Such sparseness of degenerated axon terminals visualized at a particular survival time might be attributable to variable time course of degeneration process; fibers of different diameters were reported to degenerate at different rates (51). In view of these considerations, the following experiments were performed:

In two cats, one was hemicordotomized in the second cervical segment and the other was destroyed stereotaxically in the red nuclear regions of the midbrain (Figs. 2-2,2-3), the survival period was extended up to the thirty-fifth day after the operation, when all axon terminals of injured neurons were considered to be in detectable stages of degeneration process or to have already disappeared. The ratio of the two types of *intact*

Table 2-7. Ratio of Area of Axodendritic Axon Terminals to Total Nuclear Area Examined

Subdivision	*Number of Unit Areas Examined (μm^2)*	*Total Nuclear Area Examined (μm^2)*	*Area of Axodendritic Axon Terminals*			
			Total Area (μm^2)		*Ratio to Nuclear Area*	
			R-type	*P-type*	*R-type*	*P-type*
Medial accessory olive						
Controls	40	2696	368.1	194.9	13.7%	7.2%
35 days' survival	40	2696	208.0	193.6	7.7%	7.2%
Dorsal accessory olive						
Controls	40	2696	452.9	190.7	16.8%	7.1%
35 days' survival	45	3033	181.5	223.1	6.0%	7.4%

Table 2-8. Ratio of Area of Axodendritic Axon Terminals to Total Nuclear Area Examined

Subdivision	*Number of Unit Areas Examined (μm^2)*	*Total Nuclear Area Examined (μm^2)*	*Area of Axodendritic Axon Terminals*			
			Total Area (μm^2)		*Ratio to Nuclear Area*	
			R-type	*P-type*	*R-type*	*P-type*
Principal olive						
Controls	50	3370	418.6	174.2	12.4%	5.2%
35 days' survival	75	5055	154.1	298.8	3.0%	5.9%

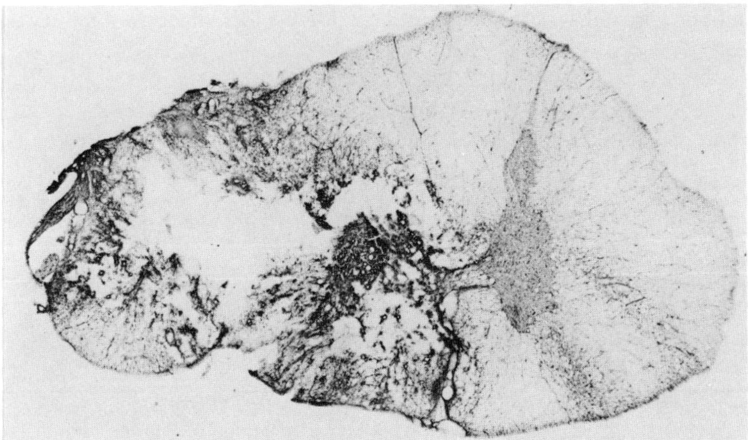

Figure 2-2. Cross section through a lower level of the second cervical cord segment, showing the lesion in the cat with survival period of 35 days after hemicordotomy.

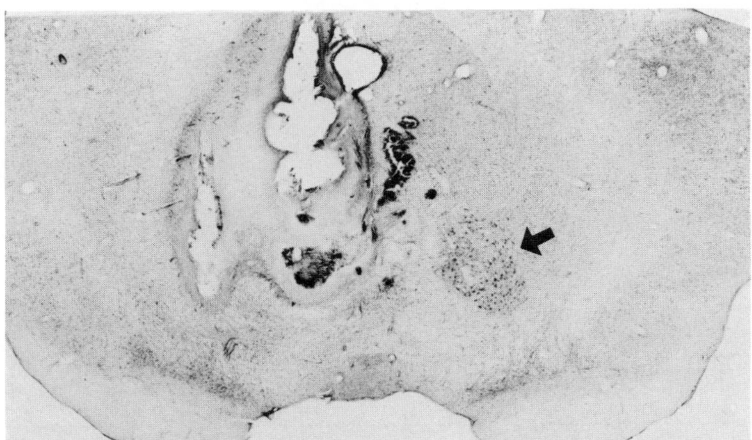

Figure 2-3. Cross section through the red nucleus, showing the extensive lesion in the cat allowed to survive for 35 days after the operation. Arrow points to the red nucleus in the normal side.

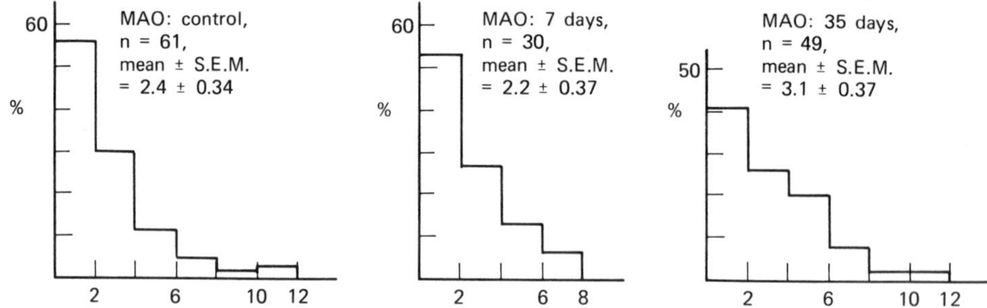

Figure 2-4. Distribution of the density of AS terminals on somatic profiles of MAO neurons cut through nuclear plane. The distribution patterns of the AS terminal density in the cats allowed to survive for seven and 35 days after hemicordotomy in the second cervical cord segment are not different significantly from that in the unoperated cat ($P > 0.5$ by Kolmogorov-Smirnov test).

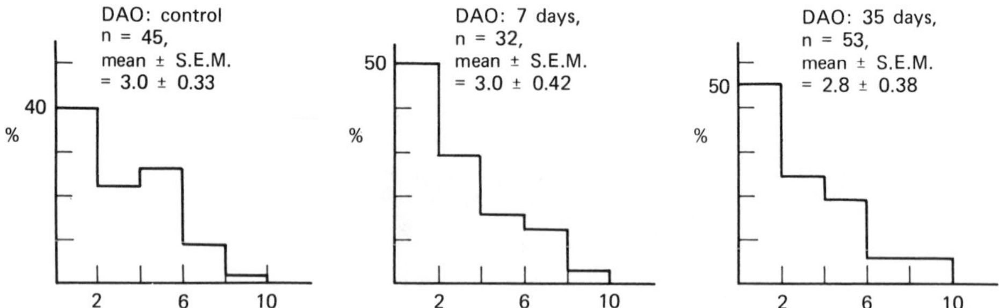

Figure 2-5. Distribution of the density of AS terminals on the somatic profiles of DAO neurons cut through nuclear plane in the same cats as used in Figure 2-4. The distribution patterns are not different significantly between the operated and the unoperated cats ($P > 0.9$).

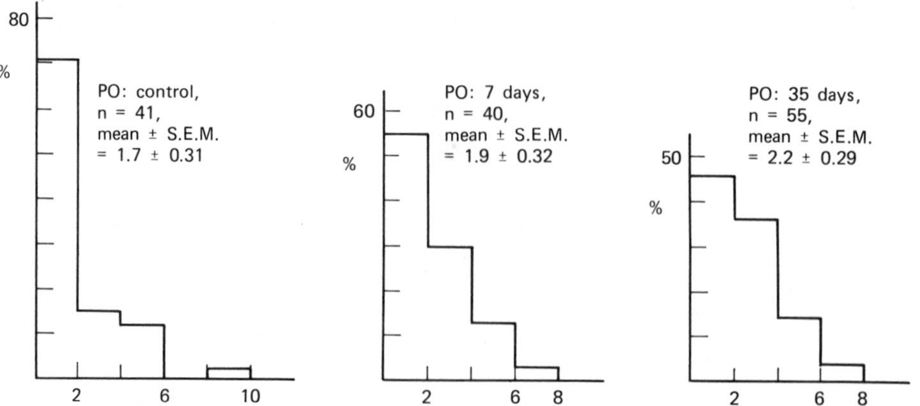

Figure 2-6. Distribution of the density of AS terminals on the somatic profiles of PO neurons cut through nuclear plane. The distribution patterns of the AS terminal density in the cats with survival period of seven and 35 days after placing lesion in the red nuclear regions are not different significantly from that in the unoperated cat ($P > 0.09$ by Kolmogorov-Smirnov test).

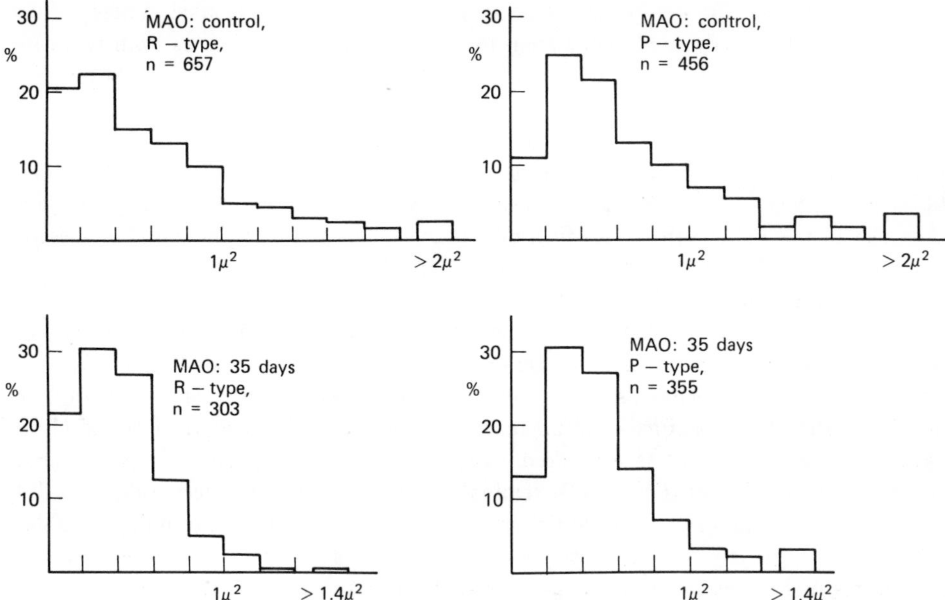

Figure 2-7. Distribution of profile areas of AD terminals in the spinal areas of the MAO. The distribution pattern of R-type terminals in the cat allowed to survive for 35 days after hemicordotomy in the second cervical cord segment is different significantly from that in the unoperated cat ($P < 0.05$ by Kolmogorov-Smirnov test). In the distribution pattern of P-type terminals no significant difference is noted between the operated and the unoperated cat ($P > 0.1$).

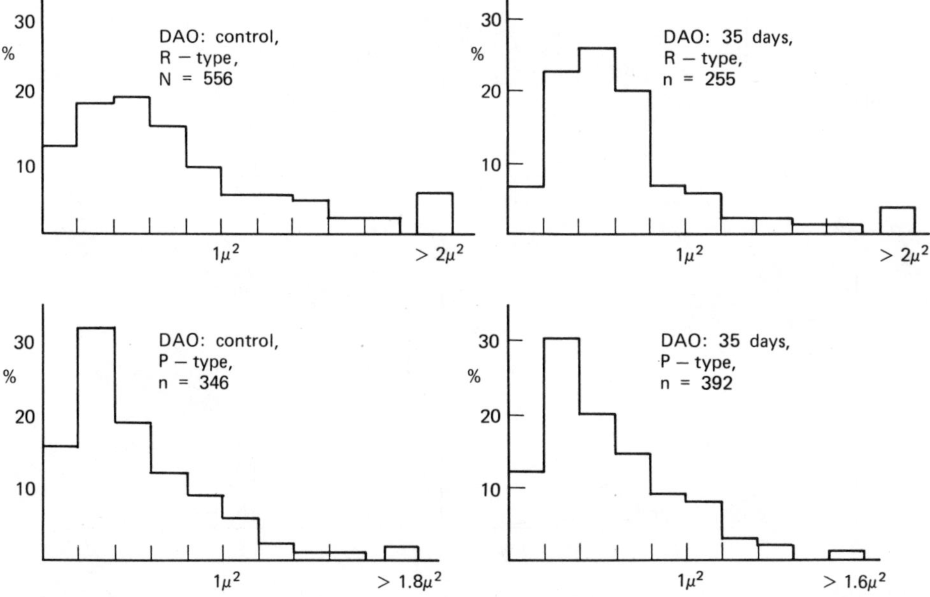

Figure 2-8. Distribution of profile areas of AD terminals in the spinal areas of the DAO in the same cats as used in Figure 2-7. Significant difference in the distribution pattern between the operated and the unoperated cat is noted in R-type terminals ($P < 0.03$) but not in P-type terminals ($P > 0.7$).

axon terminals and the density of *intact* axon terminals were calculated. These values were compared with those obtained from the unoperated cats as well as from two cats that were subjected to a similar operation in the spinal cord or the midbrain and allowed to survive for 7 days.

As regards AS terminals, no significant differences were noted between data obtained from the operated cats and those from the controls (Tables 2-1,2-2; Figs. 2-4–2-6). The ratio of AD terminals of R-type to those of P-type was decreased in the MAO and DAO, or in the PO, on the thirty-fifth day after deafferentation from spinal or mesencephalic fibers, although it was somewhat increased in the MAO on the seventh day after hemicordotomy (Tables 2-3,2-4). The density of AD terminals was also decreased in the cats allowed to survive for 35 days after the operations; decrease of the density of AD terminals appears to be due to decrease of AD terminals of R-type (Tables 2-5,2-6).

A decrease in AD terminals of R-type in the IO areas deafferented from spinal or mesencephalic fibers was further confirmed in the two cats with a survival period of 35 days after the operation. As compared with the control value, the ratio of the area occupied with profiles of R-type AD terminals to the total area was decreased in all IO areas examined, whereas no substantial changes were noted in P-type terminals (Tables 2-7,2-8). The patterns of size distribution of profiles of AD terminals are shown in histograms in Figures 2-7 through 2-9. In all IO areas examined, the patterns of size distribution of R-type terminals are different between the unoperated and the operated

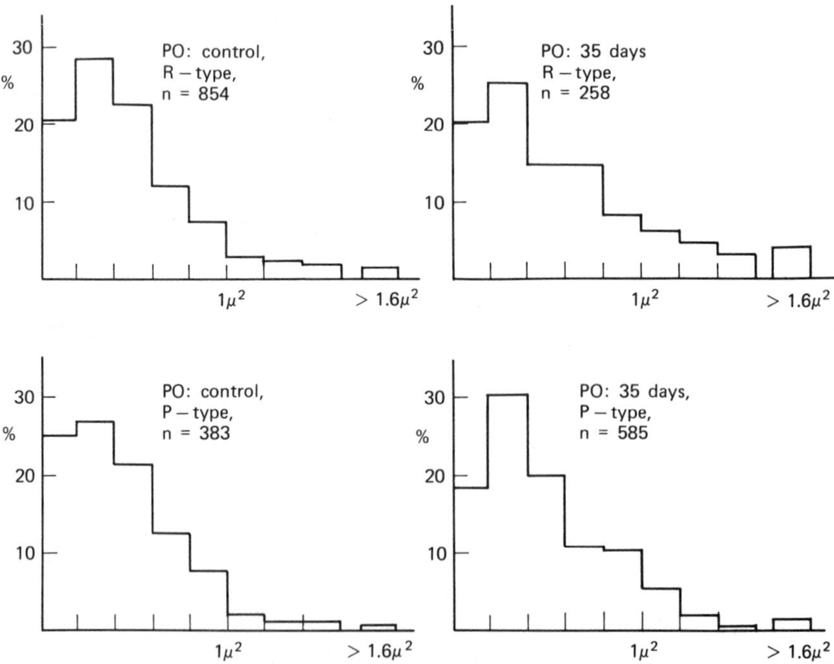

Figure 2-9. Distribution of profile areas of AD terminals in the red nuclear areas of the PO. The distribution pattern of R-type terminals in the cat allowed to survive for 35 days after placing lesion in the red nuclear regions of the midbrain is different significantly from that in the unoperated cat ($P < 0.05$ by Kolmogorov-Smirnov test). The distribution pattern of P-type terminals in the operated cat is not different significantly from that in the unoperated cat ($P > 0.2$).

cats ($P < 0.05$ by Kolmogorov-Smirnov test), while the patterns of size distribution of P-type terminals in the operated cats are not significantly different from those in the controls ($P > 0.1$ by Kolmogorov-Smirnov test).

DISCUSSION

Within the IO areas examined in this study, spinal and mesencephalic fibers were shown to be profuse at their termination; the spinal IO areas are the caudolateral portions of the MAO and the lateral portions of the DAO (38–41) and the red nuclear IO area is the dorsal lamella of the PO (42–45). Since large reticular neurons that send their dendrites into the IO domain were reported to exist around the perimeter of the cat IO (46), the examination of the IO areas in the present study was limited to the central portions of the spinal and the red nuclear IO areas.

In all cats with a survival period of 2 to 7 days after the operation, electron-dense degenerated axon terminals were found in the IO areas examined ipsilaterally to the lesions. In addition to these electron-dense axon terminals, other features of possible degeneration of axon terminals, such as an increase in the number of neurofilaments, the paleness of matrix, the accumulation of glycogen granules, and the enlargement of synaptic vesicles, were observed. Similar features, however, were also seen in the normal cat, although only infrequently and in lower grades. In the present study, therefore, these features of the axon terminals were not considered to be definite reliable signs of degeneration of axon terminals.

In the IO areas examined in the present study, almost all the electron-dense degenerated axon terminals were on dendritic profiles. These degenerated terminals, however, constituted only a small fraction of the total number of axon terminals seen in the IO areas examined; they never exceeded more than 7% of the total even in the region where degenerated axon terminals were observed most frequently. On the other hand, a decrease in R-type axon terminals was disclosed quantitatively in the spinal and the red nuclear IO areas in two cats with a survival period of 35 days after the operation, although no substantial changes were observed in P-type axon terminals. Even in these cats, however, many axon terminals still remained intact in the IO areas examined, and the subjective impression was that the number of the intact axon terminals did not seem to be decreased.

In one of these cats, the lesion in the midbrain was so extensive that all of mesencephalo-olivary (42,44,45) and mesodiencephalo-olivary fibers (43) appeared to be damaged. The existence of fibers from the striopallidum to the dorsal lamella of the PO (44) appears to be questionable. On the other hand, many cerebellar fibers were proven to terminate in the dorsal lamella of the cat IO (38,52–54). Extraspinal fibers to the spinal IO areas of the MAO and DAO were reported in the cat to arise from the mesodiencephalic areas (43,45), from the cerebellar nuclei (38,52–54), and from the posterior column nuclei (38,39,55–58). Although cerebral cortical fibers were also reported to terminate in the spinal IO areas (44), such fibers appear to be few (38,59,60). Other possible sources for the remaining intact axon terminals in the spinal and the red nuclear IO areas of the two cats were fibers of intrinsic origin. The presence of axon collaterals of IO neurons terminating within the confines of the IO was indicated electrophysiologically (61,62) as well as histologically (63), whereas no clear evidence suggested the existence of internuncial neurons within the IO (cf. ref. 64).

Thus, afferent fibers of various origins were thought to converge in the spinal and the red nuclear IO areas examined in the present study. In these IO areas, however, no evidence for sprouting or shifting of remaining intact axons was obtained after chronic deafferentation from the spinal or the mesencephalic fibers.

SUMMARY

The influence of deafferentation on the synaptic organization in the inferior olive (IO) of the adult cat was studied quantitatively by electron microscopy in the IO areas where red nuclear and spinal fibers were known to terminate with high frequency; the red nuclear IO area examined was the dorsal lamella of the principal olive, and the spinal IO areas were the caudolateral portions of the medial and dorsal accessory olive.

In the cats allowed to survive for 2 to 7 days after the placement of lesions in the red nuclear regions in the midbrain or after hemicordotomy in the second cervical cord segment, electron-dense degenerated axon terminals were found in the red nuclear or the spinal IO areas ipsilateral to the lesions. These degenerated axon terminals were seen almost exclusively on dendritic profiles and never reached 7% of the total population of axon terminals in the IO areas examined.

In the cats allowed to survive for 35 days after the placement of large lesions in the red nuclear regions of the midbrain or after hemisection in the second cervical cord segment, quantitative data showed a decrease in intact axodendritic axon terminals filled with round synaptic vesicles in the red nuclear or the spinal IO areas ipsilateral to the lesions. In the red nuclear or the spinal IO areas of these cats, however, many axon terminals filled with round synaptic vesicles still remained intact, and no substantial changes were found in axon terminals containing pleomorphic synaptic vesicles. Thus, in the partially deafferented IO areas, no conclusive evidence for synaptic reorganization by sprouting or shifting of remaining intact axons was found in the present study.

REFERENCES

1. Guth L: Axonal regeneration and functional plasticity in the central nervous system. *Exp Neurol* 45:606–654, 1974.
2. Guth L: History of central nervous system regeneration research. *Exp Neurol* 48:3–15, 1975.
3. Guth L, Windle WF: The enigma of central nervous regeneration. *Exp Neurol* 28 (suppl 5):1–43, 1970.
4. Kerr FWL: Structural and functional evidence of plasticity in the central nervous system. *Exp Neurol* 48 (3, pt 2):16–31, 1975.
5. Watson WE: *Cell Biology of Brain*. London, Chapman and Hall, 1976, p 527.
6. Donoghue JP, Wells J: Synaptic rearrangement in the ventrobasal complex of the mouse following partial cortical deafferentation. *Brain Res* 125:351–355, 1977.
7. Gentschev T, Sotelo C: Degenerative patterns in the ventral cochlear nucleus of the rat after primary deafferentation. An ultrastructural study. *Brain Res* 62:37–60, 1973.
8. Sotelo C, Palay L: Altered axons and axon terminals in the lateral vestibular nucleus of the rat. Possible example of axonal remodeling. *Lab Invest* 25:653–672, 1971.
9. Lund RD, Lund JS: Synaptic adjustment after deafferentation of the superior colliculus of the rat. *Science* 171:804–907, 1971.
10. Raisman G: Neuronal plasticity in the septal nuclei of the adult rat. *Brain Res* 14:25–48, 1969.

11. Raisman G, Field PM: A quantitative investigation of the development of collateral reinnervation after partial deafferentation of the septal nuclei. *Brain Res* 50:241–264, 1973.

12. Lee K, Stanford E, Cotman C, et al: Ultrastructural evidence for bouton proliferation in the partially deafferented dentate gyrus of the adult rat. *Exp Brain Res* 29:475–485, 1977.

13. Matthews DA, Cotman C, Lynch G: An electron microscopic study of lesion-induced synaptogenesis in the dentate gyrus of the adult rat. II. Reappearance of morphologically normal synaptic contacts. *Brain Res* 115:23–41, 1976.

14. Westrum LE: Electron microscopy of degeneration in the lateral olfactory tract and plexiform layer of the prepyriform cortex of the rat. *Z Zellforsch* 98:157–187, 1969.

15. Ralston HJ III, Chow KL: Synaptic reorganization in the degenerating lateral geniculate nucleus of the rabbit. *J Comp Neurol* 147:321–350, 1973.

16. Rustioni A, Sotelo C: Some effects of chronic deafferentation on the ultrastructure of the nucleus gracilis of the cat. *Brain Res* 73:527–533, 1974.

17. O'Neal JT, Westrum LE: The fine structural synaptic organization of the cat lateral cuneate nucleus. A study of sequential alterations in degeneration. *Brain Res* 51:97–124, 1973.

18. Westrum LE, Black RG: Fine structural aspects of the synaptic organization of the spinal trigeminal nucleus (pars interpolaris) of the cat. *Brain Res* 25:265–287, 1971.

19. Nakamura Y, Mizuno N, Konishi A, et al: Synaptic reorganization of the red nucleus after chronic deafferentation from cerebellorubral fibers: an electron microscope study in the cat. *Brain Res* 82:298–301, 1974.

20. Bernstein JJ, Bernstein ME: Neuronal alteration and reinnervation following axonal regeneration and sprouting in mammalian spinal cord. *Brain Behav Evol* 8:135–161, 1973.

21. Bernstein ME, Bernstein JJ: Synaptic frequency alteration on rat ventral horn neurons in the first segment proximal to spinal cord hemisection: an ultrastructural statistical study of regenerative capacity. *J Neurocytol* 6:85–102, 1977.

22. Bernstein JJ, Gelderd JB, Bernstein ME: Alteration of neuronal synaptic complement during regeneration and axonal sprouting of rat spinal cord. *Exp Neurol* 44:470–482, 1974.

23. Raisman G: A comparison of the mode of termination of the hippocampal and hypothalamic afferents to the septal nuclei as revealed by electron microscopy of degeneration. *Exp Brain Res* 7:317–343, 1969.

24. Tsukahara N, Kosaka K: The mode of cerebral excitation of red nucleus neurons. *Exp Brain Res* 5:102–117, 1968.

25. Tsukahara N, Toyama K, Kosaka K: Electrical activity of red nucleus neurones investigated with intracellular microelectrodes. *Exp Brain Res* 4:18–33, 1967.

26. Toyama K, Tsukahara N, Kosaka K, et al: Synaptic excitation of red nucleus neurons by fibers from interpositus nucleus. *Exp Brain Res* 11:187–198, 1970.

27. Nakamura Y, Mizuno N: An electron microscopic study of the interposito-rubral connections in the cat and rabbit. *Brain Res* 35:283–286, 1971.

28. Tsukahara N, Hultborn H, Murakami F: Sprouting of corticorubral synapses in red nucleus neurones after destruction of the nucleus interpositus of the cerebellum. *Experientia* (*Basel*) 30:57–58, 1974.

29. Tsukahara N, Hultborn H, Murakami F, et al: Electrophysiological study of formation of new synapses and collateral sprouting in red nucleus after partial denervation. *J Neurophysiol* 38:1359–1372, 1975.

30. Murakami F, Fujito Y: Physiological properties of the newly formed cortico-rubral synapses of red nucleus neurons due to collateral sprouting. *Brain Res* 103:147–151, 1976.

31. Murakami F, Tsukahara N, Fujito Y: Analysis of unitary EPSPs mediated by the newly-formed corticorubral synapses after lesion of the nucleus interpositus of the cerebellum. *Exp Brain Res* 30:233–243, 1977.

32. Murakami F, Tsukahara N, Fujito Y: Properties of synaptic transmission of the newly formed corticorubral synapses after lesion of the nucleus interpositus of the cerebellum. *Exp Brain Res* 30:245–258, 1977.

33. Nakamura Y, Mizuno N, Konishi A: A quantitative electron microscope study of cerebellar axon terminals on the magnocellular red nucleus neurons in the cat. *Brain Res* 147:17–27, 1978.

34. Mizuno N, Konishi A, Nakamura Y: An electron microscope study of synaptic organization in the lateral reticular nucleus of the medulla oblongata in the cat. *Brain Res* 94:369–381, 1975.

35. Mizuno N, Konishi A, Nakamura Y: An electron microscope study of synaptic terminals of the spino-olivary fibers in the cat. *Brain Res* 104:303–308, 1976.

36. Millonig G: A modified procedure for lead staining of thin sections. *J Biophys Biochem Cytol* 11:736–739, 1961.

37. Venable JH, Coggeshall R: A simplified lead citrate stain for use in electron microscopy. *J Cell Biol* 25:407–408, 1965.

38. Berkley KJ, Worden IG: Projections to the inferior olive of the cat. I. Comparisons of input from the dorsal column nuclei, the lateral cervical nucleus, the spino-olivary pathways, the cerebral cortex and the cerebellum. *J Comp Neurol* 180:237–252, 1978.

39. Boesten AJP, Voogd J: Projections of the dorsal column nuclei and the spinal cord on the inferior olive in the cat. *J Comp Neurol* 161:215–238, 1975.

40. Brodal A, Walberg F, Blackstad ThW: Termination of spinal afferents to inferior olive in cats. *J Neurophysiol* 13:431–454, 1950.

41. Mizuno N: An experimental study of the spino-olivary fibers in the rabbit and the cat. *J Comp Neurol* 127:267–292, 1966.

42. Edwards SB: The ascending and descending projection of the red nucleus in the cat: An experimental study using an autoradiographic tracing method. *Brain Res* 48:45–63, 1972.

43. Mabuchi M, Kusama T: Mesodiencephalic projections to the inferior olive and the vestibular and perihypoglossal nuclei. *Brain Res* 17:133–136, 1970.

44. Walberg F: Descending connections to the inferior olive. An experimental study in the cat. *J Comp Neurol* 104:77–173, 1956.

45. Walberg F: Descending connections from the mesencephalon to the inferior olive: An experimental study in the cat. *Exp Brain Res* 20:145–156, 1974.

46. Sotelo C, Llinás R, Baker R: Structural study of inferior olivary nucleus of the cat: morphological correlates of electronic coupling. *J Neurophysiol* 37:541–559, 1974.

47. Chandler RL, Willis R: An intranuclear fibrillar lattice in neurons. *J Cell Sci* 1:283–286, 1966.

48. Feldman ML, Peters A: Intranuclear rods and sheets in rat cochlear nucleus. *J Neurocytol* 1:109–127, 1972.

49. Siegesmund KA, Dutta CR, Fox CA: The ultrastructure of the intranuclear rodlet in certain nerve cells. *J Anat (Lond)* 98:93–97, 1964.

50. Němecěk St, Wolff J: Light and electron microscopic evidence of complex synapses (glomeruli) in oliva inferior (cat). *Experientia (Basel)* 25:634–635, 1969.

51. LaMotte C: Distribution of the tract of Lissauer and the dorsal root fibers in the primate spinal cord. *J Comp Neurol* 172:529–561, 1977.

52. Beitz AJ: The topographical organization of the olivo-dentate and dentato-olivary pathways in the cat. *Brain Res* 115:311–317, 1976.

53. Graybiel AM, Nauta HJW, Lasek RJ, et al: A cerebello-olivary pathway in the cat: an experimental study using autoradiographic tracing techniques. *Brain Res* 58:205–211, 1973.

54. Tolbert DL, Massopust LC, Murphy MG, et al: The anatomical organization of the cerebello-olivary projection in the cat. *J Comp Neurol* 170:525–544, 1976.

55. Berkley KJ: Different targets of different neurons in nucleus gracilis of the cat. *J Comp Neurol* 163:285–304, 1975.

56. Berkley KJ, Hand PJ: Efferent projections of the gracile nucleus in the cat. *Brain Res* 153:263–283, 1978.

57. Berkley KJ, Hand PJ: Projections to the inferior olive of the cat. II. Comparisons of input from the gracile, cuneate and the spinal trigeminal nuclei. *J Comp Neurol* 180:253–264, 1978.

58. Ebbesson SOE: A connection between the dorsal column nuclei and the dorsal accessory olive. *Brain Res* 8:393–397, 1968.

59. Sousa-Pinto A: Experimental anatomical demonstration of a cortico-olivary projection from area 6 (supplementary motor area?) in the cat. *Brain Res* 16:73–83, 1969.

60. Sousa-Pinto A, Brodal A: Demonstration of a somatotopical pattern in the cortico-olivary projection in the cat. *Exp Brain Res* 8:364–386, 1969.

61. Armstrong DM, Harvey RJ: Responses in the inferior olive to stimulation of the cerebellar and cerebral cortices in the cat. *J Physiol* (*Lond*) 187:553–574, 1966.

62. Eccles JC, Llinás R, Sasaki K: The excitatory synaptic action of climbing-fibers on the Purkinje cells of the cerebellum. *J Physiol* (*Lond*) 182:268–296, 1966.

63. Ramón y Cajal S: *Histologie du Système Nerveux de l'Homme et des Vertébrés,* vol 1. Paris, Maloine, 1909, reprinted in 1952, Madrid, CSIC, pp. 919–933.

64. Brodal A: Experimentelle Untersuchungen über die Olivocerebellare Lokalisation. *Z Ges Neurol Psychiat* 169:1–153, 1940.

3

Possible Mechanism for Long-Lasting Potentiation of Hippocampal Synaptic Transmission

P. Andersen
H. Wigström

INTRODUCTION

In their search for useful functional models for long-lasting plastic changes in the nervous system, such as memory and learning, neurophysiologists have used a variety of preparations. The task has proved difficult. Many investigators have searched for a cortical substrate for such functions, but those cortical preparations in which plastic changes do occur within a short time are often difficult to record adequately. The animal preparations have to be nearly intact and under shallow (or no) anesthesia. Recording for the prolonged time necessary to study the phenomena in question is often hampered by difficult access and mechanical instability. A major obstacle is the frequent lack of input control. At the other end of the scale, the more easily studied cells in lower forms, particularly in invertebrates, have the disadvantage that the plastic changes occurring there may not necessarily be similar to those that occur in higher animal forms.

The long-lasting potentiation (LLP) of synaptic transmission described by Bliss and Lømo (6) is an interesting model. The potentiation is of considerable size and duration, even after a short tetanic stimulation at physiological frequencies. It occurs in intact animals and is present during anesthesia, although its duration is greatly prolonged in nonanesthetized animals (5). However, because of the long time course of the LLP (several hours), recording from single cells has been difficult in such nearly intact preparations.

In this context, the transverse hippocampal slice may offer certain advantages. In 1970, Blackstad et al (4) found that the mossy fibers of the dentate granule cells run nearly normal to the longitudinal axis of the hippocampus. Independently, Andersen et al (2) found that this organization applied to all main neuronal elements of the hippocampal formation and their axons. Thus, the hippocampus was seen as composed of a large number of parallel lamellae, each representing a miniature hippocampal cortex, containing the major neuronal elements and their interconnecting axons. With the advent of in vitro brain preparations (13) it occurred to us that it might be possible to cut a slice along the plane of the lamella, thus preserving not only the essential neuronal elements but also their interconnecting axons, and to treat the preparation as a short-term tissue culture. Introducing this preparation, Skrede and Westgaard (12) found that the hippocampal neurons survived well, and that all four major neuronal elements could be excited for several hours. Later, Schwartzkroin and Wester (11) showed that this preparation had an LLP similar to that found in intact animals after a short train of stimuli given to the perforant path/granule cell synapse (6). Therefore, this situation offered the possibility of studying the neuronal mechanisms underlying LLP.

For this purpose, the advantages of the transverse hippocampal slice are manifold. First, the major features of the cortical layers with the different afferent fiber systems can be seen directly under a microscope. This facilitates direct placement of recording, stimulation, and iontophoretic electrodes. Second, by use of small knives, microsurgery can be performed on the slice to restrict the afferent input to any given part of the dendritic tree. Third, due to the absence of the blood-brain barrier, the environment of the cells can be freely manipulated. Finally, the mechanical stability of the preparation allows intracellular recording from the small cells for several hours.

We have found that short-term tetanic stimulation (10 to 50 Hz for 5 to 10 seconds) gives a marked and prolonged (several hours) facilitation of synaptic transfer in the tetanized pathway. The effect is specific, since another input to the same cell does not elicit any change.

METHODS

Adult guinea pigs were anesthetized with ether. The brain was removed and cut in two. The hippocampus was quickly dissected out by rolling it out from the lateral ventricle with a spatula. Slices, 350–400 μm thick, were cut at right angles to the ventricular surface and at an angle of 15° from a plane normal to the longitudinal axis of the hippocampus (rostral edge tilted toward the septal end). The slices were quickly transferred to a tissue bath where they were placed on a nylon net covered with lens paper with artificial cerebrospinal fluid underneath and humidified gas (95% O_2, 5% CO_2) from above. The composition of the artificial cerebrospinal fluid was (in mM): NaCl 124, KCl 5.0, KH_2PO_4 1.25, $CaCl_2$ 2.0, $MgSO_4$ 2.0, $NaHCO_3$ 26.0, glucose 10. The pH was adjusted to 7.4. After an initial period of shock, lasting for about one hour, the slices survived well and showed good extra- and intracellular responses for periods from four to 15 hours. The placement of the electrodes was verified by micrometer measurements and by a moving electrode having its tip dipped in an Alcian blue solution before placement. The blue marks were used for identification both during the experiment and in the histological preparation. After the experiments, the slices were quickly transferred to a mixture of 1% glutaraldehyde and 4% formalaldehyde, embedded in Araldite. One-μm thick sections were cut and stained with paraphenylene-diamine for control of electrode placements and lesions.

RESULTS

One of the advantages of the transverse hippocampal slice preparation is that several afferent lines to the same population of cells can be excited, and that virtually all fibers course parallel to the cell body (pyramidal) layer (10). In the diagram in Figure 3-1(*a*) a symbolic CAl cell is shown in a box.

In this investigation we studied only CAl neurons. The inputs we used were fibers located in the layer of basal dendrites, str. oriens (or), and fibers in the layer of the apical dendrites, str. radiatum (rad). Figure 3-1(*b*) shows a diagrammatic CAl

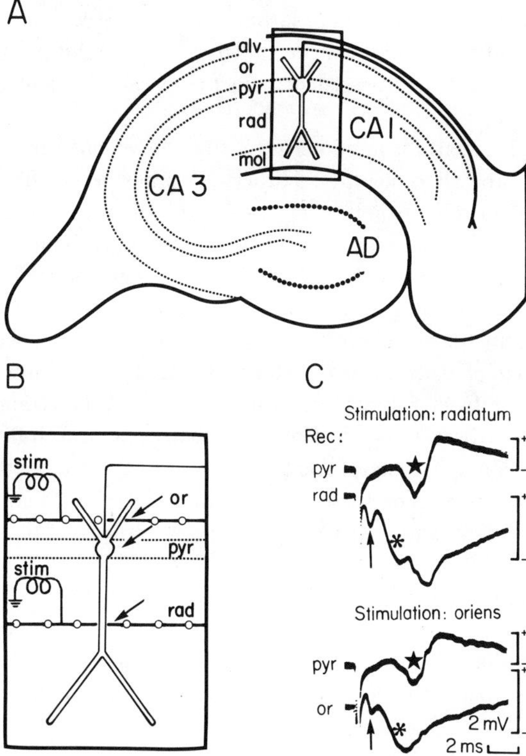

Figure 3-1. (*a*) Diagram of a hippocampal slice. A symbolic CAl pyramid is boxed in and shown in greater detail in (*b*). Afferent fibers in str. oriens and radiatum are symbolized by two fibers with boutons en passage (open circles). (*c*) Extracellular record taken from the pyramidal layer (pyr) and from the region of activated dendritic synapses (rad) in response to stimulation of radiatum afferent fibers. The star marks the population spike; the arrow indicates the pre-synaptic volley; and the asterisk the extracellular EPSP. The lower pair shows the corresponding records for activation of oriens fibers. alv:alveus, or:str. oriens, pyr:str. pyramidale, rad:str. radiatum, mol:str. moleculare.

pyramidal cell with two sets of stimulated fiber systems, one in str. oriens and the other in str. radiatum. Two recording electrodes were placed at the appropriate levels to record the incoming afferent activity of the two inputs. In addition, electrodes were recording extracellularly from the cell bodies in the pyramidal layer (pyr) or intracellularly from CAl pyramids. These could be antidromically identified by stimulation of the alveus (alv). In Figure 3-1(*c*) the upper record shows an extracellular potential recorded from the pyramidal layer with a population spike (star). This deflection represents the near synchronous discharge of many neighboring pyramidal neurons (1). The second trace shows the extracellular potential recorded at the point of impact of the stimulated afferent radiatum fibers. This trace shows an initial diphasic wave (arrow) followed by a slower negative wave (asterisk). The latter wave is associated in time with the intracellular EPSP and will henceforth be called the extracellular EPSP. Figure 3-1(*c*) shows the corresponding traces recorded from the pyramidal and oriens layers after oriens fiber stimulation.

An important requirement for any long-term study of synaptic transmission is to have a reliable measure of the afferent input. Hitherto this has been difficult to acquire, and researchers have had to rely on delivering a constant stimulus current. However, with the time course in question (several hours) it would be much better if one could have a more adequate measure of the number of activated afferent fibers. The initial deflection shown in Figure 3-1(*c*) (arrow) fulfills the criteria for a compound action potential in the presynaptic afferent fibers: There was a linear relationship between the size of the deflection and the size of both the extracellular EPSP and the intracellular EPSP. By removing calcium ions from the bathing fluid, this initial deflection survived without change in amplitude, whereas the subsequent responses, extracellular EPSP (asterisk) and reversed population spike (star), were removed as expected. Both reappeared after readministration of calcium. For these reasons the initial deflection will be called the presynaptic afferent volley, and we shall use this as a measure of the afferent input to a given cell or cell population.

When the presynaptic volley was continuously monitored (Fig. 3-2), there was often a slight change in its amplitude with time in spite of a constant stimulus current. After a short tetanizing stimulus (at o) to the afferent radiatum fibers (50 Hz, 5 seconds), there was no change in the size of the prevolley but a clear and lasting increase of the popula-

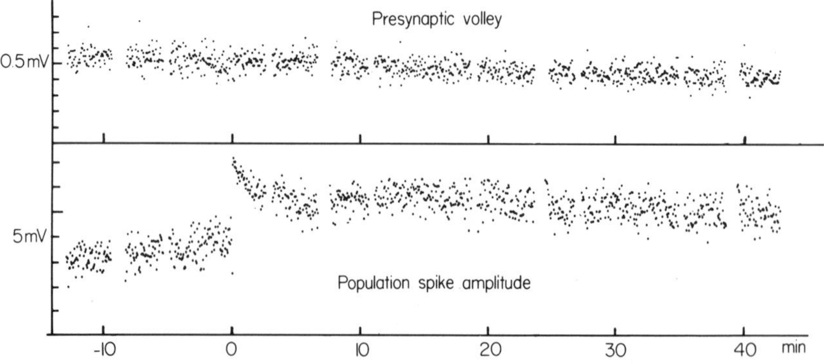

Figure 3-2. Continuous plot of the size of the presynaptic fiber volley and the population spike amplitude after 0.5-Hz stimulation of radiatum fibers. At 0 a tetanizing stimulus (50 Hz, 5 seconds) was delivered to the same fibers.

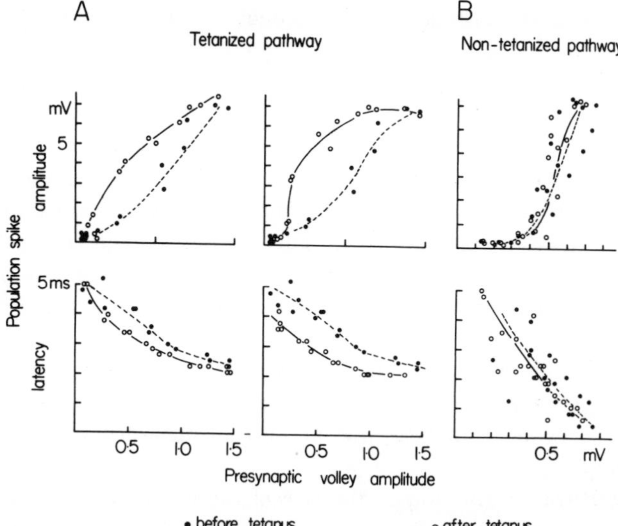

Figure 3-3. (*a*) The upper two panels show the relationships between the amplitudes of the presynaptic volley and of the population spike before (*filled circles*) and 10 minutes (left) and 40 minutes (right) after a tetanizing stimulus (20 Hz, 10 seconds) was delivered to the afferent (radiatum) fibers (open circles). The lower two panels show the corresponding peak latency of the population spike. (*b*) Similar data for the nontetanized (oriens) pathway. Lines fitted by eye.

tion spike amplitude indicating that many new cells were recruited to discharge by the same afferent volley. To study whether the effect was due to a general change in the excitability of the cells or to a change in the tetanized pathway or synapses, we tested the effect of two independent afferent volleys, one being tetanized and the other serving as a control. In the control period before tetanization and in the test period afterward, constant current stimuli were delivered alternately to the two inputs. At specific times, input-output curves were constructed by gradually increasing the stimulus strength.

In Figure 3-3(*a*) the upper panels show the input-output graphs for the population spike amplitude versus the input volley size, measured 10 and 40 minutes after the tetanization. The lower panels give the corresponding values for the peak latency of the population spike. For a given size of the input volley, the population spike is increased and its latency decreased after the tetanizing stimulus. Figure 3-3(*b*) shows the corresponding values for the control pathway 40 minutes after the tetanizing stimulus.

The changes induced in the population spike are clearly related to the tetanized pathway and do not seem to be due to a generalized excitability increase.

A study of the mechanisms involved required a more detailed study with intracellular recording. Because of the stability of the preparation adequate recording can be made for several hours.

The strategy of the experiments was to deliver every 2 seconds, a triad of test stimuli consisting of an orthodromic stimulus, a long hyperpolarizing current pulse to measure the membrane resistance, and a depolarizing pulse of constant size to test the soma membrane excitability. After a control period of 10 to 30 minutes, a tetanizing stimulus of 10–50 Hz was given, lasting 5 to 10 seconds. After the tetanic period, the triple stimulation was repeated.

The process was followed by on-line analysis. An excerpt of the computer graph on a storage oscilloscope is seen in Figure 3-4. The size of the presynaptic volley, the EPSP amplitude, the firing level of the action potential, and the latency of the orthodromically activated spike appears in the four upper rows. The three lower rows show the membrane resistance as measured from the middle line downward (crosses), the firing level of the directly evoked spike, and the latency of this spike, all for a period of 2.5 minutes before tetanization. The arrow and the black bar indicate the period of tetanic stimulation and the time immediately after. The excerpts in Figure 3-4(*a,b*) show the responses after 15 and 24 minutes, respectively. There is an increase in the EPSP and in the probability of discharge of the cell and a corresponding decrease of the orthodromic latency. This display was used mostly to indicate that the experiment was proceeding satisfactorily. The detailed analysis was performed afterward with the data replayed from magnetic tape.

Although there was fluctuation in the size of the presynaptic volley in spite of the application of constant stimulation current, the mean level was not changed after the tetanic period. Experiments in which the mean size of the presynaptic volley changed were discarded.

After tetanization there was an immediate reduction in the membrane resistance and an increase in the latency of the directly elicited spikes. This was due to the summating effect of synaptic activation, creating a large conductance change across the membrane. However, this change usually did not last for more than 0.5 to 8 minutes. Afterward there was no change in the membrane resistance from the control level. Nor was there any change in the general excitability of the membrane as shown by the response to depolarizing pulses. This rules out any general excitability change as an explanation for the long-term potentiation.

After the tetanic period, the tetanized input showed an increase in the size of the population spike and a decrease in its latency and an increased probability of firing of

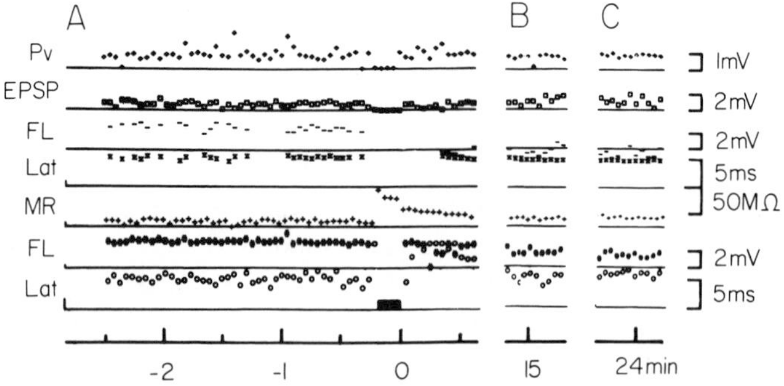

Figure 3-4. (*a*) Computer graph on a storage oscilloscope of data analysed on-line from a CAl pyramidal cell, before, during, and just after a tetanizing stimulus (50 Hz, 5 seconds) to radiatum afferent fibers. The data were calculated automatically from responses to orthodromic volleys and to depolarizing and hyperpolarizing pulses. (*b*) and (*c*) show values taken 15 and 24 minutes after the tetanizing stimulus, respectively.

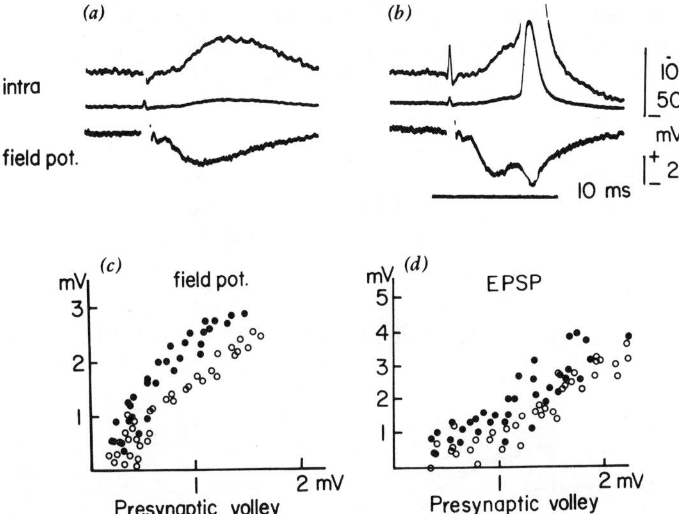

Figure 3-5. (*a*) Upper and middle trace give EPSP of a CAl pyramidal cell to an afferent volley along radiatum fibers, taken with high and low gain, respectively. Lower trace shows the extracellular field potential at the activated dendritic synapses with a small presynaptic volley and an extracellular EPSP. (*b*) shows the corresponding responses 40 minutes after a periods of tetanic stimulation (50 Hz, 5 seconds). (*c*) Plot of extracellular EPSP amplitude against size of presynaptic volley before (open circles) and 40 minutes after the tetanizing stimulus (filled circles). (*d*) Similar relationship for the intracellular EPSP.

single units (3). There was also an increased EPSP in the intracellular records. The firing level of the action potential was not changed. The control afferent line to the same group of cells (or cell) did not show any significant change, neither in size nor latency of the population spike nor in the probability of discharge of individual units.

Although there was no change in the membrane potential or resistance, there was a marked increase in the probability of discharge of individual cells or a marked reduction in the discharge latency to a given afferent volley (Fig. 3-5*a*,*b*). Plotted in relation to the presynaptic volley as a measure of the afferent input, the open circles in Figure 3-5(*c*) indicate the size of extracellular EPSP produced by different presynaptic volleys. The filled circles give the corresponding data 40 minutes after tetanization. There was also a clear increase in the intracellular EPSP in response to corresponding presynaptic volley amplitudes (Fig. 3-5*d*). However, the percentage change was not quite as large with this measure, in part due to the concomitant increase in synaptic noise created by the conductance change across the membrane. When calculating linear regression lines for the relationship between the presynaptic volley and the extracellular EPSP, the steepness of the line increased significantly between pretetanic and posttetanic values.

The described effect was seen after a single period of tetanization lasting for 5 to 10 seconds. The duration of the process lasted from 30 to 75 minutes. In no cases did we follow the process until it decayed naturally. We are therefore unable to tell the total duration of the process.

A possible mechanism could involve the effect of tetanization on the afferent fibers.

Because of their small diameter, their surface-to-volume ratio is considerably larger than for thicker nerve fibers. Therefore, the intra-axonal content of ions, which penetrates during the action potential, could increase fast. To test whether intracellular calcium accumulation could be involved in LLP, we removed calcium ions extracellularly during the tetanic period. Figure 3-6(*c*) shows the normal response to a radiatum volley recorded from the cell body layer (upper trace) and from the synaptic layer (lower trace). Removal of Ca^{2+} and addition of 2 mM Mn^{2+} (Figure 3-6*d*) leaves only the pre-volley intact. During this stage a tetanizing stimulus (50 Hz, 10 seconds) was delivered. Figure 3-6(*e*) shows the restoration after washing with normal Ca^{2+}-containing Ringer's solution. No potentiation occurred. A new tetanization (tet 2) at 50 Hz for 10 seconds gave a clear and long-lasting potentiation of both the extracellular EPSP (asterisk) and

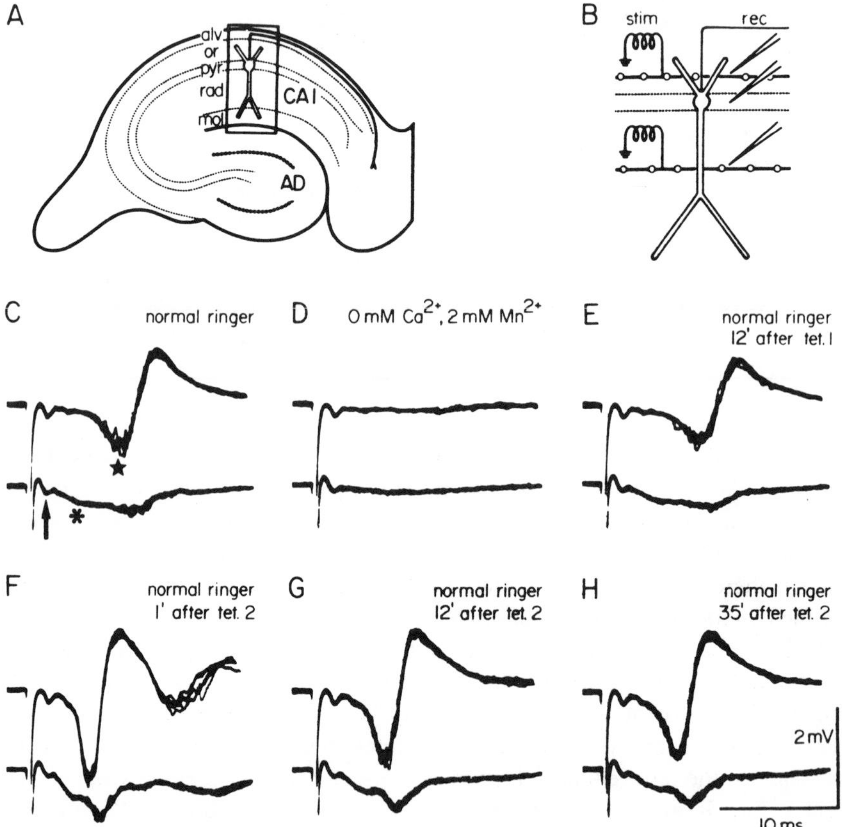

Figure 3-6. Diagram of a hippocampal slice. The boxed-in area is enlarged in (*b*) where the positions of the stimulating (left) and recording electrodes (right) are given. (*c*). Five superimposed records in response to radiatum fiber stimulation, taken from the pyramidal and radiatum layers (upper and lower trace, respectively), showing the presynaptic volley (arrow), the extracellular EPSP (asterisk) and the population spike (star). (*d*) Removal of Ca^{2+} and addition of 2 mM Mn^{2+} abolished synaptic transmission, recorded immediately before the first tetanizing stimulus (50 Hz, 5 seconds) was delivered. (*e*) Recovery, showing lack of LLP 12 minutes after the tetanization. (*f*), (*g*), (*h*). Potentiated records taken 1, 12, and 35 minutes after a second tetanizing stimulus (tet 2) was delivered in normal Ringer's.

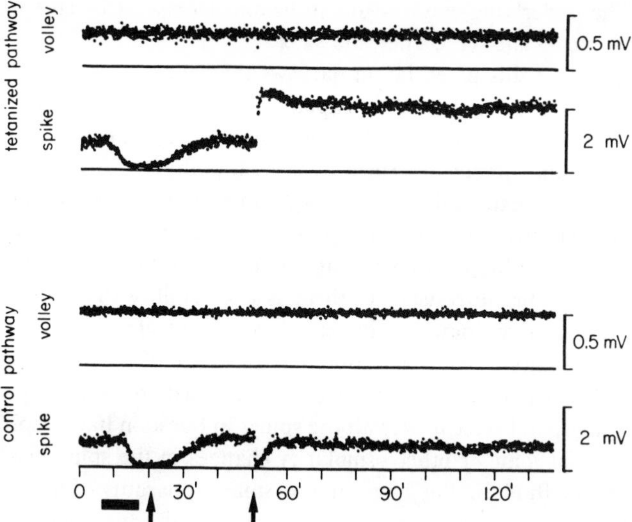

Figure 3-7. Presynaptic volleys and population spike in response to stimulation of oriens fibers (tetanized pathway, upper plots) and of radiatum fibers (control pathway, lower plots). Bar indicates perfusion with the calcium-free solution. Arrows mark two tetanizing stimuli (50 Hz, 5 seconds) delivered to str. oriens; the first during calcium-free condition, the second during normal Ringer's with 2 mol Ca^{2+}. Stimulus strength was computer adjusted to maintain constant presynaptic volley amplitudes.

the population spike (star) (Figure 3-6*f-h*). Figure 3-7 gives the time course of the calcium interference. The two panels give the size of the prevolley and population spike for the tetanized (upper part) and the control pathway (lower part). The heavy bar indicates Ca^{2+} removal. The first tetanizing stimulus was delivered while the postsynaptic responses had disappeared. The lack of potentiation is obvious when compared with the clear potentiation after the second tetanizing stimulus which was delivered during normal calcium concentration. The lack of change in the prevolley and the specificity of the potentiation is also striking.

DISCUSSION

The main finding in the present investigation was that short periods of stimulation at moderate frequencies are able to increase selectively the synaptic transmission in a tetanized pathway. Since there was no change in the membrane resistance, membrane potential, or in the response to depolarizing current pulses, the effect can not be due to a general change in the cell because of potassium accumulation or any similar nonspecific cause. Apart from a short initial period of 1 to 8 minutes, we can, therefore, not confirm the postulate by Lynch et al (1977) that the potentiation should be associated with a decrease in the general excitability of the nerve cells.

The increase in the population spike was well matched by the changes seen in individual units. The underlying cause seems to be an increased efficiency so a moderately increased EPSP excites the cell earlier and safer.

The short latency of this potentiation narrows the choice for possible interpretations. There are two main possibilities for an explanation of the phenomenon. One is that the increased EPSP is due to an increased amount of released transmitter, possibly related to the delayed calcium current described by several authors (7). This interpretation fits with the increase in the extracellular EPSP signaling an increased synaptic current.

However, an alternative explanation is that the same amount of transmitter produced a larger depolarization due to a change in the postsynaptic membrane. In spite of an unchanged soma membrane resistance, there is a possibility that local stretches of the dendritic membrane may show an increased resistance. In particular, Rall (9) has pointed to the possibility that the longitudinal resistance of the spine neck may change during periods of plastic behavior. Since the large majority of excitatory synapses in this region end on spines, and since nearly all the spines in question have a spine apparatus, it appears possible that ionic or other osmolarity changes in the spine head may induce a changed amount of fluid in the bags in the spine apparatus. This would lead to a shrinkage of the bags with a decreased neck resistance and, consequently, to an increased central effect of the injected synaptic current. More of the synaptic current would be available to depolarize the soma where the action potential probably starts.

An important problem is whether LLP may occur under physiological circumstances and whether this process takes part in learning processes. No assertions are possible. However, recordings from awake rats and rabbits have shown that hippocampal neurons often discharge for an adequate time and at an appropriate frequency for eliciting LLP. Furthermore, LLP may be elicited in awake rabbits where it lasts longer than in anesthetized preparations (5). Clearly, the simple homosynaptic facilitation of transmission can not by itself be compared with or even equated to memory processes. However, as a procedure for changing individual elements in a neuronal network which undergoes plastic changes during learning situations, LLP has a potential role. Unquestionably clarification of this important point requires prolonged recording from individual cells and their input lines in awake, behaving animals, a demanding task.

SUMMARY

Tetanic stimulation (10–50 Hz for 5–10 seconds) of afferent fibers to CAl pyramidal cells in hippocampal slices causes long-lasting potentiation (LLP) of synaptic transmission (more than one hour). The effect is seen as an increased amplitude and reduced latency of the population spike, an increased probability of discharge and decreased latency of single units, and intracellularly increased EPSP with reduced spike latency. Continuous recording of the presynaptic afferent volley ensured a constant input volley. The described effects are specific to the tetanized pathway, a control pathway to the same cells showing no change. Neither were there any significant changes in the membrane potential, in the firing level of the action potential, in the membrane resistance, or in the response to depolarizing current pulses across the soma membrane, thus ruling out a general excitability change of the membrane as a likely explanation. The effect is abolished by removing calcium ions from the extracellular medium during tetanization. The effect may be due to an increased release of transmitter due to increased and protracted calcium influx, or to a change in the postsynaptic spine neck resistance, or to both.

REFERENCES

1. Andersen P, Bliss TVP, Skrede KK: Unit analysis of hippocampal population spikes. *Exp Brain Res* 13:208–221, 1971.
2. Andersen P, Bliss TVP, Skrede KK: Lamellar organization of hippocampal excitatory pathways. *Exp Brain Res* 13:222–238, 1971.
3. Andersen P, Sundberg SH, Sveen O, et al: Specific long-lasting potentiation of synaptic transmission in hippocampal slices. *Nature* 266:736–737, 1977.
4. Blackstad TW, Brink K, Hem J, et al: Distribution of hippocampal mossy fibers in the rat: An experimental study with silver impregnation methods. *J Comp Neurol* 138:433–449, 1970.
5. Bliss TVP, Gardner-Medwin AR: Long-lasting potentiation of synaptic transmission in the dentate area of the unanaesthetized rabbit following stimulation of the perforant path. *J Physiol* (*London*) 232:357–374, 1973.
6. Bliss TVP, Lømo T: Long-lasting potentiation of synaptic transmission in the dentate area of the anaesthetized rabbit following stimulation of the perforant path. *J Physiol* (*London*) 232:331–356, 1973.
7. Heyer CB, Lux HD: Properties of a facilitating calcium current in pace-maker neurones of the snail, Helix pomatia. *J Physiol* (*London*) 262:319–348, 1976.
8. Lynch GS, Dunwiddie T, Gribkoff V: Heterosynaptic depression: a postsynaptic correlate of long-term potentiation. *Nature* 266:737–739, 1977.
9. Rall W: Cable properties of dendrites and effects of synaptic location, in Andersen P, Jansen JKS (eds): *Excitatory Synaptic Mechanisms*. Oslo, Universitetsforlaget, 1970, pp 175–187.
10. Ramón y Cajal S: *Histologie du Système Nerveux de l'Homme et des Vertébrés*. Paris, A Maloine, 1911.
11. Schwartzkroin PA, Wester K: Long-lasting facilitation of a synaptic potential following tetanization in the *in vitro* hippocampal slice. *Brain Res* 89:107–119, 1975.
12. Skrede KK, Westgaard RH: The transverse hippocampal slice: A well-defined cortical structure maintained *in vitro*. *Brain Res* 35:589–593, 1971.
13. Yamamoto C, McIlwain H: Electrical activities in thin sections from the mammalian brain maintained in chemically-defined media *in vitro*. *J Neurochem* 13:1333–1343, 1966.

4

Mechanisms of Cerebellar Motor Learning

Yasushi Miyashita

The cerebellum has long been assumed to be involved in a kind of learning by which an animal adapts to changes in environmental conditions or in accidental body status due to injury or disease and by which it acquires skills for various volitional movements. The structures of the cerebellum have been investigated in some detail (8). Five types of neurons are contained in the cerebellar cortex: granule cells, Golgi cells, basket cells, stellate cells, and Purkinje cells. There is considerable information on their mutual connections and on chemical transmitters that they release. These neurons compose a network, each small compartment of which (the microzones of Andersson and Oscarsson, ref. 2) may be involved specifically in controlling a subfunction of living body. Mathematical models of the cerebellum (1,28) could provide an interpretive link between the activities of single cerebellar neurons and the performance of the cerebellar neuronal networks. The central problem now is to learn how this cerebellar neuronal machine operates to perform the learning of motor controls.

This chapter summarizes recent experimental data on adaptive modification of the horizontal vestibulo-ocular reflex (HVOR). This phenomenon can be induced in a relatively easy and reproducible manner and is related specifically to a small area of the cerebellar cortex called the flocculus. The data have been accumulated along three lines of investigations: (*1*) the overall performance of the system concerned is analyzed by measuring eye movements in alert animals with or without lesions in the cerebellar and related structures; (*2*) relevant neuronal networks are dissected and their localization is determined; (*3*) discharges of cerebellar neurons are recorded while the animal is executing the adaptive control of the HVOR. The aim of these investigations is to formulate a hypothetical cerebellar learning mechanism.

VESTIBULO-OCULAR REFLEX (VOR)

The VOR induces eye movements that compensate for head movements to stabilize retinal images. Guided by vision, unsatisfactory performance of the VOR can be readily improved adaptively (12,22,29,33).

Simple trineuronal pathways from vestibular organ to eye muscles are the skeleton of the VOR system (Figure 4-1). The cerebellar flocculus is in the position to control this reflex, since it receives vestibular signals as a mossy fiber input and in turn projects to relay neurons of the VOR.

Ito (13,14) has pointed out that this VOR arc, by itself, had no means to improve its performance, that is, there is no feedback from eye position to vestibular input, while retinal blur signals misperformance of the VOR. It is thus proposed that the flocculus, by referring to visual information, exerts a fine adaptive adjustment of the VOR dynamics to guarantee a satisfactory ocular compensation.

Adaptive modification of the VOR thus appears to be a good model of the cerebellar motor learning.

Adaptive Gain Change of the Horizontal Vestibulo-Ocular Reflex (HVOR)

To evoke the HVOR, an alert albino rabbit was rotated sinusoidally on a horizontal turntable with his head fixed to the table, while a vertical slit light presented in front of the left eye provided visual stimuli. Eye movement was observed through a television camera (3). The HVOR was modified with vision under two experimental conditions. First, in the Fixed Slit Light (FSL) condition as it may be called, the slit light was attached to the floor, while the turntable was rotated. While a rabbit was rotated continuously for 12 to 13 hours under the FSL condition, the gain of the HVOR, as defined by the amplitude ratio of horizontal eye movement to head rotation, increased gradually (Fig. 4-2*a*,*b*). The net gain of the HVOR, g_v was measured in temporary darkness.

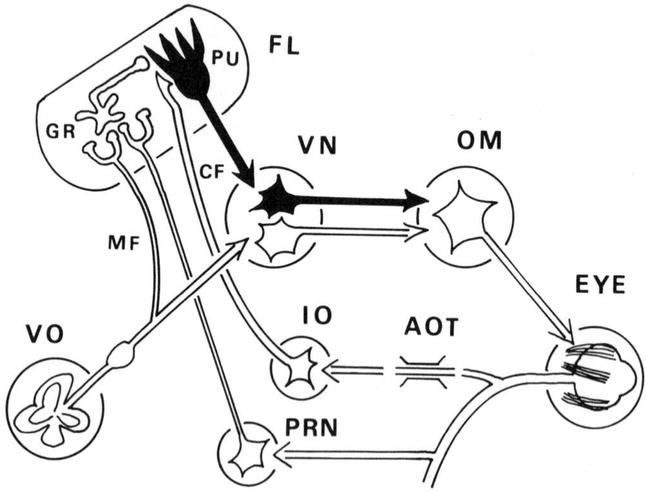

Figure 4-1. Neuronal schema showing relationships between the vestibulo-ocular reflex arc and the cerebellar flocculus. FL: flocculus, VO: vestibular organ, VN: vestibular nuclei, OM: oculomotor nuclei, IO: inferior olive, PRN: pontine reticular nucleus (Bechterew), AOT: accessory optic tract, PU: Purkinje cell, GR: granule cell, CF: climbing fiber, MF: mossy fiber. Black neurons are inhibitory ones.

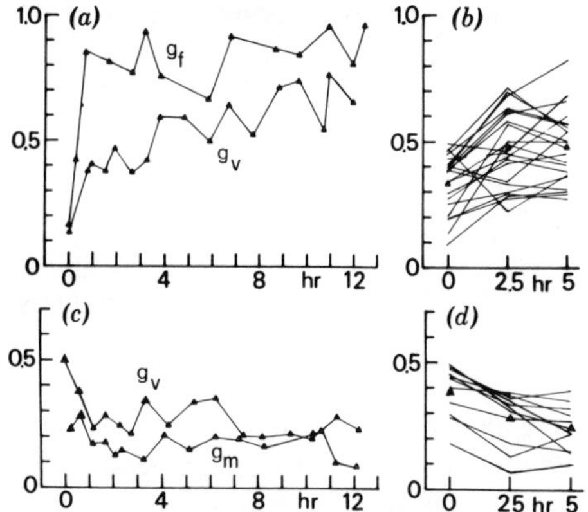

Figure 4-2. Adaptive changes of eye movements under sustained rotation with combined visual stimuli. (*a*) Five-degree (peak-to-peak) whole body rotation at 1/10 Hz on the horizontal turntable with the fixed slit light (FSL). ▲: g_v—net reflex gain measured in temporary darkness, Δ: g_f—reflex gain instantaneously modified with fixed slit light on. (*b*) Same condition as in (*a*) superimposing 22 measurements in 22 different rabbits at three times, before rotation and 2.5 hours and 5 hours after the onset of rotation. Triangles give the mean values. (*c*) Similar to (*a*) but with moving slit light (MSL) by 10° in phase with 5° turntable rotation. ▲: g_v—net reflex gain measured in temporary darkness, Δ: g_m—reflex gain modified with MSL. (*d*) Same condition as (*c*) superimposing measurements in the first runs on 11 rabbits. (Modified from Ito et al, ref. 16.)

Second, in the Moving Slit Light (MSL) condition, the slit light was moved in phase with the turntable by an angular amplitude twice as large as that of turntable. Continuous rotation for 12 to 13 hours under the MSL condition resulted in a gradual decrease of g_v (Figure 4-2*c,d*). These plastic changes of g_v under the sustained FSL or MSL condition continued for 24 to 48 hours after rotation, while the rabbit was kept in darkness.

It is important that these changes are not only plastic but also *adaptive*; that is, g_v can be increased or decreased, in the optimal direction for stabilizing retinal images (3,29). In those rabbits in which the ipsilateral flocculus was ablated beforehand, no adaptive change occurred in the HVOR gain. To the contrary, the adpative gain change was preserved after ablations of the contralateral flocculus, ipsilateral paraflocculus, bilateral nodulus and uvula, bilateral lobule VI and VII, and cerebral visual cortex (M. Ito, P. J. Jastreboff, and Y. Miyashita, in preparation). Hence, the adaptive modification of the HVOR in rabbits is specifically related to the ipsilateral flocculus. In cats the adaptation of the HVOR was influenced rather diffusely from the entire vestibulo-cerebellum (33).

FUNCTIONAL LOCALIZATION FOR THE HVOR IN THE FLOCCULUS

A difficulty in the attempt to know what occurs in the flocculus neurons during the adaptation of the HVOR, has been that the flocculus contains many neurons unrelated to the HVOR. Recent knowledge of the functional localization in the flocculus helps to overcome this difficulty.

In Figure 4-1, the VOR arc is represented by single pathway from vestibular organ to eye muscle. The actual VOR system contains many component pathways from three semicircular canals and two otolith receptors on each side to six ipsilateral and six contralateral extraocular muscles. The flocculus inhibits only some specific components among them (19). The HVOR consists of excitatory pathways (*1*) from the ipsilateral horizontal canal (HC) to the medial rectus muscle (MR), (*2*) from the contralateral HC to the lateral rectus muscle (LR), and inhibitory pathways (*3*) from the ipsilateral HC to the LR 4) from the contralateral HC to the MR. The flocculus inhibits pathways *1* and *3* specifically.

Purkinje cells inhibiting each component of the VOR are localized in their own strip-like area in the flocculus. This can be demonstrated by a study using retrograde axonal transport of the horseradish peroxidase (35), as well as by observing eye movements evoked from the flocculus (5).

In the experiments where Purkinje cell activities were recorded from the flocculus, electric pulse trains were applied through the microelectrode to each recording site (frequency: 500 Hz, duration: 1 second, pulse width: 0.2 msec, current intensity: 5–40μA). When the stimulation induced abduction of the ipsilateral eye, as in Figure 4-3(*a*) or (*f*), the recorded Purkinje cells were taken as inhibiting the HVOR and specified as H-zone Purkinje cells, because the inhibition of both pathways *1* and *3* of the HVOR mentioned above can induce the abduction. H-zone Purkinje cells were found in a strip-like area localized relatively ventrally in the flocculus (Figure 4-3*h*). When a ventral eye movement was induced in the ipsilateral eye, as in Figure 4-3(*b*) or (*g*), recorded Purkinje cells were related to the vertical VOR; they are called V-zone Purkinje cells. If no eye movement occurred in the ipsilateral eye, the recorded Purkinje cells were lumped together as N-zone Purkinje cells, which might be related to the rotatory reflex in the contralateral eye (Figure 4-3*c*), or which might have nothing to do with the VOR.

RESPONSES OF PURKINJE CELLS TO HEAD ROTATION IN DARKNESS

Using glass microelectrodes, two types of spikes were recorded extracellularly from flocculus Purkinje cells, that is simple and complex spikes (10). Simple spikes, separated from complex spikes by a slicer device, were taken as major output from Purkinje cells. While the rabbits were rotated sinusoidally by 5° or 10° in darkness, each period was divided into 18 bins, and the number of spikes occurring during each bin was counted and averaged for 10 periods. Spike density histograms thus constructed for simple spikes for rotation in darkness were often modulated, either in phase or out of phase with head velocity. The best-fitting sine curve was determined for each spike density histogram by Fourier analysis. A mathematical method was used for removing influences of a linear drift involved in the histogram, and for evaluating the statistical significance of fitness of the derived sine curves (23); only those curves with statistical significance at $P < 0.05$ were selected. The amplitude of the sine curves relative to the mean discharge frequency and its phase shift relative to the head velocity were plotted on polar diagrams (Figure 4-4). The cells plotted in the quadrant for the phase angle of 180° ± 45° are called outphase cells and those in the quadrant for 0° ± 45°, inphase cells.

The relationship between sampled Purkinje cells and types of the VOR was revealed by applying electric pulse trains to each recording site as described above. In most H-zone Purkinje cells thus specified (84 of 93 cells), head rotation in darkness induced significant modulation of simple spikes (Figure 4-4*a*). Surprisingly, many Purkinje cells in the other zones, which were not related to the HVOR, responded to horizontal rotation

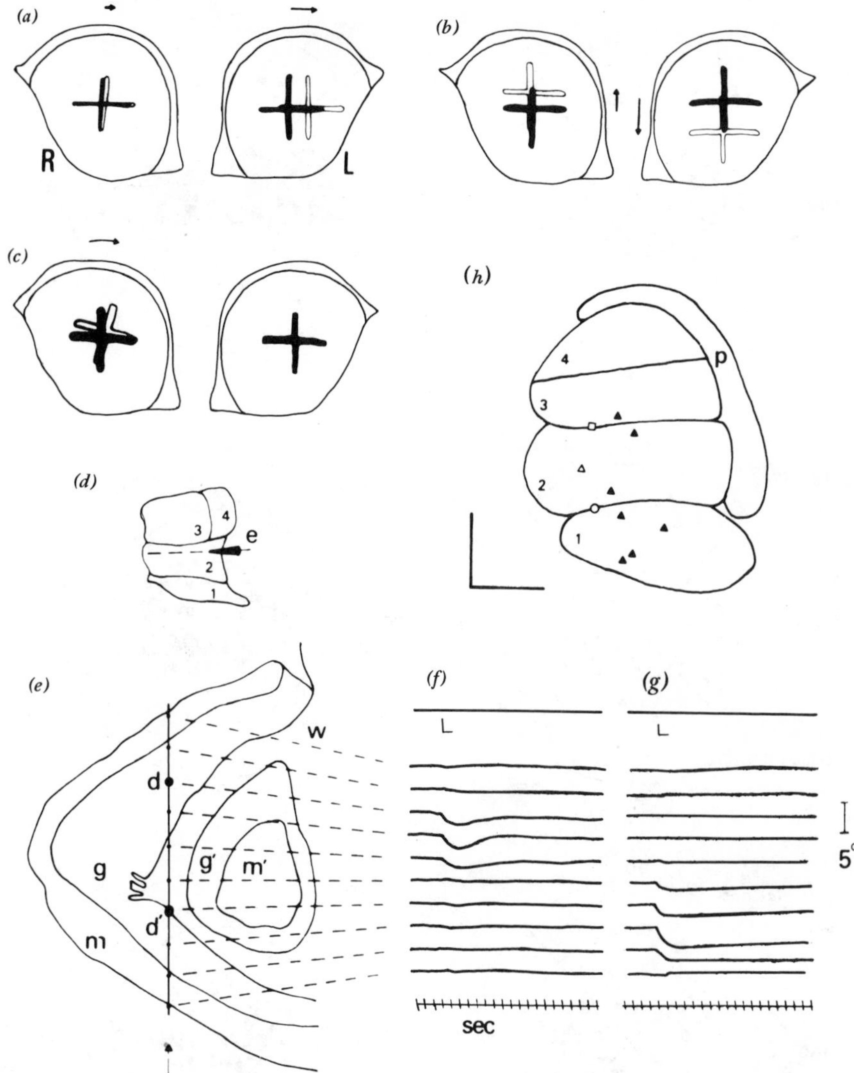

Figure 4-3. Eye movements induced by stimulation of the left flocculus. (*a*), (*b*), (*c*) Line drawings of the right (R) and left (L) eyes to which cross marks were attached. Images of the crosses at the beginning of flocculus stimulation (for parameters, see text) are filled in and those at 3 seconds thereafter are hollow. (*d*) Side-view of the flocculus studied in (*e*), (*f*), and (*g*) Broken line indicates direction of tracking with the microelectrode (e). (*e*) Tracing of the section of the flocculus along the electrode track in (*d*). m and m′ : molecular layers, g and g′ : granule layers, w: white matter, d and d′: dye spots. The electrode track is shown by a straight line on which dots mark the stimulated sites. The rostral side is represented upward. (*f*), (*g*) Horizontal (*f*) and vertical (*g*) movements of a corneal mark. Each pair of records is connected with a broken line to the spot stimulated. Downward deflections in (*f*) signify abductions and those in (*g*) downward movements of the left eye. Downward deflections in top traces indicate application of train pulse stimulation. (*h*) Side view of the flocculus systematically explored with a microelectrode. Scale, 1mm. (From Dufosse[1], et al, ref. 5.)

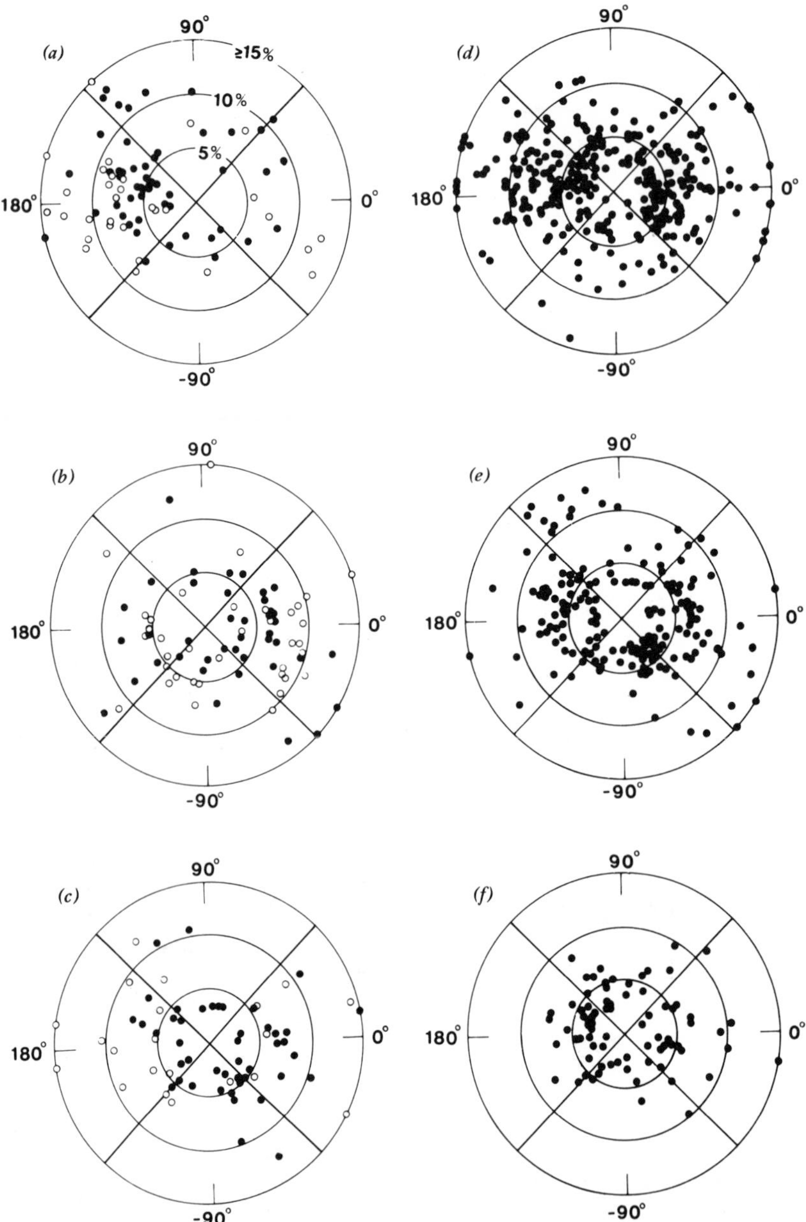

Figure 4-4. Modulation of simple spikes induced in flocculus Purkinje cells by rotation in darkness at 1/10 Hz. (*a*), (*b*), (*c*) and (*e*) were obtained in control experiments. ○: rotation by 10° (peak-to-peak), ●: rotation by 5°. (*a*) Diagram for H zone, (*b*) for V zone, (*c*) for N zone and (*e*) for all controls with 5° rotation including not only those plotted in (*a*), (*b*), and by ● but also those for which relevant eye movement types were not identified. (*d*) was obtained under adaptive enhancement of the HVOR by sustained 5° rotation with the fixed slit light. (*f*) Similar to (*d*), but under depression of the HVOR with the moving slit light. While recording spikes, the slit light was turned off temporarily. (From Dufossé et al, ref. 4.)

(80 of 135 cells in the V-zone, 72 of 123 cells in the N-zone). However, the H-zone was characterized by the fact that in more than half of the H-zone Purkinje cells, simple spike discharges were modulated out of phase with head velocity (49 outphase cells of 82 cells), as shown in Figure 4-4(*a*). In the V- and N-zones, outphase cells formed only minor groups (Figure 4-4*b,c*).

The dominance of outphase cells in the H-zone means that the flocculus is normally exerting a facilitatory action on the HVOR. Since impulse discharges from primary vestibular afferents are modulated in phase with head velocity (9), outphase modulations of inhibitory Purkinje cells would cooperate with them in activating secondary vestibular neurons (see Figure 4-1). This conclusion is consistent with the fact that ipsilateral flocculectomy induced not only the loss of adaptive gain change of the HVOR but also a slight reduction of the HVOR gain (M. Ito, P. J. Jastreboff, and Y. Miyashita, in preparation).

ADAPTIVE CHANGE OF PURKINJE CELL RESPONSES

To demonstrate any change occurring in the flocculus in connection with adaptation of the HVOR, simple spike modulations of the H-zone Purkinje cells were compared before and after the adaptation with FSL or MSL.

In the FSL condition, the net gain of the HVOR, g_v, gradually increased, attaining a plateau in 5 hours after the onset of rotation (Figure 4-2*a*). In the MSL condition, on the other hand, there was a gradual gain reduction (Figure 4-2*c*). Sampling of flocculus Purkinje cells started when g_v had changed in 5 hours by more than 20% of the initial value, and continued thereafter for 7 to 8 hours. While impulses were recorded, the slit light was temporarily turned off.

In these adaptation experiments, local stimulation of the flocculus for specifying the three zones was not attempted, because some preliminary experiments suggested the possibility that the stimulation interfered with adaptive processes in the flocculus. Hence, Purkinje cells sampled from the whole flocculus were pooled for each of the three conditions of the HVOR evoked by 5° rotation: (*a*) adaptively depressed with MSL, (*b*) control, and (*c*) adaptively enhanced with FSL. However, as described in the preceding section, H-zone cells are contained mainly on the outphase quadrant. When attention is focused on the outphase modulation, an appreciable and systematic difference is found in the amplitudes of modulation, as shown in Figure 4-4(*d*),(*e*), and (*f*). In the FSL-adapted group, the points plotted in the outphase quadrant diverge from the center of the diagram (Figure 4-4*d*), and in the MSL-adapted group, they converge onto the center (Figure 4-4*f*), as compared with those in the control (Figure 4-4*e*).

To quantify this observation, we constructed Figure 4-5, which shows cumulative distribution curves for amplitudes of the outphase modulation under the three conditions of the HVOR. The distributions shift from the left to the right in the order: (*a*) MSL-adapted, (*b*) control, and (*c*) FSL-adapted. According to Smirnov's one-side test, the differences between the curves (*a*) and (*b*) and between the curves (*b*) and (*c*) were statistically significant at 1% level. Since the rightward shift of the curves in Figure 4-5 means an increase of the population of larger outphase modulation, the results of the experiment may be summarized as in Table 4-1. The outphase modulation of the H-zone Purkinje cells has an facilitatory action on the HVOR as discussed in the preceding section. Hence, the direction of the changes in modulation (Table 4-1) is consistent with the direction of the gain change of the eye movements.

In summary, three lines of evidence, that is, studies of eye movements, analyses of neuronal connectivity, and recordings from Purkinje cells, all support the initial hypothesis that the flocculus is the site of visually induced adaptive and plastic modification of the vestibulo-ocular reflex (VOR).

However, in recording from the primate flocculus, some Purkinje cells were found to discharge in connection with eye velocity (30). It has been proposed that visual inputs to the primate flocculus are of minor importance, and that the primate flocculus is not a site for visual-vestibular interaction (24). Before ascribing this seeming contradiction to a difference of animal species, it is necessary to obtain more data about visual and eye velocity inputs to the flocculus. In the rabbit, visual inputs to the flocculus, mediated not only by climbing fiber afferents (25) but also by mossy fiber afferents (26), were revealed by both electric and flashlight stimulation. Recently it has been confirmed that visual signals, via both climbing and mossy fiber afferents, reach the H-zone of the flocculus, which is specifically related to the HVOR (31; Ito, M., Orlov, 1. and Yamamoto, M., to be published). The origin of the visual mossy fibers in the rabbit has recently been localized in the nucleus reticularis pontis (Bechterew) by Maekawa and Takeda (27) and by Yamamoto (to be published). In primate experiments, an important question to be answered is whether eye velocity inputs reach the H-zone of Purkinje cells, because

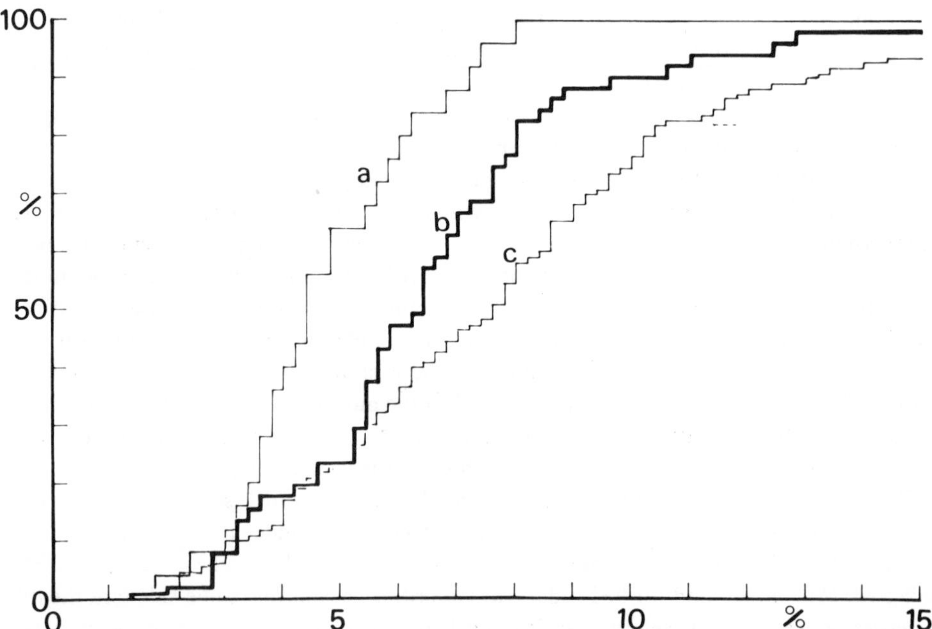

Figure 4-5. Cumulative distribution curves for amplitudes of the outphase modulation of sample spikes. Abscissa: amplitude of modulation; ordinate: cumulated number of cells in percentage of the total number of cells involved in each group of the outphase Purkinje cells. (*a*) Curve for the points plotted in the outphase quadrant (180° ± 45°) of Figure 4-4 (*f*); (*b*), (*c*) for Figure 4-4 (*e*), (*d*). (From Dufossé et al, ref. 4.)

Table 4-1. Diagrammatic Summary of Mechanism of Cerebellar Motor Learning

	HVOR GAIN	FLOCCULUS H-ZONE PURKINJE CELLS
FSL-ADAPTED	INCREASE	MORE OUT PHASE
MSL-ADAPTED	DECREASE	LESS OUT PHASE

more than two thirds of flocculus Purkinje cells in the rabbits are unrelated to the HVOR as discussed above. Further work in evaluating the relative contribution of vestibular and eye velocity inputs to H-zone Purkinje cells is needed to answer this controversial question.

CONJUNCTION HYPOTHESIS OF CEREBELLAR LEARNING

At the present stage of our knowledge, there are several possibilities for explaining the mechanisms of adaptability of the VOR system. An attractive hypothesis is that climbing fiber afferents originating from the inferior olive (IO) play the teacher's role in modifying the responsiveness of Purkinje cells to mossy fiber inputs (1,28). In this hypothesis, the essential structure of cerebellar neuronal network was considered to have much in common with the "simple perceptron," which is a mathematical model of technological "pattern recognizor" with learning capability (34). If the following two assumptions are valid, that is, (*1*) if synaptic transmission efficacies between granule cells and Purkinje cells are modifiable and (*2*) if activities in the climbing fibers control this modifiability, then, the cerebellum could work as a "programmable" controller for any movements: that is, the cerebellar cortical networks could be organized through learning to respond with any specific output pattern of Purkinje cell discharges to each input pattern of mossy fiber activities. This type of hypothesis for learning is called the "conjunction theory" (7).

In the adaptive control of the HVOR, any misperformance of the system can be detected through vision (13,14). The IO indeed relays visual signals to the flocculus (25). Hence, the adaptability of the HVOR system provides a good model for testing the validity of the hypothesis.

ROLE OF THE INFERIOR OLIVE IN ADAPTIVE CHANGE OF THE HVOR

The first step in the investigation of the role of the inferior olive (IO) in the HVOR was to interrupt visual pathways to the IO beforehand and to observe the effect on eye movements. Visual signals to the flocculus via climbing fibers are relayed in a localized portion of the IO, that is, the dorsal cap (25,32).

In one group of rabbits, electrolytic lesions were placed relatively rostrally to interrupt visual inputs to dorsal cap without impairing neurons of the source of climbing fibers to the flocculus (Figure 4-6). In them no adaptive modification of the HVOR

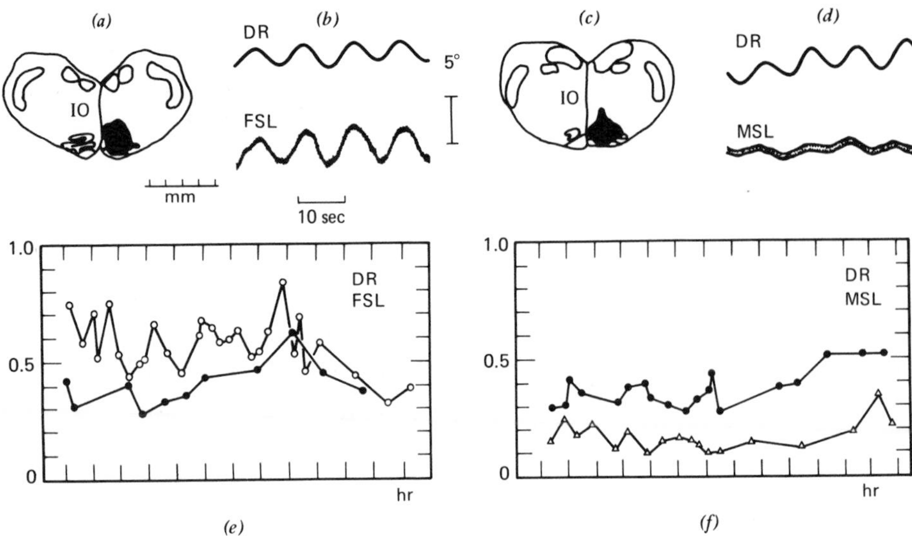

Figure 4-6. The horizontal vestibulo-ocular reflex combined with visual stimuli after destruction of rostral portion of the inferior olive. (*a*) Frontal section of the medulla through the rostral part of the inferior olive (IO). The electrolytic lesion is filled in. (*b*) Pen-writer record of horizontal rotation of the left eye measured in darkness (DR) or with the fixed slit light (FSL). The turntable was rotated by 5° (peak-to-peak) at 1/10 Hz. (*c*), (*d*) Similar to (*a*) and (*b*) but in another preparation with the lesion at the rostral pole of the inferior olive and tested with moving slit light (MSL). (*e*) Effects of sustained rotation with FSL, for the rabbit shown in A (compare with Figure 4-2a). ●: g_v—net reflex gain measured in temporary darkness, O: g_r—reflex gain modified with FSL. (*f*) Effects of sustained rotation with MSL, for the rabbit shown in (*d*) (compare with Fig. 4-2*c*). ●: g_v—net reflex gain measured in temporary darkness, Δ: g_m—reflex gain modified with MSL. (Modified from Ito and Miyashita, ref. 17.)

could induced with either the FSL (Figure 4-6*e*) or the MSL (Figure 4-6*f*) conditions. This result is favorable for the hypothesis that the IO plays the teacher's role in the adaptation.

Instantaneous change induced in the HVOR with FSL (Figure 4-6*b*) or with MSL (Figure 4-6*d*) was not affected by the interruption of visual inputs to the dorsal cap; it should be mediated by some other structures.

In another group of rabbits, electrolytic lesion involved the dorsal cap. Then, adaptive changes of the HVOR were abolished with the exception of an abnormal later change. Moreover, dynamics of the HVOR were seriously impaired just as in the case of flocculectomy; the net gain of the HVOR was reduced, and instantaneous visual effect on the HVOR was diminished. Why olivectomy resembles cerebellectomy in its effect has been explained by the recent experiments described below, which also reveal an important role of the IO in maintaining cerebellar functions.

IMPAIRMENT OF PURKINJE INHIBITION AFTER OLIVECTOMY

When electric stimuli are applied to the flocculus, downward shift or horizontal abduction is frequently induced in the ipsilateral eye. Destruction of the dorsal cap (DC)

(Figure 4-7*a*), or the adjacent area of the ventrolateral outgrowth (VLO) of the IO, alters the effect of flocculus stimulation drastically (6).

When an electrolytic lesion covered the rostral parts of the DC and VLO (Figure 4-7*b*), horizontal eye movements evoked by stimulation of the flocculus appeared normal, but vertical eye movements were reduced and changed in direction, that is, upward (Figure 4-7*e*; compare with the normal case shown in Figure 4-3*g*). On the other hand, when a lesion partially involved the caudal half of the DC (Figure 4-7*d*), the evoked movements were often, although not always (depending on the stimulated site), slightly adducted (Figure 4-7*f*), whereas vertical eye movements were downward as in normal rabbits.

The rostral parts of the DC and VLO project to flocculus Purkinje cells that inhibit relay cells of the vertical components of the VOR (18). Since the downward shift of the ipsilateral eye evoked in the normal rabbits is presumed to be affected by excitation of these Purkinje cells (5), reduction and reversal of the evoked vertical eye movements should indicate that, after deprivation of the climbing fiber afferents, the inhibitory action of Purkinje cells can no longer be actuated by the flocculus stimulation and thus is replaced by a facilitation, which is presumably mediated by axon collaterals of cerebellar afferents innervating subcortical cells and which is normally masked by that

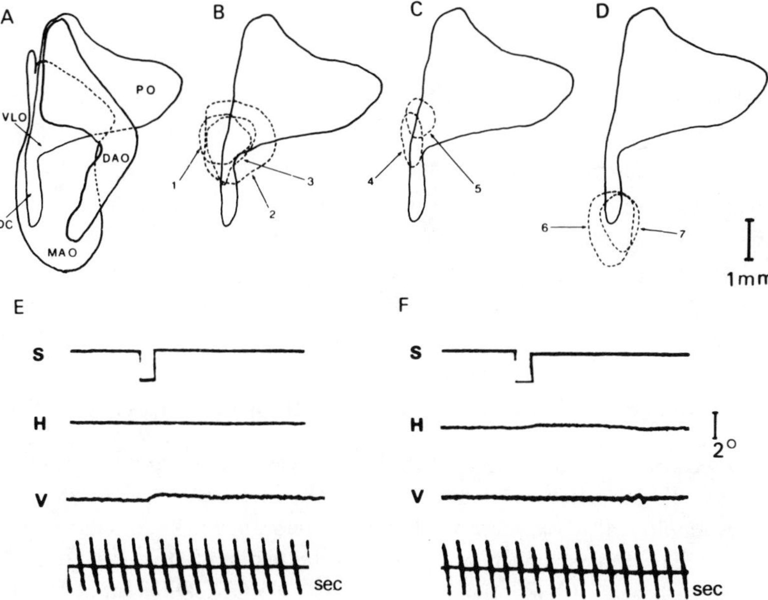

Figure 4-7. Eye movements induced by stimulation of the left flocculus after destruction of the right inferior olive. (*a*) Schematically drawn dorsal view of the right inferior olive of the rabbit. The rostral side is represented upward. PO: principal olive, MAO and DAO: medial and dorsal accessory olives. (*b*), (*c*), (*d*) Locations of the electrolytic lesions indicated by broken lines on the PO. Numbers specify contours of lesions on different rabbits. (*e*), (*f*) pen-writer record of eye movements (compare with Fig. 4-3*f*,*g*). H: horizontal movement with adduction upward, V: vertical movements with dorsal shift upward, S: monitoring the period of flocculus stimulation (for parameters, see text). (*e*) was obtained from the rabbit No. 4 (*c*) and (*f*) from No. 6 (*d*). (From Dufossé et al, ref. 6.)

inhibition. The caudal part of the DC, on the other hand, projects to Purkinje cells, the inhibit relay cells of the horizontal VOR. Diminution of horizontal abduction and its conversion to adduction after destruction of the caudal part of the DC can be explained similarly by assuming impairment of the Purkinje cell inhibition of relay cells of the HVOR and consequent unmasking of the collateral facilitation.

The above interpretation was supported by the recent experiments of Ito et al (20,21), which demonstrated that the monosynaptic inhibition of Deiters neurons by Purkinje cells was rapidly depressed after the destruction of the IO.

Apparently the IO plays an important role in maintaining the normal activities of cerebellar neurons. An interesting problem is whether or not this maintenance function of the IO is related to the role assumed in the adaptive modification of the HVOR.

DISCUSSION

Adaptive modification of the HVOR by the cerebellar flocculus now appears to be a good model of cerebellar motor learning. The system is relatively simple, so it can be subjected to extensive analyses at each level of behavioral performance, neuronal networks, cellular discharges, and synaptic events. The major experimental results presented above can be summarized as follows:

1. In rabbits, the FSL stimulus condition enhances and the MSL depresses the HVOR, adaptively and plastically.
2. Ablation of the cerebellar flocculus abolishes this adaptation.
3. Interruption of visual inputs to flocculus Purkinje cells via the inferior olive (IO) also abolishes the adaptation.
4. Purkinje cells in the flocculus inhibit the relay neurons of the HVOR, while they receive both visual and vestibular inputs, which are prerequisite for controlling the HVOR.
5. Flocculus Purkinje cells related to the HVOR change their responsiveness to vestibular stimuli adaptively in the direction consistent with changes in the HVOR.

A key procedure in establishing the fifth finding was to select and to record from only the Purkinje cells intimately related to the HVOR. Involvement of irrelevant Purkinje cells in the sample will mask adaptive changes in relevant Purkinje cells. Such selection will be particularly important when we try to evaluate quantitatively the contribution of Purkinje cell discharges to adaptive changes of the HVOR. Differential localization of such Purkinje cells inhibiting the HVOR in a strip-like area of the flocculus would correspond to the recent concept of *microzone.* In the cerebellar vermal cortex, Andersson and Oscarsson (2) have localized narrow strips of a millimeter wide and a few millimeters long as receiving specific climbing fiber inputs from the inferior olive and as projecting to specific subgroups of Deiters neurons. Each of these subgroups of Deiters neurons receives collaterals of the same climbing fibers that project to the Purkinje cells of the microzone, projecting in turn to it. The cerebellar cortex now appears to have a mosaic structure with a number of microzones, each of which behaves as a unit in cerebellar functions.

The recent finding that destruction of the IO neurons induces rapid depression in Purkinje cell inhibition revealed a new role of the IO in the maintenance of synaptic action of cerebellar Purkinje cells. An interesting question, when we note the close structural interrelationships among the three types of neurons mentioned above (i.e., IO neurons, cerebellar Purkinje cells, and their common target neurons), is whether or not the direct olivovestibular fibers influence the synaptic action of Purkinje cells on the vestibular neurons. Another question still to be answered is whether or not that maintenance role contributes to the learning function of the IO.

The results obtained in the experiments with rabbit flocculus support the hypothesis that climbing fiber afferents play the teacher's role in cerebellar learning by modifying the transmission efficacies between granule cells and Purkinje cells, even though granule-cell to Purkinje-cell transmission has not been directly tested. It is worth noting that, in many cases, simple spikes and complex spikes of a Purkinje cell modulate their discharge frequencies in a reciprocal manner. Sinusoidal rotation of the slit light, for example, increased the discharge rate of simple spikes of a Purkinje cell during its backward movement, as seen in many H-zone Purkinje cells, when that of complex spikes was increased during forward movement (15,31). This would suggest that climbing fiber inputs, represented by complex spikes, reduce the transmission to the Purkinje cells from the granule cells, which fire simultaneously with the complex spikes (1). Our results on adaptive changes of simple spike modulation during the HVOR adaptation, as summarized in Table 4-1, are consistent with the above view, because complex spikes modulate the discharge rate inphase with head velocity under FSL condition, and outphase under MSL condition, in most H-zone Purkinje cells (15,31). A similar view of a suppressive effect of complex spikes was presented recently, based on an experiment of primate motor learning (11). Further investigations are necessary to examine the underlying synaptic events directly.

In summary, the adaptation of the HVOR appears to be a good model for investigating not only cerebellar learning mechanisms but also the mechanisms of memory and learning in general.

ACKNOWLEDGMENTS

The author gratefully acknowledges the essential guidance and collaboration given by Professor Masao Ito. He is also obligated to Drs. M. Dufossé, P. J. Jastreboff, C. Batini, and R. T. Kado for their collaboration during parts of the series of experiments presented in this chapter.

REFERENCES

1. Albus JS: A theory of cerebellar function. *Math Biosci* 10:25–61, 1971.
2. Andersson G, Oscarsson O: Climbing fiber microzones in cerebellar vermis and their projection to different groups of cells in the lateral vestibular nucleus. *Exp Brain Res* 32:565–580, 1978.
3. Batini C, Ito M, Kado RT, et al: Interaction between the horizontal vestubulo-ocular reflex and optokinetic response in rabbits. *Exp Brain Res* (to be published).

4. Dufossé M, Ito M, Jastreboff PJ, et al: A neuronal correlate in rabbit's cerebellum to adaptive modification of the vestibulo-ocular reflex. *Brain Res* 150:611–616, 1978.
5. Dufossé M, Ito M, Miyashita Y: Functional localization in the rabbit's cerebellar flocculus determined inrelationship with eye movements. *Neurosci Lett* 5:273–277, 1977.
6. Dufossé M, Ito M, Miyashita Y: Diminution and reversal of eye movements induced by local stimulation of rabbit cerebellar flocculus after partial destruction of the inferior olive. *Exp Brain Res* 33:139–142, 1978.
7. Eccles JC: *The Understanding of the Brain.* New York, McGraw-Hill, 1973.
8. Eccles JC, Ito M, Szentágothai J: *The Cerebellum as a Neuronal Machine.* New York, Springer, 1967.
9. Fernandez C, Goldberg JM: Physiology of peripheral neurons innevating semicircular canals of the squirrel monkey. II. Response to sinusoidal stimulation and dynamics of peripheral vestibular system. *J Neurophysiol* 34:661–675, 1971.
10. Ghelarducci B, Ito M, Yagi N: Impulse discharges from flocculus Purkinje cells of alert rabbits during visual stimulation combined with horizontal head rotation. *Brain Res* 87:66–72, 1975.
11. Gilbert PFC, Thach WT: Purkinje cell activity during motor learning. *Brain Res* 128:309–328, 1977.
12. Gonshor A, Melvill Jones G: Extreme vestibulo-ocular adaptation induced by prolonged optical reversal of vision. *J Physiol (London)* 256–381–414, 1976.
13. Ito M: Neurophysiological aspects of the cerebellar motor control system. *Internat J Neurol* 7:162–176, 1970.
14. Ito M: Neural design of the cerebellar motor control system. *Brain Res* 40:81–84, 1972.
15. Ito M: Neuronal events in the cerebellar flocculus associated with an adaptive modification of the vestibulo-ocular reflex of the rabbit, in Baker R, Berthoz A (eds): *Control of Gaze by Brain-stem Neurons.* Amsterdam, Elsevier, 1977.
16. Ito M, Jastreboff PJ, Miyashita Y: Adaptive modification of the rabbit's horizontal vestibulo-ocular reflex during sustained vestibular and optokinetic stimulation. *Exp Brain Res* (to be published).
17. Ito M, Miyashita Y: The effects of chronic destruction of the inferior olive upon visual modification of the horizontal vestibulo-ocular reflex of rabbits. *Proc Japan Acad* 51:716–720, 1975.
18. Ito M, Miyashita Y, Ueki A: Functional localization in the rabbit's inferior olive determined in connection with the vestibulo-ocular reflex. *Neurosci Lett* 8:283–287, 1978.
19. Ito M, Nishimaru N, Yamamoto M: Specific patterns of neuronal connexions involved in the control of the rabbit's vestibulo-ocular reflexes by the cerebellar flocculus. *J Physiol (London)* 265:833–854, 1977.
20. Ito M, Nishimaru N, Shibuki K: Destruction of inferior olive induces rapid depression in synaptic action of cerebellar Purkinje cells. *Nature* 277:568–569, 1979.
21. Ito M, Orlov I, Shimoyama I: Reduction of the cerebellar stimulus effect on rat Deiters neurons after chemical destruction of the inferior olive. *Exp Brain Res* 33:143–146, 1978.
22. Ito M, Shiida T, Yagi N, et al: Visual influence on rabbit's horizontal vestibulo-ocular reflex presumably effected via the cerebellar flocculus. *Brain Res* 65:170–174, 1974.
23. Jastreboff PJ: Evaluation and statistical judgment of neural responses to sinusoidal stimulation in cases with superimposed drift and noise. *Biol Cybern* 33:113–120, 1979.
24. Lisberger SG, Fuchs AF: Role of primate flocculus during rapid behavioral modification of vestibulo-ocular reflex. I. Purkinje cell activity during visually guided horizontal smooth pursuit eye movements and passive head rotation. *J Neurophysiol* 41:733–763, 1978.
25. Maekawa K, Simpson JI: Climbing fiber responses evoked in vestibulocerebellum of rabbit from visual system. *J Neurophysiol* 36:649–666, 1973.
26. Maekawa K, Takeda T: Mossy fiber responses evoked in the cerebellar flocculus of rabbits by stimulation of the optic pathway. *Brain Res* 98:590–595, 1975.
27. Maekawa K, Takeda T: Origin of the mossy fiber projection to the cerebellar flocculus from the optic nerves in rabbits, in Ito M, et al: *Integrative Control Functions of the Brain,* vol 1. Tokyo, Kodansha-Scientific, 1978, pp 110–112.
28. Marr D: A theory of cerebellar cortex. *J Physiol (London)* 202:437–470, 1969.
29. Miles FA, Fuller JH: Adaptive plasticity in vestibulo-ocular responses of the rhesus monkey. *Brain Res* 80:512–516, 1974.

30. Miles FA, Fuller JH: Visual tracking and the primate flocculus. *Science* 189:1000–1002, 1975.

31. Miyashita Y: Interaction of visual and canal inputs on the oculomotor system via the cerebellar flocculus. *Progress in Brain Res* (to be published).

32. Mizuno N, Mochizuki K, Akimoto C, Pretectal projections to the inferior olive in the rabbit. *Exp Neurol* 39:498–506, 1973.

33. Robinson DA: Adaptive gain control of vestibulo-ocular reflex by the cerebellum. *J Neurophysiol* 39:954–969, 1976.

34. Rosenblatt F: *Principles of Neurodynamics: Perceptrons and the Theory of Brain Mechanisms.* Washington, DC, Spartan Books, 1962.

35. Yamamoto M, Shimoyama I: Deferential localization of rabbit's flocculus Purkinje cells projecting to the medial and superior vestibular nuclei, investigated by means of the horseradish peroxidase retrograde axonal transport. *Neurosci Lett* 5:279–283, 1977.

5
Neuronal Mechanisms of Visual Cortical Plasticity

Keisuke Toyama

COLUMNAR AND LAMINAR ORGANIZATION IN THE VISUAL CORTEX

Visual cortical plasticity has been intensively studied during the last decade (2,3,5,7,11,23). It has been established that responsiveness of the cortical cells is highly modifiable according to visual experience. The modifiability is exhibited only during the early infancy of the animal (3,11,24). Once the responsiveness of the cortical cells, either normal or abnormal, has been established, it persists for life. It is likely that neuronal networks in the visual cortex are still immature in infancy and that their structures can be modified by visual experience, within certain limitations.

In contrast to its remarkable modifiability during infancy, the visual cortex of the adult animal is characterized by orderly fixed organizations. One of them is the columnar organization. As schematically illustrated in Figure 5-1, cells reponding to the inputs through the right eye are clustered into a slab perpendicular to the cortical surface (R columns) and those responding through the left eye into another slab (L columns). Orthogonal to these slabs of ocular dominance are relatively smaller slabs in which cells are clustered according to their preference for the orientation of light stimuli. The orientation slabs are arranged in a well-ordered sequence, from the one for the vertical orientation to that for the horizontal one and further back to the vertical one (7,12).

Finally there is a tangential organization. Cells of similar efferent connectivity are arranged in a lamina. Cells whose axons project to the contralateral visual cortex or to the ipsilateral visual association cortex are located in layer III (E_1 in Figure 5-2*a*); those projecting to the superior colliculus, in layer V (E_2); and those to the lateral geniculate body, in layer VI (E_3). A similar tangential organization is also found for afferent inputs. Only cells in layers III to V (E_1, E_2, and I_1 in Figure 5-2*b*) receive excitatory input from the geniculate body directly. Cells in layers II and VI (I' and E_3) receive the input indirectly through an excitatory interneuron in layer IV (I_1). Inhibition from the lateral geniculate body is exerted on cells in layers III to V (E_1, E_2, and I_1 in Figure 5-2*c*) through an inhibitory interneuron in layer IV (I_2). On those in layers II and VI

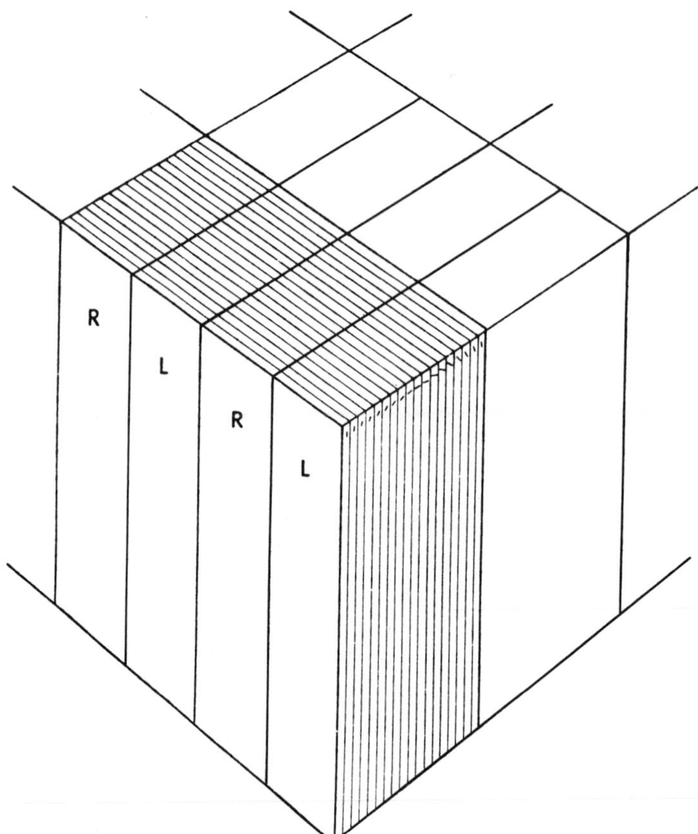

Figure 5-1. Three-dimensional schema of columnar structures in the visual cortex. Two organizations, ocular dominance and orientation columns, are represented along the two coordinates orthogonal to each other. The columns denoted by L and R are those for the inputs through the left and right eyes; those denoted by vertical and horizontal bars represent the columns for the vertical and horizontal orientation, respectively. (From Hubel and Wiesel, ref. 12.)

(I′ and E_3) inhibition is exerted through additional inhibitory interneurons (I_3 and I_4) located nearby (20).

These perpendicular and tangential organizations in the visual cortex can be viewed either functionally, as clusters of cells with a similar responsiveness to light stimuli (7,12), or structurally, as cells with similar input-output connections (20).

We attempted to correlate structural and functional factors in perpendicular and tangential organizations of the visual cortex. For this purpose we used cross-correlation analysis of activities in two cortical cells. This technique reveals the ongoing interaction between two cells during their responses to visual stimuli and allows us to study responsiveness and neuronal connectivity of cortical cells at the same time. Another advantage of the cross-correlation technique is that it does not use electrical stimuli, which often introduce complications such as artifact potentials and spread of stimulus currents to the neighboring brain structures. This advantage is important in the study of the intrinsic connectivity in the visual cortex where the distance of the intercellular connections are extremely small (13,16).

This chapter describes the perpendicular and parallel frameworks in the visual cortex, as revealed by this cross-correlation study, and discusses the possible relevance of these structures to the visual cortical plasticity.

CROSS-CORRELATION TECHNIQUE

As illustrated in Figure 5-3(*a*), impulse discharges were recorded simultaneously from two cells using two microelectrodes. One of the microelectrodes was double barreled (m_2 in Figure 5-3*a*). One barrel, filled with 2M NaCl, was used for recording, while the other one, filled with 0.2M sodium glutamate, was used for ejecting glutamate ions. The other, single-barreled microelectrode (m_1) was used for recording.

These two microelectrodes were inserted into area 17 of a cat's visual cortex; the single-barreled one, perpendicularly, and the double-barreled one, obliquely, at 10° to the former. The tips of these electrodes were set about 200 μ apart from each other on the cortical surface, so that they approached each other to within a few tenths of a micron at 1 mm below.

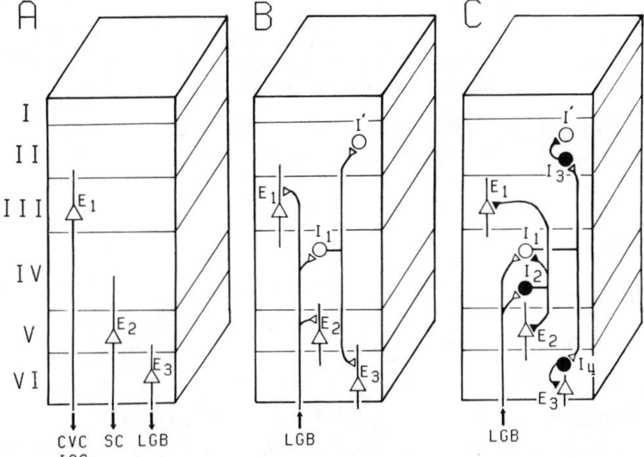

Figure 5-2. Laminar structures in cat's visual cortex. (*a*) Efferent organization. E_1: efferent cell projecting to the contralateral visual cortex (CVC) or to the ipsilateral association cortex (IAC), E_2: corticotectal cell to the superior colliculus (SC), E_3: corticogeniculate cells to the lateral geniculate body (LGB). (*b*), (*c*) Organizations of geniculate inputs; (*b*) for excitation, (*c*) for inhibition. I_1: interneuron mediating disynaptic excitation of cells in layers II (I′) and VI (E_3), I_2: interneuron mediating disynaptic inhibition of cells in layers III–V (E_1, E_2, I_1); I_3 and I_4: interneurons mediating trisynaptic inhibition of cells in layers II and VI (I′ and E_3). (Modified from Toyama et al, ref. 20)

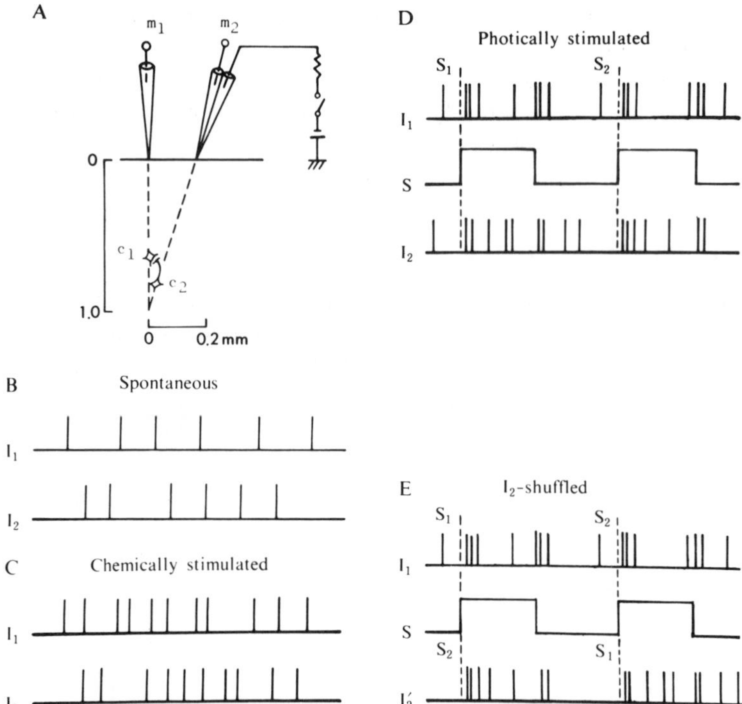

Figure 5-3. Schema of experimental arrangement for cross-correlation study. (*a*) Arrangement for simultaneous recording of impulse discharges from two cells. m_1 and m_2: single- and double-barreled microelectrodes, C_1 and C_2: two cells recorded simultaneously. (*b*) Impulse trains occurring in C_1 and C_2 with no stimulus. (*c*), (*d*) Similar to (*b*) but with chemical and photic stimulation. Bottom trace represents phobic stimulation. Upward and downward deflections indicate the onset and offset of light stimuli. (*e*) Similar to (*d*) but after the shuffling of the impulse train in C_2, (From Toyama, ref. 16).

Responses of a pair of neurons were studied simultaneously, using moving and stationary light stimuli. These neurons were classified into four response types (*1*) simple cells with discrete ON and OFF areas; (*2*) complex cells, with superposed ON and OFF areas; (*3*) hypercomplex cells, with a receptive area similar to that of the complex cell but bounded with zones of end-stop inhibition (1,6,9); and (*4*) cells with ON or OFF areas only. The last type of cell had only one kind of receptive area, either ON or OFF, and it was differentiated from the simple cell by this exclusive nature of its receptive field organization (15,17,21). Cortical cells discharged spontaneously at a relatively low frequency, so a relatively long period of recording was needed to obtain a reliable correlogram. This difficulty was overcome by activating the cortical cells in two ways: by electrophoretic ejection of glutamate ions and by photic stimulation. As an additional advantage, the chemical or photic activation enhanced the interaction between the two cells, and hence the cross correlation of their activities.

Figure 5-3(*b*),(*c*),(*d*) illustrates impulse trains recorded from two cells (C_1 and C_2) under the following three experimental conditions: (*1*) with no stimulus; (*2*) with chemical stimulation, and (*3*) with photic stimulation. The ejection of glutamate ions onto C_2 raised the rate of impulse discharges to several times that of the spontaneous discharges (cf. Figure 5-3*c* with *b*); concomitantly there was a facilitative effect on C_1. The latter might be due to an excitatory synaptic action exerted by C_2 on C_1, but the possibility cannot be excluded that it might be due to a direct action of glutamate ions, which reached C_1 by diffusion. Photic stimulation activated the two cells conjointly at the moments of exposure and withdrawal of the light stimuli (Figure 5-3*d*). Therefore, a cross-correlogram of their impuse discharges should represent the gross correlation which is the sum of the pseudocorrelation due to the coincident activation and net correlation due to the synaptic interaction. The pseudocorrelation can be obtained in isolation by fractionating the impulse train of C_2 at each moment of the stimulus presentation, shuffling the fractionated trains (Figure 5-3*e*) and computing a cross-correlogram (14). The net correlation is determined by subtracting the pseudocorrelogram from the gross correlogram.

INTERNEURONAL INTERACTIONS

Common Excitation

Cross-correlation analysis revealed three types of interactions. The first type was conjoint activation of cortical cells due to common exitatory inputs. Figure 5-4(*a*) illustrates the receptive areas of two complex cells. The receptive area of C_1 (solid line in Figure 5-4*a*) was mostly overlapped with that of C_2 (dotted line). The cross-correlogram obtained for the spontaneous discharges revealed a slight positivity around zero time (Fig. 5-4*b*). This positive correlation was greatly enhanced during photic stimulation. Figure 5-4(*c*),(*d*) shows the gross and the pseudocorrelograms obtained when a stationary light slit (thick solid lines in A) was exposed at a part of the receptive areas of the two cells. In Figure 5-4(*e*) the net correlogram was determined as described above. A sharp rise in positive correlation is seen extending only for three bins, that is, 0.9 msec around zero time. This precise coincidence of activities is probably due to common excitatory inputs that are transmitted monosynaptically from the lateral geniculate cells.

Intracortical Excitation

The second type of interaction obtained was the intracortical excitation of one cell by another. In Figure 5-5(*a*) are shown the receptive areas of two complex cells, one of which (C_1) is completely overlapped with the other (C_2). No significant interaction was detected between the two cells in the cross-correlogram of their spontaneous discharges (not shown). When C_2 was chemically stimulated, a positive correlation appeared in the correlogram (Fig. 5-5*b*). A greater positivity was obtained during photic stimulation (Fig. 5-5*c*). The positive correlation usually occurred around −0.6 msec, attained a maximum in a few milliseconds, and declined gradually. This positive correlation signifies that impulse discharges in C_1 are facilitated after those in C_2 with a time lag comparable to a monosynaptic delay. This excitatory interaction is explicable by assuming excitatory synaptic connections from C_2 to C_1.

Intracortical Inhibition

The third type of interaction was the intracortical inhibition. As judged by their receptive fields (Fig. 5-5*d*), C_1 is a complex cell and C_2 is a simple cell. The correlogram

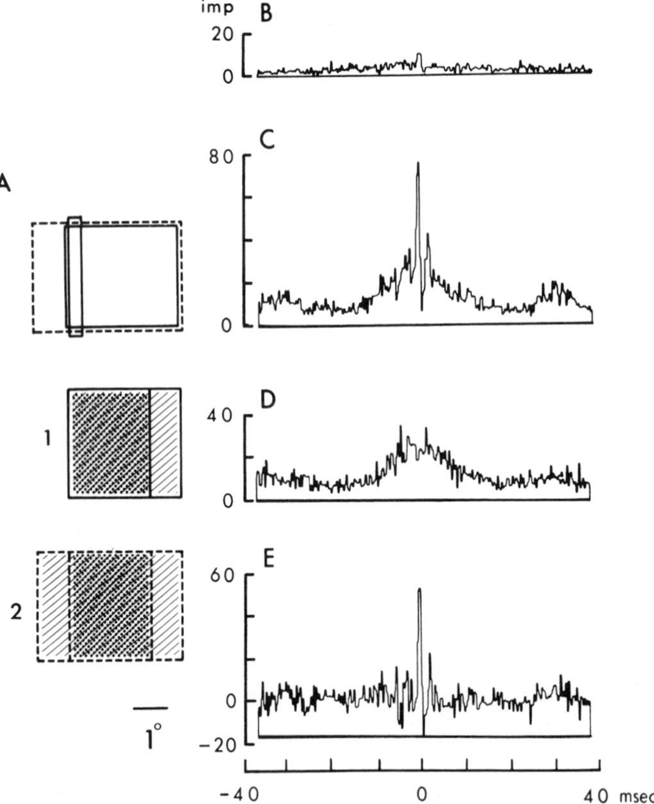

Figure 5-4. Common excitation of two cortical cells. (*a*) Diagram illustrating a stationary light slit exposed on the receptive areas of two complex cells (C_1 and C_2). Solid line represents the receptive area of C_1; dotted line that of C_2; and thick solid line, a stationary light slit. Internal structures of the receptive areas are shown below. Dots: ON area, hatches: OFF area. (*b*) Cross-correlogram for spontaneous discharges of the two complex cells. (*c*), (*d*), (*e*) Gross, pseudo-, and net correlograms obtained under photic stimulation, (From Kimara et al., ref. 13).

obtained with chemical stimulation revealed a tendency for a correlation to fall below the baseline at the left half of the correlogram (Fig. 5-5*e*). The negative correlation starts in a few bins after zero time, which is equivalent to about −1 msec and continues for more than 40 msec. The early onset of the negative correlation indicates that the simple cell depresses the complex cell with a monosynaptic delay. A comparable negativity also occurred in the net correlogram using photic stimulation (Fig. 5-5*f*).

FACTORS RELEVANT TO INTERNEURONAL INTERACTIONS

Response Type

The relationship between the neuronal interactions and the response types of cortical cells was studied for 145 neuronal pairs. Common excitation occurred most frequently, in more than half the neuronal pairs (in 83 of the 145 pairs) and in all combinations except those involving hypercomplex cells, that is, in 13 of 21 pairs between simple cells, in 25 of 32 pairs between simple and complex cells, in 21 of 41 pairs between complex cells, and so on (Table 5-1). By contrast, the intracortical excitation was specific to response types. It was found only in two combinations, that is, from complex to complex cells (12 of 41 pairs) and from complex to hypercomplex cells (4 of 5 pairs). The intracortical inhibition was also confined to only four combinations, that is, from a cell with an exclusively ON or OFF area to the same type of cell (2 of 11 pairs), from that type of cell to a simple cell (8 of 15) and also to a complex cell (3 of 12) and from a simple to a complex cell (10 of 32).

Cellular Location

Another factor related to the interneuronal interactions is the location of cells. This matter was studied by sampling a number of cells with the vertical electrode, while the oblique

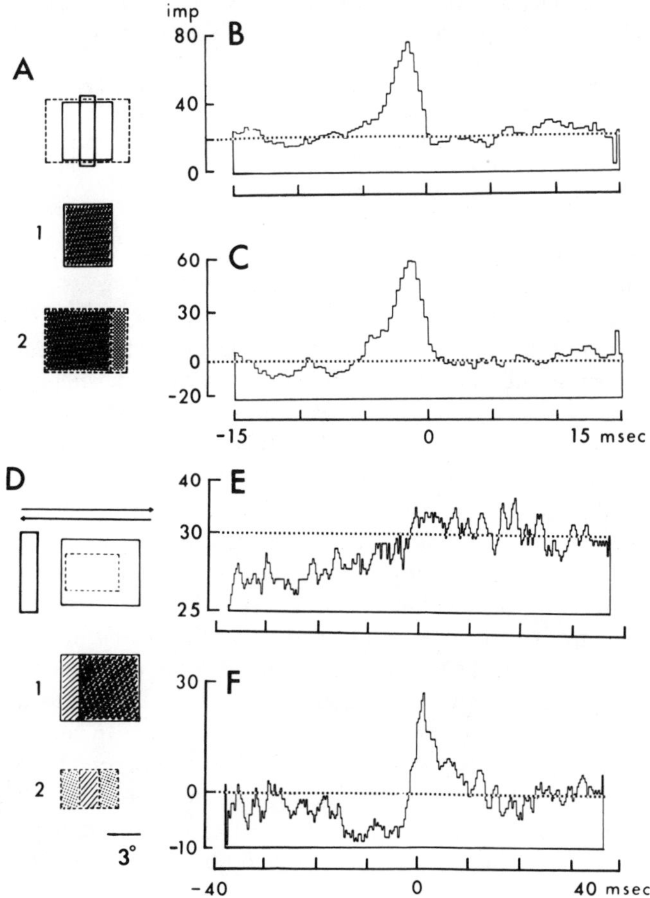

Figure 5-5. Intracortical excitation and inhibition. (*a*) Diagram similar to that in Figure 5-4(*a*) for two complex cells. (*b*) Cross-correlogram obtained during chemical stimulation of C_2. (*c*) Net correlogram obtained under photic stimulation. (*d*), (*e*), (*f*) Similar to (*a*), (*b*), and (*c*) but for complex (C_1) and simple cells (C_2).

Table 5-1. Statistics of Neuronal Pairs Exhibiting Common Excitation

Between	E	S	C	H
E	8(11)	7(15)	6(12)	0(2)
S		13(21)	25(32)	0(3)
C			21(41)	2*(5)
H				1(3)

E: Cell with exclusively ON or OFF area, S: Simple cell, C: complex cell, H: hypercomplex cell. Figures in the table represent the number of neuronal pairs exhibiting common excitation for each combination of the response types; figures in brackets are the total number of pairs. The figure with the asterisk indicates the number of pairs in which one partner was a special hypercomplex cell whose receptive field organization is similar to that of a simple cell but was bounded by end-stop inhibition.

electrode was holding one cell continuously (Fig. 5-6*a*). A cross-correlogram was computed for the former cells with reference to the latter cell. In Figure 5-6(*a*), indicating the results of such an experiment, the reference cell in the middle part of layer IV is a simple cell. A very strong common excitation was seen with simple cells in close proximity, while a smaller excitation occurred with complex cells and cells with exclusively ON or OFF area within a distance of 300 μ (Fig. 5-6*b*). No excitation was obtained with complex cells at greater distances.

In Figure 5-6(*a*), those cells sharing a common excitation with the reference cell are enclosed by a blank rectangle, in which those sharing a very strong common excitation are circumscribed by the hatched area. It can be seen that the blank rectangle area extends for almost the whole extent of layers IV and V. Common excitation occurred in all cells enclosed in this rectangle, with a tendency that the smaller the distance between a cell and the reference cell, the greater the excitation. This was regularly found in all similar trackings. Sometimes the tracking was not exactly aligned to the orientation columns and penetrated through different orientation columns. In such a case, a common excitation was shared even with the cells whose orientation preference differed by more than 30° from that of the reference cell, if that cell had the same ocular preference. In other words, common excitation occurs even between cells belonging to different orientation columns when they belong to the same ocular dominance column. The area within which two cells share a common exciation with each other thus seems to extend over at least several orientation columns and, to a considerable extent, through an ocular dominance column and perpendicularly for the greater part of layers III to V.

The intracortical excitation was much more localized. It was exerted from cells in the middle layer to those in the superficial layer. As illustrated in Figure 5-7(*a*), the reference cell is a complex cell in the upper part of layer IV. Monosynaptic excitation was exerted from the reference cell to complex and hypercomplex cells in the stippled area. No intracortical excitation was induced in cells outside this area, but there was common excitation in cells below this area (blank rectangle). In all trackings that revealed the intracortical excitation, the source cell was confined around the border area between layers III and IV and the target cells in layer II, 200–400 μ upward from the source cell. In addition, intracortical excitation seemed to be exerted only onto the cell whose orientation preference was aligned with that of the source cell. Intracortical excitation was never found with cells whose orientation preference differed by more than 15° from that of the source cell. Thus, the intracortical excitation seems to be exerted onto cells belonging to the same orientation column as that of the source cell.

The specific location of the source cell was also found in the intracortical inhibition. In Figure 5-7(*b*), the source cell of the inhibition was a simple cell located in the deeper part of layer IV. The inhibition was exerted onto five complex cells, indicated in the filled rectangle. In all trackings revealing the intracortical inhibition, the source cells

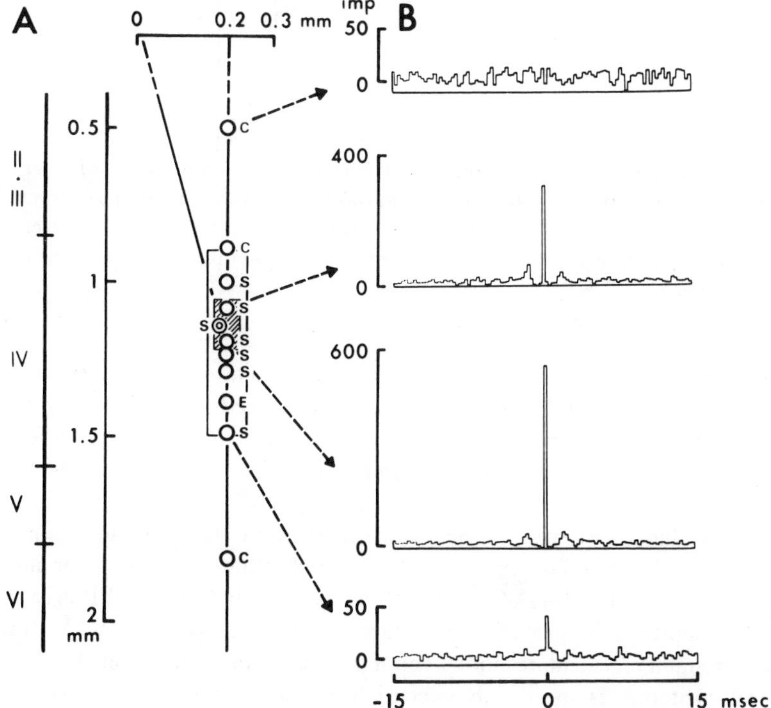

Figure 5-6. Depth profile of distribution of common excitation. (*a*) Diagram of cellular location. The locations of the sampled cells are represented along the tracks of the vertical and oblique electrodes. ◎: reference cell sampled by the oblique electrode, O: test cells sampled by the vertical electrode, letters assigned to circles: response types of the cells—S for simple and C for complex cells, E, cells with exclusively ON or OFF area, hatched rectangle: area where the test cells exhibited strong common excitation with the reference cell, blank rectangle: area for weak common excitation. (*b*) Net correlograms obtained with a moving slit light during stimulation for four representative cells.

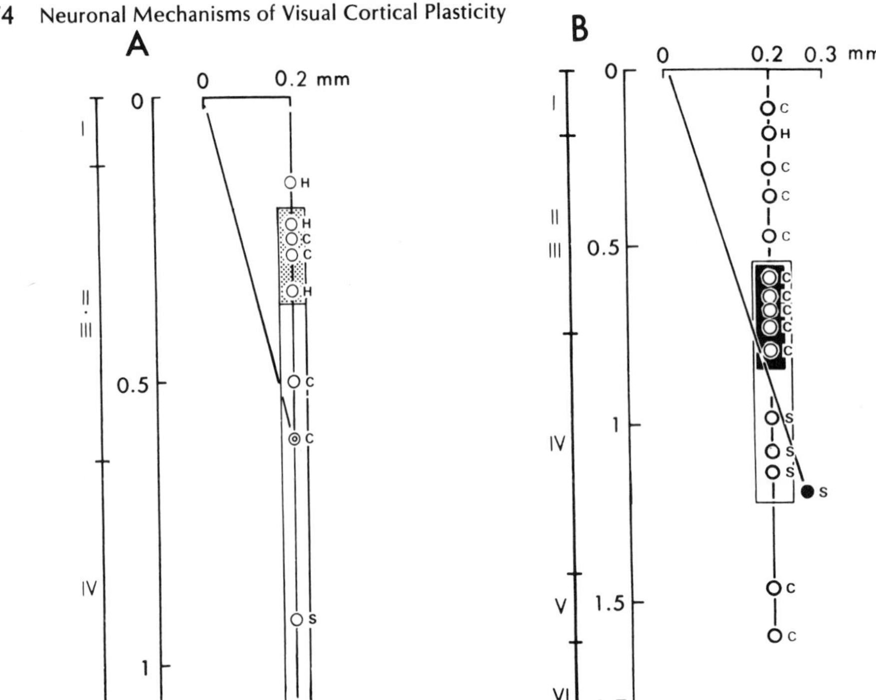

Figure 5-7. Depth profile for intracortical excitation and inhibition. (*a*) Diagram similar to that in Figure 5-6(*a*) but for intracortical excitation. Stippled rectangle represents an area where the test cells receive intracortical excitation from the reference cell. (*b*) Diagram for intracortical inhibition. Recipient area of the inhibition is indicated by filled rectangle.

were regularly found in the deeper part of layer IV. The target area extended for a few hundred microns in layers III to V. In most of the target cells, the orientation preference agreed with that of the reference cell, but in a few cells, the preference differed by as much as 25°. Therefore, the intracortical inhibition could extend through a few orientation columns.

In summary, the three types of neuronal interactions that operate among cortical neurons are related to two factors: response type and cellular location. Common excitation occurs in any combination of a cell with an exclusively ON or OFF area, a simple cell, and a complex cell, providing they are located in layers III to V (Fig. 5-8). Therefore, excitatory geniculate inputs commonly seem to impinge on these cells. The intracortical excitation is specifically exerted from the complex cell in layer IV to the complex and hypercomplex cells in layers II to III. Intracortical inhibition was also exerted specifically from the cell with an exclusively ON or OFF area to the simple cell in layer IV and from the simple cell to the complex cell in layers II to V. In addition to the major connections of the intracortical inhibition that were demonstrated in about 20 neuronal pairs, minor ones were found in several pairs. These minor connections resulted in the inhibition of the complex cells by a cell with an exclusively ON or OFF area and the mutual inhibition between a cell with an exclusively ON area and one with an OFF area.

THREE-DIMENSIONAL FRAMEWORKS AS THE BASES OF COLUMNAR AND LAMINAR ORGANIZATION

The present observations demonstrated two contrasting types of neuronal organization in the visual cortex: (*1*) organization based on a coarse geometry, for the extrinsic inputs of the geniculate excitation and (*2*) a neuronal organization based on a fine geometry, for the intrinsic inputs of intracortical excitation and inhibition. The geniculate inputs extend perpendicularly for almost the entire extent of the middle layers (III–V) and tangentially for the whole dimension of a single ocular dominance column across many orientation columns (Fig. 5-9). The source and targets of the intracortical interaction are much more restricted. The source cell of the intracortical excitation is confined to the upper part of layer IV, and the target cells are confined to a narrow block a few hundred microns thick, which extends for only a single ocular dominance and orientation column. Intracortical inhibition is also exerted from cells in the deep part of layer IV to a small block in layers III–V with dimensions similar to those for the target zone of the intracortical excitation. These specific relationships of the neuronal connectivities of the cortical cells to their perpendicular and tangential coordinates in the visual cortex suggest the existence of frameworks that determine the neuronal connectivity in the visual cortex. The most important element in determining the efferent connectivity seems to be the layer or the perpendicular coordinate in the frameworks. As has been shown, the destination of an efferent projection is closely related to a particular cell layer. Similarly, the termination of the excitatory and inhibitory interneurons might be determined by the tangential framework in the visual cortex. Those cells located in the upper part of layer IV might be destined to excite cells in layer II and those in the lower part to inhibit cells in layers III–V. The perpendicular framework may also determine the neuronal connectivity, since the target areas of the excitation and inhibition extend for only one or, at most, a few orientation columns. Altogether, it may be argued that the neuronal con-

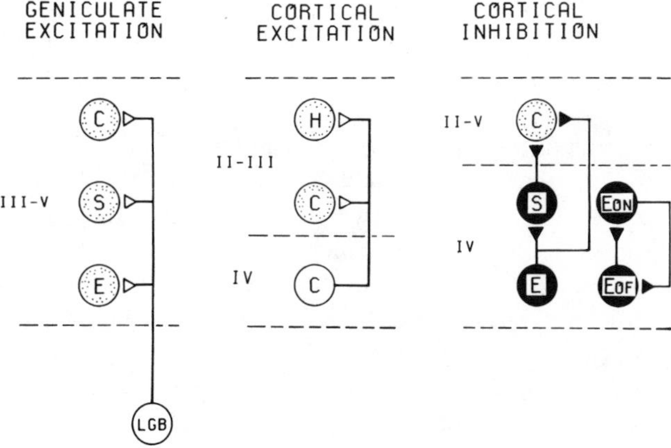

Figure 5-8. Summary diagram of interneuronal connections in the visual cortex. Pathways are illustrated separately for geniculocortical excitation, intracortical excitation, and intracortical inhibition. Conventions for response types of cortical cells are same as those in Figures 5-4(*a*) and 5-5(*a*),(*b*).

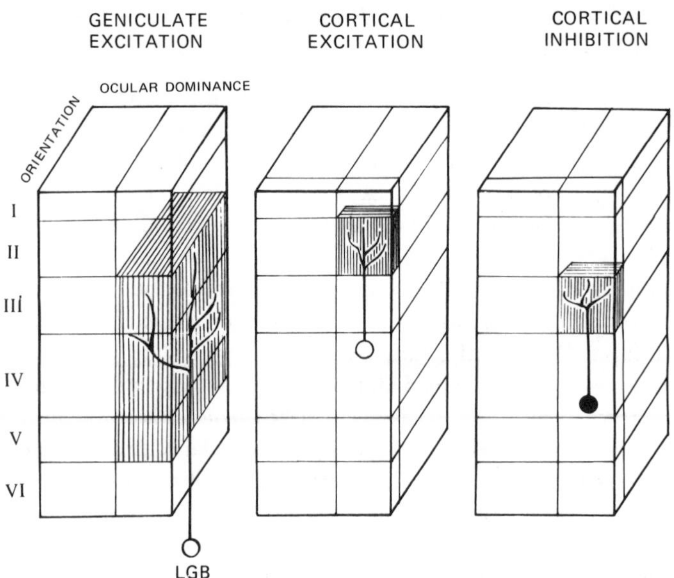

Figure 5-9. Three-dimensional illustrations of frameworks in the visual cortex. Source cell and recipient area of its innervation (hatched area) are illustrated separately for geniculocortical excitation, intracortical excitation, and intracortical inhibition.

nectivity is built up in the visual cortex along with the perpendicular and tangential frameworks, and that the intersection of these two frameworks determines the properties of cells, such as the destination of their innervation (whether they are to be efferent cells or interneurons), their synaptic action (whether it is to be excitatory or inhibitory), and even their responsiveness to visual stimuli, through the neuronal connectivity established in this way.

This view can account for the observations that those cells sharing inhibition or excitation from the same interneurons form a cluster and exhibit a similar responsiveness to visual stimuli.

The regular patterns of these perpendicular and tangential organizations in the adult animal indicate that the frameworks may be mostly innate. The striking modifiability of responsiveness in the infant animal, however, suggests that these frameworks are not absolutely rigid; possibly, they are still immature in infancy and require the nurturance of the visual environment for their sound development. This is a speculation based entirely on the structures revealed by the cross-correlation study of normal adult animals. The future extension of this study to animals with abnormal visual experience may elucidate the structural basis of the visual cortical plasticity.

ACKNOWLEDGMENT

The author thanks Professor M. Ito for his helpful discussion and constant encouragement.

This work was supported by a grant from the Japanese Ministry of Education (#348095).

REFERENCES

1. Bishop PO, Coombs JS, Henry GH: Responses to visual contours: spatio-temporal aspects of excitation in the receptive fields of simple striate neurones. *J Physiol* (*London*) 219:625–657, 1971.
2. Blakemore C, Cooper GP: Development of the brain depends on the visual environment. *Nature* (*London*) 228:477–478, 1970.
3. Blakemore C, Van Sluyters RC: Reversal of the physiological effects of monocular deprivation in kittens: further evidence for a sensitive period. *J Physiol* 237:195–216, 1974.
4. Blakemore C, Van Sluyters RC: Innate and environmental factors in the development of the kitten visual cortex. *J Physiol* 248:663–716, 1975.
5. Hirsch HVB, Spinelli DN: Visual experience modifies distribution of horizontally and vertically oriented receptive fields in cats. *Science* 168:869–871, 1970.
6. Hubel DH, Wiesel TN: Receptive fields, binocular interaction and functional architecture in the cat's visual cortex. *J Physiol* 160:106–154, 1962.
7. Hubel DH, Wiesel TN: Shape and arrangement of columns in cat's striate cortex. *J Physiol* 165:559–568, 1963.
8. Hubel DH, Wiesel TN: Receptive fields of cells in striate cortex of very young, visually inexperienced kittens. *J Neurophysiol* 26:994–1002, 1963.
9. Hubel DH, Wiesel TN: Receptive fields and functional architecture in two nonstriate visual areas (18 and 19) of the cat. *J Neurophysiol* 28:229–289, 1965.
10. Hubel DH, Wiesel TN: Binocular interaction in striate cortex of kittens reared with artificial squint. *J Neurophysiol* 28:1041–1059, 1965.
11. Hubel DH, Wiesel TN: The period of susceptibility to the physiological effects of unilateral eye closure in kittens. *J Physiol* 206:419–436.
12. Hubel DH, Wiesel TN: Sequence regularity and geometry of orientation columns in the monkey striate cortex. *J Comp Neurol* 158:267–293, 1974.
13. Kimura M, Tanaka K, Toyama K: Interneuronal connectivity between visual cortical neurones of the cat as studied by cross-correlation analysis of their impulse discharges. *Brain Res* 118:329–333, 1976.
14. Perkel H, Gerstein GL, Moore GP: Neuronal spike trains and stochastic point processes. II. Simultaneous spike trains. *Biophys J* 418–410, 1967.
15. Singer W, Tretter F, Cynader M: Organization of cat striate cortex: a correlation of receptive-field properties with afferent and efferent connections. *J Neurophysiol* 38:1080–1098, 1975.
16. Toyama K: Interneuronal connectivity in cat visual cortex: studies by cross-correlation analysis of the responses of two simultaneously recorded neurones, in *Integrative Control Functions of the Brain,* vol 1. Ito M, et al (eds): Tokyo, Kodansha-Scientific, 1978, pp 65–72.
17. Toyama K, Kimura M, Shiida T, et al: Convergence of retinal inputs into visual cortical cells: II. A study of the cells disynaptically excited from the lateral geniculate body. *Brain Res* 137:221–231, 1977.
18. Toyama K, Maekawa K, Takeda T: An analysis of neuronal circuitry for two types of visual cortical neurones classified on the basis of their responses to photic stimuli. *Brain Res* 61:395–399, 1973.
19. Toyama K, Maekawa K, Takeda T: Convergence of retinal inputs onto visual cortical cells: I. A study of the cells monosynaptically excited from the lateral geniculate body. *Brain Res* 137:207–220, 1977.
20. Toyama K, Matsunami K, Ohno T, et al: An intracelluar study of neuronal organization in the visual cortex. *Exp Brain Res* 21:45–66, 1974.
21. Toyama K, Takeda T: A unique class of cat's visual cortical cells that exhibit either ON or OFF excitation for stationary light slit and are responsive to moving patterns. *Brain Res* 73:350–355, 1974.
22. Toyama K, Tanaka K, Kimura M: On-line computer system for vision experiments: Control of visual stimuli and analysis of neuronal signals. *Brain Theory Newsletter* 3:170–171, 1978.
23. Wiesel TN, Hubel DH: Single-cell responses in striate cortex of kittens deprived of vision in one eye. *J Neurophysiol* 26:1003–1017, 1965.
24. Wiesel TN, Hubel DH: Extent of recovery from the effects of visual deprivation in kittens. *J Neurophysiol* 28:1060–1072, 1965.

6
Theories of Cortical Function and Measurements of Its Performance

Horace B. Barlow

Most investigators will probably agree that the mental abilities of higher mammals are based largely on their well-developed cerebral cortex, yet we seem to be almost as far as we have ever been from understanding the neural basis of intelligence, learning, and memory. The cortex is a surprisingly uniform structure (13,40), so one might hope that the study of one part would throw light on all of it. From the time of Hubel and Wiesel's first paper 20 years ago (29) to the present, the neuroanatomy and neurophysiology of the visual cortex have been studied intensively, and thousands of papers must have been published: surely they must tell us something about intelligence, learning, and memory!

I have set myself two tasks. The first is to try to summarize what the neurophysiological study of the visual cortex has told us about the neurobiological basis of learning and memory; the conclusion is that, although the cortex can undoubtedly be changed by experience, such plasticity is certainly not its most outstanding characteristic, and it is hard to understand its purpose. This leads directly to the second task, which is to report my progress in analyzing complex types of visual performance, in the hope that this will lead to an answer to the question, What does cortex do? As a physiologist I am strongly prejudiced to believe that, for an organ with such a uniform structure, there must be a simple answer to this question. The heart pumps blood; the lungs exchange gases; the kidney forms urine; and the retina transduces the optical image and transmits it to the brain. It must be worth searching for the appropriate succinct description of what cortex does.

As used here, d'_E is experimentally determined in a psychophysical experiment and is obtained from the proportion of detection failures and false positives. The highest value that could theoretically have been achieved in the experiment is d'_I, which is calculated from the known parameters of the populations of messages (in our case random dot figures) delivered.

For more details see Swets (53) and, for the current approach, Barlow (3).

PLASTICITY AND RIGIDITY OF THE VISUAL CORTEX

This has been a controversial topic over the past 5 or 10 years, but I think our knowledge of the facts has been consolidated in the last few years (1), and a fairly reliable picture can now be given.

It has long been known by ophthalmologists that disuse of an eye in childhood, or mismatch between the images from the eyes such as occurs with strabismus, can lead to permanently impaired vision in one eye. This was clearly an effect of experience on the function of the visual system, but it was not until Hubel and Wiesel's work on kittens, and later on monkeys, that a physiological model was available for analyzing the presumed basis for those plastic changes. Their results in kittens were, briefly, as follows (31–33,57–59). Normally the majority of cells in the primary visual cortex (area 17) receive connections from both eyes, although there are a few cells that receive excitatory connections from only one eye. If the use of one eye is prevented by occluding it during a "sensitive period" lasting between the ages of 3 weeks and 3 months, then this distribution of cells is disturbed: the occluded eye loses its connections, so the cortex of such a cat contains a large preponderance of cells connected to the eye that remained in continued use and relatively few cells connected to both eyes or to the eye whose use was interfered with. At the peak of the sensitive period definite effects of this sort can be detected after periods of monocular occlusion lasting only a day or less.

These results are robust and repeatable; the controversy has centered on the questions that arise from it. Are other aspects of the geniculocortical system also modifiable? What is the mechanism by which alterations are brought about? What is their functional significance?

RANGE OF MODIFIABILITY

Hubel and Wiesel showed that the changes brought about by deprivation could be reversed, at least partially, within the sensitive period, and this has been confirmed (9,41). Instead of deprivation, Hubel and Wiesel (32) also mimicked another condition that predisposes to amblyopia in humans, namely strabismus; this induced condition reduced the number of units connected to both eyes and increased the number connected to only one eye. This result has also been obtained by many other experimenters. In addition Hubel and Wiesel have repeated much of the deprivation work on rhesus monkeys, whose primary visual cortex is arranged in a rather more orderly way than the cat's, thus making disruptions of the pattern easier to detect. In general the results are similar, but there are interesting differences in detail which will be considered later.

Plasticity of other properties has not been so easily established. Hirsch and Spinelli (27,28) and Blakemore and Cooper (7) reported that the distribution of orientationally selective cells could be changed by exposing kittens to oriented stripes in the sensitive period, and it was claimed (8) that this occurred after very brief exposures. Stryker and Sherk (51) were unable to obtain any effects in a more thorough, computer-controlled, repetition of the experiments in which freely moving kittens were exposed in striped drums. It can probably be concluded that this is, at best, an unreliable way of modifying the cortex. Hirsch and Spinelli used goggles containing lenses and gratings in their experiments. Their first report was difficult to interpret because they used unconventional neurophysiological methods, but many of their observations have been successfully repeated, and the goggle method of exposure seems to be reliable in biasing the distribution of orientationally selective cells in the cortex (6,38,39,51). At one point it appeared that their success might have been due to another feature of their experiment, namely their exposure of one eye to vertical stripes and the other to horizontal ones. It was suggested that this was tantamount to depriving the first eye of horizontal stripes and the other of vertical ones, and that the supposed orientation effects were therefore really due to monocular deprivation. There may be an effect of this sort, but the results of Stryker et al (52) and Rauschecker (46) show that there is a genuine effect of orientation with binocular exposure, when monocular deprivation is not a possible explanation.

Another effect that has proven hard to repeat is that reported by Shlaer (49). He placed a prism in front of one eye to displace images vertically in that eye and claimed that the receptive fields were shifted in such a way as to reduce or eliminate the misalignment. Yet another example of unrepeatability is the suggestion in several of the early reports that a period of consolidation must elapse between a change of experience and a resultant change in properties of cortical neurones. Freeman's (21) results suggest that the effects of monocular occlusion are greatest immediately, without waiting for consolidation.

These misfortunes make one believe that *Nature* could speed the progress of science, and *Science* could aid the understanding of nature, if these two journals agreed to place all manuscripts on this subject in the shredder. But the danger of unreliability is now more widely appreciated, and careful repetition has established that a good deal of modification does take place in response to alterations of the visual experience of young animals; the rule appears to be that increased numbers of units respond to features that the animal has experienced, while a decreased number respond to features it has been prevented from experiencing.

Other forms of modified experience may work. Thus, several studies agree that exposure to stripes moving in one direction increases the representation of units selective for that direction (17,19,54). It is interesting that the critical period for this effect terminates before the corresponding period for monocular deprivation (20). Rearing in slow stroboscopic illumination also has some effects, although these are not very well defined (16,18,42). The experiment of rearing animals in an environment with small isolated spots of light but no lines or edges (44,55) has not been repeated, and it would be interesting to know if the claim that unusual units are produced is sustained; as originally described these units are suspiciously like the "special complex" type subsequently described by Gilbert (22) in normal cortex. However, it does seem to be possible to produce units of types not found in normal cortex. Hirsch and Spinelli's original results suggested this, and Singer (50) has described definite examples of cells with double receptive fields spaced at an angular distance from each other corresponding to the periodicity of the grating they had been exposed to. Thus, the cortex can, at least to a limited extent, gather together elements that are frequently activated synchronously and can respond when the combination occurs again. That is a potentially powerful learning mechanism of a type very like that Hebb presaged in 1949 (25).

The foregoing account has emphasized modifiability, but it must be appreciated that much of the anatomical structure of the primary visual cortex is strongly resistant to modification. The topographical map can be modified only slightly, if at all, and noone has claimed that the lamination can be altered, nor that the destinations of the long fibers leaving each lamina can be changed. Thus, a balanced overall view of the cortex would give it a rigid anatomical framework within which physiological function is slightly modified by experience; and the modifications are in the direction of "strengthening by exercise," as ophthalmologists have long realized.

To get a sense of proportion about the plasticity of cortex, it is instructive to compare its modifiability with that of subcortical structures, for in two recent studies the cortex has proved to be the more resistant to change. Singer (50) rotated one eye of a kitten about its visual axis. Confirming the work of Blakemore et al (11), he found that the cortical map remained unchanged in terms of retinal coordinates, whereas definite changes occurred in the tectal projection. Again, Ikeda and Wright (36) have reported large changes in the resolving power of neurons in the LGN after strabismus and other procedures designed to impair image quality; previously modifications of cortical neurons were thought to occur in the cortex, but it appears that the subcortical structures may be as susceptible as the cortex.

MECHANISMS OF RIGIDITY AND PLASTICITY

The main issue here has been whether experience has a positive effect in bringing about proper cortical function, or whether it acts solely by preserving genetically formed functional connections, as Hubel and Wiesel have consistently maintained. A second important issue is whether lack of experience has a deleterious effect by itself, or whether it only acts when there are competing active neurons to take over unused connections, as in the case of monocular deprivation. There are a good many other questions about the actual mechanism of experience-mediated and developmental changes: Do nerve terminals retract and sprout? Do trophic substances signal the formation of successful synapses? Do synapses form, degenerate, and displace each other? Are inoperative synapses distinguishable from working ones? These are the sort of questions one may hope to be able to answer, but the main issues are only now being settled.

No one doubts that competition is an important factor, as Wiesel and Hubel (58) and Guillery and Stelzner (24) showed by comparing changes in monocular and binocular parts of the visual field in the cat. But Sherman (48) has come to the conclusion that competition is the main cause of cell shrinkage and dysfunction only in the Y cells; the X cells are not particularly affected by competition, and for them simple disuse is a sufficient cause.

The influence of competition can also be seen in the ocular dominance stripes discovered by Hubel and Wiesel (35) in the monkey cortex. Shortly before birth there is no sign of ocular dominance columns, but they develop in the first month or two, whether or not the infant monkey uses its eyes, and in the adult the cells of layer IVc are all completely dominated by one eye or the other. However, the width of the region dominated by one eye can be increased during the first months of life if it is given a competitive advantage by occluding the other eye. Hubel and Wiesel suggest that this is due, not to active sprouting or invasion by the open eye, but to their takeover of cells that were initially binocularly connected. However, Blakemore, Garey, and Vital-Durand (10) have shown that the balance can be shifted to and fro by reverse suture during the first 2 months, which suggests a positive effect of experience as well as a purely negative effect of its lack.

The thesis that the cortex is formed entirely under genetic instructions would be firmly established if it could be shown that the inexperienced cortex functions in a fully normal way. This has not been done, partly of course because we do not really understand what the normal function is. What has been shown, and is widely accepted, is that the inexperienced cortex possess fragments of normal function. Thus, Hubel and Wiesel (31) reported that very young, inexperienced kittens have orientationally selective cells, and this has been confirmed (Blakemore and Van Sluyters (9), Buisseret and Imbert (14); Barlow and Pettigrew (4) thought there were only directionally selective cells, but this appears to be incorrect.) In inexperienced kittens and lambs there are visual cortical cells showing binocular connections, but in kittens such cells are very unselective for the amount of disparity present until visual experience is received (43), and in lambs, too, these cortical cells become more selective (45).

In addition, much of the regular arrangement of cells found in the adult visual cortex is also present without experience (34). There are regions (stripes or columns) dominated by one eye alternating with regions dominated by the other, and hints of orderly sequences of orientational selectivity are found. But in other ways the early reports overestimated the normality of the inexperienced cortex, particularly in the case of animals well into the critical period (56). Many unresponsive cells were found, and while some may be as selective for orientation as all but the most finely tuned of those found in adult (12,47), it is becoming clear that their contrast sensitivity and responsiveness remains only a fraction of that found in the best adult units (Derrington, in preparation). Furthermore, Buisseret, Gary-Bobo, and Imbert (15) have shown that a short period of exposure in a 6-week-old, binocularly deprived kitten has a dramatic effect in restoring the cortex to its normal state at that age. It is interesting that the active exploration of the visual environment using eye movements seems to be a necessary condition for this visual experience to have its restorative effect.

Some are apt to say that the disruptive or degenerative consequences of disuse are masking the proper function of a cortex developed strictly according to genetic instructions, but that is a semantic evasion. If the cortex fails to perform some important function without experience, then at least at a phenomenological level the positive or constructive effect of experience cannot be denied.

Perhaps present knowledge in this area can best be summarized in this way: The view that the cortex is genetically hard wired has been admirably productive, because it has led to our present knowledge of the microstructure of orientational and ocular dominance columns that lies within the topographical mapping of the visual field on to the cortex. However, the concept of a hard wired cortex is merely a useful prejudice, not the whole story.

FUNCTIONAL SIGNIFICANCE

There are two extreme views of the functional significance of the above facts; one is to regard the experience-mediated changes in cortical function as a paradigm of learning and memory, and thus of cortical function. The other is to deny that such changes have any functional significance whatever: the paucity of binocular neurons after strabismus or alternating occlusion is no more a functional adaptation than is the weakness of a limb when it is not exercised or the withering of a plant when it is not watered. I personally think the latter view borders on the absurd. Whatever else it does, the visual cortex has an intricate organization that seems to specialize in bringing information from the two eyes together, normally resulting in a single view of the world, together with the important additional capacity of judging relative depth. Clinically, the kind of modified visual experience that, in cats and monkeys, prevents the persistence of binocular neurons in area 17, in humans, prevents the development (or persistence) of the stereoscopic capacity. However, abnormal early experience does not usually interfere with excellent vision in one eye, and sometimes vision is excellent in both; to me that is almost as surprising as to find that you can chop a car in half to produce two motorcycles. Such a trick car might be made, but it would have to be a feature designed into the original car right from the start. In the same way the possibility of separate use, as well as joint use with stereopsis, must surely be a genetically determined option of the developing visual system, an option that is exercised in response to the appropriate environmental cue.

If the latter view is accepted, the implications are quite extensive; but before returning to this I want to report progress in the experimental analysis of the performance of a visual task in which I am sure the cortex must be involved.

EXPERIMENTS IN DETECTING VISUAL STRUCTURE

The relevance of these experiments to the problem of cortical function needs a word of explanation. Suppose that for some reason you doubt the truth of the statements that the cornea and lens of the eye form an image on the retina, and that it is the light absorbed from this image that enables one to see. One way I might try to convince you of the truth of these statements would be to say, "If there is an image, light from different points in space will be separate in the image, even though the light from both points passes through the pupil; you can see two points as separate, and this fits in with the idea of image formation." The conclusion I am coming to about the cortex is that it tests for the existence of certain types of associational structure, and to convince you of this I shall show that it does a particular task of this nature almost as well as it can be done, just as image formation in the eye separates light from different directions almost as well as diffraction allows.

The aim of the experiments I shall describe was to explore tasks more complex than those normally used in psychophysics, in the hope that such tasks might be limited by cortical function rather than by subcortical mechanisms. The first problem was to bypass the inefficiency of the peripheral steps in the visual system. The principle for doing this is as follows: One can send a message to the brain in which the individual elements get through clearly and unambiguously, but the message is nonetheless difficult to interpret because the way the elements are assembled is not understood. For instance, if I write RINGENT, the letters are clear and unambiguous, but because it is a rare English word you may still not know what it means. Similarly, if tests can be devised in which one can be sure the eye will transmit the elements, one can test how well the central mechanisms can interpret them.

I have used bright dots on an oscilloscope as the elements, using them to construct pictures with a definite regular, but also partially random, structure. Figure 6-5 shows some examples. Now the intention is to see how efficiently the structure, the regular element, is detected. To do this, a subject is shown examples with the structure and examples without. Then he is given unknowns and sorts them. He will make a few mistakes, and from the results one can calculate d'_E*. Regard this as the signal: noise ratio of the

* Signal detection theory deals with the problem of discriminating between two populations of messages, for instance, between a signal buried in a noisy background and the noisy background alone. It is postulated that a single quantity can be calculated for any message received; this quantity will follow one distribution for noise alone, another for signal plus noise. A measure of the discriminability of the two populations is given by d', defined as the ratio of the separation of the means of the two distributions to the standard deviation of the noise-alone population.

message on which the discrimination is performed. One can also sometimes calculate d'_{I} the best possible discrimination of the two populations of patterns the subject saw. Then efficiency F is simply:

$$F = (d'_{\text{E}}/d'_{\text{I}})^2 \tag{1}$$

This is a way of estimating the proportion of the sample of information presented that is actually used (3). The limiting factor is the deliberately imposed irregularity of the randomly placed dots, and the losses that cause inefficiency result from imperfect function or design in the neural mechanisms that analyze the images.

Figure 6-1 shows the task used for the first results I shall describe. The subject was presented with randomly selected targets from two populations, one of which did, while the other did not, have an average excess of dots in the left half. It is easy to tell when the excess is large, as at the right, but when it is small the judgment cannot be made correctly every time because the background number of dots in the left field, to which the excess number was added, was made to vary. Hence, although the average number exceeded the right half, particular samples from the population that had an excess on average could actually contain fewer dots than the comparison field. From the proportions correctly placed in the two classes the experimental discriminability, d'_{E} can be calculated. From the figures in Figure 6-1, one can also calculate the highest discriminability that could be achieved, d'_{E}; for example, in the third from the right the difference of means, ΔN, is 20, whereas the standard deviation of background alone is 10. Hence, $d'_{\text{I}} = \Delta N/6 = 20/10 = 2$.

Figure 6-2 shows the results obtained for two subjects. The points in the top curve are the values of d'_{E} obtained for various values of ΔN, the average excess of dots in the left half field, as abscissa. The continuous line shows the corresponding values of d'_{I}. From expression (1), the experimental values can be converted to efficiencies, and these values of F are plotted in the lower half of the figure. Where the measured values of d'_{E} are low, the relative error is very large, and the estimates of F are subject to enormous errors. However, as d'_{E} becomes larger, the relative error becomes reasonable, and it will be seen that both subjects consistently achieve efficiencies of 40% or 50%.

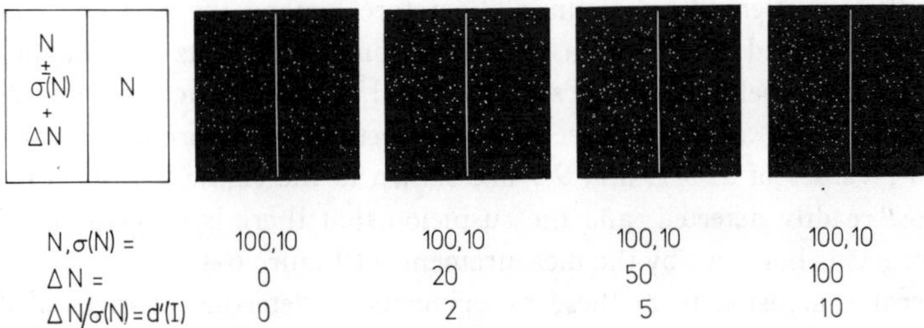

Figure 6-1. A simple perceptual task for which the absolute efficiency can be measured. The left hand square shows the scheme according to which the four pictures were constructed, and the numbers underneath give the parameters for the populations from which they are samples; the lowest gives d'_{I} the highest attainable d' for discriminating between samples from the left population ($\Delta N = 0$) and samples from each of the other three. Subjects inspected known examples from the two populations to be discriminated and then sorted 100 unknowns, knowledge of the result on each being provided. From the successes and failures of each d'_{E}, was calculated in the usual way. Efficiency is simply $(d'_{\text{E}}/d'_{\text{I}})^2$.

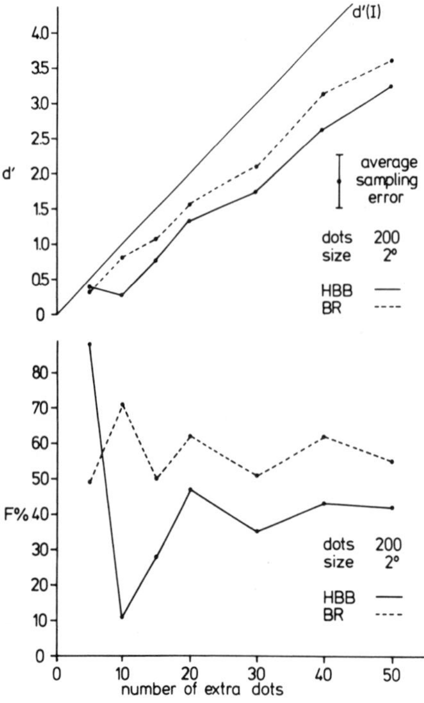

Figure 6-2. Values of d′ and efficiency on two subjects for the experiment of Figure 6-1. Since the sampling error is large, the calculated efficiencies ($< d'_E/d'_I >^2$) are very inacurrate when d'_E is low, but at high values of d'_E efficiencies of 40–50% are obtained. The difference between these two experienced subjects is probably mainly due to the duration available for the task; for HB this was 200 msecs; for BR, unlimited, but usually not longer than 1 sec.

There seems to be some sort of limit to perceptual efficiency at 50%, for we have achieved it at a variety of tasks but have never gotten anything better except when the dots could actually be counted (3). This limit is probably important in reinterpreting experiments at absolute threshold (2), but we are interested in problems of the central nervous system so I shall not go into the limit problem at threshold.

As stated earlier, it was hoped that the nature of the detection and discrimination tasks that are efficiently performed might give a clue to the nature of the neural mechanisms that lie behind our retinas. Therefore, among the first experiments I did was one that measured efficiency in detecting elongated targets that might match the receptive fields of Hubel and Wiesel's (30) cortical neurons. The targets were all of the same area and shaped as in the three left-hand sections of Figure 6-3. Examples of dot figures for d'_I values of 2, 5.1, and 9.9 are shown to the right. It is hard to say which shape is most readily detected, and the suspicion that there is no greater efficiency for elongated targets is born out by the measurements of Figure 6-4.

The general conclusion from these experiments in detecting changes of dot density was that the visual system can reach an efficiency of 50% for a wide variety of target shapes and sizes, but there was no sign of improved performance for targets tailored to match the properties of cortical receptive fields that we thought we already knew about.

Now the type of structure so far imposed on the random dot patterns, which the subject had to detect, can be called first-order structure: it consisted simply of changes in the dot density in particular parts of the picture. It is not difficult to design an optimal system for detecting such structure, so I decided to see how the eye performed with second-order structure. Here, the average dot density is uniform, but given the position

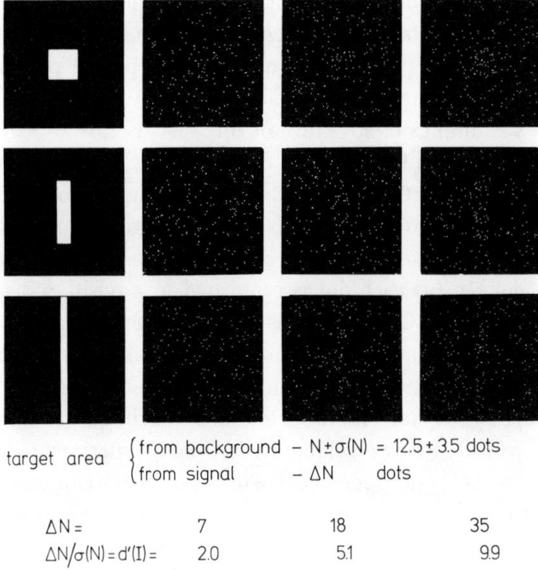

Figure 6-3. The targets at right have different shapes but the same area. The square target measured ¼° × ¼°, the longest rectangle 1° × 1/16°. Samples at various signal : noise ratios are shown at right.

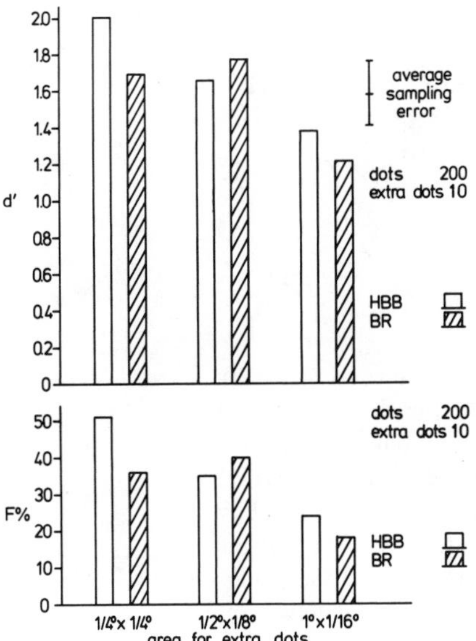

Figure 6-4. Results of the experiment in Figure 6-3 for two subjects. Long, thin rectangles are certainly not better detected than squares.

of one dot, the position of other dots is nonuniform. The simplest way of creating such structure is by placing the dots in pairs according to some paradigm; the position of one dot then determines exactly the position of its pair, but the position of other dots is nearly unaffected and hence statistically nearly uniform.

Figure 6-5 shows examples of structure of this sort. Figure 6-5(*a*) is simply an array of randomly placed dots. In Figure 6-5(*b*) each dot of (*a*) has been replicated in a position symmetric about the vertical midline; the resulting mirror symmetric structure is immediately evident. Figure 6-5(*c*) and (*d*) are similar to examples illustrated by Glass (23) a few years ago. In (*c*) each dot is replicated at a position just above and to the right of its parent dot. In (*d*) each dot is replicated in a position displaced radially and tangentially from the center. The striations in (*c*) and the spiral in (*d*) are immediately evident, but it is interesting that the random array of (*a*) creates so small an impression that it requires careful inspection to confirm that it is the parent of (*b*), (*c*), and (*d*).

The form of structure we have investigated most thoroughly is bilateral symmetry, as shown in Figure 6-5(*b*). B. Reeves collaborated in these experiments (5) and our first step was to explore the range of conditions under which symmetry can be detected.

Figure 6-6 shows that symmetry need not be complete to be immediately detectable. In the top left figure, marked 1.0, all the 100 dots are in pairs; in the top right, marked 0.7, there are 35 pairs and 30 (15 on each side) placed at random. The lower two

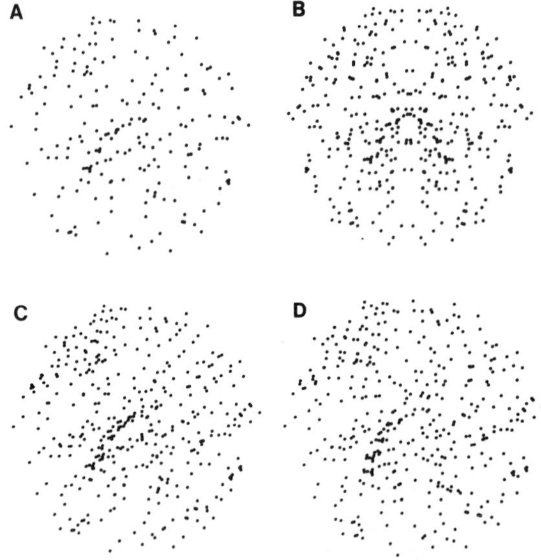

Figure 6-5. Examples of second-order structure created by pairing dots. In (*a*) the dots are placed entirely at random. In (*b*) each dot is paired in the mirror position on the opposite side on the vertical midline. In (*c*) each dot is paired at a position slightly above and to the right of its parent. In (*d*) the pairing is done in a direction spiralling outward from the center. Although it is not perceptually obvious, the dots in (*a*) are the parent dots for the pairs in all the other patterns.

figures have 40% and 10% of the dots arranged in pairs; the remainder are randomly placed. Symmetry is readily detected in the top two figures and a d' of about 1 can be achieved when discriminating the 20 pairs with 60 random dots from a population in which all were random. Clearly, symmetry gives a graded impression, and an object need not be totally symmetric to be detected as such.

Figure 6-7 shows that symmetry can be detected when the axis is horizontal or oblique instead of vertical, although it is less easily detected about these axes. Finally, Figure 6-8 shows that the axis need not be in the midline. This was a rather complex experiment, in which the subject fixated on a mark that was extinguished just before the picture was briefly displayed. The picture was displaced either to the left or to the right by the amount shown on the abscissa, or else it appeared in the central undisplaced position. Because of the uncertainty about its position, the subject could not make anticipatory eye movements, and the central position was retained to act as a control observation throughout the series with variable positions. Unfortunately, the control failed, in the sense that performance in this central position was not constant, but the main result of this experiment is to show that symmetry can be detected with the axis displaced from the midline, although less well.

Two further points should be made about Figures 6-7 and 6-8. First, an overlay of a certain proportion of random dots was used to make the task more difficult; if it is too easy, the subject may make no errors, and then the d' measure of discriminability fails. That is a purely technical matter; the other, more interesting, point is that symmetry can perfectly well be detected in a brief exposure of 100 msec, as was used for the experiment in Figure 6-8. Clearly searching eye movements are quite unnecessary.

Barney Reeves and I think these experiments show that the mechanism for detecting bilateral symmetry is surprisingly versatile. We next wanted to determine its efficiency, using the absolute measure that Hecht had used for quantum absorbtion and that I had applied to the ability to detect changes of dot density. The difficulty here is that the display produces pictures with high positional accuracy, so when it is programmed to place a pair of dots in symmetric positions they are *exactly* symmetric, with an accuracy higher than what the eye requires or can use. Because of this high accuracy, it would be easy to identify from their coordinates even a single symmetric pair among the 100 or so dots we use in most of our trials. This places the human at a disadvantage because the positional accuracy of the displays is not matched to that of his symmetry detecting mechanisms.

To investigate this point we produced pictures with degraded or "smeared" symmetry. Figure 6-9 shows the principle; instead of positioning the mate of a dot in the exactly symmetric position it is placed at a random position within a tolerance area whose size can be varied. In this way the exactness of the symmetry can be varied to see, first, what effect this has on the ability of human subjects to detect symmetry, and second, to see what effect it has on the best possible detection of symmetry.

Figure 6-10 shows measurements of d'_E for two subjects for varied values of the tolerance range. As this range is increased beyond about ± 8 minutes, performance declines rapidly, but what is perhaps surprising is that such a large amount of "smear" is needed to degrade performance. The whole picture was 126 minutes across, so the width of the tolerance area with ± 8-minute smear is already more than one quarter of the width of each symmetric half picture.

Next consider what effect the use of inexact pairing has on the best possible discrimination of symmetry. When the tolerance range is small, it is highly improbable that an

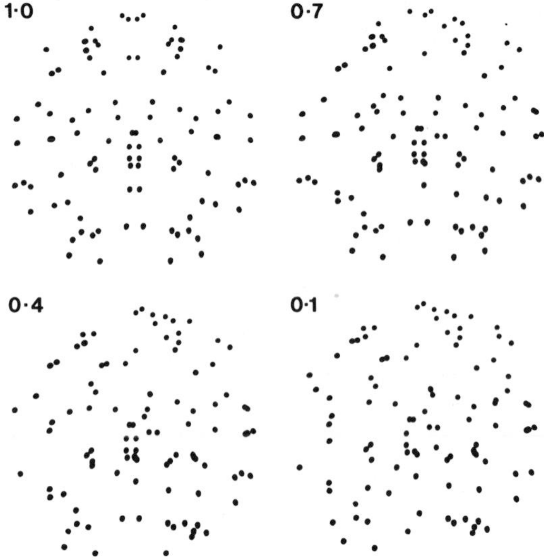

Figure 6-6. Partial symmetry is readily detected. The figures at top left of each array show the proportion of dots that are arranged in exact mirror pairs, the remainder being placed randomly. When this proportion is 0.4 (bottom left), the population can be discriminated from a completely random population with d'_{E} Ω 1.

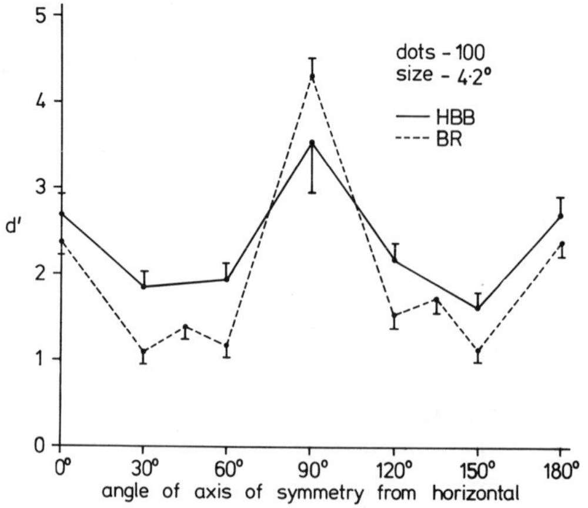

Figure 6-7. Symmetry can be detected, although less well, when the axis is horizontal or oblique. Eighty percent of dots were paired, and 90° is vertical.

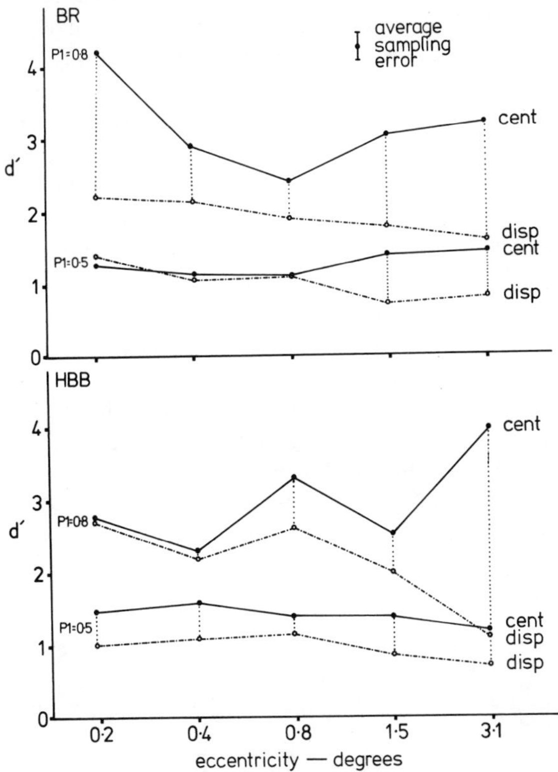

Figure 6-8. Discrimination of symmetry when the axis is displaced from the vertical midline of the visual field. The subjects fixated a central mark; when it was extinguished the pattern appeared briefly either centrally or displaced to right or left by the amount indicated on the abscissa. Symmetry can be detected above a displaced axis, although less well than for a central axis.

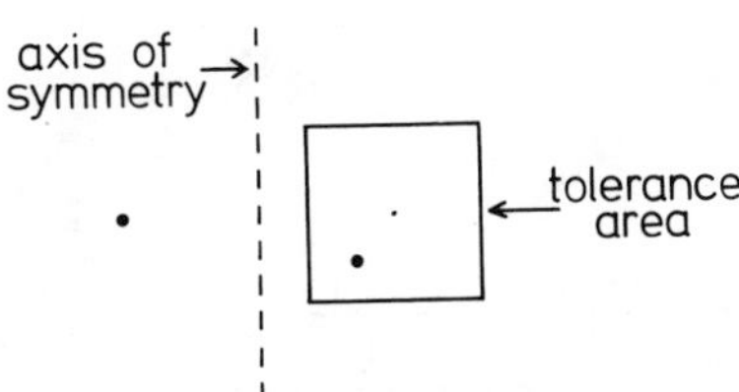

Figure 6-9. Smeared symmetry is produced by placing the pair at random in a tolerance area centered on the exact symmetric position. Because dots are liable to occur by chance in the tolerance area of other dots, errors cannot be avoided when detecting symmetry. The continuous line in Figure 6-10 shows the limiting value of d'_{I} as a function of the size of the tolerance area with which symmetric pairs were produced. The ordinate scale for d'_{I} is at right.

acceptable pair will occur by chance. For instance, if the tolerance area is only 1.0% of the total area of one half field, and if there are 50 dots in a half field, it can be seen immediately that the expected number of dots in a given tolerance area is 0.05, and few spurious pairs will occur. That is, if a dot is found in the tolerance area for a dot in the other half field, it is unlikely to have fallen there by chance and is more likely to have been deliberately placed there; hence the picture is probably from the symmetric population. On the other hand, when the tolerance area forms a substantial fraction of a half field, a tolerance area corresponding to a dot on the other side is very likely by chance to contain one or more dots that have not been placed there deliberately as a pair. Furthermore, these "spurious" pairs will vary in number from sample to sample and may on occasion be so numerous as to suggest that a pattern is from the paired population, even when it is not. In this way the discriminability of samples from paired and unpaired populations becomes imperfect, even using optimum methods.

We have estimated the ideal performance, d'_I, both by calculation and by simulation on the computer. The continuous line in Figure 6-10 shows the results, but note that the ordinate scale on the right must be used for this curve.

No adjustment of the ratio of the two ordinate scales could possibly make the experimental points fit the ideal curve over the whole range, but as plotted they agree quite well for tolerances of ± 12 minutes and greater. For smaller tolerances the optimum symmetry detector is much better, even after the adjustment of the ordinate scale that

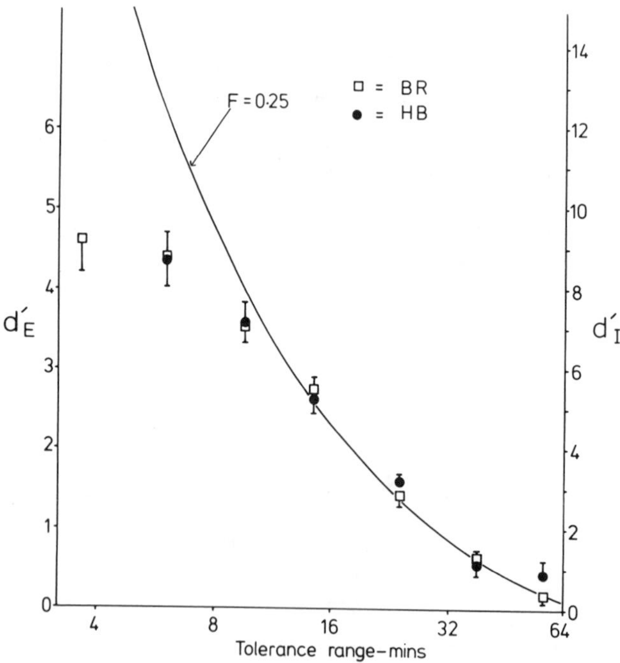

Figure 6-10. Experimental values of d'_E for two subjects as a function of tolerance range. Note that performance is strongly affected by increasing the tolerance range, but only when this has increased to about 8 minutes. For large values d'_I (right ordinate) is approximately twice d'_E (left ordinate), which corresponds to an efficiency of 25%.

makes them agree at large tolerances. This shows that the human symmetry-detecting mechanism does not demand great precision, and that when this mechanism is presented with patterns possessing precise symmetry, it does not do nearly as well at discriminating as an optimum method, which expects high precision. Of course, the fact that the symmetry-detecting mechanism does not require high precision enormously simplifies the task, as we shall see shortly.

The second point to note is the actual relationship between the scales. The scale for d'_I is exactly double that for the experimental points, so that over the range where they agree

$$d'_I = 2d'_E$$

and from expression (**1**)

$$F = (d'_E/d'_I)^2 = 0.25 \qquad (2)$$

Considering that symmetry detection is a fairly complex operation demanding coordinated pairwise comparisons, 25% seems a high figure for efficiency. We do not yet know if it is fortuitous that the best efficiency for first-order structure is 0.5 and for second-order, $(0.5)^2 = 0.25$; both could be explained by a loss of information from about half the initial sample of dots, because the second-order structure depends on pairs of dots, and the number of pairs that can be used is approximately proportional to the square of the number of dots used.

The fully efficient method for discriminating between samples from symmetric and nonsymmetric populations requires a search through all the $N(N-1)/2$ pairs of dots, asking of each pair: Could this have been produced as a deliberate pair under the specified tolerance range? It is clear that performance will be best when this specified tolerance range is equal to the tolerance range used when generating the patterns, so this is the value to specify when searching through all pairs. The optimum discrimination is achieved by classifying the pattern as symmetric when the number of qualifying pairs exceeds a selected criterion. Note in passing that the value of this criterion will not change the efficiency as we have defined it; it will change the ratio of errors of the two kinds; that is, it will increase false positives and decrease detection failures, or vice versa, and changes of criterion will also have an important effect on the *accuracy* of the efficiency estimate. For this last reason, the range within which a usable criterion must lie is always rather narrow. However, what makes this ideal method of discriminating symmetry difficult is the initial step of searching through the $\sim N^2/2$ pairs of dots. For a real image, N would of course be far larger than the 100 or so we have used and might correspond to the number of resolvable picture elements, in which case the search would become absurdly long and difficult. It is for this reason that the result with smeared symmetry seems to us important, for it suggests that the system is tolerant and works at low resolution. We have therefore devised a simple model of symmetry detection working at low resolution to see how its efficiency compares with the human.

Figure 6-11 shows the basis of the model. The picture is divided into 16 squares, 8 in each half field. The number of dots in each square is counted, and these numbers alone are used in judging symmetry; that is, the position of a dot within a subsquare is ignored entirely. Of course, we realize than an improved version of this model would not be subdivided into square regions and might use a Mexican-hat-shaped weighting function to get a relative measure of how many dots there are in a region, but let us see how the crude version works.

Having obtained the numbers, we then test the hypothesis that it is *not* symmetric about the midline. Now if that was the case, the difference between numbers in symmetrically placed squares would vary with variance equal to $2N$, and the hypothesis can be tested by calculating $\chi^2(7)$ as indicated. If symmetry is present, the variance will be less than the hypothesis postulates, and the value of χ^2 obtained will be below 7, its expected value.

Figure 6-12 shows the performance of the model, with the same experimental points as Figure 6-10 for comparison. Clearly the dotted line is not a bad fit to the data, although the model seems to outperform the human at large tolerances.

Also included is the solid line representing ideal performance, for one can look at these experiments as tests of *failure* to achieve *ideal* performance, rather than simply as tests of what can be achieved. If both model and human had performed close to ideal, clearly the fit between the two would have been attributable to the way ideal performance varies rather than to any specific properties of the model, but this is not the case, and the model gains strength as a representation of how the brain detects symmetry.

The argument and the model could be framed in the currently fashionable language of spatial frequencies. The model would then correspond approximately to one that operated on an input pattern in which higher spatial frequencies have been filtered out; it is, we suggest, the low spatial frequencies that are used in the detection of symmetry in dot patterns such as we use, and presumably in real life as well. But our model brings out immediately the virtue of operating with smeared, blurred, or low frequency information, namely, that when you do so you can operate with far fewer quantities. In our case the number of paired comparisons is reduced from 4,950, the value of $N(N-1)/2$ for $N = 100$, to 120 (the value for $N = 16$), of which only 8 paired comparisons are used in the test for symmetry about the vertical midline. We think that the advantage of removing high spatial frequencies is that it enables one to reduce the number of sample points required to define the image. Many people who talk of spatial frequency filtering do not seem to appreciate the main advantage it confers, but the relatively crude operation of integrating dots over squares performs sampling and filtering in one operation, and the advantage of reducing the number of quantities that must be handled becomes immediately obvious. Receptive fields could, of course, perform such integration in a more versatile and less crude manner.

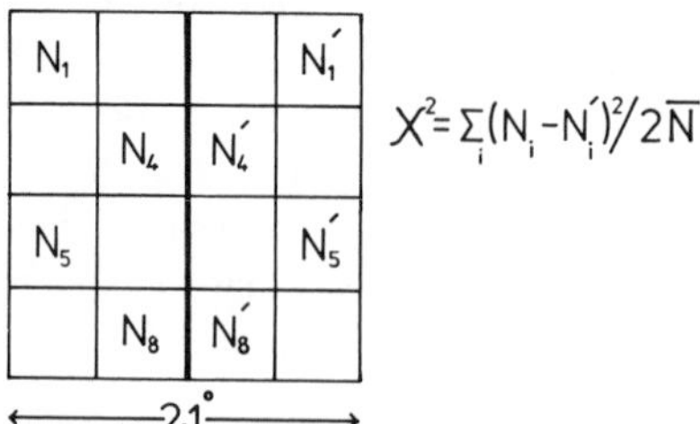

Figure 6-11. A statistical test for symmetry can be performed by dividing each side into 8 squares and counting the number of dots in each square. If there is no deliberately imposed symmetry about the midline and the arrangement of dots is otherwise random, the variance of the number in each square will be close to $\overline{N}$, the average number per small square, and the difference between a symmetric pair will have variance $2\overline{N}$. A χ^2 (7) test can be performed as shown, low values indicating symmetry. The dotted line in Figure 6-12 shows the performance of this model in a computer-simulated trial.

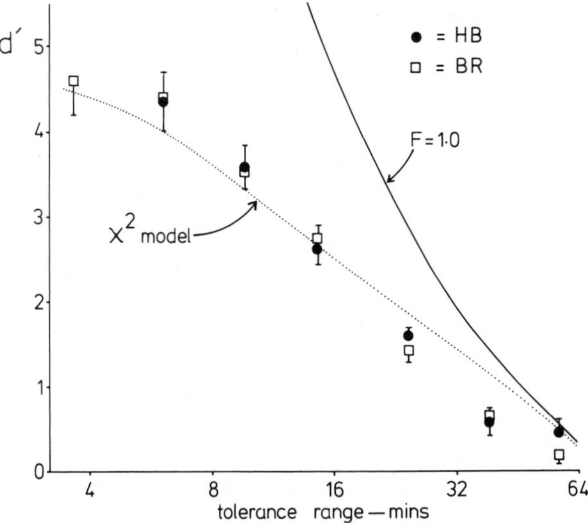

Figure 6-12. Comparison of the model in Figure 6-11 with the results in Figure 6-10. The model outperforms the human at large tolerances but matches quite well elsewhere. The solid line shows the ideal performance, using an exhaustive search through all dot pairs, plotted here using the same ordinate scale as the experimental points.

CONCLUSIONS

What have the mechanisms for detecting symmetry got to do with the neurophysiology of the cells of the visual cortex and their plasticity? It is unlikely that the primary cortex is directly involved in symmetry detection, for the following reason. Our patterns extend over two degrees, and of course symmetry can be detected in objects subtending a much greater angle. Now, the magnification factor in the center of the visual field is 6 mm of cortex per degree in rhesus monkeys, and more than this in humans. Hence, the edges of a symmetrical pattern would stimulate regions more than 12 mm apart on the cortex, and there are very few intracortical connections extending over that range. Thus, one suspects symmetry detection is a specialized operation performed in one of the many specialized parastriate regions (see ref. 60).

However, it is perhaps not too fanciful to detect some similarity in the kind of operation that cells in primary visual cortex can perform and in the kind of operation required for symmetry detection. First, the cortex depends on a very precise and orderly projection of the incoming fibers: clearly a precise and orderly system of connections is needed to bring together the regions that are paired for any given position of the axis of symmetry; it might be said that those orderly patterns of connections are unimaginable were it not for our knowledge of primary visual cortex. Second, we know that cortical neurons can respond selectively to particular patterns or associations of stimuli, such as those corresponding to a line or to joint stimulation of the two eyes, and this is the kind of capacity required to detect the similarity of two regions paired about a given axis.

If there is anything valid in these speculations on the capacity of the cortex to detect associations, the plasticity of neurons of the primary visual cortex becomes highly significant. They can switch off or detach the input from one eye if it is not stimulated concurrently with the other and thus cease to respond binocularly; one wonders, then, if a symmetry-deprived animal could detect symmetry. The more radical changes described by Singer (50), in which neurons were found with two receptive fields separated by the period of the grating to which the animal had been habitually exposed, suggests that cortical neurons may even develop new capacities in response to specific new types of regularity in their environment. Whether such capacities are called learning and memory may be a problem of terminology and semantics.

ACKNOWLEDGMENTS

My thanks are due to my colleagues Aart van Meeteren and Barney Reeves, who helped plan and perform many of the experiments described here, and also to the Medical Research Council and Royal Society, which provided financial support.

REFERENCES

1. Barlow HB: Visual experience and cortical development. *Nature* 258:199–204, 1975.
2. Barlow HB: Retinal and central factors in human vision limited by noise, in Barlow HB, Fatt P (eds): *Photoreception in Vertebrates*. London, Academic Press, 1975, p 337–358.
3. Barlow HB: The efficiency of detecting changes of density in random dot patterns. *Vision Research* 18:637–650, 1978.
4. Barlow HB, Pettigrew JD: Lack of specificity of neurones in the visual cortex of young kittens. *J Physiol* 218:98–100P, 1971.
5. Barlow HB, Reeves BC: The versatility and absolute efficiency of detecting mirror symmetry in random dot displays. *Vision Research* 19:783–793, 1979.
6. Blakemore CB: Genetic instruction and developmental plasticity in the kitten's visual cortex. *Phil trans Roy Soc Lond B* 425–434, 1977.
7. Blakemore C, Cooper GF: Development of the brain depends on the visual environment. *Nature (London)* 228:447–448, 1970.
8. Blakemore C, Mitchell DE: Environmental modification of the visual cortex and the neural basis of learning and memory. *Nature* 241:467–468, 1973.
9. Blakemore C, Van Sluyters RC: Innate and environmental factors in the development of the kitten's visual cortex. *J Physiol* 248:663–716, 1975.
10. Blakemore C, Garey LJ, Vital-Durand F: The physiological effects of monocular deprivation and their reversal in the monkey's visual cortex. *J Physiol* 283:223–262, 1978.
11. Blakemore C, Van Sluyters RC, Peck CK: Development of cat visual cortex following rotation of one eye. *Nature* 257:584–586, 1975.
12. Bonds AB: Development of orientation tuning in kitten striate cortex, in Freeman R (ed): *Developmental Neurobiology of Vision*. NATO Advanced Study Institute Series. New York, Plenum Press, 1979.
13. Braitenburg V: *Gehirngespinste. Neuroanatomie für kybernetisch Interessierte*. Heidelberg, Springer-Verlag, 1973. (Translated as "On the Texture of Brains", Heidelberg Science Library, 1977.)
14. Buisseret P, Imbert M: Visual cortical cells: their developmental properties in normal and dark reared kittens. *J Physiol (Lond)* 248:663–716, 1976.
15. Buisseret P, Gary-Bobo E, Imbert M: Ocular motility and recovery of orientational properties of visual cortical neurones in dark-reared kittens. *Nature* 272:816–817, 1978.

16. Cynader M, Berman N, Hein A: Cats reared in stroboscopic illumination: effects on receptive fields in cat visual cortex. *Proc Nat Acad Sci (Wash)* 70:1353–1354, 1973.

17. Cynader M, Berman N, Hein A: Cats raised in a one-directional world: effects on receptive fields in visual cortex and superior colliculus. *Exp Brain Res* 22:267–280, 1975.

18. Cynader M, Chernenko G: Abolition of direction selectivity in the visual cortex of the cat. *Science* 193:504–505, 1976.

19. Daw NW, Wyatt HJ: Kittens reared in a uni-directional environment: evidence for a critical period. *J Physiol (Lond)* 257:155–170, 1976.

20. Daw NW, Berman NEJ, Ariel M: Interaction of critical periods in the visual cortex of kittens. *Science* 199:565–567, 1978.

21. Freeman RD: The effects of a "consolidation" period following brief monocular deprivation in kittens, in Freeman R (ed): *Developmental Neurobiology of Vision*. NATO Advanced Study Institute Series. New York, Plenum Press 1979.

22. Gilbert CD: Laminar differences in receptive field properties of cells in cat primary visual cortex. *J Physiol* 268:391–421, 1977.

23. Glass L: Moiré effect from random dots. *Nature* 223–578–580, 1969.

24. Guillery RW, Stelzner DJ: The differential effects of unilateral lid closure upon the monocular and binocular segments of the dorsal lateral geniculate nucleus of the cat. *J Comp Neurol* 139:413–422, 1970.

25. Hebb DO: *The Organization of Behavior*. New York, Wiley, 1949.

26. Hirsch HVB, Leventhal AG: Cortical effects of early visual experience, in Cool S (ed): *Frontiers of Vision Research*. Berlin, Springer-Verlag, 1979.

27. Hirsch HVB, Spinelli DN: Visual experience modifies distribution of horizontally and vertically oriented receptive fields in cats. *Science* 168:869–871, 1970.

28. Hirsch HVB, Spinelli DN: Modification of the distribution of receptive field orientation in cats by selective visual exposure during development. *Exp Brain Res* 13:509–527, 1971.

29. Hubel DH, Wiesel TN: Receptive fields of single neurones in the cat's striate cortex. *J Physiol* 148:574–591, 1959.

30. Hubel DH, Wiesel TN: Receptive fields, binocular interaction, and functional architecture in the cat's visual cortex. *J Physiol* 160:106–154, 1962.

31. Hubel DH, Wiesel TN: Receptive fields of cells in striate cortex of very young, visually inexperienced kittens. *J Neurophysiol* 26:994–1002.

32. Hubel DH, Wiesel TN: Binocular interaction in striate cortex of kittens reared with artificial squint. *J Neurophysiol* 28:1041–1059, 1965.

33. Hubel DH, Wiesel TN: The period of susceptibility to the physiological effects of unilateral eye closure in kittens. *J Physiol* 206:419–436, 1970.

34. Hubel DH, Wiesel TN: Ordered arrangement of orientation columns in monkeys lacking visual experience. *J Comp Neurol* 158:307–318, 1974.

35. Hubel DH, Wiesel TN: Ferrier Lecture: Functional architecture of macaque monkey visual cortex. *Proc Roy Soc B* 198:1–59, 1977.

36. Ikeda H, Wright MJ: Properties of LGN cells in kittens reared with convergent squint: a neurophysiological demonstration of amblyopia. *Exp Brain Res* 25:65–77, 1976.

37. Imbert M, Buisseret P: Receptive field characteristics and plastic properties of visual cortical cells in kittens reared with or without visual experience. *Exp Brain Res* 22:25–36, 1975.

38. Leventhal AG, Hirsch HVB: Cortical effect of early selective exposure to diagonal lines. *Science* 190:902–904.

39. Leventhal AG, Hirsch HVB: Effects of early experience upon orientation sensitivity and binocularity of neurons in visual cortex of cats. *Proc Nat Acad Sci* 74:1272–1276, 1977.

40. Mountcastle V: In Schmitt FO and Worden FG (eds): *The Neurosciences: Fourth Study Program*. Cambridge, Mass, MIT Press, 1979, p 21.

41. Movshon JA: Reversal of the physiological effects of monocular deprivation in the kitten's visual cortex. *J Physiol (Lond)* 261:125–174, 1976.

42. Olson CR, Pettigrew JD: Single units in visual cortex of kittens raised in stroboscopic illumination. *Brain Res* 70:189–204, 1974.
43. Pettigrew JD: The effect of visual experience on the development of stimulus specificity by kitten cortical neurones. *J Physiol* 237:49–74, 1974.
44. Pettigrew JD, Freeman RD: Visual experience without lines; effect on developing cortical neurons. *Science* 182:599–600, 1973.
45. Ramachandran VS, Clarke PGH, Whitteridge D: Cells selective to binocular disparity in the cortex of newborn lambs. *Nature* 268:333–335, 1977.
46. Rauschecker JPJ: Orientation dependent changes in ocular dominance of neurons in the kitten's visual cortex, in Freeman R (ed): *Developmental Neurobiology of Vision.* NATO Advanced Study Institute Series. New York, Plenum Press, 1979.
47. Sherk H, Stryker MP: Quantitative study of cortical orientation selectivity in visually inexperienced kittens. *J Neurophysiol* 39:63–70, 1975.
48. Sherman M: Differential susceptibility to deprivation of X and Y systems, in Freeman R (ed): *Developmental Neurobiology of Vision.* NATO Advanced Study Institute Series. New York, Plenum Press, 1979.
49. Shlaer R: Shift in binocular disparity causes compensatory change in the cortical structure of kittens. *Science* 173:638–641, 1971.
50. Singer W: Neuronal mechanisms in developmental plasticity; the role of extrinsic gating systems, in Freeman R (ed): *Developmental Neurobiology of Vision.* NATO Advanced Study Institute Series. New York, Plenum Press, 1979.
51. Stryker MP, Sherk H: Modification of cortical orientation selectivity in the cat by restricted visual experience: a reexamination. *Science* (*NY*) 190:904–906, 1975.
52. Stryker MP, Sherk H, Leventhal AG, et al: Physiological consequences for the cat's visual cortex of effectively restricting early visual experience with oriented contours. *J Neurophysiol* 41:896–909, 1978.
53. Swets JA (ed): *Signal Detection and Recognition by Human Observers.* New York, John Wiley, 1964.
54. Tretter F, Cynader MS, Singer W: Modification of direction selectivity of neurons in the visual cortex of kittens. *Brain Res* 84:143–149, 1975.
55. Van Sluyters RC, Blakemore C: Experimental creation of unusual neuronal properties in visual cortex of kittens. *Nature* 246:506–508, 1973.
56. Watkins DW, Wilson JR, Sherman SM: Receptive field properties of neurons in binocular and monocular segments of striate cortex in cats raised with binocular lid suture. *J Neurophysiol* 41:305–321, 1978.
57. Wiesel TN, Hubel DH: Single cell responses in striate cortex of kittens deprived of vision in one eye. *J Neurophysiol* 26:1004–1017.
58. Wiesel TN, Hubel DH: Comparison of the effects of unilateral and bilateral eye closure on cortical unit responses in kittens. *J Neurophysiol* 28:1029–1040, 1965.
59. Wiesel TN, Hubel DH: Extent of recovery from the effects of visual deprivation in kittens. *J Neurophysiol* 28:1060–1072, 1965.
60. Zeki SM: Functional specialization in the visual cortex of the rhesus monkey. *Nature* 274:423–474, 1978.

7

Neuronal Activity in the Cortical Supplementary Motor Area Associated with the Development of a Preparatory Motor Set for Sensory-Triggered Responses

Jun Tanji

The achievement of motor tasks in a number of instances requires a variety of preparatory states on the part of the animal or human. For such motor acts as performing a predetermined limb movement in response to a sudden somesthetic stimulus, an adequate and immediate response to the stimulus to start the intended movement would be possible only after the subject acquires skills to be prepared to respond properly to the forthcoming stimulus. What, then, is the neural basis for the acquisition of this motor skill? Hammond (7) found that a 50-msec latency biceps response to an arm displacement involving biceps stretch was present or absent, depending on whether subjects had been instructed to resist or to let go in response to the displacement. Recent reports by Evarts and Tanji (5,6) have shown that the intention for a predetermined motor act can profoundly modify reflex responses of the cerebral motor cortex to kinesthetic inputs. Evarts and Tanji's detailed analysis of response latencies in the motor cortex and muscles provided evidence of cortical participation in the early sensory-triggered muscle response. Thus, the response of motor cortex neurons to a somesthetic stimulus could be modulated by an earlier instruction telling the animal how to respond to the stimulus, so that the short latency response of the motor cortex is appropriate in playing a part in initiating an intended movement. These reports led to the next question of what structures in the CNS are responsible for the adjustment of input-output relationships in the motor cortex. Experiments by Wiesendanger et al. (17) on anesthetized monkeys have shown that the electrical stimulation of the supplementary motor area (SMA) affects the responses to sensory inputs of neurons in the motor cortex. Thus, the SMA is a good candidate for a structure to be involved in the modulating system that provides adequate adjustments of motor cortex responses in relation to a learned motor task. To test this hypothesis, two monkeys were trained to perform essentially the same task as that reported by Evarts and Tanji (6), and single unit activity in the SMA was recorded. Observations were focused on neuronal activity during a preparatory period, when the monkey was instructed to push or pull a handle in response to a forthcoming perturbation given to the handle. To obtain information on whether the recorded area is a portion of the SMA that projects to an arm area of the motor cortex, an additional experiment was performed using two monkeys. Horseradish peroxidase (HRP) was injected in the arm area to detect retrograde labeling of projecting neurons in the SMA.

METHODS

Behavioral Procedures

To establish a pattern of behavior involving the preparatory state of the animal before starting motor tasks in response to forthcoming sensory inputs, two monkeys were trained in essentially the same manner as explained in the report by Tanji and Evarts (6). Each monkey's hand and forearm were attached by means of a padded bracket to a metal piece, which was connected to a torque motor by connecting rods and pivots. Fixation at the finger, wrist, and shoulder limited the monkey's movement of its right forelimb to pushing and pulling the metal piece largely by extension and flexion at the elbow joint. The monkey positioned the forearm together with the metal piece in a central "hold" zone, midway between the push and pull zones. The central zone corresponded to a handle excursion of 1.0 cm. Correct positioning was indicated by a white lamp. After a holding period, which varied unpredictably from 2.5 to 5 seconds, a red or a green lamp came on. *Red* was an instruction to pull when the metal piece was subsequently perturbed, and *green* was an instruction to push when the piece was sub-

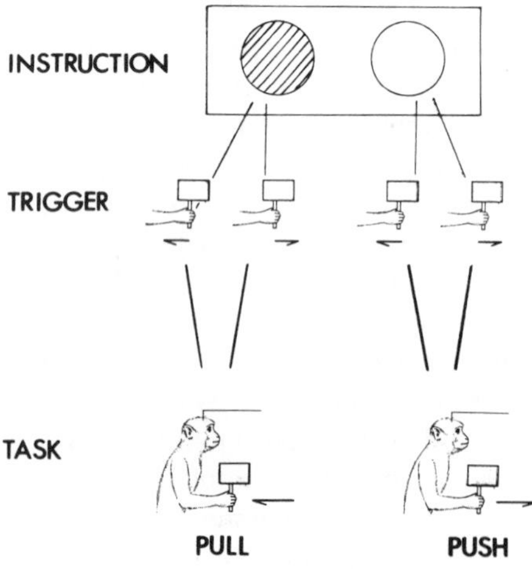

Figure 7-1. This figure shows diagrammatically the behavioral pattern that monkeys were trained to achieve. The monkey waited for one of two instructions that told him the direction of the movement he was to start in response to the forth-coming sensory stimulus to the hand. He was required not to initiate the movement when the instruction came on. Instead, he had to wait 2.5 to 5 seconds until the occurrence of the stimulus (perturbation of the handle), which served to trigger the movement.

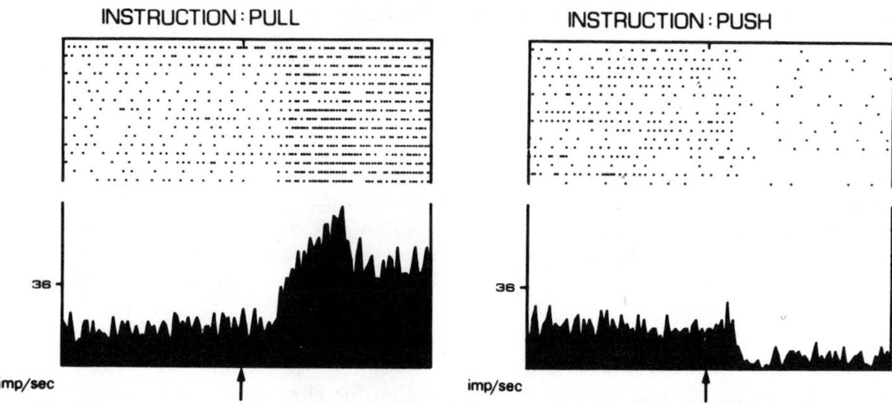

Figure 7-2. Discharge of an SMA neuron for 1024 msec before and 1024 msec after the appearance of the red signal (instruction to pull) and the green signal (instruction to push). The activity of this neuron is displayed in two different formats. At the top are rasters where each row is a trial, with dots representing individual single-unit discharges. Below are histograms, which represent summation of data in the rasters plus the data obtained from subsequent 16 trials. Bin width is 16 msec. The time of occurrence of the instruction signal is indicated by an arrow.

sequently perturbed. Push and pull instructions were varied according to a predetermined pseudorandom order. The handle perturbation serving to trigger the movement specified by the prior instruction was produced by a brushless DC torque motor (Aeroflex TQ 34W-1H), which was driven by an operational power supply (Aeroflex Am 200A). The magnitude of the torque was adjusted to a little more than that necessary to produce a short-latency tendon jerk in the biceps or triceps muscle. Once initiated, the torque output from the motor continued until the response (whether correct or incorrect) had been completed. Response completion was defined as the entrance of the handle into either the push or pull zoned, both separated from the central hold zone by 7.5 cm. When the zone specified by the earlier instruction was entered following the perturbation, a reward of fruit puree was delivered. An incorrect response did not lead to reward. In either case, a new cycle of behavior now began, with a return to the holding position of the pre-instruction holding step. The behavioral sequence is shown diagrammatically in Figure 7-1.

Data Recording and Processing

A stainless-steel cylinder allowing microelectrode recordings in a 16-mm-diameter area was attached to the skull over medial part of the premotor area of the cortex, with its center at Horseley-Clarke coordinates A 20, L 3. Histological examination of the recording sites in two monkeys confirmed that the sites covered an area defined as SMA by Penfield and Welch (13). Glass-insulated platinum-iridium electrodes were used for recording extracellular unit activity from the SMA. Details of these procedures have been described previously (4). The EMG was recorded with Teflon-coated silver wires chronically implanted in biceps, triceps, pectoralis major, supraspinatus, infraspinatus, anterior serratus, pectoralis major, and paravertebral muscle. Unit activity, EMG, output of position transducer, and signals corresponding to instructions, perturbations,

Table 7-1. Latencies of Instruction-Evoked Neuronal Response

	<200	*200–300*	*300–400*	*400–500*	*>500*	*Total*
D neurons	24	27	19	10	14	94
non-D neurons	1	9	21	31	45	107

The response latency for each neuron that showed a statistically significant response to the instruction is tabulated here. In each column are listed the numbers of neurons having latencies (in milliseconds) corresponding to each of the column headings. It is apparent that D neurons that possessed a differential relationship to two different instructions had latencies shorter than neurons that responded to them similarly (non-D neurons).

responses, and rewards were recorded on magnetic tape. A digital computer (250 System, San'ei-Nova) was used to detect poststimulus changes in neural discharge frequency and to compute the latency of these changes with respect to an instruction.

Histological Studies

Two monkeys whose neuronal activity was studied were perfused with saline followed by 10% formalin. Brain sections were stained with thionin to examine the locations of electrode tracks and electrolytic lesions.

Two other monkeys were used for the HRP study. Under pentobarbital narcosis, the precentral area was exposed and an area of lowest threshold for contraction of arm muscles was identified by repetitive electrical stimulation of the cortical surface. A 30% aqueous solution of HRP (Toyobo, 0.5 μl) was injected through a 26-gauge Hamilton microsyringe mounted on a stereotaxic instrument. Four injections, each separated by 1 mm, were made within the target area at a depth of 1.5–2.5 mm below the pia mater. The total volume injected was 2.0 μl. After 72 hours, the monkey was anesthetized and perfused with saline followed by 2 liters of fixative, which contained 0.5% glutaraldehyde and 2% paraformaldehyde in an 0.1 M phosphate buffer at pH of 7.4. The brain was then removed and placed in the same buffer to which 10% sucrose had been added for 24 hours at 4°C. At the end of this period, the brain was photographed and cut by a freezing microtome into 40-μm thick sections. Every sixth section was reacted in an incubation medium of 3,3′-diaminobenzidine tetrahydrochloride in Tris buffer. The sections were mounted on slides to counterstain with thionine.

RESULTS

Neuronal Activity Responding to Motor Instructions

Of many hundreds of neurons recorded long enough for the detection of any relationship to various aspects of the present behavioral pattern, 201 neurons were found to alter discharge activity in relation to the motor instruction, long before the start of actual movement (push or pull). Monkeys were well trained not to move the handle or to alter the way of gripping the handle in response to the instruction. EMG recordings detected no alteration of activity in the arm as well as girdle muscles in the holding period until the occurrence of the triggering stimulus. Thus, the neural response was observed in the absence of any overt change in the muscle activity. Figure 7-2 shows an example of the neuronal response to the pull as compared with the push instruction. Two kinds of displays are presented in this figure: rasters show the raw data for 16 individual trials, with the instruction occurring at the center of the raster, and histograms represent the summation of the data shown in the rasters plus the data obtained in 16 additional trials. The increase of discharge frequency after the pull instruction reached the 0.01 level of statistical significance at 182 msec, and the decrease reached the level at 168 msec. The criterion of response adopted in this study was the 0.01 level, and the latency of the response was taken as the time at which this level was attained. Thus, the response latency for the increase and decrease of activity in this unit was taken as 182 and 168 msec, respectively. Results on response latencies for the entire sample of 201 SMA neurons are shown in Table 7-1.

Each neuron was examined in relation to each of the instructions (push and pull), and in a number of cases, the responses to the two instructions differed. The differences were of two types: (*a*) presence versus absence (i.e., response for one instruction and no response for the other) and (*b*) increase versus decrease (i.e., an increase in activity for one instruction and a decrease for the other). Units showing either of these differences were classified as having differential responses to the different instructions, and their response latencies are tabulated separately (as D neurons) in Table 7-1. According to the hypothesis that the SMA is responsible for the modification of motor cortex responses to somesthetic input, there should be activity changes of SMA neurons, which

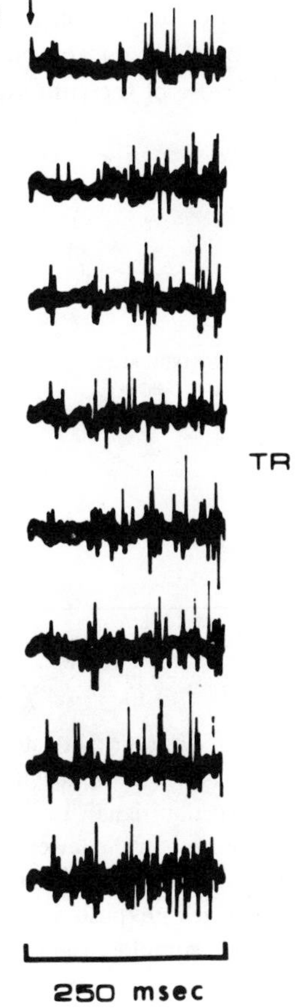

Figure 7-3. Activity of the triceps muscle recorded from chronically implanted electrodes, showing its response to a perturbing stimulus (which stretches the muscle) when the monkey initiated push movement. Each sweep was triggered at the start of mechanical displacement of the metal piece of which the monkey's forearm was attached. The top trace was obtained when the direction of the stimulus was switched from "all away from" to "all toward" the monkey. The direction remained the same in 16 successive trials, 8 of which are shown in the figure.

differs greatly depending on whether the monkey is instructed to push or to pull. The presence of the 94 D neurons seem to substantiate this hypothesis. However, this is a requisite finding and not a sufficient proof for the hypothesis. Thus, the next attempt was a more crucial test of the hypothesis.

Parallelism Between Neural Activity and the Acquisition of Motor Skills

The direction of the sensory-triggering stimulus (perturbation of the handle), coming toward or away from the monkey, was usually randomized, and it was impossible for the animal to anticipate the next stimulus direction. On some occasions, after the D neuron was obtained, this behavioral pattern was somewhat altered. The perturbation continued in one direction for 16 successive trials; then the direction was reversed for another 16 trials. After the direction was altered several times in this manner, the monkey learned to anticipate the direction of the forthcoming stimulus. The effect of the anticipation on the stimulus-evoked muscle responses is shown in Figure 7-3. The figure shows the activity of the triceps muscle when the animal pulled the metal piece in response to the stimulus, which came toward the monkey (and stretched the triceps muscle). The first tracing was obtained when the direction of the stimulus was changed. The stimulus evoked a short latency response, which seemed to be a tendon jerk, and, following a pause, later muscle activity started about 120 msec after the onset of the stimulus. The latter muscle activity was initiated progressively earlier as the stimulus direction remained the same. In the tracing at the bottom of the figure, it will be noted that the early reflex response is immediately followed by the later response, implying that the monkey acquired skills to make the most efficient use of the stimulus in trigger-

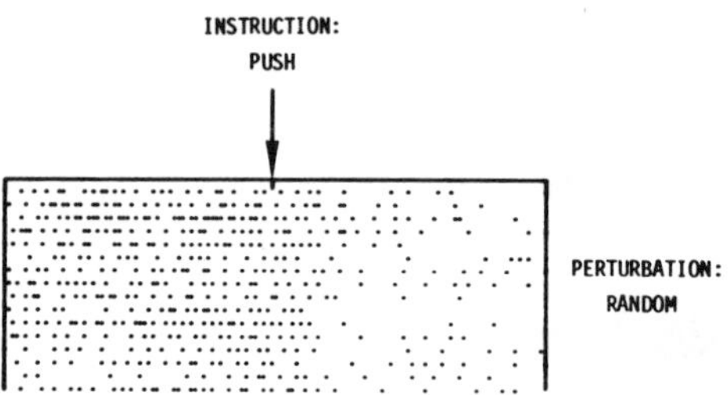

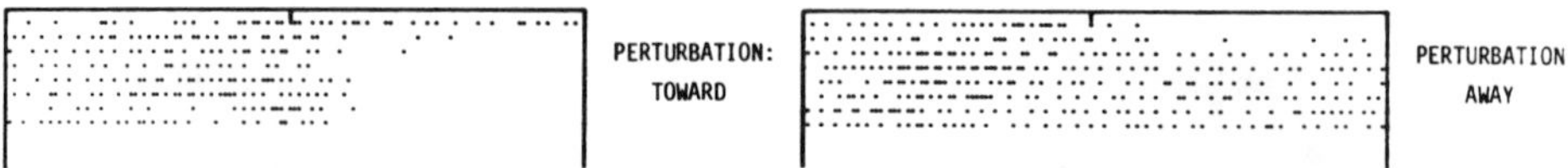

Figure 7-4. This figure shows dependence of the instruction effect (activity decrease) on the anticipated direction of the forthcoming sensory stimulus. Rasters show activity of an SMA neuron during 1024 msec before and after the onset of the instruction signal. In the upper part of the figure the direction of the purturbing stimulus was randomized. In the lower part, the direction remained the same in 16 successive trials, in half of which the instruction was to push. Hence, activity in eight trials when the monkey was instructed to push in response to all "toward" stimulus (left of the figure) and to all "away from" stimulus (right) is presented in order of successive trials.

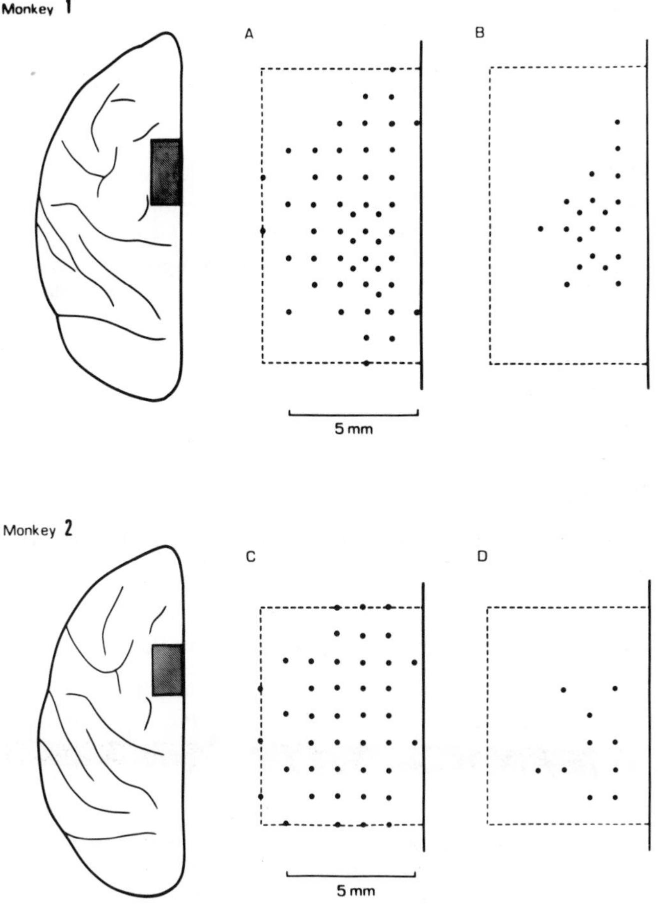

Figure 7-5. The black dots in each rectangle represent points of microelectrode penetration into the supplementary motor area. Dots in (*A*) and (*C*) show all points of penetration in monkeys 1 and 2, respectively; in (*B*) and (*D*), penetrations yielding neurons with differential responses to two instructions of push and pull. The locations of rectangles are depicted at left, showing the top view of left hemispheres of the two monkeys.

ing the intended muscle response. The neuronal activity shown in Figure 7-4 revealed a remarkable parallelism between the augmentation of the early muscle response and the response to the instruction of an SMA neuron. The neuron decreased its discharge after the instruction to push when the direction of the perturbation was randomly altered (upper part of the figure). This decrease was not at all observed with the first behavioral response when a series of "away" stimuli (which shortened the triceps) was switched unexpectedly to a series of "toward" stimuli (which stretched the triceps). Subsequently, the decrease in discharge was progressively more evident until, toward the end of the all "toward" stimulus series, the discharge completely stopped (see the lower left of the figure). In contrast, when the stimulus was switched to all "away," the instruction gave rise to a cessation of discharge only at the initial part of the sequence, and the discharge

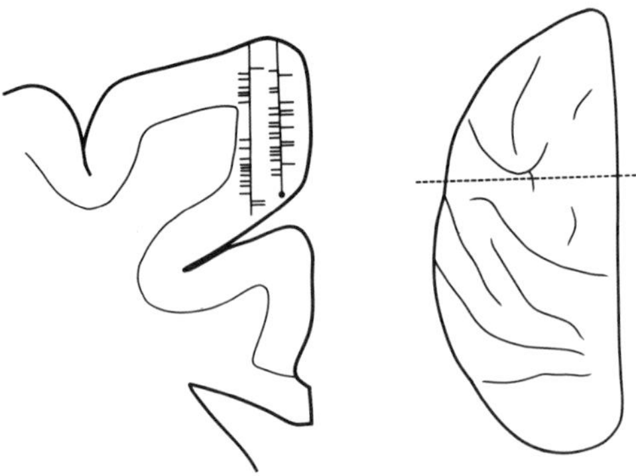

Figure 7-6. Reconstruction of two penetrations made within 100 μm of the rostrocaudal level, indicated by a dashed line in the right of the figure. Horizontal bars to the right of the electrode track indicate points where D neurons were obtained. Bars to the left indicate points where neurons other than D neurons were recorded. A black dot indicates a point where electrolytic lesion was made.

decrease was progressively less evident (lower right). Similar observations were made of 20 out of 27 D neurons, whose specificity of the effect of the instruction on its direction was tested. In the remaining seven neurons, the degree of the neural response was unrelated to the stimulus direction.

Distribution of Neurons with Differential Relationships to Two Different Motor Instructions

The points of microelectrode entrance into the SMA for recording of 94 D neurons are shown in Figure 7-5. In both monkeys it is apparent that these entry points were

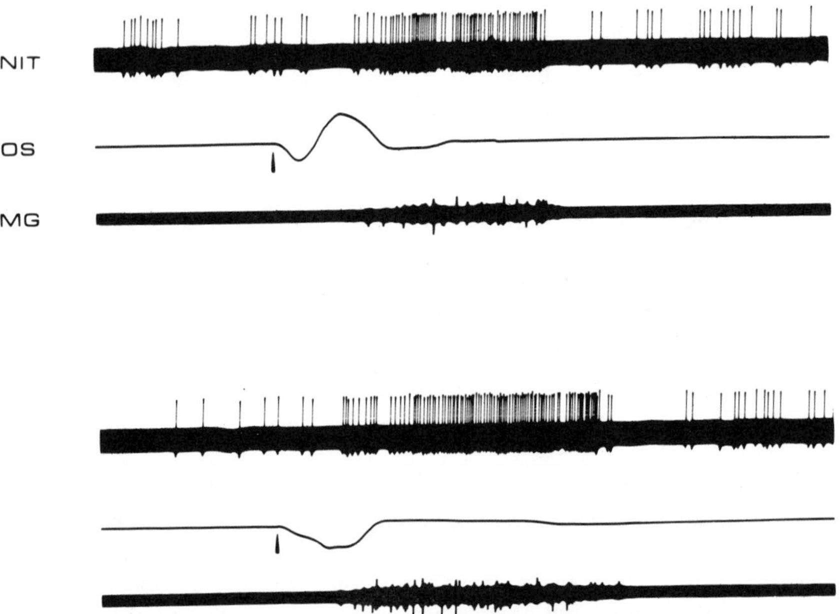

Figure 7-7. Top traces show discharges of an SMA neuron. Middle traces indicate the output of a transducer monitoring position of the metal piece to which monkey's forelimb is attached. Bottom traces show EMG activity recorded from the paravertebral muscle. This neuron possesses activity correlated with that of the paravertebral muscle and not correlated with push or pull movement. No instruction effects are detected.

confined to an area within 5 mm from the midline, extending a few millimeters anteriorly and posteriorly from a portion corresponding to the caudal end of the arcuate sulcus. Most of the recordings were obtained from penetrations located medially. As many as seventy-five neurons were obtained from microelectrodes inserted at not more than 2.5 mm from the midline. Two examples of electrode penetration are shown in Figure 7-6, in which electrode tracks were reconstructed from histological sections, and points where single neuron activity was isolated were drawn. In the medial penetration (labeled b), recordings from as many as 8 D neurons were obtained (bars protruding to the right indicate their recording points), whereas readings from only 3 neurons were obtained in the lateral penetration (labeled a). It was noted that most recordings from D neurons were obtained while the electrodes passed through the layer III of the cortex.

Neuronal Activity Related to Postural Adjustments

Among all the neurons recorded, about 24% exhibited activity changes with a constant relationship to a movement of push or pull, and about 5% responded to perturbing stimuli with latencies of less than 50 seconds. Since these neuronal responses are not relevant to the theme of this chapter, they will not be described here. However, the following observation should be mentioned. Twenty-six neurons were activated or silenced at a period when the monkey repositioned its forelimb (with the metal piece)

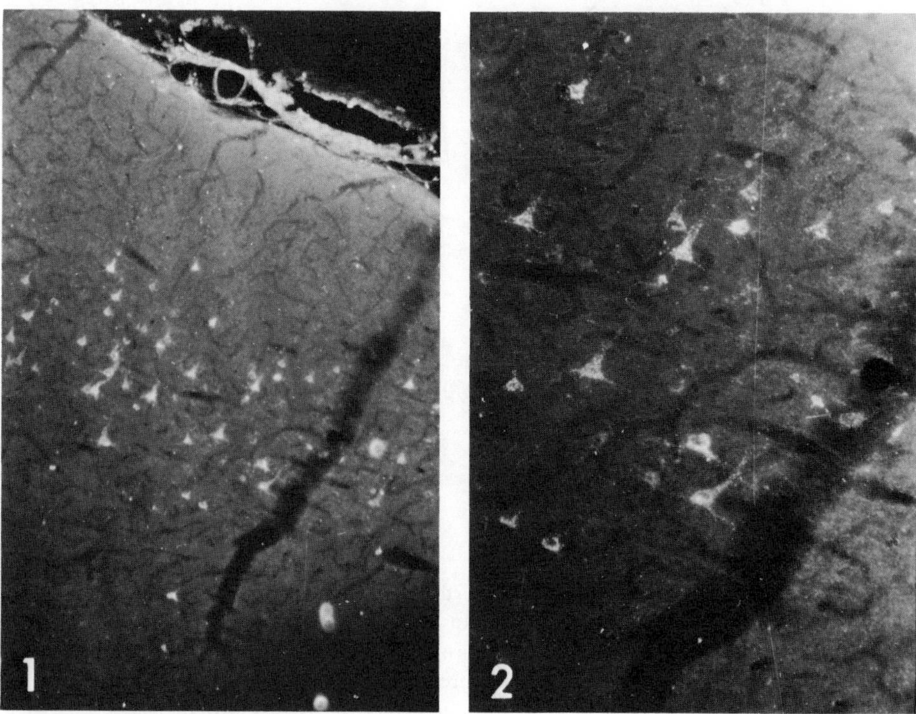

Figure 7-8. (*1*) Darkfield photomicrograph showing HRP-labeled neurons in the SMA after injection of HRP in arm area of the motor cortex. HRP-positive granules are evident in the high-power field (*2*).

into the central holding zone, after completing the push or pull response. An example is shown in Figure 7-7. This neuron was not very active when the monkey pushed or pulled the handle in response to the sensory stimulus. However, the neuron exhibited marked activity when the monkey gradually moved the metal piece back to the hold zone. This neural activity was best correlated with activity in the paravertebral muscles

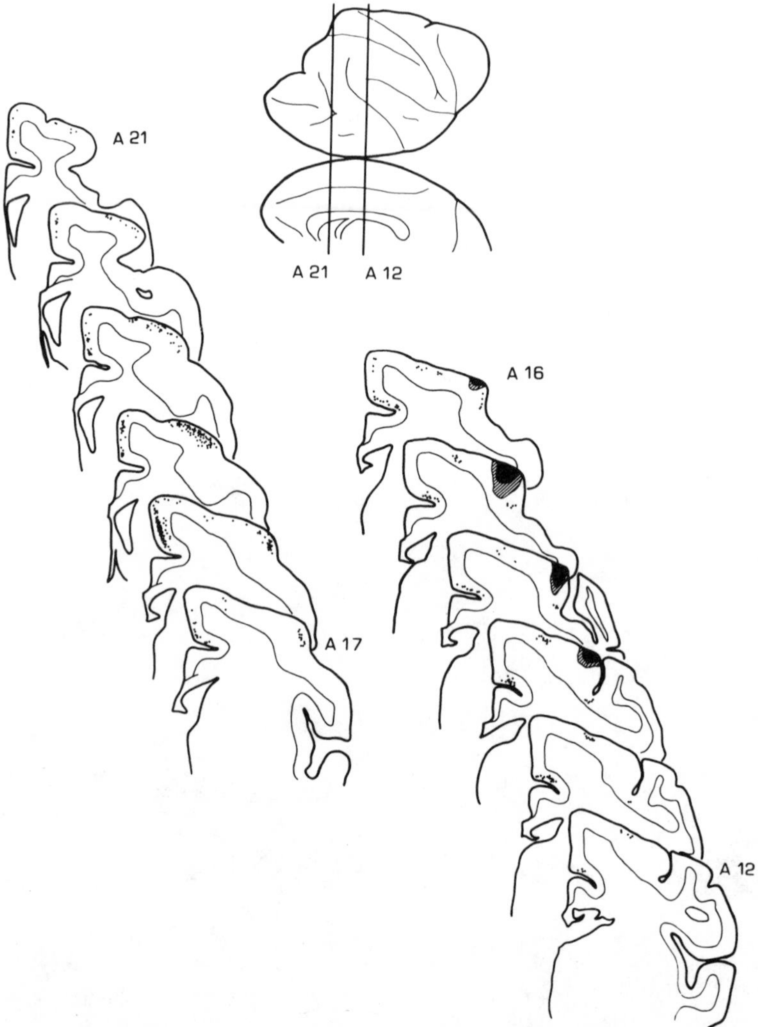

Figure 7-9. Distribution of HRP-labeled neurons in the SMA. Reconstruction of the diffusion of injected HRP into arm area of the motor cortex and of the distribution of labeled cortical neurons in coronal sections of the right hemisphere. The shaded region in the precentral area indicates faint reaction product surrounding the focus of the injected HRP (represented in black). Plotting of two sections (100 μm apart) were superimposed to obtain one coronal reconstruction. Each dot corresponds to one labeled cortical neuron. Reconstruction was made at every 800 μm from A 12 to A 21 of Horsley-Clarke coordinates.

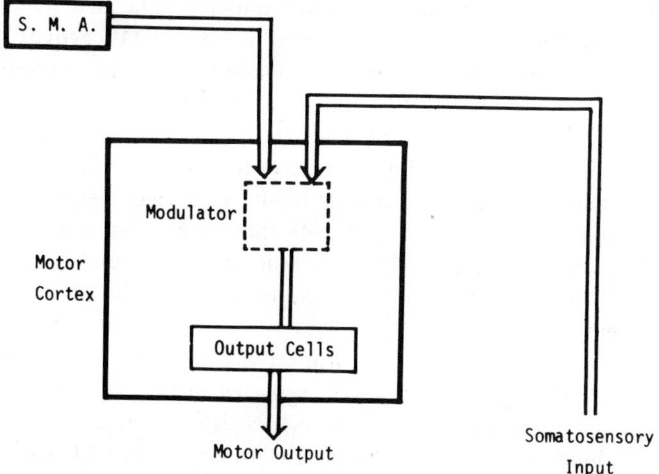

Figure 7-10. This figure shows diagrammatically the concept that the SMA functions as a modulating system that enables or shuts off the operation of transcortical reflex arcs by way of the motor cortex.

(shown in the figure). Some of the 26 neurons showed activities correlated with those of shoulder or girdle muscles. None had any response to the instruction signals.

Distribution of HRP-Labeled Neurons

The injection site of exogenous HRP was confined to the arm area of the motor cortex; diffusion of the HRP did not extend into the white matter (see Fig. 7-9). Labeled neurons were found in the SMA and in the lateral part of area 6 (posteromedial to the upper limb of the arcuate sulcus). In the SMA, labeled neurons were mostly located in the layer III of the cortex (Fig. 7-8). Their distribution in one monkey is shown in Figure 7-9. Basically the same results were obtained from the other animal. Thus, it is apparent that responses from D neurons were obtained from the area where projection neurons to the arm area of the motor cortex are massively grouped.

DISCUSSION

In the experiments discussed in this chapter, each animal was highly trained to perform a motor task that required readiness to make use of the kinesthetic stimulus to start rapid movements. Thus, the instruction light required the monkey to be prepared for a forthcoming movement in response to a perturbation of the handle. This preparatory "motor set" gave rise to activity changes of some neurons in the SMA as early as 140 msec after the onset of the instruction. During this preparatory period, the monkey kept holding the handle in a narrow zone. He was specially trained not to make any movement of the handle or postural adjustments until the occurrence of the perturbation. As a result, EMG recordings from forelimb and trunk muscles revealed no activity changes in this period. On the other hand, in association with the repositioning of the handle by the monkey after the performance of pushing or pulling, there was obvious EMG activity in the proximal forelimb and trunk muscles. The activity of 94 neurons described in this chapter was not at all associated with this EMG activity, in spite of the fact that a separate population of 26 neurons exhibited an evident relationship to the postural adjustments involving forelimb and trunk muscles. Therefore, it is unlikely that the response of 94 neurons to the instruction light is related to the postural adjustments. Rather, their response seems to reflect the development in the brain of a preparatory state to respond adequately to the stimulus input. This view was strengthened by the observation (indicated in Figs. 7-3 and 7-4) that there was a parallelism between neuronal activity changes and the development of early muscle response during a sequence in which the animal learned to make better use of the stimulus to initiate the intended movement.

The neural pathway with which the neural activity in the SMA could influence motor activities includes such efferent connections, reported in the literature, as to the motor cortex (2,8), the pontine nuclei (2), the red nucleus (10), the striatum (9), and the spinal cord (1,11). All these efferent connections could provide a neural basis for the development of the prepared responsiveness. However, the following facts suggest that the connection to the motor cortex plays a significant role: (*a*) electrical stimulation of the SMA modulates sensory responses of the motor cortex (17); and (*b*) responses from a large number of D neurons were recorded while the electrode seemed to be in the layer III of the cortex, which gives rise to corticocortical connection to the motor cortex (8).

In conclusion, the neuronal response in the SMA described in this chapter substantiates the hypothesis that the SMA actually plays a part in modifying the input-output relationship in the motor cortex, in a behavioral context in which the use of sensory input is essential for proficient performance of a motor task. The concept is shown diagrammatically in Figure 7-10. Thus, the transcortical reflex loop by way of the motor cortex, proposed by Phillips (15), seems to be equipped with a powerful gain control system, which allows the operation of the loop only when it is needed.

Numerous reports have described that the ablation of the SMA in humans (3,12) or in animals (14,16) give rise to forced grasping. On the basis of the present findings this phenomenon may be interpreted as an outcome, at least in part, of removing the neural mechanism that provides the preparatory setting for the responsiveness of the motor cortex to sensory inputs for its purposeful operations.

REFERENCES

1. Coulter JD, Jones EG: Differential distribution of corticospinal projections from individual cytoarchi tectonic fields in the monkey. *Brain Res* 129:335–340, 1977.
2. DeVito JL, Smith OA: Projections from the mesial frontal cortex (supplementary motor area) to the cerebral hemispheres and brain stem of the *Macaca mulatta. J Comp Neurol* 111:261–278, 1959.
3. Erickson TC, Woolsey CN: Observations of the supplementary motor area of man. *Trans Amer Neurol Ass* 76:50–52, 1951.
4. Evarts EV: A technique for recording activity of subcortical neurons in moving animals. *Electroenceph Clin Neurophysiol* 24:83–86, 1968.
5. Evarts EV, Tanji J: Gating of motor cortex reflexes by prior instruction. *Brain Res* 71:479–494, 1974.
6. Evarts EV, Tanji J: Reflex and intended responses in motor cortex pyramidal tract neurons of monkey. *J Neurophysiol* 39:1069–1080, 1976.

7. Hammond PH: The influence of prior instruction to the subject on an apparently involuntary neuro-muscular response. *J Physiol (London)* 132:17P–18P, 1956.

8. Jones EG, Coulter JD, Hendry HC: Intracortical connectivity of architectonic fields in the somatic sensory, motor and parietal cortex of monkeys. *J Comp Neurol* 181:291–348, 1978.

9. Kemp JM, Powell TPS: The cortico-striate projection in the monkey. *Brain* 93:525–546, 1970.

10. Kuypers HGJM, Lawrence DG: Cortical projections to the red nucleus and the brain stem in the rhesus monkey. *Brain Res* 4:151–188, 1967.

11. Nyberg-Hansen R: Corticospinal fibres from the medial aspect of the cerebral hemisphere in the cat. An Experimental study with the Nauta method. *Exp Brain Res* 7:120–132, 1969.

12. Penfield W, Jasper H: *Epilepsy and the Functional Anatomy of the Human Brain.* Boston, Little, Brown, 1954, pp 88–106.

13. Penfield W, Welch K: The supplementary motor area in the cerebral cortex of man. *Trans Amer Neurol Assn* 179–184, 1949.

14. Penfield W, Welch K: The supplementary motor area of the cerebral cortex. A clinical and experimental study. *Arch Neurol Psychiat* 66:289–317, 1951.

15. Phillips CG: Motor apparatus of the baboon's hand. *Proc Roy Soc (London B)* 173:141–174, 1969.

16. Travis AM: Neurological deficiencies following supplementary motor area lesions in *Maca mulatta. Brain* 78:155–173, 1955.

17. Wiesendanger M, Rüegg DG, Lucier GE: Why transcortical reflexes? *Can J Neurol Sci* 2:295–301, 1975.

8

Functional Relations Between Primate Motor Cortex Cells and Forelimb Muscles: Coactivation and Cross-Correlation Patterns

Eberhard E. Fetz

INTRODUCTION

A more complete understanding of the neural basis of learning and memory will depend in part on further knowledge about the neural mechanisms underlying voluntary movements. Before we can begin to analyze the neural events that mediate the effects of reinforcers and stimuli on operant behavior, we need to know more about the way the nervous system generates and controls simple motor responses.

In higher mammals, the cerebral cortex clearly plays a major role in the control and performance of appropriate movements. Clues about the behavioral functions subserved by different regions of cortex may be obtained by their ablation or stimulation (5). Specific hypotheses about the relationship between cortical cells and behavior may be further elucidated by recording activity of single units in animals trained to make relevant responses, as illustrated by the contributions of others in this symposium. This chapter will review recent studies of the functional relationships between precentral motor cortex cells and forelimb muscles; their coactivation was investigated by operantly conditioning response patterns in these elements, and their interaction was tested by cross-correlation techniques.

That many motor cortex cells discharge during voluntary limb movement has now been well established, but the specific parameters of movements, which are coded in precentral cell activity, remain to be elucidated satisfactorily. Experiments have shown

This research was supported by NIH grants RR00166, NB5082, NS12542, and NS11027.

that precentral cell activity may be related to active force (3,4,6,7,13,15,16,18), direction of movement (7,9,13–15,18), contraction of muscles (7,9,12,13,18), and preparation for responding (17,18), not to mention their sensory responses to passive limb movements and cutaneous stimulation (9,12,14). In a recent study, comparing the relations between motor cortex cells and three different behavioral variables, Thach (18) concluded that "all the types of neurons that were looked for were found, in nearly equal numbers." One may hope that this baffling variety of relationships is due, in part, to complexities in the arrangement of forelimb muscles, and that some clarification might come from further analysis of the functional relations between these cells and their relevant muscles. Documenting the response patterns of motor cortex cells during complex movement sequences is somewhat analogous to observing the responses of sensory cortex cells to complex stimulus patterns. Just as the functional organization of sensory systems has been elucidated by systematically comparing the response properties and receptive fields of cells at successive levels and relating these to peripheral receptors, so also might the functional organization of cells in motor systems be clarified by analyzing their relation to specific muscles.

OPERANTLY CONDITIONED RESPONSE PATTERNS OF MUSCLES AND PRECENTRAL CELLS

To investigate the coactivation of single motor cortex cells with isolated contraction of different forelimb muscles, we have recorded their activity in monkeys trained to contract different sets of forelimb muscles isometrically (12). The four muscles chosen were a flexor and an extensor of the wrist and of the elbow. Their activity was recorded over several months with implanted pairs of EMG electrodes. The activity of the same cortical units and limb muscles was also documented during active elbow movements, as illustrated for one precentral cell in Figure 8-1. This motor cortex cell fired before active elbow flexion and preceded the activity of the agonist muscle, the biceps. The fact that both wrist muscles were also coactivated with elbow flexion illustrates a basic problem in relating cell and muscle activity during a single movement sequence. Most movements involve coactivation of many muscles, making it impossible to known which ones, if any, the unit may be affecting.

To resolve further which of these forearm muscles the unit was consistently related to, the monkey was operantly reinforced for contracting each of the four muscles in relative isolation. With the arm held fixed, this cell fired with isometric contractions of both the biceps and flexor carpi radialis, that is, the flexors of the elbow and wrist (Fig. 8-2); the unit was inactive during contraction of the wrist and elbow extensor muscles. This result illustrates a property of other precentral cells recorded in this region under these conditions: most cells fired with isometric activation of more than one of the muscles. Some cells were activated with both the biceps and triceps, and others fired with all four muscles.

To explore the relationship between this unit and the forelimb muscles further, the monkey was also rewarded for activating the cell in "operant bursts" and was allowed to coactivate any of the muscles. Under these conditions, the monkey activated the biceps and both wrist muscles with operant bursts of the unit (Fig. 8-2*e*). Such a pattern was representative of results obtained with other cells whose activity was operantly rewarded: usually, the monkey coactivated several muscles with operant bursts. The set of coactivated muscles—the so-called "motor field"—could be quite different for

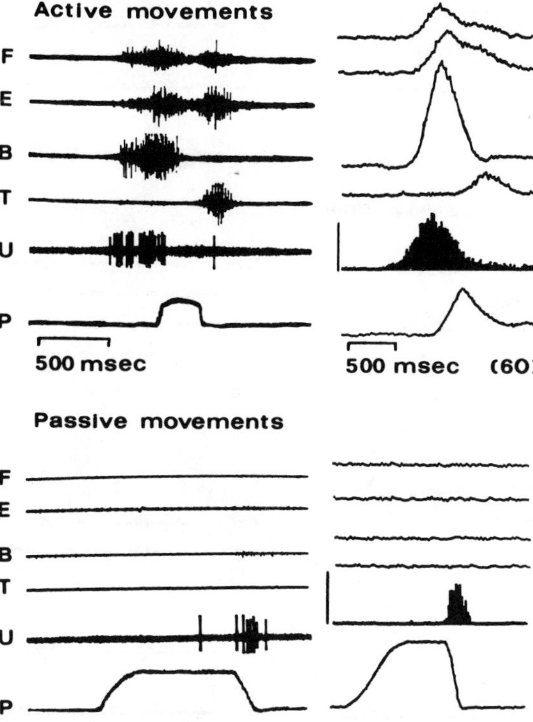

Figure 8-1. Responses of precentral unit and arm muscles during active and passive elbow movements. Muscles recorded with implanted EMG electrodes are, from top, flexor carpi radialis (F), extensor carpi radialis (E), biceps (B), and triceps (T). Precentral unit activity (U) and elbow position (P) recorded with potentiometer at the pivot point of the forearm cast. Single trials are shown at left and response averages compiled over 60 responses at right. With the forearm held in a cast, this cell responded before active elbow flexion and responded to passive elbow extension. The adequate natural stimulus for the cell was passive elbow extension and passive wrist flexion. Vertical bars calibrate a firing rate of 50 impulses per second. (From Fetz and Finocchio, ref. 12.)

adjacent motor cortex cells in the same cortical region (8,12). Indeed, some precentral cells were activated in operant bursts without any observed muscle activity or movements (9,12).

In other experiments, monkeys were operantly rewarded for activating motor cortex cells under relatively unrestrained conditions to determine which limb movements might be associated with cell activity (9). For some cells, operant bursts were associated with specific joint movements; however, many other cells were associated with more generalized and variable movements, with no obvious relation between the cell and any particular component of the movements. Thus, although operant reinforcement of cell activity may be a convenient technique for eliciting the movements associated with dif-

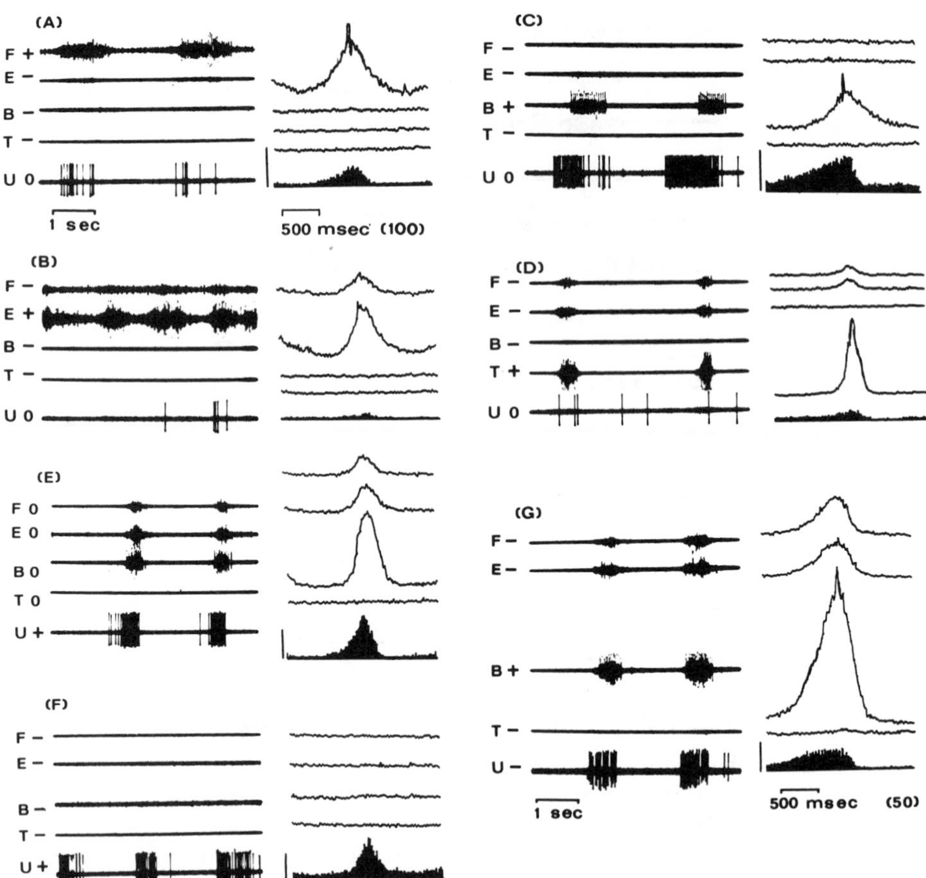

Figure 8-2. Operantly conditioned response patterns of the unit in Figure 8-1 and forearm muscles under isometric conditions. Responses at left show successive reinforced patterns, and response averages at right show reinforced responses. The elbow was held fixed at an angle of 90° and the wrist at an angle of 180°. The muscles and unit are labeled as in Figure 8-1. A + indicates elements whose activation was rewarded; a − indicates elements whose simultaneous suppression was required; 0 indicates elements whose activity was not included in the reinforcement contingency. (*a*), (*b*), (*c*), (*d*) Differential reinforcement of isolated bursts of EMG activity in each arm muscle, with no contingency on cortical unit. (*e*) Operant unit bursts were reinforced with no contingency on the muscles. (*f*) Reinforcement of operant unit bursts and simultaneous muscle suppression. (*g*) Responses when isolated biceps activity and unit suppression were reinforced. Vertical bar calibrates firing rate of 50/sec. Response averages include 100 events for (*a*) through (*d*) and 5 responses (*e*) through (*g*). (From Fetz and Finocchio, ref. 12.)

ferent cells, such movements sometimes turned out to involve complex and variable sequences. However, when the same unit was continuously reinforced over many minutes, certain components of these movements often dropped out, until relatively specific movements were repeatedly emitted with each burst.

Observing the same unit-muscle pairs during different responses revealed a considerable variability in patterns of unit-muscle coactivation, which was strongly dependent on the behavioral conditions. Some cells were consistently coactivated with a given muscle under isometric conditions, but did not fire with that muscle, or were in fact suppressed when the muscle was activated during limb movements. Activity of the cell shown in Figure 8-2 provides an example. This cell was activated with the extensor carpi radialis (ECR) during elbow movements and during operant unit bursts but did not fire during isometric contractions of the ECR muscle. This indicates that unit-muscle correlations may depend considerably on the behavioral circumstances, and they should be tested under a variety of conditions to determine those which are the most consistent.

As discussed elsewhere, we might consider the "strongest" unit-muscle correlations to be those that involve the most intense coactivation of cell and muscle activity and those that appear most consistently under different behavioral conditions (8,12). However, even the strongest unit-muscle correlations could be changed by operantly reinforcing their dissociation. Thus, for the cell used in Figure 8-2, the unit-biceps correlation, which appeared during isometric biceps activity, unit reinforcement, and active elbow flexion, could be dissociated when the monkey was reinforced for activating the cell and suppressing all muscle activity (Fig. 8-2*f*). Similar dissociation was achieved for all precentral cells tested in this study and appeared to be as easy to condition as the isolated muscle activity. Thus, operant reinforcement of the dissociation revealed a degree of plasticity in these correlations which was not apparent when either the units, or the muscles, or the movements were the reinforced responses. In retrospect, this result might not be considered surprising since the effect of a single precentral cell—even one that has direct corticomotoneuronal connections—is subthreshold for firing the motoneuron and could, in principle, be easily overridden by the combined effects of other descending pathways. Nevertheless, the fact that these cells and motor units can be so independently activated does reveal an unexpected degree of flexibility in their relationships. When the reverse dissociation—biceps activation and unit suppression—was attempted (Fig. 8-2*g*), the monkey produced more intense biceps bursts but did not consistently suppress unit activity. Failure to shape this reverse dissociation may well have been due to behavioral causes such as fatigue or satiation.

In addition to relatively simple patterns of coactivation of units with muscles, some precentral cells exhibited more complex firing patterns. As an example, Figure 8-3 shows the response pattern of a non-PT neuron which exhibited a biphasic sequence of suppression as muscle activity increased, followed by activation as muscle activity was decreasing. This temporal pattern is most clearly evident in relation to the ECR muscle (Fig. 8-3*b*), but a similar sequence was apparent with each of the other muscles as well. The fact that this cell showed a similar response pattern with all four muscles may be interpreted in several ways. This cell's activity might be thought to be related to a common component of each response, such as orienting to the feeder. However, this did not appear to be the case, since free food delivery did not evoke activation of the cell, and since the suppression of cell activity began well before onset of muscle activity. Moreover, other cells in the same cortical region showed similar "off" response patterns with certain muscles, but not with other muscles. A second alternative is that this cell was simply coactivated with some other unrecorded muscle in another part of the body which underwent a similar response sequence. Such a hypothesis could conceivably be tested by recording activity of every muscle, but this becomes practically impossible. Besides being experimentally untestable, the notion that the response pattern of every motor cortex cell must mirror the response of some muscle is ultimately theoretically sterile. A single class of cells provides no basis for explaining how response patterns may be initiated and controlled. A third and perhaps more interesting alternative is that

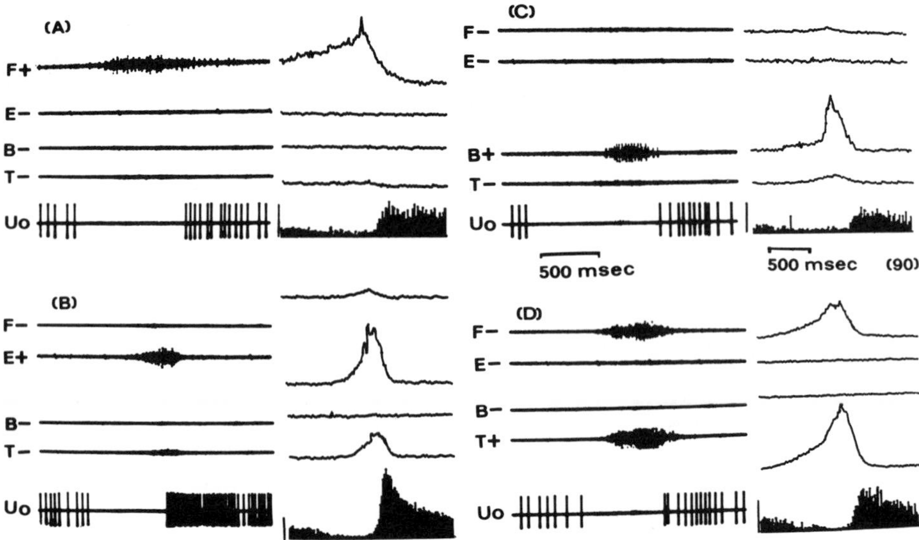

Figure 8-3. Response patterns of precentral non-PT neuron with isometric contractions of different forearm muscles. Single trials are illustrated at left, and response averages over 90 successive reinforced responses are shown at right. This unit exhibited a similar pattern of suppression and excitation with each of the muscles. (From Fetz and Finocchio, ref. 12.)

some cortical cells may have higher-order relationships to muscle activation—both temporally, in being related to changes in muscle activity, and spatially, in being related to more than one muscle. The biphasic pattern of this cell, then, might indicate that it could be related to turning muscle activity off; the fact that the pattern was similar for all four muscles suggests that it may be more related to the occurrence of a response than its topography. Such speculations are clearly tentative until convincingly confirmed. The point is that the last two alternatives cannot be resolved without some independent means, other than covariation, to establish causal relationships between cell and muscle activity.

CROSS-CORRELATION PATTERNS

To determine whether causal connections between precentral cells and forelimb muscles might be detected by cross-correlation techniques, we have used spike-triggered averages (STAs) of rectified EMG activity as a convenient approximation to true cross-correlations. Such STAs have revealed that action potentials of certain precentral neurons are followed by a transient postspike facilitation (PSF) of average motor unit activity in certain forelimb muscles. The latency and the time course of most PSF are consistent with their mediation by direct corticomotoneuronal (CM) connections, so we have referred to these precentral cells as CM cells.

In these experiments, monkeys were trained to alternately flex and extend the wrist against elastic loads. To provide periods of tonic coactivation of cells and agonist forelimb muscles, the ramp-and-hold movements involved a static hold period of at least 1 second (Fig. 8-4). Wrist and finger muscles were identified by their relative locations and their response to intramuscular stimulation through the implanted pairs of recording electrodes. Action potentials of precentral cells that discharged tonically during either flexion or extension were used to compile STAs of full-wave rectified EMG activity of covarying agonists. For example, the cell shown in Figure 8-4 fired consistently during extension of the wrist and was recorded with six extensor muscles. STAs of two of the six covarying muscles (EDC and ED4,5) showed clear postspike facilitation. Two additional muscles (ECR-L and ED2,3) also showed evidence of a weaker augmentation of EMG activity after the spike. Averages of the remaining two muscles showed no significant spike-related effects in the number of events averaged.

The flexion-related cell shown in Figure 8-5 illustrates some further features of these cells. STAs show that action potentials of this cell were followed by postspike facilitation in all three implanted flexor muscles, as well as the flexor EMG recorded by surface electrodes. The remarkable response pattern of this cell is shown in the response averages (upper right). This unit exhibited an intense peak of activity at movement onset followed by a pause and a gradually increasing ramp of activity during the static hold period. Such a "phasic-ramp" pattern was characteristic of 8% of the CM cells (3). It illustrates the fact that the firing pattern of some CM cells may differ appreciably from the average activity of the muscles that they facilitate. Clearly, this cell had a particularly potent effect at movement onset when its firing was highest. This cell also illustrates the fact that the postspike facilitation was independent of triggering at onset

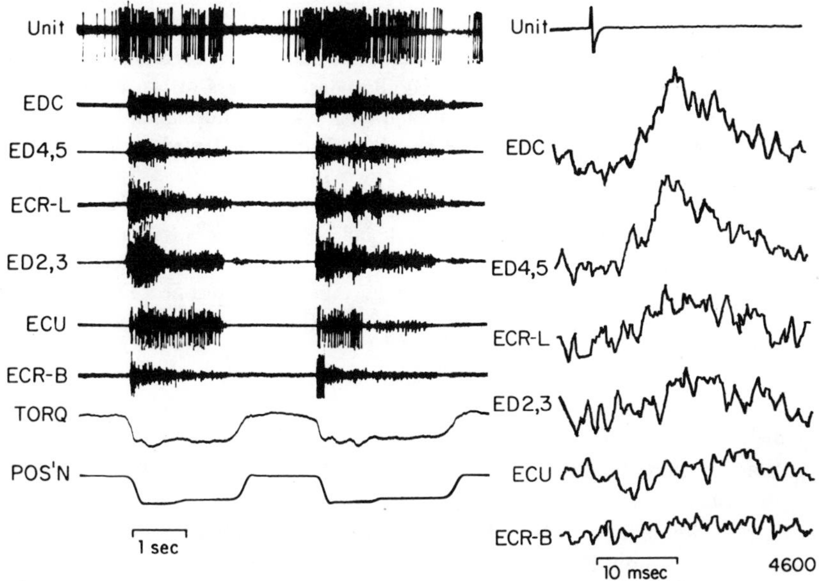

Figure 8-4. Responses of precentral CM cell that covaried with wrist extension and facilitated activity of extensor muscles. Responses at left show activity of unit and six coactivated extensor muscles, torque, and position. Muscles whose activity was recorded with implanted electrodes included extensors of the digits (EDC: ED4,5; Ed2,3) and extensors of the wrist (ECR-L; ECR-B; ECU). Spike-triggered averages at right indicate averages of full-wave rectified EMG activity from 4600 action potentials. Bin width was 250 μsec, and the analysis period included 5 msec before and 25 msec after triggering action potential. (From Fetz and Cheney, ref. 10.)

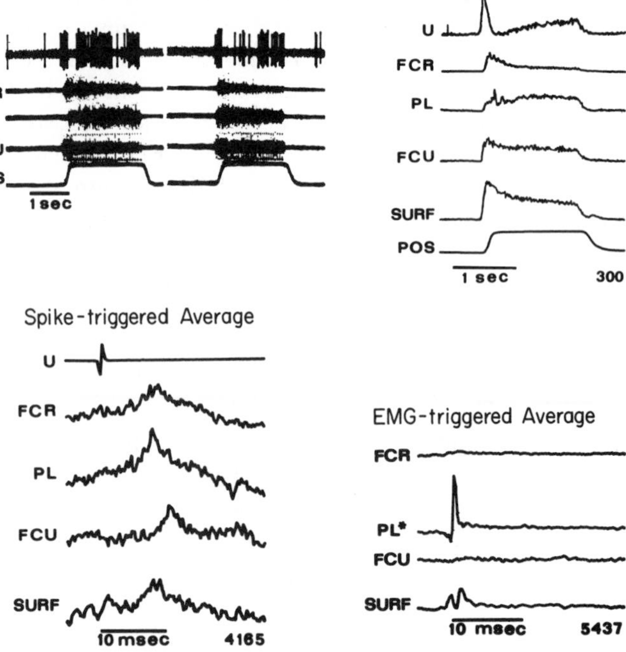

Figure 8-5. Precentral CM cell related to wrist flexion. Top left illustrates examples of two flexion responses showing EMG of flexor carpi radialis (FCR), palmaris longus (PL), and flexor carpi ulnaris (FCU) and wrist position (POS). Response averages at top right illustrate average pattern of unit and muscle activity during 300 successive flexion responses. The muscle activity of implanted muscles and surface-recorded EMG activity was full-wave rectified. Spike-triggered average at lower left was compiled for 4165 action potentials occurring during the tonic hold period, that is, excluding spikes during the phasic peak of unit activity. The EMG-triggered average at lower right shown an average of the rectified EMG activity triggered from motor units in PL. (From Fetz and Cheney, ref. 10.)

of movement, when muscle activity is increasing. The STAs (lower left) were compiled only from action potentials occurring during the tonic hold period, when muscle activity was relatively constant.

To confirm the independence of the EMG records, muscle activity was routinely cross-correlated by compiling EMG-triggered averages. As shown in Figure 8-5 (lower right), an average triggered from motor units in the PL muscle showed no evidence of common pickup of the same units in either of the adjacent muscles, FCR or FCU; the peak in the surface record indicates that the surface electrodes over PL did record some units in common. Similar averages triggered from each of the other muscles confirmed that the implanted electrodes had indeed recorded independent motor units. Such controls were routinely done when multiple PSFs were observed. In a few cases, EMG-triggered averages revealed evidence of common pickup; in those cases, one of the potentially redundant EMG records was eliminated from the data base.

When STAs were compiled simultaneously from several agonist muscles, the cells that produced PSF generally facilitated more than one muscle. Of 370 precentral neurons, which covaried strongly with either flexion or extension, and which were used to compile STAs of five or six nonredundant covarying forelimb muscles, less than half (43%) produced any evidence of PSF. Of those that produced PSF, 70% facilitated more than one muscle. This suggests that the set of facilitated muscles, that is, the cell's "muscle field," typically includes more than one synergist forelimb muscle. Whether the PSF is mediated by monosynaptic corticomotoneuronal connections remains to be proved. If it is, the muscle field would represent the set of target muscles whose motoneurons are contacted by terminals of the CM cell (1). In any case, the muscle field is a measure of the extent of facilitation of different muscles correlated with action potentials of single motor cortex cells.

CONCLUSION

In summary, the functional relations between motor cortex cells and muscles have been elucidated in different ways by their coactivation and their cross-correlation patterns. When specific patterns of cell and muscle activity were operantly reinforced, single motor cortex cells were found to be coactivated with several different muscles; moreover, the coactivation of a given unit-muscle pair could be quite flexible, depending on the behavioral conditions. Even "strong" unit-muscle correlations, which appeared consistently during a variety of different response patterns, could be dissociated by differential reinforcement of unit activity and muscle suppression (12).

In contrast to the widespread and variable coactivation patterns, the cross-correlation patterns, that is, the short latency postspike facilitation of EMG activity revealed by STAs, provides more secure evidence for a causal relation between cell and muscle activity. Whether or not they are mediated by monosynaptic connections, PSF provides a direct measure of the output effects on muscle activity correlated with action potentials of the precentral cell. The set of facilitated muscles, or "muscle field," usually included more than one of the covarying forelimb muscles. However, even CM cells were coactivated with more muscles than they facilitated, and many other precentral cells were coactivated with muscles that they did not facilitate. Interestingly, the firing patterns of CM cells were sometimes distinctly different from the activity of their facilitated target muscles.

Clearly, the most challenging work lies just ahead, namely, to combine the operant conditioning and STA techniques and to investigate further the interdependence, if any, of the covariation and cross-correlation patterns. For example, to test the mediation of the PSF it would be important to determine whether it is a function of different response patterns. To test the independence of CM cells and their target muscles, it would be interesting to see if their activity can be bidirectionally dissociated.

ACKNOWLEDGMENTS

These experimental results were due in large part to the skill and perseverance of my colleagues, Dr. Dom V. Finocchio and Dr. Paul D. Cheney. We gratefully acknowledge the technical assistance of Mr. Jerrold D. Maddocks and the Bioengineering Division of the Primate Center.

REFERENCES

1. Asanuma H, Zarzecki P, Jankowska E, et al: Projections of individual pyramidal tract neurons to lumbar motor nuclei of the monkey. *Exp Brain Res* 34:73–89, 1979.
2. Cheney PD, Fetz EE: Comparison of spike-triggered averages and stimulus-triggered averages of forearm muscle activity from identical motor cortex sites in behaving monkeys. *Society for Neuroscience Abstracts* 3:269, 1977.
3. Cheney PD, Fetz EE: Functional properties of primate corticomotoneuronal cells. *Society for Neuroscience Abstracts* 4:293, 1978.
4. Conrad B, Wiesendanger M, Matsunami K, et al: Precentral unit activity related to control of arm movements. *Exp Brain Res* 29:85–95, 1977.
5. Denny-Brown D: *The Cerebral Control of Movement.* Liverpool, Liverpool University Press, 1966.
6. Evarts EV: Relation of pyramidal tract activity to force exerted during voluntary movement. *J Neurophysiol* 31:14–27, 1968.
7. Evarts EV, Activity of pyramidal tract neurons during postural fixation. *J Neurophysiol* 32:375–385, 1969.
8. Fetz EE: Operant control of single unit activity and correlated motor responses, in Chase M (ed): *Operant Control of Brain Activity.* Los Angeles, UCLA Press 1974, pp 61–90.
9. Fetz EE, Baker MA: Operantly conditioned patterns of precentral unit activity and correlated responses in adjacent cells and contralateral muscles. *J Neurophysiol* 36:179–204, 1973.
10. Fetz EE, Cheney PD: Muscle fields of primate corticomotoneuronal cells. *J Physiol (Paris)* 151:239–245, 1978.
11. Fetz EE, Cheney PD, German DC: Corticomotoneuronal connections of precentral cells detected by post-spike averages of EMG activity in behaving monkeys. *Brain Res* 114:505–510, 1976.
12. Fetz EE, Finocchio DV: Correlations between activity of motor cortex cells and arm muscles during operantly conditioned response patterns. *Exp Brain Res* 23:217–240, 1975.
13. Humphrey DR, Schmidt EM, Thompson WD: Predicting measures of motor performance from multiple cortical spike trains. *Science* 170:758–762, 1970.
14. Lemon RN, Hanby JA, Porter R: Relationship between the activity of precentral neurones during active and passive movements in conscious monkeys. *Proc Roy Soc* B194:341–373, 1976.
15. Schmidt EM, Jost RG, Davis KK: Reexamination of the force relationship of cortical cell discharge patterns with conditioned wrist movements. *Brain Res* 83:213–223, 1975.
16. Smith AM, Hepp-Reymond MC, Wyss UR: Relation of activity in precentral cortical neurons to force and rate of force change during isometric contractions of finger muscles. *Exp Brain Res* 23:315–332, 1975.
17. Tanji J, Evarts EV: Anticipatory activity of motor cortex neurons in relation to direction of an intended movement. *J Neurophysiol* 39:1062–1068, 1976.
18. Thach WT: Correlation of neural discharge with pattern and force of muscular activity, joint position and direction of intended next movement in motor cortex and cerebellum. *J Neurophysiol* 41:654–676, 1978.

9
Prefrontal Unit Activity and Delayed Conditional Discrimination

Masataka Watanabe

INTRODUCTION

Since Jacobsen (9) reported large cognitive-learning deficits after ablation of the monkey's prefrontal cortex, many studies have been carried out to investigate the function of this area. In monkeys, dorsolateral prefrontal lesions severely impair spatial delayed alternation (DA) (12) and spatial delayed response (DR) (1). On the other hand, monkeys whose orbitofrontal cortex, including the inferior frontal convexity, was removed were shown to have severe deficits on go/no-go tasks (8), on delayed matching tasks (18), and on reversal tasks (2). On the basis of these results, it has been suggested that dorsolateral and orbital sectors of the prefrontal cortex subserve different functions, with the dorsolateral more involved in spatial memory and the orbital more involved in the inhibition or control of dominant response tendencies (3).

Recently dorsolateral prefrontal units were observed to show changes in discharge rate in relation to the performance of the DA or DR tasks (5,11). Quite recently Niki (14,16) found units in the principalis area that exhibited differential activity during the delay period for right and left trials in DA and DR. (These units were called differential delay units.) Furthermore, he demonstrated that the activity of these differential delay units was related to the relative position of the two choice keys rather than to their absolute position in space (15).

An example of activity of a differential delay unit is shown in Figure 9-1. The monkey was trained in delayed alternation using a panel containing four choice keys, which were arranged horizontally as shown. Only two keys were used at any one time. For example, when the 2-3 pair was used, the monkey had to make alternation responses to the choice keys of 2 and 3, and this particular unit had a higher discharge rate before the choice of 3. When the activity in the 2-3 pair was compared with that in the 3-4 pair (in the 2-3 pair, 3 was in the relative right, and in the 3-4 pair, 3 was in the relative left), greater activity was observed before the choice of the relative right choice key in both cases. Thus, the activity of this unit before the choice of 3 showed

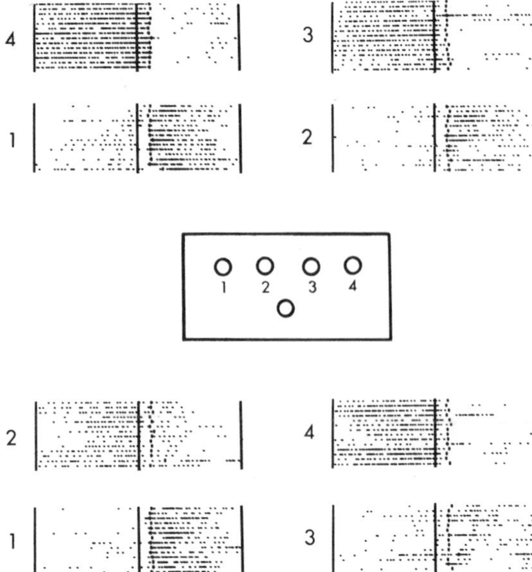

Figure 9-1. Prefrontal unit responses showing directional selectivity during delay periods before pressing the choice keys illustrated in central panel. Each dot indicates one spike discharge. Each raster shows 2 seconds of activity before and after the stimulus. The center line indicates the time of the onset of illumination of choice keys, and the heavy dot indicates the occurrence of response. Position number of the choice key in a panel corresponds to the number shown on the left side of each raster. The upper raster of the pairs is for relative right and the lower, for relative left. (From Niki, ref. 15.)

specificity depending on the relative location of this key in space. The significance of the relative position is also evident if one compares the activity associated with pressing of key 2 in the 1-2 pair and in the 2-3 pair. These results indicate that dorsolateral units might be related to information processing that is dependent on the context and that has no direct relationship with physical features of the stimulus nor with specific muscular movements.

Two studies described in this chapter are extensions of previous studies (14,15,16) in which characteristics of the differential delay units were analyzed. The studies presented here were done to investigate further the kind of information processing performed by the prefrontal cortex. The first study was designed to determine whether the differential activity during the delay period in the DR reflects the difference of cue location or the direction of the impending response. It was not possible to differentiate the two in the previous studies on DR, since the animal had to respond to the same window in which the cue was presented. The second study was conducted to elucidate the neuronal correlates of the delayed conditional discrimination task in which the animal must make his choice depending on the "context" (i.e., difference of the instruction). The main aim of this study was to discover which units, if any, might show activity changes in relation to the significance of the stimulus or to the intention of the animal.

INFORMATION PROCESSING IN THE PREFRONTAL CORTEX DEPENDING ON SPATIAL CONTEXT

The results of the first study have been published elsewhere (17). Two monkeys were trained in the performance of three kinds of spatial tasks (right-left DR, up-down DR, and conditional position task with delay). Diagrams of the sequence of events of these three tasks are illustrated in Figure 9-2. The monkey faced a panel containing a central hold lever and four choice keys (right, left, up, and down). In the right-left DR (R-L DR) task, the cue was presented on the right or left choice key for 1 second, and after a delay period of 3 seconds, a go signal was presented on the right and left choice keys simultaneously. The animal was required to depress a hold lever during the intertrial interval (ITI), cue, and delay periods. The animal received a drop of fruit juice as a reward when it depressed the choice key at which the cue had been presented after the end of the delay period. In the up-down DR (U-D DR) task, the cue was presented on the upper or lower choice key, and the correct response was depressing the choice key at which the cue had been presented. In the conditional position (CP) task with delay, the

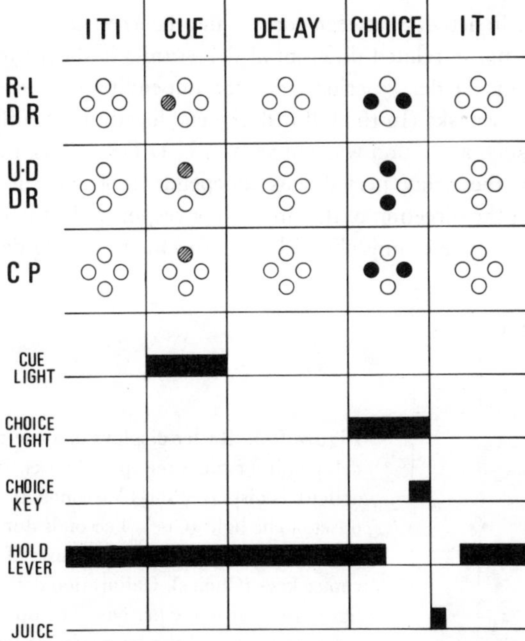

Figure 9-2. Diagrams of the sequence of events in the spatial delayed choice tasks. R-L DR: right-left delayed response, U-D DR: up-down delayed response, CP: conditional position discrimination with delay, ITI: intertrial interval. (From Niki and Watanabe, ref. 17.)

cue was presented on the upper or lower choice key, and the go signal was presented on the right and left choice keys. The monkey was required to depress the right (left) choice key when the cue had been presented on the upper (lower) choice key.

Units were sought in the dorsolateral prefrontal area (A26–34, L14–18). When a unit was found that showed differential activity during the delay period for right and left (or up and down) trials in the R-L DR or U-D DR, the same unit was tested in the other tasks. Among many task-related units, two kinds of differential delay units were found: one was related to the cue location, and the other was related to the direction of the impending response. The former will be called "cue-related differential delay unit" and the latter, "response-related differential delay unit."

Figure 9-3 shows an example of the cue-related differential delay units. This unit showed greater firing during the delay period on down trials than on up trials during U-D DR. In the CP task, greater firing was observed when the cue was presented on the lower choice key. There was no difference in discharge rate during the delay period in R-L DR for right and left trials. It should be noted that cue position was the same for U-D DR and CP tasks (up-down) although the direction of response was different (up-down vs. right-left). On the other hand direction of response was the same in the CP and R-L DR tasks although the cue was presented in a different position. Thus, in this particular unit an activation during delay was seen only when the cue was presented in the lower position. Differential activation of these units during the delay period for the specific cue location disappeared when either no cue light or two cue lights were presented during the cue period as a control. This type of differential delay unit showed little or no difference in activity between correct and incorrect trials.

An example of response-related differential delay units is shown in Figure 9-4. Activation was seen during the delay period when the impending response was "right" both in the R-L DR and CP tasks (In the CP task the cue location was different from that in R-L DR), whereas such activation was not seen in U-D DR. Thus, the activation of this type of unit during the delay period was independent of the cue location and was dependent instead on the direction of the impending response. In the no-cue and two-cue control conditions, this type of unit showed some specificity during delay with respect to

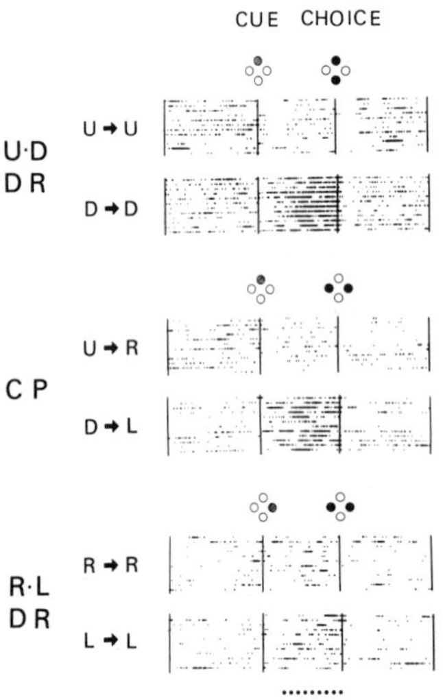

Figure 9-3. Raster displays of a cue-related differential delay unit for the three spatial tasks. In each raster the activity is displayed for 13 seconds, that is, 4.5 sec before onset of cue light (Cue), 4 seconds during cue and delay periods, and 4.5 seconds after onset of illumination of choice keys (Choice). Calibration dots at bottom of the figure indicate delay periods. The upper raster of U-D DR is for up trials and the lower, for down trials. In CP the upper raster is for up trials on which cue is presented in the upper choice key and the animal is required to respond to the right choice key and the lower, for down trials. In R-L DR the upper raster is for right trials and the lower for left trials. For explanation of abbreviations, see key to Figure 9-2. (From Niki and Watanabe, ref. 17.

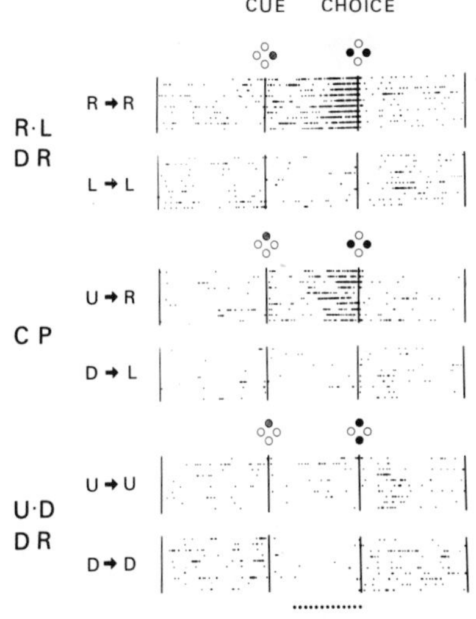

Figure 9-4. Raster displays of the response-related differential delay unit for three kinds of spatial tasks. In both R-L DR and CP, upper rasters are for activity to the right choice key and upper raster, for the left choice key. In U-D DR the upper raster is for the upper choice key response and the lower, for the lower choice key response. Conventions are the same as in Figure 9-3. (From Niki and Watanabe, ref. 17.)

the direction of the impending response. Thus, it was possible to predict the direction of the response, and, therefore, the occurrence of errors whenever they occurred, from the activity of this type of unit during the delay period. This type of unit often showed a gradual increase in firing rate before the time of the response. The anticipatory change in firing during the preparatory period of push-pull movement has been also observed in the supplementary motor area (SMS) (Chapter 8).

From the characteristics of the activity it can be deduced that cue-related differential delay units may be involved in the central processes, which hold the information on the position of the cue previously presented, and response-related differential delay units may be related to a preparatory set for responding to a certain position where the animal is required to respond after the delay period is over. Because of the existence of these units, especially the response-related differential delay units whose activity is independent of the cue location, the dorsolateral prefrontal cortex is thought to participate in the information processing, depending on the spatial context.

INFORMATION PROCESSING IN THE PREFRONTAL CORTEX DEPENDING ON NONSPATIAL CONTEXT

The second study was designed to investigate whether prefrontal unit activity depends on nonspatial context. Units were recorded in an area within A20–36, L9–21, covering the dorsolateral and orbital frontal areas. The orbitofrontal area was explored in this experiment because unit activity of this area has not been studied in relation to discrimination learning, and it has not been clear what kind of information processing occurs in this area.

Two monkeys were trained to perform a delayed conditional discrimination task using a test panel with a central hold lever and two choice keys. As illustrated in Figure 9-5, the monkey first had to depress the hold lever for 5 seconds to start the trial. After the 5-second intertrial interval, a red or green light was presented for 1 second on both choice keys simultaneously as a conditional cue (CC). the CC period was followed by

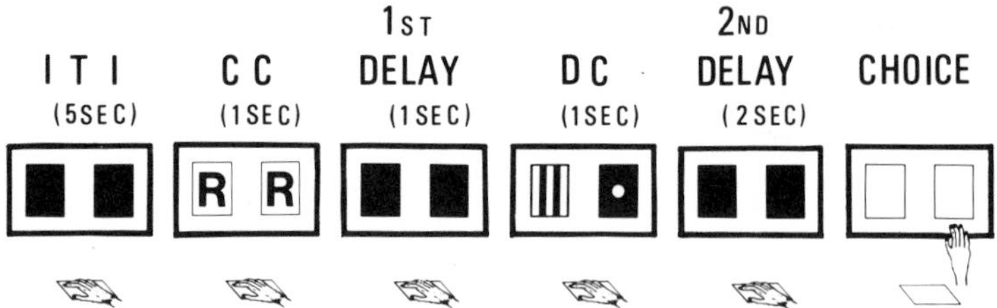

Figure 9-5. Schema of events of the delayed conditional discrimination. Each event occurs sequentially from left to right. ITI: intertrial interval, CC: conditional cue, DC: discriminative cue.

the first delay period (1 second), after which two pattern stimuli were presented for 1 second as a discriminative cue (DC). The two patterns were presented in a configuration of either circle-right and stripe-left or of circle-left and stripe-right. A preset semi-random sequence determined which CC and which pattern configuration as the DC were presented in each trial. The DC period was followed by a second delay period of 2 seconds. If the monkey continued to depress the hold lever during all these periods, a white light was presented on right and left choice keys simultaneously as a go signal. The circle (stripe) was the positive pattern when the red (green) light had been presented as the CC in this task. If the monkey depressed the correct key after the go signal was presented, he was rewarded with fruit juice.

Context-dependent information processing was required for the correct performance of this task, because the positive pattern was dependent on the CC. Two delay periods were introduced in this experiment to differentiate unitary changes related to the three events of the task, that is, CC, DC, and the choice response.

In this experiment a total of 424 prefrontal units showed changes in discharge rate in relation to the task performance. One hundred sixty-nine of them showed differential activity, depending on the difference of the CC and/or that of the DC. Differential units were classified into three main types (type A, n = 9; type B, n = 124; type C, n = 36) according to the epoch in which the differential activity was observed.

Examples of differential activity of each type of units are shown in Figure 9-6. Type A units showed the differential activity depending on the difference in the CC at the time of the CC presentation or during the first delay period. The unit in Figure 9-6(*A*) showed greater discharge when the CC was green than when it was red (3 and 4).

In the type B units the differential activity was observed during the DC and/or the second delay period. Type B units consisted of 4 subtypes: type B1 (n = 9), B2 (n = 1), B3 (n = 87), and B4 (n = 27). The activity of type B1 units was related to the difference in the configuration of the two pattern stimuli, that is, dependent on whether it was the circle-right and stripe-left (1 and 3) or the circle-left and stripe-right (2 and 4). The example in Figure 9-6(*B1*) showed greater activity in case 1 and case 3 at the time of the DC presentation.

Type B2 units showed differential activity, not during the CC nor during the first delay period, but during the DC period depending on the difference of the CC. The unit in Figure 9-6(*B2*) showed a greater firing when the CC had been green (3 and 4).

Type B3 units showed differential activity depending on the side on which the positive pattern appeared. The unit in Figure 9-6(*B3*) showed a higher rate of firing when a positive pattern appeared on the left side (2 and 3) than when it appeared on the right side (1 and 4) during the DC period. Type B3 units showed the similar activity to the different DC (1 and 4 or 2 and 3) or showed the different activity to the same DC (1 and 3 or 2 and 4) if the CC had been different. Gradual buildup of firing rate was often observed in those type B3 units that showed changes in discharge rate during the second delay period. Such a gradual buildup of firing rate is very similar to that found in the response-related differential delay units in the first study. Because the activity of type B3 units was dependent on the location of the positive pattern, it reflected the direction of the impending response. Thus, it was possible to predict the occurrence of errors, whenever they occurred, from the activity of this type of units, just as it was possible from the activity of the response-related differential delay units of the first study.

Activity of type B4 units was dependent on both the CC and DC. Units of this type showed unique activity during certain combinations of CC and DC. The unit in Figure

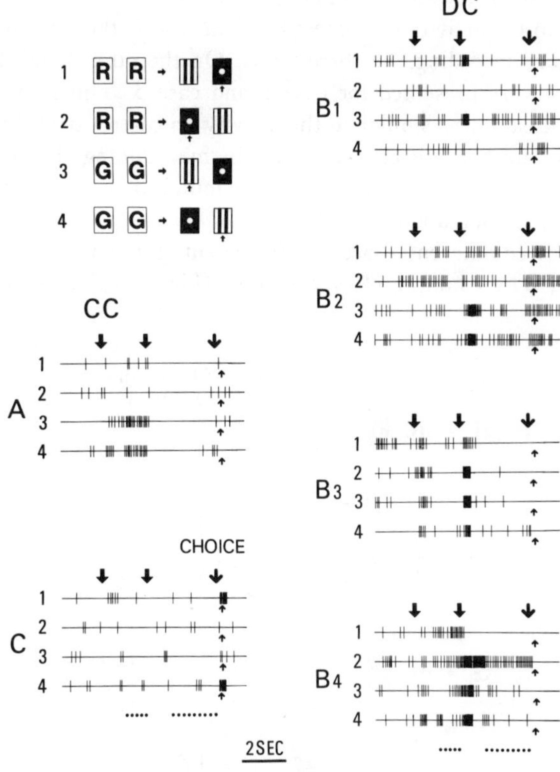

Figure 9-6. Activity of each type of differential units in the delayed conditional discrimination. Unit discharge is shown by shaped pulses. The upper left illustrates the four combinations of CC and DC. The activity of each type of unit is shown for each of these four cases. For the display of each unit, the left arrow indicates the time of the CC presentation; the center arrow, the time of the DC presentation; and the right arrow, the time of the go signal presentation. Small upward arrows indicate the time of the response. Dotted lines indicate delay periods.

9-6(*B4*) showed the greatest increased activity in case 2 during the DC and second delay periods. Firing was suppressed after the DC presentation in case 1. Increased firing rate was observed at the time of the DC presentation in case 3 and case 4.

Another example of a type B4 unit is shown in Figure 9-7. This unit showed specificity in firing for each case during both the DC and second delay periods. The greatest increase in firing (in case 4) and decreased firing (in case 1) were observed during these periods. Firing change was weak in case 2, and negligible firing change was observed in case 3. The specificity in the responses of type B4 units is noteworthy considering that the same DC was presented in case 1 and case 3 or in case 2 and case 4, and that the direction of the response was the same in case 1 and case 4 and in case 2 and case 3. It was possible to predict the occurrence of errors from the activity of type B4 units as it was possible from the activity of the type B3 units. Furthermore, the activity on erroneous trials appeared to indicate the type of error. The same CCs and the different DCs were presented for case 1 and case 2. Therefore, when the activity on erroneous trials in case 1 was similar to the activity on correct trials in case 2, the error may have occurred because of the failure in coding the correct DC. On the other hand, the different CCs and the same DCs were presented for case 1 and case 3. Thus, when the activity on erroneous trials in case 1 was similar to the activity on correct trials in case 3, the error was supposed to occur because of the failure in maintaining the correct information about the CC. More than 95% of the errors were found to be correlated with failures in maintaining the information about the CC.

Type C units showed differential activity dependent on the direction of the response at the time of choice. The example of type C unit (Fig. 9-6*C*) showed increased firing

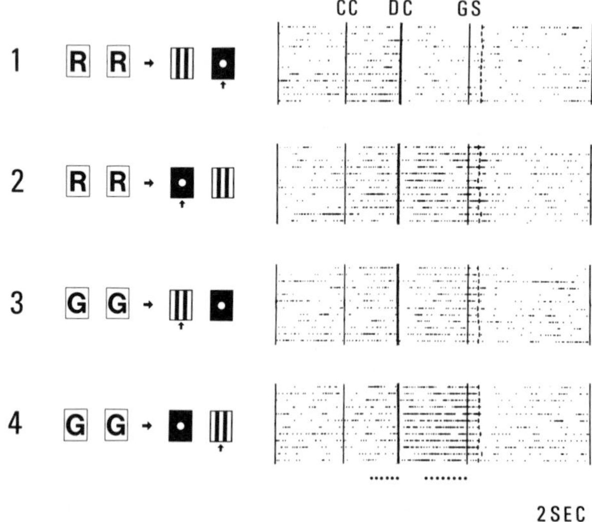

Figure 9-7. Raster displays of type B4 unit for the four cases. CC line indicates the time of CC presentation and DC line, the time of DC presentation. GS is the abbreviation for go signal. Heavy dots indicate the time of the response. Calibration dots on bottom indicate delay periods. Duration of the second delay period was 1.6 seconds in this particular case.

when the animal depressed the right choice key (1 and 4). Similar differential activity at the time of choice has been reported in other task situations (14–16).

These differential units were found in both the dorsolateral and orbital frontal cortices. Prefrontal localization of each type of units was difficult to determine due to a limited number of samples.

A control experiment was done to determine whether the activity of these differential units was related to the specific cues used in the experiment. After completion of training on the original task, the two monkeys received additional training of four different delayed conditional discrimination tasks in which different CCs and DCs were used. For example, "plus" and "square" patterns were used instead of "circle" and "stripe" patterns as a DC in one task. In another task the same two patterns (plus or square) were presented on both choice keys instead of red or green light as a CC. The results of these control experiments indicate that the activity of most of these differential units was independent of physical features of the cue but dependent on the meaning of the cue, although the activity of some units reflected both the meaning and certain aspects of features of the stimulus.

From the above results, possible functional roles of each type of differential units could be postulated as follows: Type A units may be involved in coding the information about the CC at the time of the CC presentation or holding that information during the first delay period. Type B1 units may participate in coding and/or holding the information about which DC was presented. Type B2 units may be related to the retrieval of the information about the CC at the time of the DC presentation. Activity of the type B3 units that showed phasic changes at the time of the DC presentation may be associated with the decision about which side is positive. Those type B3 units that showed changes during the second delay period may be related to the preparatory set for responding to the particular direction. Because type B4 units showed unique activity to each case, these units are considered to be related to the recognition of the DC, depending on the context and/or the retention of that information during the second delay period.

Type C units may be associated with the initiation and execution of the pressing response of the particular choice key.

It has been well documented that the sensory cortical unit activity is dependent on physical features of the stimulus (7) and motor cortical unit activity is connected with specific muscle movements (4). Furthermore, the unit activity of the temporal and parietal association cortices has been shown to be related to specific features of the stimulus or specific muscular movements although the specific features of the stimulus or the muscular movement have been found to be much more complex in these association cortices than in the sensory or motor cortex (6,13).

However, unit activity of the prefrontal cortex seems to be not so much related to specific features of the stimulus or specific muscular movements as the unit activity of other cortices does. In this experiment, type B2 units showed activity independent of the stimulus that was shown but dependent on the stimulus that had been presented. The activity of type B3 units was dependent on the side that the monkey recognized as positive and was independent of the features of the DC. Type B4 units showed activity dependent on the meaning of the DC determined by the context (information retained about the CC), irrespective of whether it was correct or not. These results indicate that the activity of type B2, B3, and B4 units is context dependent. The activity of type A and type B1 units is also considered to be context dependent, since these units showed responses related to the meaning but not to the physical features of the stimulus in the control experiment involving other CCs and DCs. The differential activity of type B3 units may be related only to the spatial information processing, while the activity of type A, B1, B2, and B4 units was found to be related to the nonspatial information processing.

Additional support for the notion that prefrontal units are not directly related to specific features of the stimulus or to specific muscular movements comes from the following observations. Kojima and Tobias (10) have observed that prefrontal units showed the differential activity in response to the same cue, depending on whether the cue was meaningful or meaningless, that is, whether the presentation of the cue signals the opportunity for response followed by reward or not. Suzuki and Azuma (19) have shown that the activation of their "G neuron" (which showed increase in discharge rate when the monkey gazed at a small spot) was little influenced by stimulus parameters, such as the size, intensity, and position of the light spot. As was described before, Niki (15) showed that prefrontal units exhibited the differential activity before the same response (depressing the same choice key), depending on the task situation.

In conclusion, prefrontal units are considered to be related to processing information about both the spatial and nonspatial context and are not associated with specific features of the stimulus or specific limb movements.

ACKNOWLEDGMENTS

The author expresses his gratitude to Dr. H. Niki for his guidance throughout the experiments and in preparing the manuscript, and to Dr. E. E. Fetz for his comments on the manuscript.

The author thanks Elsevier/North-Holland Biomedical Press and Dr. H. Niki for permission to reproduce copyrighted materials.

REFERENCES

1. Blum RA: Effects of subtotal lesions of frontal granular cortex on delayed reaction in monkeys. *Arch Neurol Psychiat* 67:375–386, 1952.
2. Butter CM: Perseveration in extinction and in discrimination reversal tasks following selective frontal ablations in *Macaca mulatta. Physiol Behav* 4:163–171, 1969.
3. Butters N, Pandya D, Stein D, et al: A search for the spatial engram within the frontal lobes of monkeys. *Acta Neurobiol Exp* 32:305–329, 1972.
4. Evarts EV: Representation of movements and muscles by pyramidal tract neurons of the precentral motor cortex, in Yahr MD, Purpura DP (eds): *Neurophysiological Basis of Normal and Abnormal Motor Activity.* New York, Raven Press, 1967, pp 215–251.
5. Fuster JM: Unit activity in the prefrontal cortex during delayed response performance: neuronal correlates of short-term memory. *J Neurophysiol* 36:61–78, 1973.
6. Gross CG, Rocha-Miranda CE, Bender DB: Visual properties of neurons in inferotemporal cortex of the macaque. *J Neurophysiol* 35:96–111, 1972.
7. Hubel DH, Wiesel TN: Functional architecture of the striate cortex, in Carlson FD (ed): *Physiological and Biochemical Aspects of Nervous Integration.* Englewood Cliffs, NJ, Prentice-Hall, 1968, pp 153–161.
8. Iversen SD, Mishkin M: Perseverative interference in monkeys following selective lesions of the inferior prefrontal convexity. *Exp Brain Res* 11:376–386, 1970.

9. Jacobsen CF: An experimental analysis of the frontal association areas in primates. *Arch Neurol Psychiat* 33:558–569, 1935.
10. Kojima S, Tobias TJ: Reward related visual stimuli: single unit recording in monkey prefrontal cortex (PFC). *Exp Brain Res* 23(suppl):111, 1975.
11. Kubota K, Niki H: Prefrontal cortical unit activity and delayed alternation performance in monkeys. *J Neurophysiol* 34:337–347, 1971.
12. Mishkin M: Effects of small frontal lesions on delayed alternation in monkeys. *J Neurophysiol* 20:615–622, 1957.
13. Mountcastle VB, Lynch JC, Georgopoulos A, et al: Posterior parietal association cortex of the monkey: command functions for operations within extrapersonal space. *J Neurophysiol* 38:871–908, 1975.
14. Niki H: Prefrontal unit activity during delayed alternation in the monkey. I. Relation to direction of response. *Brain Res* 68:185–196, 1974.
15. Niki H: Prefrontal unit activity during delayed alternation in the monkey. II. Relation to absolute *versus* relative direction of response. *Brain Res* 68:197–204, 1974.
16. Niki H: Differential activity of prefrontal units during right and left delayed response trials. *Brain Res* 70:346–349, 1974.
17. Niki H, Watanabe M: Prefrontal unit activity and delayed response: relation to cue location *versus* direction of response. *Brain Res* 105:79–88, 1976.
18. Passingham R: Delayed matching after selective prefrontal lesions in monkeys (*Macaca mulatta*). *Brain Res* 92:89–102, 1975.
19. Suzuki H, Azuma M: Prefrontal neuronal activity during gazing at a light spot in the monkey. *Brain Res* 126:497–508, 1977.

10

Biochemical Events Mediating the Formation of Short-Term and Long-Term Memory

Bernard W. Agranoff

I have taken advantage of the intimacy of the setting of this meeting to give you a somewhat personal view of the progress and problems of studying memory formation from the standpoint of a biochemist. What can I say, after having pondered this question for some 15 years? Perhaps a better first question is one that I asked myself at the onset: Has biochemistry, or for that matter, our entire body of scientific knowledge, yet progressed to the point that the study of memory is suitable for attack by present-day concepts and methods? History has taught us that this latter question is a moot one. Man's quest to understand how his mind works has always been with us, through fads and fancies, including "reverberating circuits," engrams, "smart pills," and memory-transfer molecules. Because of this intrinsic irresistibility, we here address ourselves not so much to the question of whether the time is yet ripe but to how we can most constructively approach the problem. In the context of this interdisciplinary group, I would like to summarize what the biochemical approach has taught us, and what we might reasonably expect in the future. Lest one conclude that curiosity alone motivates the behavioral neuroscientist in his study of memory, I hasten to emphasize the growing biomedical implications of memory research. As medical science makes gains in maintaining our bodies and achieving longevity, we find increasing numbers among the aged who develop serious brain disorders—the senile dementias—associated with specific memory deficits. If we can block memory formation, there is hope that we will eventually be able to augment it.

THE TWO BIOCHEMICAL APPROACHES

Behavior memory as we ordinarily conceive of it, that is, enhanced performance of an experimental subject on the basis of prior experience, can be studied with the tools of the biochemist in two principal ways: we may use either interventive or correlative approaches.

In the interventive approach, an agent that has known specific biochemical actions is administered. From the observed effect of the agent on behavior, we make inferences about the nature of the disrupted or altered process. An example is the blocking of retention of a learned task produced by the injection of an inhibitor of protein synthesis. This has been a major theme in our laboratory, and our findings and conclusions are summarized below. Other commonly used interventive agents that block memory include inhibitors of RNA synthesis, antibodies to specific brain proteins or lipids, neurotransmitter agonists and antagonists, various convulsant agents (including electroconvulsive shock), and as reported at this meeting, agents that bind specific classes of brain proteins.

Interventive agents have been reported that enhance memory formation (1). In this category I include so-called memory-transfer experiments, in which it is claimed that injection of material obtained from the brain of a trained animal (donor) can be injected into an untrained animal (recipient) with a resultant enhanced behavior not seen if the donor had not been trained (2). Because there has been much controversy and little evidence to support memory transfer, these experiments will not be discussed further. They should, however, be clearly distinguished from experiments in which various peptides are reported to have behavioral effects of a less specific nature, for example, to block extinction of a learned task (3). These latter experiments bear promise that they will provide new knowledge about the interface between the brain's cognitive functions and its neuroendocrine machinery, that is, about processing rather than about information-specific mechanisms, as distinguished later.

The interventive agents are, at best, pharmacological tools, in that what we observe is the effect of the application of a nonphysiological agent or of a naturally occurring substance under nonphysiological conditions. The great strength of the interventive approach is that it permits us to ask rather broad questions about whole animals engaged in processes generally accepted as learning and memory formation. The interventive approach has the inherent disadvantage, on the other hand, that while it can point us in a general direction, it cannot provide us with the precise answers we would like, nor can it give us definitive proof of a hypothesis. Conclusions drawn are also limited by the specificity of the agent used. For example, an inhibitor of protein synthesis could have side effects that account for its observed influence on behavior. Even if it can be convincingly demonstrated by the use of a number of agents of varying structure, all of which block protein synthesis, that protein synthesis is indeed required for memory formation, our answer is not as informative as we would like, considering the complexity of the brain and the myriad structural and catalytic proteins in every cell. Despite these serious drawbacks, the interventive techniques, as we shall see, have served to tell us something about *where* and *when* memory is formed in the brain.

Studies in fishes (4), rodents (5,6), and birds (7) confirm the contention that there is a critical period of time just after a training session, during which processing necessary for the formation or survival of long-term memory occurs. Where in the brain these agents are producing their effects has been relatively little studied. In his initial pioneering experiments, Flexner (8) showed that newly formed memory was most susceptible to bitemporal (and not to frontal or occipital) sites of intracerebral injection of puromycin, and that unilateral injections were ineffective. Our studies in the goldfish have involved injection of various inhibitors of macromolecular synthesis into the cranial fluid bathing the entire brain. Intracerebral injection of antibiotic blocking agents into the brain substance of the goldfish is technically difficult, so we chose to pursue the question of brain localization in the mouse, both because of its larger brain and because its anatomy more closely approximates that of the primate, our ultimate interest. While there have been extensive studies on the effects of inhibitors of protein synthesis on memory formation in the mouse, there have been few attempts to localize the site of action anatomically. This is partly beause, under some circumstances, the insertion of a cannula into the brain substance can itself have an amnestic effect, and partly because it became apparent that certain inhibitors of protein synthesis could be injected parenterally into mice both to block brain protein synthesis and to produce profound amnesia. While interventive studies using parenteral injections have been convenient, they tell us little about the possible regional localization of the site of action of the agents. Our experiments on regional localization used a step-through task in the mouse. Initial studies with cycloheximide in a 30 μl volume (injected bilaterally) indicated that hippocampus and, possibly, striatum, amygdala, and medial anterior thalamic areas were primarily involved (9). Localization of the inhibition was estimated by radioautography in unilaterally injected subjects. In a more recent reinvestigation of this problem we have greatly reduced the volume injected (0.05 μl) and have used a potent blocker of protein synthesis, streptovitacin A. We have confirmed the hippocampal site and have ruled out overlying cortex as a possible site of action (10).

In the correlative approach, one observes changes in the brain without physiological perturbation. Almost invariably, this means that radioisotopic precursors are injected into experimental and control animals with the aim of finding differences in incorporation that can be related to the behavioral manipulation. A well-known example of this is the double-label approach as applied to behavioral studies by Glassman (11). One isotopic form of labeled uridine was injected into experimental mice trained in a jump-up task while another form was injected into various control subjects. After the experiment, the experimental and control brains were combined and RNA was extracted. The hope was to find a species of RNA in which the double-label ratio was selectively altered. Instead, a uniform increase was seen throughout the spectrum of separated RNAs in trained mice, relative to resting or yoked controls. The results suggest that increases in RNA labeling associated with learning may have resulted from altered precursor pools, cerebral blood flow, brain metabolism, and so on, rather than to a selective increase in a particular RNA population. Even when careful attempts are made to measure precursor pools, one can never be certain whether the appropriate precursor pool has indeed been measured. An increase in labeling can also indicate decreased destruction, rather than an increase in synthesis of RNA. Furthermore, if an alteration in labeling is seen as a result of a behavioral manipulation, it is necessary to rule out various interpretations of how the behavior is related to the change, since the altered metabolism can be epiphenomenal, for example, related to stress or to sensorimotor aspects of the training, rather than to learning and memory mechanisms themselves. These criticisms should not be taken to denigrate correlative studies. It is my contention that further progress in memory research will result from a combined interventive and correlative approach (see also Chapter 13). While information about the time and, perhaps, the gross anatomical localization within the brain of critical steps in memory formation can be derived from interventive experiments, such findings will be strengthened by further correlative studies in the same experimental animal and behavioral paradigm. That is, the interventive approach gives us strong hints about where and when to look for expected altered biochemical correlates of memory.

EXPERIMENTS ON MEMORY IN THE GOLDFISH

My interest in memory began some 20 years ago when I was at the National Institutes of Health, as a result of casual observations on imprinted Mallard ducklings provided me by Eckhardt Hess of the University of Chicago. At the University of Michigan, I had many interesting discussions with Ralph Gerard but was nevertheless loathe to make a foray into the field, until I read Flexner's interesting report (8) on the effects of puromycin on memory in mice. In the years that followed, Flexner proposed a number of alternative explanations for his earlier results (e.g., 12). In the meantime, many laboratories have used a wide variety of blockers of macromolecular synthesis and have concluded that the agents have selective effects on memory formation. Studies in goldfish (*Carrasius auratus*) have used inhibitors of protein synthesis (primarily puromycin and acetoxycycloheximide), inhibitors of RNA synthesis (primarily actinomycin D and camptothecin), and electroconvulsive shock.

The behavioral apparatus used is a shuttlebox, shown in Figure 10-1. The apparatus consists of a water-filled plastic tank separated by an opaque barrier with a rectangular opening 30 mm high and 40 mm wide. The water level is 10 mm below the top of the opening. After 5 minutes of acclimation in the dark, the light on the opposite side of the box goes on; 15 seconds later, a repetitive mild electrical shock is administered through the water by means of grids on the sides of the box. The fish initially swims through the opening only after receiving several shocks (the escape response), at which time the light goes off and the shocking ceases. After a variable period of time in the dark, there is a light signal, again on the side of the box opposite to the fish's location, that is, the side from which the fish had just escaped, and the sequence is repeated. The fish shuttles back and forth, receiving one trial per minute. An entire session, including the 5-minute pretrial acclimation takes 20 minutes. During the session, the fish learns that by swim-

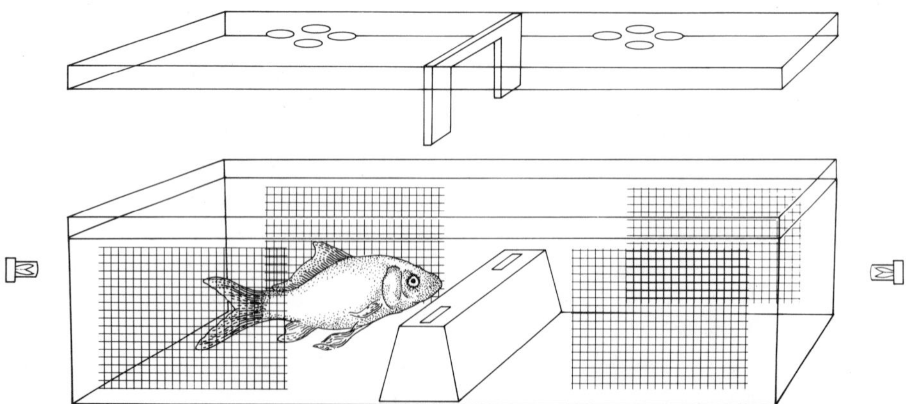

Figure 10-1. Goldfish shuttlebox used for training of light avoidance coupled to shock.

ming through the barrier in the first 15 seconds he avoids the shock. This active avoidance is the learned response. Ten shuttleboxes are operated simultaneously by a computer, which also records latencies, avoidances, and escapes (as well as failures to escape). The position of the fish is recorded by four infrared detectors, which bracket the barrier (not shown in Fig. 10-1).

We have consistently used partial training, that is, our "trained" fish do not generally exceed 50–70% of avoidance responding. This avoids "ceiling" effects, which might otherwise obscure amnestic actions and has, in our experience, ensured the detection of minimal amnestic effects. The advantage of a multitrial task, compared with a one-trial task, such as the one-trial step-through avoidance task commonly used in the mouse, is that in the former we can measure both short-term memory (STM) and long-term memory (LTM) formation, while in the latter one can measure only LTM formation. A great advantage of single trial training tasks is that each session is brief, and many animals can be trained quickly. Also, one can hope to correlate the precise times of learning and memory formation with purported biochemical changes. The simultaneous use of 10 computerized shuttleboxes overcomes the "through-put" problem and, as detailed below, we believe that formation of LTM does not begin until just after the animal has been returned to his home tank after session I. The shuttlebox task thus has very favorable characteristics for the study of STM and LTM. Figure 10-2 is a diagrammatic summary of information obtained with a number of different shuttleboxes over the past 15 years.*

In Figure 10-2(*1*), the increased probability of avoidance responding during the day 1 of session I can be seen, indicating that STM is formed. Fish that were returned immediately to their home tanks and retrained 1 week later show additional improvement. If an amnestic agent, such as a blocker of protein synthesis, is injected intracranially (IC) just before the session (time A), normal acquisition (learning, STM formation) is seen, but there is a profound deficit in performance on retraining 1 week later. If the agent is administered sufficiently in advance of session I, (time B), normal retention is seen on day 8. By varying the time of injection before training (B), the duration of a given agent's amnestic affect can be established. Intracranial injection of puromycin is effective when given 24, but not 72, hours before session I. This compares well to its duration of action as an inhibitor of brain protein synthesis, as measured by inhibition of labeled amino acid incorporation into brain protein. Fish exhibiting a retention decrement in session II can be given a third session (not shown) on day 15. In this case, they show the usual improvement in performance seen between sessions I and II. This result indicates that the induced blocking of memory does not permanently damage the fish's ability to learn or to form memory. These experiments clearly indicate a difference between STM and LTM formation. That is, the blocking agents thus far used have had no effect on STM but prevent the development of LTM.

The effects of amnestic agents administered after training are shown in Figure 10-2(*2*). Injection of an amnestic agent immediately after session I (time C) results in pro-

* The training task has been systematically altered over the years in attempts to maximize retention differences between sessions I and II, to minimize seasonal variability in goldfish performance (12), to decrease occasional photodetector error, and so on. Fish were initially given 20 trials in session I and the CS-US interval was 20 seconds. They were retrained 3 days later (4). The barrier used was as shown in the box in Figure 10-1, but the partition attached to the lid was absent. The partition greatly reduces the possibility of spontaneous crossing. The apparatus as shown is currently in use.

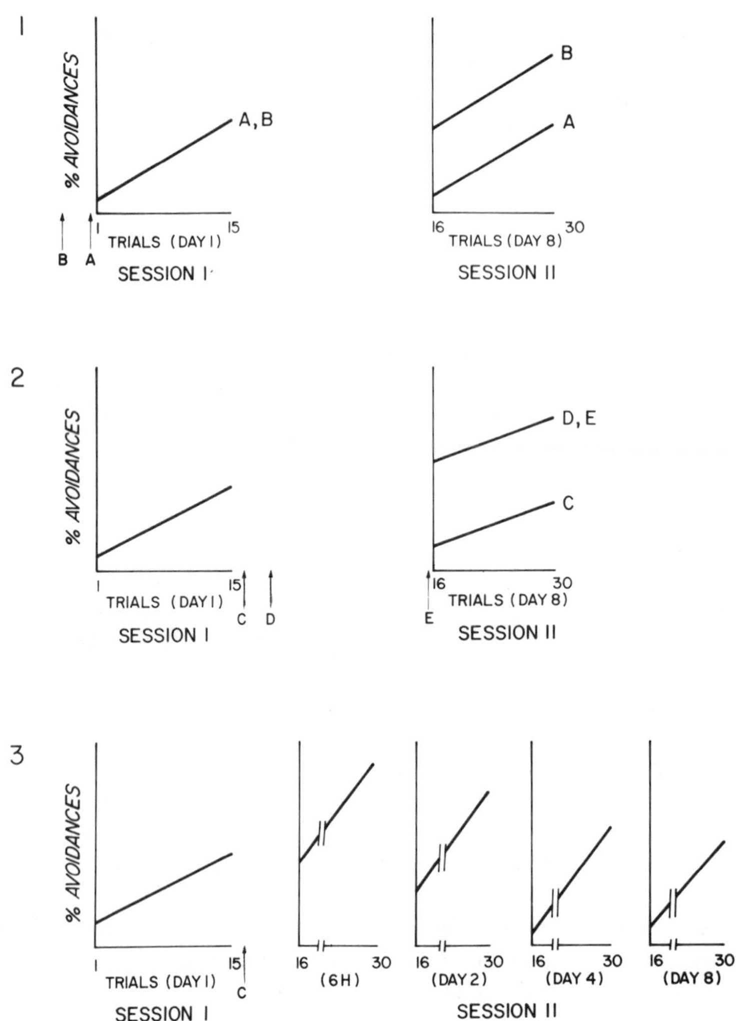

Figure 10-2. Composite representation of effects of agents that block long-term memory (LTM) formation of a multitrial task—goldfish shuttle box shock-avoidance paradigm. Fish were given to sessions of 15 trials each (see text).

found deficits on retraining 1 week later. The process is time dependent. If the fish are returned to their home tanks and are given the injection a few hours later (time D), no deficit is seen on retraining on day 8. In fact, fish not treated previously and given the amnestic agent just before retraining on day 8 (time E), show the learned response. This time dependency of the treatment rules out both chronic (lingering) and acute toxic effects of the amnestic agents as possible explanations for the observed reduced responding rates. The decrement in performance is thus attributed to a specific memory loss.

Since the injection at time C lowers performance to the naive (session I level), we infer that LTM formation is completely blocked. This means that all LTM is formed *after* the training session. This important conclusion has its analogy in the retrograde amnesia seen clinically. After head trauma associated with unconsciousness, there is usually a loss of memory for events occurring immediately before the trauma.

If fish are not returned to home tanks promptly after session I but are detained in the training apparatus, the interval (C → D) during which they are susceptible to memory block is prolonged, as discussed below in the section on the environmental trigger.

The decay of STM can be seen in Figure 10-2(*3*). Injection of blocking agents just before or just after training will result in failure to form LTM. Individual groups of animals so treated and retrained at various times earlier than 8 days (e.g., 6, 24 or 48 hours after session I) demonstrate the learned habit even though they would have lost their ability to perform it within a few days. The experiments constitute evidence for a decay of STM. They do not tell us whether STM is normally converted to LTM or whether LTM arises separately. That is, we do not know whether the blocking agents weaken a unitary process, in which STM is "hardened" into LTM, or whether STM ordinarily decays in this fashion, while the blocking agents prevent the independent formation of LTM. In either event, it is clear that STM is not obliterated by the treatments—its presence can be detected after the amnestic agent has been administered.

It is important to note that the time required for the consolidation of memory (Fig. 10-2(*2*), C → D), varies with the conditions of the paradigm, such as the number of trials per session, shock intensity, and so on, and also to some extent with the amnestic agent used. For example, the susceptibility of memory to acetoxycycloheximide after session I appears to outlast susceptibility to puromycin. Thus, while we talk about the fixation of memory (or its "consolidation"), what we actually measure is the artificial interaction of a physiological process and an interventive agent.

What we can say about the physiological process is that it is temperature dependent. Since fish are poikilothermic, they can be cooled or warmed (within limits) after a training session with few untoward effects. By combining a temperature experiment with the injection of a disruptive agent such as puromycin, we established that cooling slows fixation, while warming accelerates it, as is expected for a biochemical process (14). Cooling fish for 24 hours slows down brain protein synthesis. The magnitude and duration of the inhibition mimics that seen with protein-synthesis blockers, yet there is no memory loss as a result of the prolonged cooling. Disruption of memory apparently requires normally ongoing brain metabolism in the presence of the selective block.

The various phenomena observed in Figure 10-2 can be generated by one of several inhibitors of protein synthesis or of RNA, but not of DNA, synthesis (15). It is also seen after electroconvulsive shock (ECS), administered by transorbital electrodes (16). While there may be a common mechanism for the effect of the chemical agents and of ECS, it is yet not apparent what it might be. Blocking agents do not result in convulsions nor do they potentiate the action of convulsant agents (15). Correspondingly, while ECS produces some decrease in protein synthesis, the decrement is not sufficient to explain its amnestic action (17). An especially interesting aspect of the action of ECS is that it can also produce an anterograde amnesia (16). That is, previously untrained fish given ECS and permitted to recover briefly before session I show normal acquisition but poor LTM formation (Fig. 10-2,*7*A). By varying the interval between ECS and the onset of training (B → A), we were able to demonstrate that the amnestic effects of ECS are present for about 2 hours after the convulsion. Thus, it is not the convulsion itself, but some metabolic consequence that is responsible for its amnestic action. The increased turnover of catecholamines in rats for many hours after a single ECS treatment may be relevant (18).

THE ENVIRONMENTAL TRIGGER

Since the interventive agents can restore animals to the naive performance level when given after session I (time C) Fig. 10-2,*2*), it is apparent that no memory fixation occurs during session I. Yet, within a few minutes of being returned to the home tanks, measurable fixation has taken place, as judged by the rapid development of insusceptibility to amnestic treatments. This prompted Roger Davis to ask: What is it about the training apparatus that prevents fixation, or about the home tank that promotes it? (19). He conducted experiments in which animals were not returned to their home tanks but were detained in the apparatus after the session. While detention in the training apparatus had no effect on retention in control animals, LTM in fish remained susceptible to amnestic agents for over an hour—a time at which, we had previously shown, they would have fixed memory. It thus appeared that the act of removing fish from the training apparatus and their return to the home environment signaled the onset of the physiological fixation process. A number of subsequent studies showed that this delay in onset of LTM fixation was not mediated by a chemical change in the environment, such as the action of substances in the training apparatus water, but primarily by visual stimuli that informed the fish of whether it was in the threatening environment of the training apparatus or in the safe environment of the home tank. We referred to the underlying process as *dearousal,* as seen in Figure 10-3. We should perhaps find another term, since the word *dearousal,* aside from being unaesthetic, bears the connotation of rest or sedation. In fact, anesthesia with Finquel (MS-222) after training does not trigger fixation. The fish must apparently experience the return to safety. A similar detention effect has been observed in mice (20). The "environmental trigger" in fish may be related to observations in mice that the action of antibiotic blocking agents on memory is in some cases antagonized by amphetamine (21). We have speculated elsewhere that the amphetamine exerts its action by delaying the "dearousal" process

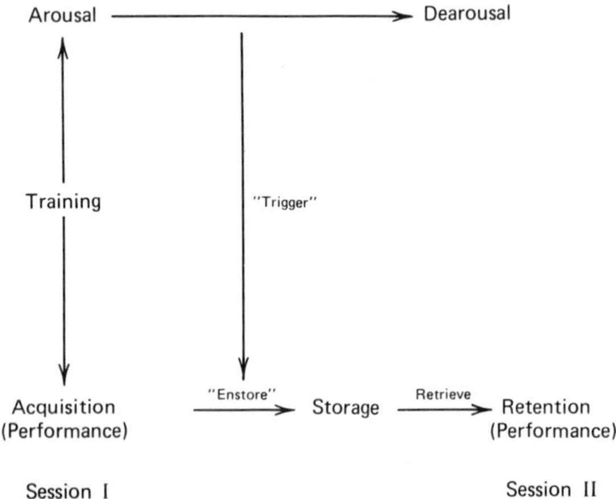

Figure 10-3. Representation of events mediating LTM formation of an avoidance task. The model, based primarily on shuttlebox experiments in goldfish in the author's laboratory, is also applicable to studies using the antibiotic blocking agents in other species. (From 32. Reproduced with permission of Raven Press).

(22). Since the block in mouse brain protein synthesis produced by the inhibitors is of a rather short duration, it is possible that by the time the fixation signal is issued in amphetamine-treated mice, protein synthesis has returned to normal, and thus LTM formation is not impeded. We have not observed such an effect of amphetamine in the fish. However, we have recently performed studies in fish that have previously been treated with 6-hydroxydopamine (6-OH-DA), an agent known to destroy catecholaminergic terminals. If the fixation signal is mediated by a catecholaminergic process, one might observe a difference in susceptibility to LTM formation in the treated animals. Indeed, 6-OHDA-treated fish show normal acquisition and retention but remain susceptible to blocking agents for over 6 hours after session I (unpublished results).

INFORMATION-SPECIFIC AND NONSPECIFIC PROCESSES

Little reference has been made up to now of the vast body of knowledge gained from neuroanatomical and ultrastructural investigations on the brain. The ability to store behavioral information undoubtedly resides in the chemical synapses by which neurons communicate. We biochemists, to paraphrase from our western film classics, have the reputation of homogenizing first and asking questions later. This propensity could doom the correlative approach, since the correlate we seek may be the block of the synthesis of a rather prevalent protein in a specific group of cells. Destruction of morphologic features would destroy the evidence. On the other hand, the blocking agents may be involved in a non-information-containing process—perhaps even at some distance from synapses mediating memory. STM and LTM may both be considered to be information-containing states analogous to the latent image in film and the finished photograph, respectively. The fixative process, which preserves the latent image, need not in itself be information-containing. Protein inhibitors could block the fixative—the enstoring process shown in Figure 10-3. That the brain could issue such a fix signal via neural or neurohumoral pathways has been entertained previously and has support from human studies (23). Our blocking studies thus may be relevant not to behavioral specificity but to the fixation process.

What then can we learn about the development of behavioral specificity, presumably borne in synaptic connections? Before we can learn much about how synaptic relationships are altered with learning, it will probably be necessary to learn how they are determined initially—a question that awaits advances in our understanding of the biochemistry of form and development. In fact, the brain is often cited as an example of one of the thornier problems in developmental biology, since it is clear that there is insufficient DNA to code for the human brain to the last bouton on the last neuron without invoking some hierarchical program of instruction (24). At the microscopic level there is considerable variability from one side of the brain to the other, and among clonal (gynogenetic) "sibs," there is considerable variability in specific brain structures (25,26). One biochemical correlate of the brain's diversity is the presence of more unique sequence RNA than in any other organ yet examined (27).

To gain further information on how neurons recognize brain targets, we have been studying regeneration in the goldfish retina following crush of one optic nerve. Ganglion cells are known to have specific target sites in the optic tectum, and, by means of biochemical probes, we have been examining alterations in the ganglion cell body that reflect the regrowth. Thus far, the earliest changes we have detected relate to nucleoside phosphorylation (28,29). We have also successfully demonstrated the release of tubulin messenger and tubulin synthesis after crush (30). These and other biochemical "handles" should eventually prove useful in studying the mediation of behavioral plasticity in the goldfish brain, an even more complex system.

INFERENCES FROM KNOWN TIME PARAMETERS OF LEARNING AND MEMORY FORMATION

For many years memory was thought to have an early electrical manifestation, which is then converted to a permanent chemical form. The concept was based on the evanescent nature of STM—it can be formed in a fraction of a second and is not necessarily converted to LTM—and on the relatively slow rate of development of LTM, inferred from various observations on the retrograde nature of memory disruption. There is also, of course, the known stability of both memory and of covalent chemical linkages over long time periods. The demonstration of disruption of memory formation by ECS, and the evidence that genetic information is stored in the covalent sequences of DNA, both served to reinforce further the dual (electrical → chemical) concept of memory formation. This simplistic view has long since outlived its usefulness. Over the years, neurophysiologists engaged in studies on memory have searched for, and have found, long-lasting electrical changes in brain, such as heterosynaptic facilitation, while biochemists are becoming increasingly interested in, and are finding, rapid biochemical reactions, such as phosphorylation of enzymes that regulate metabolic cascades in nanosecond time frames. Both STM and LTM undoubtedly have electrical and chemical consequences in the brain, even though their precise nature remains far from clear. While extensive stimulation is reported to produce alterations of brain structure, such as increased arborization of dendritic spines (31), it has not been possible to demonstrate accretion of a class of brain proteins with training, age, and so on. The altered cell presumably maintains itself by positive feedback switches, such as are invoked for theories of development.

We have speculated elsewhere that both STM and LTM may be mediated by chemical processes, posttranslational and de novo macromolecular synthesis, respectively. The original idea came from a consideration of time constraints, based on the fact that memory exists in a metastable form followed by a long-lasting form. The dual chemical model is made further attractive by the identification of a number of posttranslational alterations known to occur at the synapse, including phosphorylation, methylation, and glycosylation. We have reviewed elsewhere a number of known posttranslational alterations of protein, which have been proposed to play a role in brain function, and then have considered them as possible mediators of STM (32). Let us consider then the possible behavioral consequences on shock avoidance training of a hypothetical interventive agent that blocks posttranslational reactions that mediate STM, and that has no effect on LTM (Fig. 10-4). Treated animals are predicted to show no acquisition, but should perform the escape response normally. On retesting, they should learn normally, assuming that the effect of the agent had worn off by the second session. If previously trained, animals should demonstrate the learned behavior, but should show no further acquisition, while under the effects of the agent (time E).

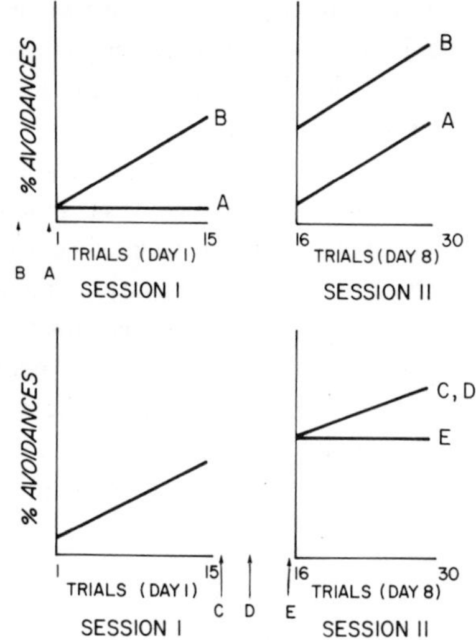

Figure 10-4. Actions predicted of an agent that blocks short-term memory formation, but has no effect on long-term memory (see text and Fig. 10-2).

While it would be convenient for the biochemist if the putative post-translational effect mediating STM involved covalent linkages, noncovalent changes such as conformational alterations in proteins on calcium binding, and so on, are equally valid candidates at present.

An interesting model of posttranslational and de novo synthetic alterations leading to a similar physiological result in a single neuron may have relevance here. It has been reported that nerve growth factor (NGF) is released from target organs of sympathetic neurons after stimulation. At first, NGF reacts with presynaptic receptors, presumably by posttranslational activation of tyrosine hydroxylase at the synapse. Prolonged stimulation results in retrograde transport of NGF to the cell nucleus, where new tyrosine hydroxylase messenger is released and translated (33).

FUTURE TRENDS

This rather personal account, in addition to emphasizing primarily the work of our own laboratory, has also dealt only with the use of whole animal behavior. Much progress has been made and is being made in reductionist models. Studies on habituation and sensitization in the Aplysia gill-withdrawal reflex strongly indicate that altered neurotransmitter release accompanies the changes (34). Electrophysiological and biochemical studies in incubated hippocampal slices also bear promise that long-lasting changes can be induced in vitro (35, Chapter 3).

An ultimate goal of memory studies is their application to human disease. Nowhere is the experimental animal less appropriate to the human model than in studies on higher brain functions. Memory deficits in humans are almost invariably described in terms of ideational (verbal) behavior for which there is no adequate animal model. Ultimately we must study the biochemistry of the human brain. A promising field for the future is the use of noninvasive techniques for studying human brain biochemistry. Most recently, the positron-emitting scanner has evolved. By using cyclotron-produced nuclides, relatively large amounts of radioactivity can be safely administered, and, because of their short half-life, the total radiation dose to patients is small. By means of detectors coupled to a computer, a brain cross section can be reconstructed showing distribution of injected positron-emitting materials. For example, ^{11}C- or ^{18}F-deoxyglucose, positron-emitting glucose analogs, are phosphorylated by hexokinase but are not metabolized further. Like ^{14}C-deoxyglucose, they leave a time trace in the brain of glucose metabolism at the time of injection. Gray matter can presently be distinguished from white matter in living humans (36). Cortical areas undergoing stimulation should eventually be detectable, as has been successfully shown in contact radioautograms from brains of rats or monkeys injected with ^{14}C-deoxyglucose (37). Furthermore, by means of ^{11}C- or ^{18}F-tagged amino acids, it should be possible to see amino acid uptake and, eventually, protein synthesis in brain regions (38), a prediction made several years ago. Such tools will prove to be important adjuncts in the evaluation of brain disease and in the development of therapeutic agents.

REFERENCES

1. Dawson RG, McGaugh JL: Drug facilitation of learning and memory, in Deutsch JA (ed): *The Physiological Basis of Memory.* New York, Academic Press, 1973, p 77.
2. Ungar G, Desiderio DM, Parr W: Isolation, identification, and synthesis of a specific behavior-inducing peptide. *Nature* 238:198, 1972.
3. DeWied D, Gispen WH: Behavioral effects of peptides, in Gainer H (ed): *Peptides in Neurobiology.* New York, Plenum Press, 1977, p 397.
4. Agranoff BW, Klinger PD: Puromycin effect on memory fixation in the goldfish. *Science* 146:952, 1964.
5. Barondes SH: Cerebral protein synthesis inhibitors block long-term memory. *Int Rev Neurobiol* 12:177, 1970.
6. Flood JF, Rosenzweig MR, Bennett EL, et al: Influences of duration of protein synthesis inhibition on memory. *Physiol Behav* 10:55, 1973.
7. Mark RF, Watts ME: Drug inhibition of memory function in chickens, *Proc Roy Soc Lond* 178:439, 1971.
8. Flexner JB, Flexner LB, Stellar E: Memory in mice as affected by intracerebral puromycin. *Science* 141:57, 1963.
9. Eichenbaum H, Quenon BA, Heacock AM, et al: Differential behavioral and biochemical effects of regional injection of cycloheximide into mouse brain. *Brain Res* 101:171, 1976.
10. Boast CA, Agranoff BW: Biochemical and behavioral effects of streptovitacin A in mice, abstract. Society for Neuroscience Eighth Annual Meeting, p 255, 1978.
11. Glassman E: The biochemistry of learning: an evaluation of the role of RNA and protein. *Ann Rev Biochem* 38:605, 1969.
12. Flexner LB, Goodman RH: Studies on memory: inhibitors of protein synthesis also inhibit catecholamine synthesis. *Proc Nat Acad Sci* 72:4660, 1975.
13. Agranoff BW, Davis RE: More on seasonal variations in goldfish learning. *Science* 186:65, 1974.
14. Neale JH, Klinger PD, Agranoff BW: Temperature-dependent consolidation of puromycin-susceptible memory in the goldfish. *Behav Biol* 9:267, 1973.
15. Agranoff BW: Biochemical concomitants of the storage of behavioral information, in Jaenicke L (ed): *Biochemistry of Sensory Functions,* 25 Mosbacher Colloquium der Gesellschaft fur Biologische Chemie. Springer-Verlag, 1974, p 597.
16. Springer AD, Schoel WM, Klinger PD, et al: Anterograde and retrograde effects of electroconvulsive shock of puromycin on memory formation in the goldfish. *Behav Biol* 13:467, 1975.

17. Dunn AJ: The chemistry of learning and the formation of memory, in Gispen, WM (ed): *Molecular and Functional Neurobiology*. Amsterdam, Elsevier, 1976, p 347.

18. Kety SS, Jovoy F, Thierry AM, et al.: A sustained effect of electroconvulsive shock on the turnover of norepinephrine in the central nervous system of the rat. *Proc Natl Acad Sci USA* 58:1249, 1967.

19. Davis RE, Agranoff BW: Stages of memory formation in foldfish: evidence for an environmental trigger. *Proc Natl Acad Sci* 55:555, 1966.

20. Robestelli F, Geller A, Jarvik ME: Retrograde amnesia from detention. *Physiol Behav* 3:543, 1968.

21. Barondes SH, Cohen HD: Arousal and the conversion of "short-term" to "long-term" memory. *Proc Natl Acad Sci* 61:923, 1968.

22. Springer AD, Agranoff BW: Puromycin-induced retention deficit in goldfish as a function of attained training performance level. *Behav Biol* 17:547, 1976.

23. Milner B: Amnesia following operation on the temporal lobes, in Whitty CWN, Zangwill OL (eds): *Amnesia*. London, Butterworth, 1966, p 109.

24. Changeux JP, Danchin A: Selective stabilization of developing synapses as a mechanism for the specification of neuronal networks. *Nature* 264:705, 1976.

25. Agranoff BW, Davis RE, Gossington RE: Esoteric fish. *Science* 171:230, 1971.

26. Leventhal F, Macagno E, Levinthal C: Anatomy and development of identified cells in isogenic organisms. *Symposium on Quant Biol* 40:321, 1975.

27. Soga K, Takahashi Y: Transcription of repeated and unique DNA sequences in brain nuclei. *J Neurochem* 26:89, 1976.

28. Dokas LA, Burrell HR, Agranoff BW: Altered RNA precursor metabolism in the goldfish retina during optic nerve regeneration, abstract. *Fed Proc* 37:1785, 1978.

29. Burrell HR, Dokas LA, Agranoff BW: RNA metabolism in the goldfish retina during optic nerve regeneration. *J Neurochem* 31:289, 1978.

30. Burrell HR, Heacock AM, Water RD, et al: Increased tubulin messenger RNA in the goldfish retina during optic nerve regeneration *Brain Res* 168:628, 1979.

31. Scheibel ME, Scheibel AB:, Some thoughts on the ontogeny of memory and learning, in Rosenzweig MR, Bennett EL (eds): *Neural Mechanisms of Learning and Memory,* Cambridge, Mass., MIT Press, 1976, p 241.

32. Agranoff BW, Burrell HR, Dokas LA, et al: Progress in biochemical approaches to learning and memory, in Lipton M, DeMascio A, Killam K (eds): *Psychopharmacology: A Generation of Progress.* New York, Raven Press, 1978, p. 623.

33. Black I: Regulation of autonomic development. *Ann Rev Neurosci* 1:183, 1978.

34. Brunelli M, Castelluci V, Kandel ER: Synaptic facilitation and behavioral sensitization in *Aplysia:* possible role of serotonin and cyclic AMP. *Science* 194:1176, 1976.

35. Andersen P, Sundberg SH, Sveen O, et al: Specific long-lasting potentiation of synaptic transmission in hippocampal slices. *Nature* 266:736–737, 1977.

36. Gallagher BM, Fowler JS, Gutterson NI, et al: Metabolic trapping as a principle of radiopharmaceutical design: Some factors responsible for the biodistribution of ^{18}F 2-deoxy-2-fluoro-D-glucose. *J Nucl Med* 19:1154, 1978.

37. Sokoloff L, Reivich M, Kennedy C, et al: The ^{14}C-deoxyglucose method for the measurement of local cerebral glucose utilization: theory, procedure, and normal values in the conscious and anesthetized albino rat. *J Neurochem* 28:897, 1977.

38. Agranoff BW: Biochemical strategies in the study of memory formation, in Tower DB, Brady RO (eds): *The Nervous System, Basic Neurosciences, vol 1.* New York, Raven Press, 1975, p 585.

11

Neurochemical Correlates of Discriminative Learning Disabilities in Experimental Phenylketonuric Rats and in Postnatally Undernourished Rats

Shin-ichi Kohsaka
Yasuzo Tsukada

INTRODUCTION

The formation of the neuronal network in the central nervous system during development is not only a genetically programmed event but it is also highly modulated by environmental factors such as somatosensory inputs, hormonal secretion, and nutritional state. Human mental retardation is in some instances thought to be the outcome of the aberrant patterns of brain development. Some forms of mental retardation, such as Down's syndrome, are the result of genetic abnormalities, and other forms are the result of changes in response to metabolic abnormalities or nutritional inbalances.

It is well known that severe mental retardation accompanies phenylketonuria and that growth restriction due to undernutrition at an early developmental stage results in irreversible deficit of mental function (11,23,25).

In this chapter, the relationship between neurochemical changes and behavioral abnormalities in experimental phenylketonuric rats and in postnatally undernourished rats was investigated to clarify some possible neurochemical mechanisms involved in higher nervous activities, such as learning and memory.

MATERIALS AND METHODS

Preparation of Experimental Animals

Experimental Phenylketonuric Rats (PKU Rats)

Pregnant Wistar albino rats were obtained from an animal dealer. After delivery, the pups were nursed eight to each dam for 21 days. Thereafter, they were divided into two groups at random. One group of pups was fed a normal diet from the twenty-second day of age for several months (control rats). The other group of pups was fed a high phenylalanine diet containing 7% L-phenylalanine from the twenty-second day of age for several months (PKU rats). Some PKU rats were fed the high phenylalanine diet from the twenty-second day of age up to 3 months of age, after which they were "rehabilitated" be feeding them the normal diet (R-PKU rats).

Postnatally Undernourished Rats (C-D Rats)

From the first day of gestation, one group of pregnant Wistar albino rats was fed the normal diet containing 25% casein (control dams), and the other group of pregnant rats was fed a low-protein diet containing 12% casein (deprived dams). After delivery, the pups from the control dams were divided into two groups at random. One group of the pups was nursed by the control dams, which were fed the normal diet, and after weaning the pups were continuously fed the normal diet for several months (control rats). The other group of the pups was nursed by deprived dams, which were fed the low-protein diet, and after weaning they were continuously fed the low-protein diet for several months (Continuously-Deprived rats).

The diagram of the procedure for preparation of experimental rats is shown in Figure 11-1. The calories of both the normal diet and the low protein diet were adjusted to the same level (3.5 Kcal/gm) by adding cornstarch to the low protein diet. The normal diet,

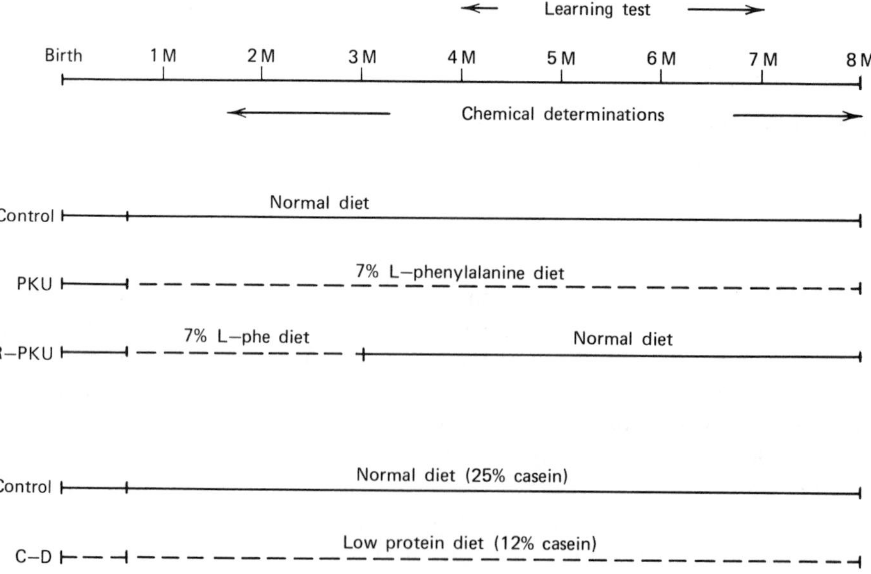

Figure 11-1. Diagram of the experimental procedure for preparation of experimental phenylketonuric rats and of postnatally undernourished rats.

the low protein diet, and the high phenylalanine diet were purchased from Oriental East Co. Ltd. (Tokyo).

Chemical Determinations

Chemical determinations were carried out in rats 50 days, 4 months, 7 months, or 8 months of age. After decapitation, brain tissue was rapidly removed and separated into several regions (pallium cerebri, brain stem, and cerebellum) under cold conditions. DNA content in the cerebrum was measured by the method of Burton (1) after the extraction procedures of Schmidt and Thannhauser (21), and Schneider (22). The concentration of free amino acids in the ethanol-chloroform extract of the pallium cerebri and plasma was determined using an automatic amino acid analyzer (Nihon Denshi Co. Ltd., JLC-6AH). The tryptophan content in the brain stem was measured by the method of Denckla and Dewey (3). The 5-hydroxytryptamine (5-HT) and the 5-hydroxyindolacetic acid (5-HIAA) content in the cerebrum was determined by the fluorometric method of Fischer et al (6), and the dopamine (DA) and the norepinephrine (NE) content was measured by the method of Chan (2). The activity of 2′,3′-cyclic nucleotide 3′-phosphohydrolase (CNPase) in several brain regions was assayed by the method of Kurihara and Tsukada (10) or by the method of Tsukada et al (27). The tryptophan hydroxylase activity in the brain stem was measured by the method of Martin and Patterson (12) using 30,000 gm of supernatant of the homogenate.

Operant Brightness Discriminative Learning Test

When the experimental rats reached 4 months of age, a brightness discriminative learning test was performed. Subjects were housed individually, and their body weights were maintained at about 80% of their free feeding weight throughout the learning experiment.

On the first day of the training, the rats were conditioned to press a bar under a continuous reinforcement schedule (CRF-80) during which bright light (8000 lux) was displayed on the front wall of a Skinner box, and food pellets were used (36 mg) as the reinforcer. From the second day of the learning test, they were trained under a schedule of variable interval (VI). In this training, when bright light (8,000 lux) was displayed on the stimulus panel as a positive stimuls (S^+), bar-pressing responses were reinforced under a VI schedule. On the other hand, when dim light (8 or 80 lux) was displayed as a negative stimulus (S^-), reinforcement was not available even after bar-pressing responses. Each daily session consisted of 20 S^+ and 20 S^- presentations, one presentation being 25 to 30 seconds. These conditioned stimuli were presented at random in accordance with a Gellerman series. In some learning tests, a blackout period (darkness) of 5 seconds was used between each conditioned stimulus. The length of the variable interval of reinforcement was gradually increased from 5 seconds to 15 or 30 seconds. The correct response ratio ($R^+/R^+ + R^-$) was calculated from the number of correct responses (R^+) during S^+ presentations and the number of incorrect responses (R^-) during S^- presentations in each session. The criterion was set at a correct response ratio of 85% in three successive sessions. The training was continued until the subjects were able to attain the criterion of the learning test or for 25 to 40 sessions. The apparatus was controlled by a microcomputer (Unitec Electronics Co. Ltd., UP-8).

RESULTS AND DISCUSSION

Phenylketonuric Rats

Amino Acid Concentrations

Table 11-1 shows the amino acid content in the pallium cerebri and in plasma of 50-day-old rats. High phenylalanine levels were observed in both the pallium cerebri and plasma of the PKU rats. The tyrosine content was also significantly elevated in both the pallium cerebri and plasma of the PKU rats. The percent increase of phenylalanine in plasma was much higher than that of tyrosine. The content of other amino acids such as aspartate, glutamate, and GABA was decreased to varying extents. This was thought to be due to the inhibition of carbohydrate metabolism by the accumulation of phenylalanine in the cerebrum (17). In the urine of the PKU rats, 5mg/dl of phenylpyruvate, which is excreted in the urine of PKU patients, was detected. From these results, it was concluded that a useful model of phenylketonuria could be produced by feeding rats a high phenylalanine diet, even though it was accompanied by hypertyrosinemia.

Body Weight, Cerebral Weight, and DNA Content

The body weight gain was significantly lowered in the PKU rats at the age of 50 days and 7 months, as shown in Table 11-2. This result might be due to the nutritional inbalance of amino acids. The cerebral weight of the PKU rats tended to be low, but not significantly. The DNA content per cerebrum of the PKU rats did not differ from that of the control rats at either age. In the rat, it was believed that the proliferation of neuronal and glial cells in the cerebrum are finished at an early postnatal stage of development (13). Therefore, in PKU rats fed the high phenylalanine diet after the age of 22 days, proliferation of neuronal and glial cells was assumed to be unaffected. But the slight decrease in the cerebral weight might indicate that the cerebral cells are a little smaller than those of the controls.

Indolamine Content and its Metabolism

5-HT is thought to be a neurotransmitter in the central nervous system. Many investigators have reported a decrease in the content of 5-HT in plasma and in the brain of

Table 11-1. Amino Acid Concentration in the Pallium Cerebri and in the Plasma of 50-Day-Old Rats

	Pallium Cerebri (μmole/gm)		*Plasma (μmole/ml)*	
	Control (4)[b]	*PKU (4)*	*Control (4)*	*PKU (4)*
Aspartate	3.41 ± 0.09[a]	1.79 ± 0.16[c]		
Glutamate	8.82 ± 0.29	6.45 ± 0.22[c]		
GABA	2.53 ± 0.25	1.86 ± 0.18		
Tyrosine	0.10 ± 0.03	0.67 ± 0.17[c]	0.09 ± 0.01	0.48 ± 0.13[c]
Phenylalanine	0.10 ± 0.02	0.73 ± 0.17[c]	0.08 ± 0.02	2.01 ± 0.69[c]

[a] Mean ± SE.

[b] ( ): Number of rats used.

[c] The values were significantly different from the controls ($P < 0.01$ by t test).

Table 11-2. Body Weight, Cerebral Weight, and DNA Content per Cerebrum of 50-Day-Old and 7-Month-Old Rats

	Body Weight (gm)	*Cerebral Weight (gm)*	*DNA Content (mg)*
50-day-old			
Control (4)[a]	210 ± 17[b]	1.17 ± 0.04	1.08 ± 0.03
PKU (4)	84 ± 9[c]	1.06 ± 0.01	1.03 ± 0.01
7-month-old			
Control (4)	374 ± 14	1.33 ± 0.03	1.16 ± 0.03
PKU (4)	265 ± 6[c]	1.21 ± 0.03	1.13 ± 0.02
R-PKU[d](4)	311 ± 15[c]	1.28 ± 0.05	1.13 ± 0.04

[a] ( ): Number of rats used.

[b] Mean ± SE.

[c] The values were significantly different from the controls ($P < 0.01$ by t test).

[d] Rehabilitated PKU rats.

PKU animals and of PKU patients (8,14,15,20,29), and it was assumed to be one of the possible factors leading to mental retardation in PKU.

The 5-HT and 5-HIAA content in the cerebrum of the PKU rats was measured to learn whether or not serotonergic neurons develop normally in the high phenylalanine environment. As shown in Table 11-3, the 5-HT and 5-HIAA content decreased remarkably in both the pallium cerebri and the brain stem of the PKU rats measured at ages of 50 days and 4 months. In addition, the tryptophan content and the tryptophan hydroxylase activity in the brain stem of the PKU rats at the age of 5 months were measured. Both the tryptophan content and the tryptophan hydroxylase activity were decreased significantly in the PKU rats compared with those of the controls. The decrease in the tryptophan content can be explained by the competitive inhibition of tryptophan uptake into the brain due to the high phenylalanine concentration in the plasma. Also, tryptophan hydroxylase activity might be competitively inhibited by the high phenylalanine concentration in the brain (9,24,30). Consequently, the decreases in 5-HT and 5-HIAA might be explained by the lack of precursor and the low activity of tryptophan hydroxylase. In either event, it appeared that the serotonergic neuronal function could be suppressed in the PKU rat brain.

2′,3′-Cyclic Nucleotide 3′-Phosphohydrolase (CNPase) Activity

CNPase activity is associated with the central myelin sheath and is thought to be a good marker enzyme of myelin in the central nervous system, as was reported by Kurihara and Tsukada (10). The CNPase activities in the various brain regions of the PKU rats were measured as a marker of myelination in the central nervous system. Table 11-4 showed the CNPase activities in the pallium cerebri, the brain stem, and the cerebellum of 4-month-old and 8-month-old rats. in the PKU rats, a significant decrease in CNPase activity was observed in the pallium cerebri and in the brain stem at both ages. But a significant decrease of CNPase activity was not found in the cerebellum. It was therefore considered that myelin formation in the PKU rat cerebrum was disturbed during postnatal development by the high phenylalanine environment. As is well known,

Table 11-3. The Content of 5-HT, 5-HIAA, Tryptophan, and Tryptophan Hydroxylase Activity in the Cerebrum of the Rats

	Pallium Cerebri		*Brain Stem*	
	5-HT (*μg/gm w/w*)	*5-HIAA* (*μg/gm w/w*)	*5-HT* (*μg/gm w/w*)	*5-HIAA* (*μg/gm w/w*)
50-day-old				
Control (5)[a]	0.79 ± 0.01[b]	0.56 ± 0.02	1.04 ± 0.04	0.88 ± 0.02
PKU (5)	0.33 ± 0.05[c]	0.11 ± 0.03[c]	0.43 ± 0.07[c]	0.17 ± 0.04[c]
4-month-old				
Control (3)	0.75 ± 0.02	0.39 ± 0.02	1.12 ± 0.03	0.67 ± 0.02
PKU (3)	0.54 ± 0.04[c]	0.12 ± 0.02[c]	0.71 ± 0.07[c]	0.23 ± 0.02[c]
R-PKU[d](3)	0.90 ± 0.05	0.41 ± 0.01	1.28 ± 0.05	0.73 ± 0.05
	Tryptophan Content[e] (*nmole/gm w/w*)		*Tryptophan Hydroxylase Activity*[e] (*nmole/mg protein/hr*)	
7-month-old				
Control	13.5 ± 0.4 (3)		1.49 ± 0.07 (5)	
PKU	10.9 ± 0.3[c] (3)		1.13 ± 0.07[c] (5)	

[a] ( ): Number of rats used.

[b] Mean ± SE.

[c] The values were significantly different from the controls ($P < 0.01$ by t test).

[d] Rehabilitated PKU rats.

[e] Measured only in the brain stem.

Table 11-4. 2′, 3′-Cyclic Nucleotide 3′-Phosphohydrolase Activities in Several Regions of the Rat Brain[a]

	Pallium Cerebri (*units/mg protein*)	*Brain Stem* (*units/mg protein*)	*Cerebellum* (*units/mg protein*)
4-month-old			
Control (3)[b]	3.25 ± 0.02[c]	5.33 ± 0.02	3.05 ± 0.17
PKU (3)	2.79 ± 0.08[d]	4.67 ± 0.01[d]	2.78 ± 0.11
8-month-old			
Control (5)	3.16 ± 0.04	5.34 ± 0.06	2.90 ± 0.07
PKU (5)	2.76 ± 0.06[d]	4.26 ± 0.19[d]	2.59 ± 0.05
7-month-old			
Control (4)	3.18 ± 0.14	5.66 ± 0.13	3.18 ± 0.10
R-PKU[e](4)	2.57 ± 0.09[d]	5.05 ± 0.04[d]	3.21 ± 0.05

[a] The activity was assayed using the method developed by Kurihara and Tsukada (10). One unit of enzyme activity was defined as the amount that produces 1 μmole of adenosine 2′-phosphate in 1 minute.

[b] ( ): Number of rats used.

[c] Mean ± SE.

[d] The values were significantly different from the controls ($P < 0.01$ by t test).

[e] Rehabilitated PKU rats.

myelin is formed by oligodendroglia in the central nervous system. However, the proliferation of glial cells in the cerebrum is believed to occur in the early postnatal period (13). Therefore, in the PKU rats, the amino acid imbalance due to the high phenylalanine diet given after the age of 22 days might have an effect on the process of the maturation of glial cells but not on that of the proliferation of oligodendrocytes. In other experimental rats that were produced in our laboratory, such as hypothyroid rats (19,26) and neonatally hydrocortisone intoxicated rats (18), the decrease of CNPase activity was also found only in the pallium cerebri and in the brain stem. From these obervations, it was assumed that cerebral myelination was more sensitive to environmental factors than were other brain elements.

Rehabilitated PKU Rats (R-PKU Rats)

The rehabilitation of the PKU rats was achieved by the schedule shown in Figure 11-1. The rats were fed the high phenylalanine diet from the twenty-second day up to 3 months of age, and thereafter they were fed the normal diet for several months (R-PKU rats).

In the R-PKU rats, the body weight gain was slightly restored but still was lower than that of the controls at the age of 7 months. The cerebral weight and the DNA content per cerebrum did not differ from those of the controls. Therefore, the cell population and the cell size in the cerebrum of the R-PKU rats seemed to be normal.

In the R-PKU rats, the 5-HT and 5-HIAA content in the pallium cerebri and in the brain stem was normal, compared with that of the control rats (Table 11-3). Hence, the suppression of the serotonergic function of the PKU rats seemed to be restored by feeding a normal diet after the age of 3 months. This might be due to the normalization of amino acid inbalance in the brain and in the plasma of the R-PKU rats.

The CNPase activity in the pallium cerebri, the brain stem, and the cerebellum was determined at the age of 7 months. As shown in Table 11-4, the CNPase activity still remained low in the pallium cerebri and in the brain stem of the R-PKU rats. It seems that the disturbance of myelination caused by amino acid inbalance during the early postnatal period could not be reversed by feeding a normal diet after the age of 3 months.

Discriminative Learning Ability and Its Correlation to Neurochemical Changes

Operant brightness discriminative learning abilities of the PKU and R-PKU rats were tested. Figure 11-2 shows the mean correct response ratio of the subjects throughout the learning test. In the control rats, the mean correct response ratio increased with daily training, and all the control subjects were able to attain the learning criterion within 40 sessions. In the PKU and R-PKU rats, the mean correct response ratio also increased gradually with training, but none of the subjects could attain the learning criterion within 40 sessions. After 40 sessions, the mean correct response ratio of the PKU and R-PKU rats remained at 70% or 80%. We concluded that the discriminative learning ability of both PKU and R-PKU rats was considerably poorer than that of the control rats. T-maze learning ability was examined in our laboratory using rats that were fed a high tyrosine diet and had hypertyrosinemia (7). The rats with hypertyrosinemia showed normal learning ability. It is well known that patients who have a high plasma tyrosine concentration, such as in albinism, have normal mental functions. Therefore, these considerations further suggest that the learning disabilities of the PKU and R-

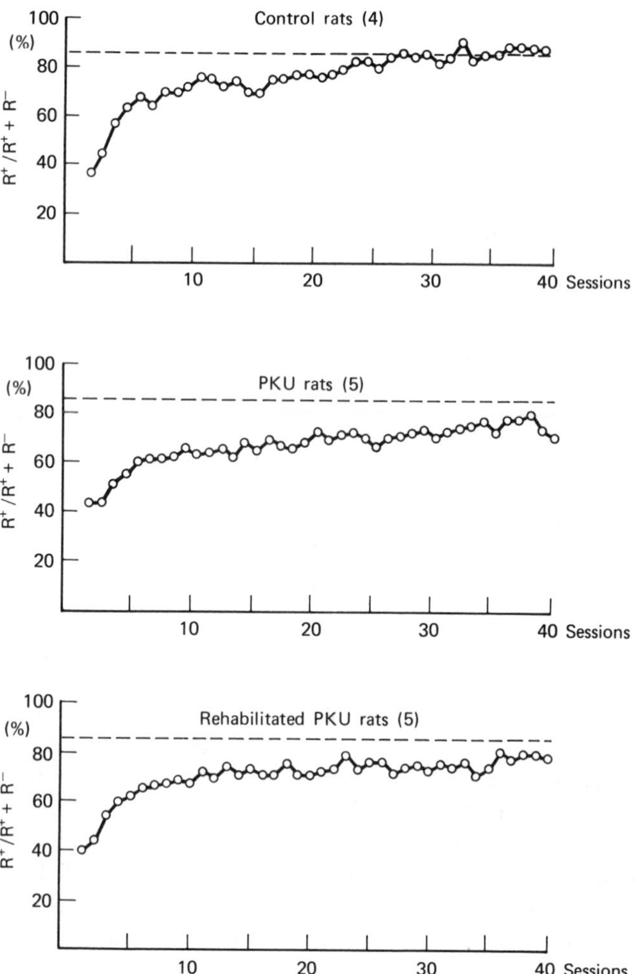

Figure 11-2. Changes in the mean correct response ratio. In this learning test, bright light (8000 lux) was used as S^+ and dim light (80 lux) was used as S^-, one presentation being 30 seconds. No blackout period was used. The final length of the variable interval was 30 seconds. Each point represents the mean correct response ratio of the subjects. ( ): number of rats used.

PKU rats are probably caused by the hyperphenylalaninemia during the early postnatal stage of development. These results make it clear that the low activity of cerebral CNPase, which seems to reflect the dysmyelination in the cerebrum, is closely related to discriminative learning disability in the PKU and R-PKU rats.

Postnatally Undernourished Rats (C-D Rats)

To confirm the relationship between the decrease in cerebral CNPase activity and the learning disability, further investigations were made with postnatally undernourished rats (C-D rats).

Neurochemical data are shown in Table 11-5. The body weight gain was lowered in the C-D rats, but cerebral weight and DNA content per cerebrum did not differ from those of the control rats at the age of 4 months. In this case, cell proliferation in the cerebrum seemed to be unaffected by postnatal undernourishment.

The 5-HT and 5-HIAA content decreased significantly in the pallium cerebri and in the brain stem of the C-D rats. tryptophan content and tryptophan hydroxylase activity in the brain stem of the C-D rats also decreased considerably. This could be attributed to a decrease in the size of the amino acid pools and in protein synthesis resulting from protein restriction in the diet. It might further be considered that the serotonergic neuronal function was impaired in the C-D rats by the protein restriction during postnatal development.

A significant decrease in CNPase activity was observed in the pallium cerebri and in the brain stem of the C-D rats. However, there was no change in CNPase activity in the cerebellum of the C-D rats. It is probable that the myelin formation in the cerebrum was disturbed by the protein restriction in the postnatal stages.

Figure 11-3 shows the mean correct response ratio during training of the control rats and the C-D rats. In this learning test, the mean correct response ratio of the control rats increased day by day, and they were able to attain the learning criterion within 15 sessions. In the C-D rats, the mean correct response ratio increased gradually with daily training, but the subjects could not achieve the learning criterion within 25 sessions.

Table 11-5. Neurochemical Data on Postnatally Undernourished 4-Month-Old Rats

	Control	*C-D*
Body weight (gm)	369 ± 14[a] (4)[b]	304 ± 8[c] (5)
Cerebral weight (gm)	1.35 ± 0.03 (4)	1.30 ± 0.04 (5)
DNA (mg)/cerebrum	1.11 ± 0.03 (4)	1.10 ± 0.06 (5)
5-HT content (μg/gm w/w)		
Pallium cerebri	0.70 ± 0.02 (6)	0.57 ± 0.03[c] (4)
Brain stem	1.06 ± 0.03 (6)	0.88 ± 0.05[c] (4)
Tryptophan content (nmole/gm w/w)	11.4 ± 0.3 (12)	8.5 ± 0.6[c] (5)
Tryptophan hydroxylase (nmole/mg protein/hr)	1.71 ± 0.05 (6)	1.42 ± 0.07[c] (4)
CNPase[d] (units/mg protein)		
Pallium cerebri	2.35 ± 0.06 (4)	1.62 ± 0.07[c] (5)
Brain stem	3.99 ± 0.13 (4)	2.39 ± 0.12[c] (5)
Cerebellum	2.37 ± 0.13 (4)	2.26 ± 0.06 (5)

[a] Mean ± SE.

[b] ( ): Number of rats used.

[c] The values were significantly different from the controls ($P < 0.01$ by t test).

[d] CNPase activity was assayed using the method developed by Tsukada et al (27). One unit of enzyme activity was defined as the amount that produces 1 μmole of adenosine 2′-phosphate in 1 minute.

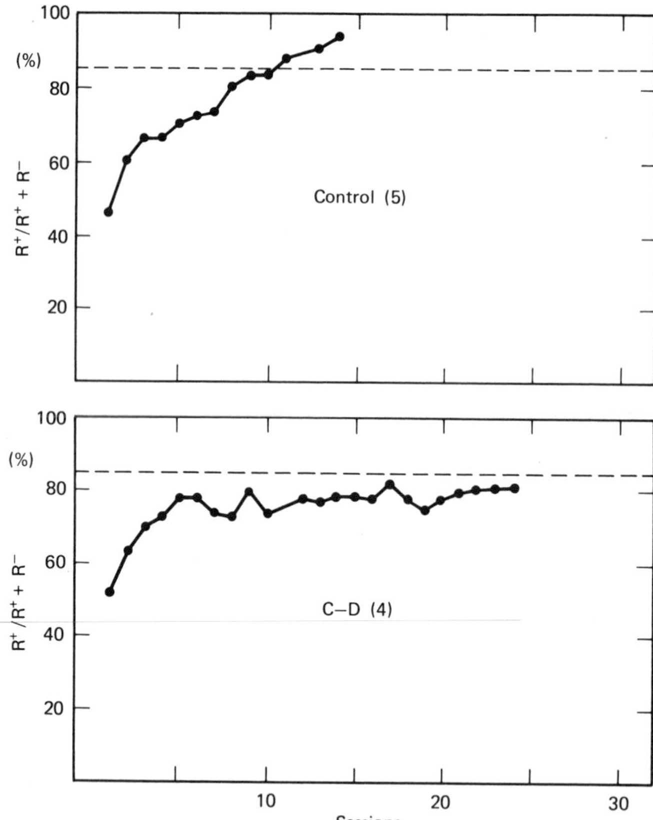

Figure 11-3. Changes in the mean correct response ratio. In this learning test, bright light (8000 lux) was used as S^+ and dim light (8 lux) was used as S^-, one presentation being 25 seconds. A blackout period of 5 seconds was used between each stimulus. The final length of the variable interval was 15 seconds. Each point represents the mean correct response ratio of the subjects. ( ): number of rats used.

Thus, it seems that learning ability is retarded in the C-D rats compared with the control rats.

In these results, the decrease in cerebral CNPase activity again seems to correlate with the learning disability of the C-D rats. However, correlation of the serotonergic dysfunction in the brain to the learning disability can not be excluded.

We next examined the correlation between the monoamine content in the cerebrum and learning ability.

Correlation Between Cerebral Monoamine Content and Learning Ability

Figure 11-4 shows a diagram of the experimental procedure. Male Wistar albino adult rats were used as experimental animals. After they were taught to press a bar, they were trained for 2 or 3 weeks according to the method described in this chapter. In this learning test, a small lamp (24 VDC) in the Skinner box was used as S^+, and darkness was used as S^-. After a training period of 2 or 3 weeks, all the rats were able to attain the learning criterion. Therefore, they were overtrained for an additional 2 weeks to obtain a stable correct response ratio. Then the effect of changes of the monoamine content in the brain on the learning ability was examined. In this experiment, to increase the monoamine content in the brain, several doses of amine precursors such as 5-hydroxytryptophan (5-HTP) and L-dihydroxyphenylalanine (L-dopa) were administered orally, and 2 hours later the learning abilities of the rats were examined. On the other hand, to decrease the monoamine content in the brain, 2 mg/kg of reserpine was injected subcutaneously 24 hours before the learning test.

In another experiment, the effect of changes of cerebral monoamine contents on the learning process was examined. 5-HTP (50 mg/kg) or L-dopa (200 mg/kg) was administered to untrained rats daily 2 hours before training, and the training process was observed from the point of view of correct response ratio.

Table 11-6 shows the content of 5-HT, 5-HIAA, dopamine (DA), and norepinephrine (NE) in the pallium cerebri and in the brain stem 2 hours after the administration of 5-HTP or L-dopa and 24 hours after the injection of reserpine. After the administration of 320 mg/kg of L-dopa, the DA content increased remarkably, but the NE content decreased. There were no changes in the 5-HT and 5-HIAA content. After the administration of 25 mg/kg and 100 mg/kg of 5-HTP, the 5-HT and 5-HIAA content increased, and a dose response could be seen, but the DA and NE content decreased slightly. Twenty-four hours after the injection of 2 mg/kg of reserpine, the 5-HT, DA, and NE content decreased significantly, but the 5-HIAA content remained

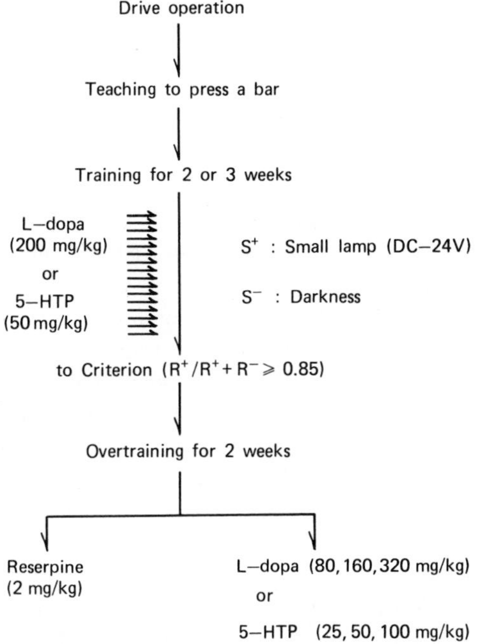

Figure 11-4. Diagram of the experimental procedure.

Table 11-6. The Content of 5-HT, 5-HIAA, DA, and NE in the Pallium Cerebri and in the Brain Stem After the Administration of Amine Precursors and Reserpine

	5-HT (*μg/gm w/w*)	*5-HIAA* (*μg/gm w/w*)	*DA* (*μg/gm w/w*)	*NE* (*μg/gm w/w*)
Pallium Cerebri				
Control (6)[a]	1.01 ± 0.04[b]	0.49 ± 0.03	0.23 ± 0.02	0.11 ± 0.01
L-dopa (3) (320 mg/kg)	1.02 ± 0.02	0.54 ± 0.03	1.96 ± 0.18[c]	0.06 ± 0.02
5-HTP (6) (25 mg/kg)	1.17 ± 0.05	1.02 ± 0.01[c]	0.11 ± 0.01[d]	0.09 ± 0.01
5-HTP (9) (100 mg/kg)	1.39 ± 0.03[c]	1.95 ± 0.14[c]	0.11 ± 0.01[d]	0.08 ± 0.01
Reserpine (3) (2 mg/kg)	0.31 ± 0.09[c]	0.55 ± 0.04	0.14 ± 0.02[d]	0.03 ± 0.01[c]
Brain stem				
Control (6)	1.42 ± 0.03	0.85 ± 0.04	0.45 ± 0.03	0.15 ± 0.01
L-dopa (3) (320 mg/kg)	1.52 ± 0.03	1.03 ± 0.05	0.64 ± 0.03[d]	0.08 ± 0.01[d]
5-HTP (6) (25 mg/kg)	1.59 ± 0.04	1.39 ± 0.02[c]	0.15 ± 0.02[c]	0.09 ± 0.01[d]
5-HTP (9) (100 mg/kg)	1.84 ± 0.02[c]	2.86 ± 0.25[c]	0.17 ± 0.03[c]	0.08 ± 0.01[d]
Reserpine (3) (2 mg/kg)	0.40 ± 0.10[c]	1.20 ± 0.12[d]	0.23 ± 0.01[c]	0.03 ± 0.01[c]

[a] ( ): Number of rats used.

[b] Mean ± SE.

[c,d] The values were significantly different from the controls ([c] $P < 0.01$, [d] $P < 0.05$ by *t* test).

unchanged. Under these conditions, the discriminative learning ability of the rat was tested.

Figure 11-5(*a*) shows the changes in the number of correct responses (R^+) of the overtrained rats that were given 5-HTP, L-dopa, or reserpine. There was no change in the number of correct responses after the administration of L-dopa regardless of the size of the dose (80 mg, 160 mg, and 320 mg/kg). There was also no change in the number of correct responses observed after the administration of 5-HTP in small doses (25 mg or 50 mg/kg). However, the number of responses clearly decreased after the administration of 100 mg/kg of 5-HTP or 2 mg/kg of reserpine. Figure 11-5(*b*) shows the correct response ratio of the rats that were given 5-HTP or L-dopa. There was no change in the correct response ratio after the administration of L-dopa or 5-HTP, even after the administration of 100 mg/kg of 5-HTP. However, in the case of reserpine injection, it seemed useless to calculate the correct response ratio, since the total number of responses was so small.

Thus, it can be concluded that changes in cerebral monoamine content have no effect on the learning ability of rats that have already attained the learning criterion. However, a significant increase in 5-HT content in the cerebrum caused suppression of motor activity. Although Essman (4,5) reported an amnestic effect of 5-HT on learning performance in mice, we did not observe any such effect as far as discriminative learning was concerned.

Figure 11-6 shows the effect of amine precursor administration on the process of learning. 5-HTP or L-dopa was administered daily 2 hours before training. In this case, the rats attained the learning criterion just as well as the control rats. This indicates that the elevation of monoamine content in the cerebrum had no effect on the learning process.

GENERAL DISCUSSION

In this experiment, neurochemical changes and discriminative learning abilities were examined using experimental phenylketonuric rats, rehabilitated experimental phenylketonuric rats, and postnatally undernourished rats. The results suggested that the low activity of CNPase in the cerebrum was more closely correlated with discriminative learning disability in cerebral impaired rats than with cerebral weight, number of cells in the cerebrum, or monoamine content in the cerebrum.

Consequently, we believe that myelination in the cerebrum during early postnatal development is important for supporting higher nervous activities. The reason why myelination in the cerebrum is so important for attainment of discriminative learning needs to be studied further, particularly in regard to synaptogenesis and glial function.

The correlation between discriminative learning ability and the monoamine content in the cerebrum was also investigated. No causal relationship was found as far as discriminative learning was concerned, although it has been reported that the changes in the monoamine content of the cerebrum control affect, mood, and emotional behavior in rats and mice (16,28).

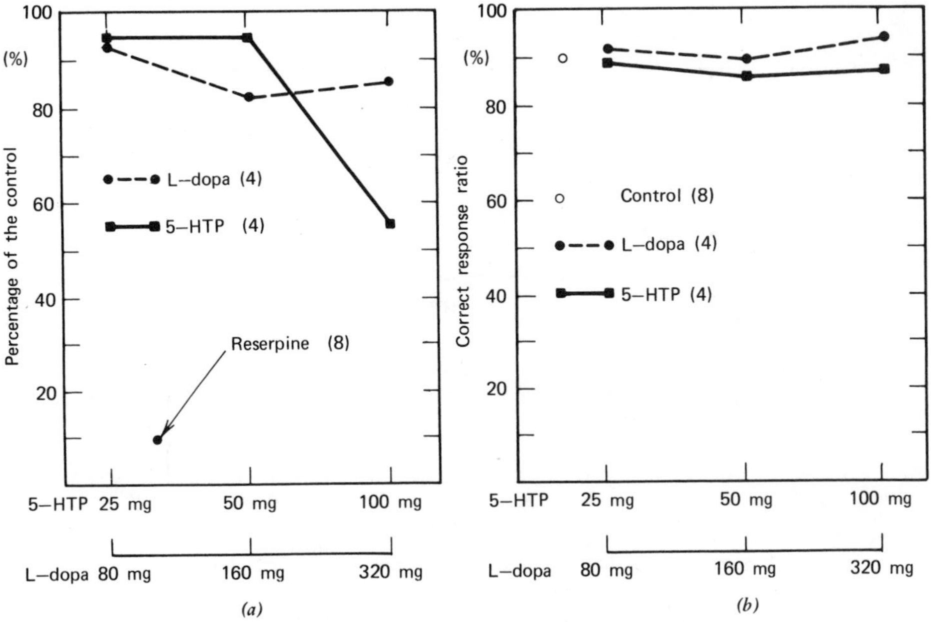

Figure 11-5. (*a*) Number of correct responses. (*b*) Correct response ratio. ( ): number of rats used.

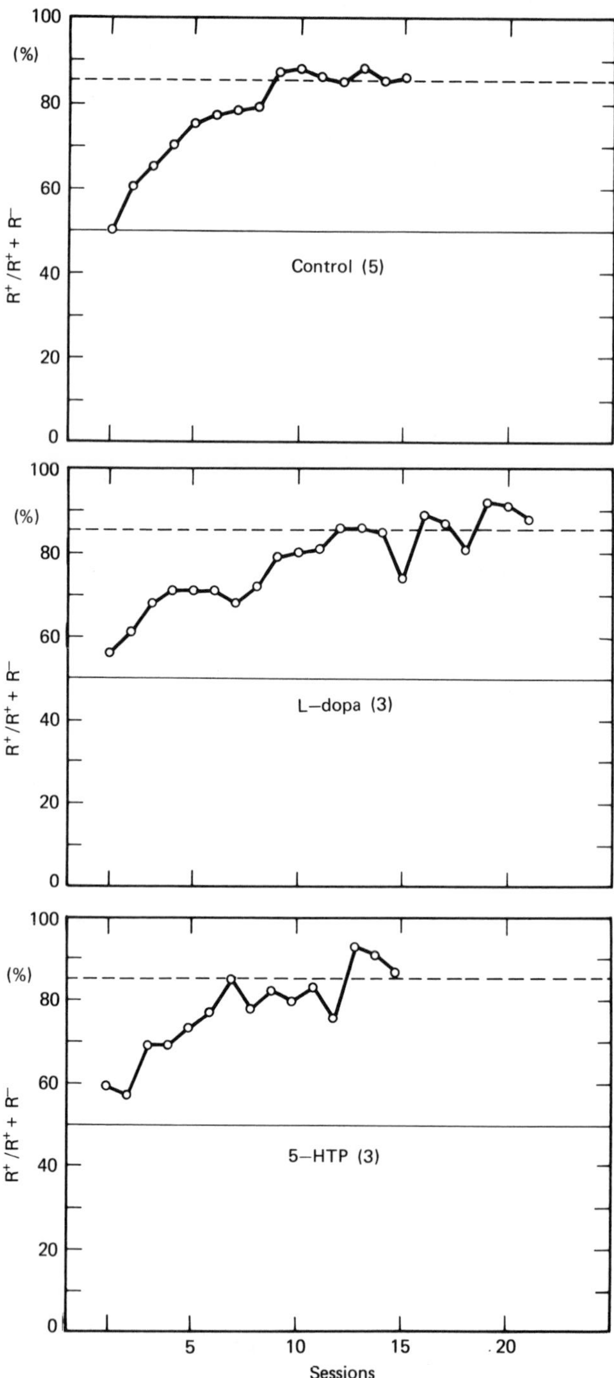

Figure 11-6. Changes in the mean correct response ratio. In this learning test, a small lamp (DC-24V) was used as S^+, and darkness was used as S^-, one presentation being 30 seconds. The final length of the variable interval was 15 seconds. Each point represents the mean correct response ratio of the subjects. ( ): number of rats used.

SUMMARY

The correlation between discriminative learning ability and neurochemical changes such as cerebral weight, DNA content, monoamine content, and CNPase activity was investigated in PKU (high phenylalanine diet), R-PKU (rehabilitated after 2 months on the diet), and C-D rats (malnourished postnatally).

Body weight gain was clearly lowered in the PKU, R-PKU, and C-D rats, but cerebral weight and DNA content per cerebrum did not differ from those of the control rats. The 5-HT, 5-HIAA, and tryptophan content and tryptophan hydroxylase activity in the cerebrum of the PKU and C-D rats were significantly decreased, while the R-PKU rats showed normal values. The activity of CNPase, a marker enzyme of central myelin, decreased significantly in the cerebrum of the PKU, R-PKU, and C-D rats. We concluded that cerebral myelin formation was disturbed in the experimental rats. Brightness discriminative learning ability was impaired in the PKU, R-PKU, and C-D rats compared with the control rats.

Our results strongly suggest that the decrease in CNPase activity is more closely related to discriminative learning disability in these cerebrally impaired rats than cerebral weight, number of cells in the cerebrum, or cerebral monoamine content.

The relationship between the monoamine content in the cerebrum and learning ability was also examined. Changes in monoamine content in the cerebrum had no effect on the learning ability of rats that had already attained the learning criterion. Furthermore, when monoamine precursors were administered during training, the resulting elevation of monoamine content in the cerebrum had no effect on the learning process.

REFERENCES

1. Burton K: A study of the conditions and mechanism of the diphenylamine reaction for the colorimetiric estimation of deoxyribonucleic acid. *Biochem J* 62:315–323, 1956.
2. Chan CC: A sensitive method for spectrofluorometric assay of catecholamines. *Int J Neuropharmacol* 3:643–649, 1964.
3. Denckla WD, Dewey HK: The determination of tryptophan in plasma, liver and urine. *J Lab Clin Med* 69:160–169, 1967.
4. Essman WB: Experimentally induced retrograde amnesia; some neurochemical correlates. In: *Current Biochemical Approaches to Learning and Memory*. New York, Spectrum Pub, 1973, pp 159–188.
5. Essman WB: Serotonin in learning and memory, in Essman W. B. (ed) *Serotonin in Health and Disease*. Vol 3: *The Central Nervous System*. Spectrum Pub, 1978, pp 145-201.
6. Fischer CA, Kariya T, Aprison MH: A comparison of the distribution of 5-hydroxyindol acetic acid and 5-hydroxytryptamine in four specific areas of the rat and pigeon. *Comp Gen Pharmacol* 1:61–68, 1970.
7. Hirano S, Noguchi T, Tsukada Y: Studies on experimental phenylketonuria using rat and monkey. *Bull Japanese Neurochemical Society* 3:77–80, 1964 (in Japanese).
8. Hsia DY, Nishimura K, Brenchley Y: Mechanisms for the decrease of brain serotonin. *Nature* 200:578, 1963.
9. Kohsaka S: Studies on neurochemical changes and behavioral abnormality in experimental phenylketonuric rats. *J Keio Medical Society* 54:173–192, 1977 (in Japanese).
10. Kurihara T, Tsukada Y: The regional and subcellular distribution of 2′,3′-cyclic nucleotide 3′-phosphohydrolase in the central nervous system. *J Neurochem* 14:1167–1174, 1967.
11. Latham MC: Protein-calorie malnutrition in children and its relation to psychological development and behavior. *Physiol Rev* 54:541–565, 1974.

12. Martin GE, Patterson K: Rapid non-isotopic assay of tryptophan-5-hydroxylase activity in tissues. *Analytical Biochem* 52:625–629, 1973.

13. McIlwain H, Bachelard HS: Chemical and enzymic make-up of the brain during development, in *Biochemistry and the Central Nervous System.* Edinburgh, Churchill Livingstone Press, 1971, pp 406–444.

14. McKean CM, Schanberg SM, Giarman NJ: Aminoacidurias; effects on maze performance and cerebral serotonin. *Science* 157:213–215, 1967.

15. McKean CM: The effects of high phenylalanine concentrations on serotonin and catecholamine metabolism in the human brain. *Brain Res* 47:469–476, 1972.

16. Murphy DL, Redmond DE Jr: The catecholamines; possible role in affect, mood, and emotional behavior in man and animals. in: *Catecholamines and Behavior,* vol 2. New York, Plenum Press, 1975, pp 73–104.

17. Noguchi T: Regulation of phenylalanine and tyrosine metabolism in vivo and the effects of phenylalanine on the amino acid metabolism in rat brain. *Bull Japanese Neurochemical Society* 6:131–146, 1967 (in Japanese).

18. Noguchi T, Kohsaka S, Aoki E, et al: The effect of bovine growth hormone on the retarded growth in the neonatal hydrocortisone-treated rat. *Neurochem res* 3(5):660–661, 1978.

19. Nomura M, Tsukada Y: Correlation between cerebral CNPase and discriminative learning ability in the rats. *Bull Japanese Neurochemical Society* 12:24–27, 1973 (in Japanese).

20. Pare CM, Sandler M, Stacey RS: 5-Hydroxytryptamine deficiency in phenylketonuria. *Lancet* 272:551–553, 1957.

21. Schmidt G, Thannhauser SJ: A method for determination of deoxyribonucleic acid, ribonucleic acid and phosphoproteins in animal tissues. *J Biol Chem* 161:83–89, 1945.

22. Schneider WC: Phosphorus compounds in animal tissues. I. Extraction and estimation of deoxypentose nucleic acid and pentose nucleic acid. *J Biol Chem* 161:293–303, 1945.

23. Scrimshaw NS: Malnutrition, learning and behavior. *Amer J Clin Nutr* 20:493–502, 1967.

24. Siegel FL, Aoki K, Colwell RE: Polyribosome disaggregation and cell-free protein synthesis in preparations from cerebral cortex of hyperphenylalaninemic rats. *J Neurochem* 18:537–547, 1971.

25. Smart JL, Dobbing J: Vulnerability of developing brain. II. Effects of early nutritional deprivation on reflex ontogency and development of behavior in the rats. *Brain Res* 28:85–95, 1971.

26. Tsukada Y, Nomura M, Nagai K, et al: Neurochemical correlates of learning ability, in: Delgado JMR and DeFeudis FV (eds): *Behavioral Neurochemistry.* New York, Spectrum Pub 1977, pp 63–84.

27. Tsukada Y, Nagai K, Suda H: A new method for the measurement of 2′,3′-cyclic nucleotide 3′-phosphohydrolase (CNPase) by high performance liquid chromatography, and an attempt at partial purification of the enzyme from rat brain. *Neurochem Res* 3(5):662–663, 1978.

28. Valzelli L: Affective behavior and serotonin, in Essman WB (ed): *Serotonin in Health and Disease.* Vol 3 in Essman WB (ed): *The Central Nervous System.* Jamaica, NY, Spectrum Pub, 1978, pp 145–201.

29. Yuwiler A, Louttit RT: Effects of phenylalanine diet on brain serotonin in the rats. *Science* 134:831–832, 1961.

30. Yuwiler A, Geller E, Slater GG: On the mechanism of the brain serotonin depletion in experimental phenylketonuria. *J Biol Chem* 240:1170–1174, 1965.

12
Microtubules and Memory: Effects of Vinblastine on Avoidance Training

Tetsuhide H. Murakami

INTRODUCTION

Recently, a number of reports have been published on the structure and function of microtubules in various cells. Microtubules are present in flagella, cilia, and neurons and probably play some role in cellular motility, in the mechanical strength and rigidity of cells, in the transport of solute, and in the direction of axoplasmic organelles within cells. The cyclic formation and breakdown of microtubules is most obvious during mitosis. With the electron microscope, three fibrous forms have been identified in neurons: microtubules, neurofilaments, and microfilaments. Microtubules are about 26 nm in diameter with a wall thickness of 6 nm; neurofilaments are 10 nm in diameter with a wall thickness of 3 nm; and microfilaments are 5 nm in diameter.

The antimitotic drug, vinblastine, belongs to a class of chemically related alkaloids known commonly as vinca alkaloids. These chemicals can destroy microtubules in a wide variety of cells, thereby disrupting the many biological functions that depend on this class of subcellular organelle. In many cases, the dissolution of microtubular structures in vivo is accompanied by the formation of paracrystals as aggregates of various molecular organizations. The effect of vinblastine on neurofilaments and on microfilaments is still unclear. It is reported that vinblastine induces blockage of orthograde and retrograde axonal transport in axons, raises the miniature end-plate potential frequency, and causes giant spontaneous potentials. No changes in membrane resistance occur, but the shape of the action potentials and their rate of rise are somewhat affected.

Taking all of this into consideration, it seems likely that disruption of the structure of microtubules with colchicine or vinblastine could alter the acquisition and retention of

This work was supported by the grant-in-aid "Genetic Improvement of Laboratory Mouse" No. 111,504, 1976, No. 210,704, 1977 and was also supported by the grant-in-aid "Integrative Control Functions of the Brain" No. 212,103, 1977, No. 311,404, 1978, for scientific research from the Ministry of Education, Japan.

learning behavior as a summarized function of higher nervous activity. This chapter deals with the effect of vinblastine on the acquisition and retention of avoidance training in mice.

TRAINING APPARATUS AND TRAINING PROCEDURE

Learning was tested with a training apparatus called a jump-box (Fig. 12-1). It was made of opaque plastic board (30 × 30 × 30 cm), with an electric grid floor of 8-mm brass rods, the centers of which were 30 mm apart. An escape shelf, 15 cm wide, was located 10 cm above the floor and ran completely around the inside of the walls. The conditional stimulus consisted of a light (60 watt lamp) and buzzer (75 phon). Exposure of the animal to the stimulus for 3 seconds was followed by an electric shock, which constituted an unconditional stimulus. The shock was 40 V (AC) and was given for 20 seconds through the grid floor. The average time from the start of one trial.to the start of the next trial was approximately 30 seconds. If the mouse did not respond by jumping up on the escape shelf, the conditional stimulus and electric shock were given for another 20 seconds. If the animal jumped up onto the escape shelf before the onset of the unconditional stimulus, an avoidance response was judged to have occurred. The animal was allowed to remain on the edge of the outside of the box for 20 seconds and was then placed on the grid floor by hand for the next trial. Each animal was given either 30 trials of avoidance training in 15 minutes or 60 trials in 30 minutes. The duration of each training session was 1 week. The schedule of training is shown in Figure 12-1. The apparatus and training procedures were based on those reported by Zemp et al (33).

ANIMALS USED IN THE EXPERIMENTS

Mice of the ddN-F10 strain ranging in age from 6 to 10 weeks and weighing between 20 and 30 grams were used. The mice were handled for 5 minutes to accustom them to

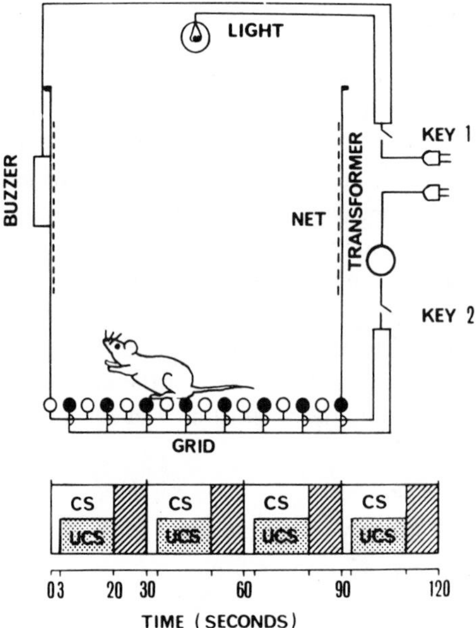

Figure 12-1. Side view of training apparatus and schedule of training.

being handled. This was done on consecutive days before an experiment. Their open-field activity was recorded by an automatic counter over a 5-minute interval.

The standard deviation in learning experiments based on avoidance training in highly inbred mice is greater than that for individuals of the same strain. In view of this, ddN-strain mice, which have a large litter size and high training scores, were selected for breeding based on avoidance training. Such mice were allowed to mate if they had learned to jump up on the escape shelf before the onset of the unconditional stimulus for at least 20 of the first 60 trials. Further improvements were achieved by the mating of full siblings and by a rotation system. From the seventh and later generations of brother and sister matings, mice responding more than 15 times in the first 30 trials were allowed to mate. The standard deviation of scores for the twelfth generation (ddN-F12) was significantly different in comparison with earlier generations of these inbred mice. No remarkable difference in avoidance ability was evident between males and females. The results of these experiments on genetic improvement, some of which have been reported by Murakami (21,22) and Hara (13), are shown in Figure 12-2.

The effect of the administration of drugs on learning ability was tested with a counter specially designed to measure open-field activity of mice. The counter measured crossing of infrared beams (Fig. 12-3). The open-field activities were studied in ddN-F10 mice and several other inbred strains of mice during a 5-minute period. The results are shown in Figure 12-4. The rate of open-field activity decreased with progressive sessions. In addition, no relationship between the rate of open-field activity and the learning ability was noted.

Memory formation was compared using avoidance training between the ddN-F10 strain and the following inbred strains: C3H, DBA, C57-BL, RF, AKR, C58, D103, C6, and CBA. The results are shown in Figure 12-5. The ddN-F10, DBA, C58, and C3H strains were the fastest learners, while RF, D103, C6, and CBA strains were the slowest learners. The ddN-F10, DBA, C58, C57-BL, and C3H strains gave performances superior to RF and D103 in long-term memory tests. All strains except ddN-F10 showed large standard deviations (Fig. 12-5).

EFFECT OF VINBLASTINE ON LEARNING

Vinblastine sulfate was purchased from the Eli Lilly & Co., Indianapolis, Indiana. It was dissolved in physiological saline solution. Animals were injected intraperitoneally with 50 μg/0.5 ml before or after training sessions. Control mice received the same volume of physiological saline solution. Each experimental group consisted of a total of 24 mice. The intraperitoneal injection of 50 μg of vinblastine in 0.5 ml of saline solution resulted in a slight decrease in body weight within the next 3 days, but this was followed by recovery to the initial level by the seventh day. The injected mice did not show any appreciable change in their open-field activities.

In mice given 50 μg of vinblastine intraperitoneally 1 week before the first training session (Fig. 12-6*a*), learning ability in the first training session was much less than that of the control group. In the second and third training sessions, learning ability gradually increased to reach a normal rate. As shown in Figure 12-6(*b*), mice given 50 μg of vinblastine intraperitoneally immediately after the first training session showed no difference from saline-injected animals in the second and third training sessions. The same results were obtained for the previously trained animals (Fig. 12-6*c*). Animals exposed

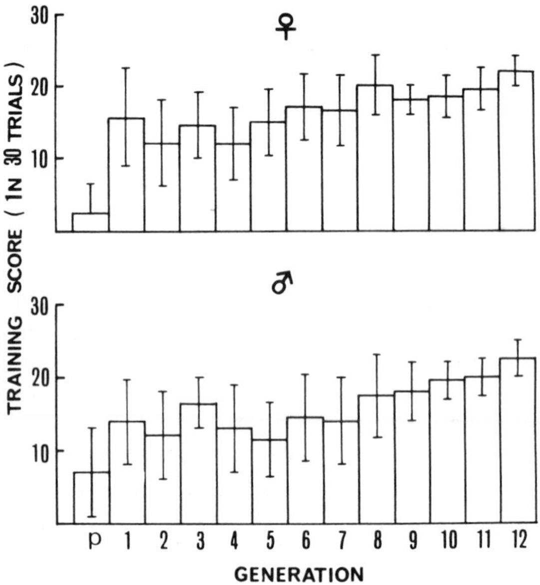

Figure 12-2. Genetic improvement of ddN strain mice in terms of avoidance training. The ordinate indicates the training score in the first 30 trials. The standard deviation gradually decreased, and the training scores increased.

to the fourth training session reached a consolidated state. Vinblastine did not cause any loss of memory in the second and third training sessions after injection.

Animals were lightly anesthetized with ether and placed in a stereotaxic head holder. Holes were drilled in the skull 2 mm lateral to the midsagittal plane and 2 mm anterior to the caudal suture of the parietal bone. Slow bilateral intracerebral injections were given at a depth of 3 mm from the surface of the skull using 10 μl Hamilton syringes. Each animal received 1 μl of solution containing 0.5 μg of vinblastine. The scalp incision was sutured. The entire procedure took less than 10 minutes.

Animals given a dose of 2 μg or more of vinblastine showed an increase in body weight after 7 days of hyperphagia. The injected mice, however, did not show any appreciable change in their open-field activity (Table 12-1).

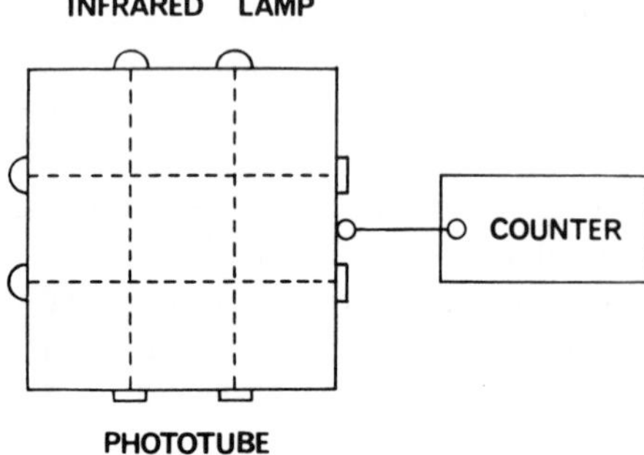

Figure 12-3. Block diagram and a top view of the counter used to measure open field activity.

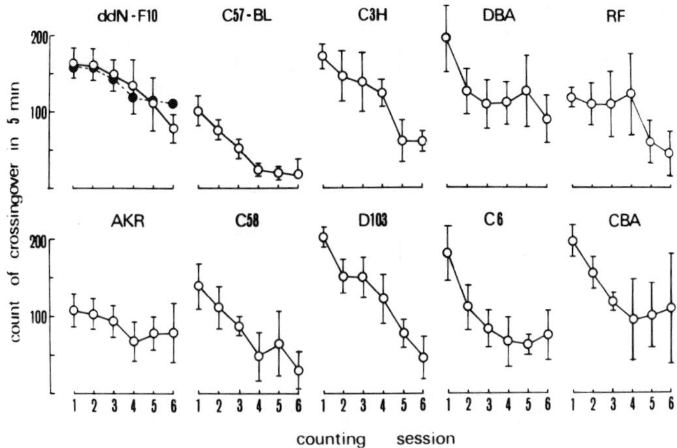

Figure 12-4. Changes in open field activity of different inbred strains of mice. Avoidance training was begun with the third estimation. In ddN-F10 (●) indicates no training. The ordinate indicates the count for crossing of infrared beams during 5 minutes. Open field activities gradually decreased. (From Hara, ref. 13.)

Intracerebral administration 1 week before the first training session significantly affected the learning ability and the retention of avoidance training (Fig. 12-7*a*). The same result was obtained when animals were given vinblastine immediately after the first training session (Fig. 12-7*b*). Even "consolidated" mice given the drug, however, showed a profound loss of memory (Fig. 12-7*c*).

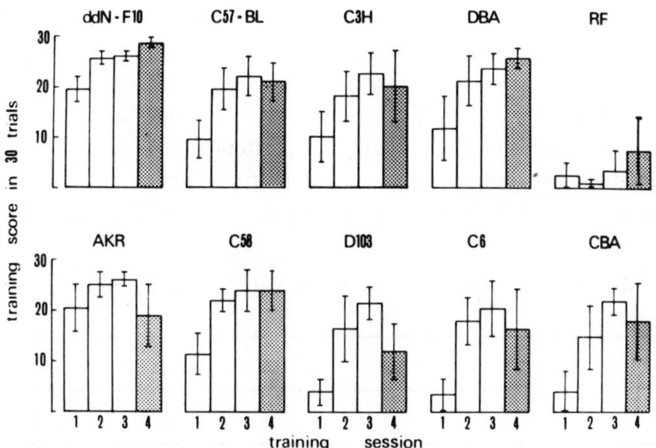

Figure 12-5. Comparison of memory formation in avoidance training with an average of 24 mice for each group in 10 inbred strains. The ordinates show training scores in 30 trials. White columns are for three sessions performed at 1-week intervals. Stippled columns indicate 4 weeks after the third training session. The bar attached to each column shows the standard deviations. (From Hara, ref. 13.)

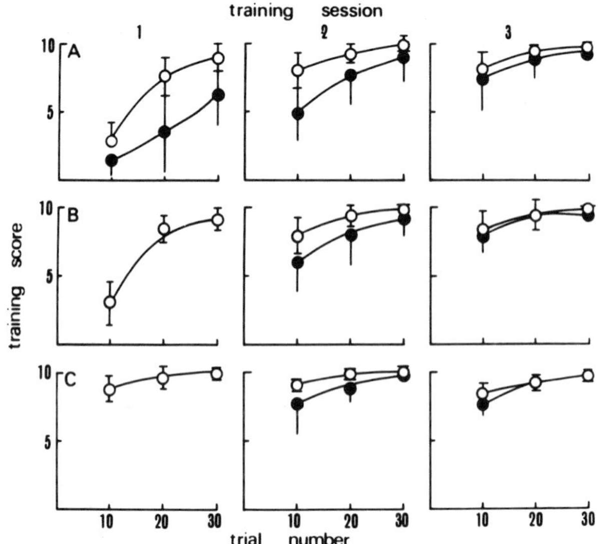

Figure 12-6. Learning curve in ddN-F10 strain mice injected intra-peritoneally with saline (O) and vinblastine (●) at a dose of 50 μg in 0.5 ml of saline. (*a*) Injected 1 week before the first training session. (*b*) Injected immediately after the first training session. (*c*) Injected after consolidation. The ordinates show the mean of training scores in trials. The bars indicate standard deviation. Training sessions performed at 1-week intervals.

AUTORADIOGRAPHICAL OBSERVATIONS

Approximately 36 mice of the ddN-F10 strain were used in this experiment. Radioactive (G-^{3}H)-vinblastine sulfate (specific activity 17.7 Ci/mmole), was purchased from the Radiochemical Centre, Amersham, Great Britain, dessicated to dryness with nitrogen gas through a Millex with a 0.45 μ pore size (Millipore Co.), and resuspended in saline. Animals were given either a single intraperitoneal dose of (G-^{3}H)-vinblastine (40 μCi in 0.5 ml of saline solution) or an intracerebral injection (2.5 μCi of (G-^{3}H)-vinblastine in 5 μl) into both frontal lobes at a depth of 3 mm. The animals were killed 1

Table 12-1. Changes in Open Field Activity During Progressive Trial Sessions[a]

	Trial Session				
	1	2	3	4	5
Saline	154 ± 40	148 ± 39	159 ± 38	129 ± 45	125 ± 40
Vinblastine	148 ± 40	159 ± 46	144 ± 43	112 ± 47	102 ± 40

[a] Mice were given saline and vinblastine intracerebrally after the third estimation. The time from the third to the fifth measured intervals was 1 week. Administration of vinblastine did not produce any remarkable differences in open field activity.

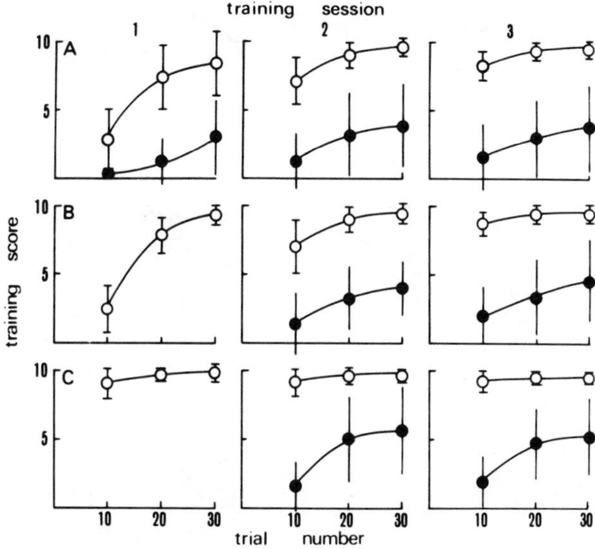

Figure 12-7. Learning curve in ddN-F10 strain mice given intracerebral administration of saline (O) and vinblastine (●) at a dose of 0.5 μg in 1 μl saline. (*a*) Injected 1 week before the first training session. (*b*) Injected immediately after the first training session. (*c*) Injected after consolidation. The ordinates show the mean training scores for 10 trials. The bars indicate standard deviation. Training sessions performed at 1-week intervals.

hour, 24 hours, or 1 week later by cervical dislocation. The brains were fixed in Carnoy Solution (acetic acid : ethanol, 1 : 3) for 12 hours, dehydrated, and embedded in paraffin. Sections were cut at a thickness of 8 μm in the coronal and horizontal planes. The sections were deparaffinized in xylene, rehydrated in alcohol and water, then dipped in Sakura autoradiographic emulsion, type NR-M2. This was followed by development in Konidol X and fixation of the emulsion. The slides were stained with 0.1% toluidine blue, dehydrated in a graded alcohol series, cleared in xylene, and mounted in Canada balsam. The exposure time was 4 weeks at 4°C.

Autoradiographic analysis confirmed that ^{3}H-vinblastine injected either intraperitoneally or intracerebrally was incorporated into the brain. The labeled cells were most numerous in the vicinity of the third ventricle and the lateral ventricles. Intracerebral administration of ^{3}H-vinblastine also resulted in numerous labeled cells in the medial parts of the hippocampus. There was no evidence of any migration of labeled cells within the first week after injection; on the contrary, the number of grains in all areas decreased progressively during this period. Figure 12-8 is a schematic representation of these brain slices. The ^{3}H-vinblastine incorporated areas are shown as dots.

ELECTRON MICROSCOPIC OBSERVATION

Animals were given vinblastine intracerebrally in both frontal lobes at a depth of 3 mm. Each dose was 0.5 μg of vinblastine in 1 μl of saline. Control animals received the same

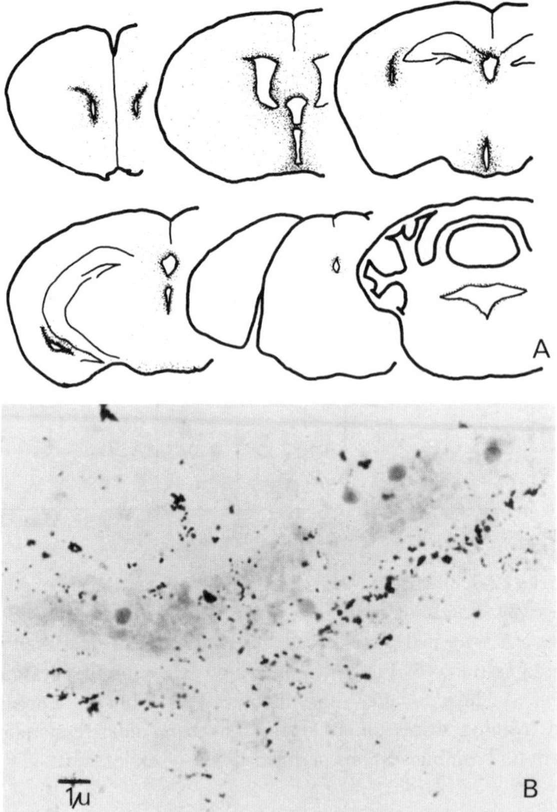

Figure 12-8. (*A*) Schema of mice brain showing areas where ^{3}H-vinblastine was incorporated. Silver grains in the cells are shown by dots. (*B*) ^{3}H-vinblastine autoradiograph in the vicinity of the third ventricle (original magnification, ×400). The brain specimen was fixed 24 hours after the intracerebral administration of vinblastine (2.5 μCi in 5 μl) into each frontal lobe at a depth of 3 mm.

volume of physiological saline solution. The animals were sacrificed by perfusion at various intervals from 5 hours to 1 week thereafter.

The perfusing fixative consisted of 5% glutaraldehyde in 0.1 M phosphate buffer, pH 7.3. The tissue blocks were selected from the cerebral hemispheres, the hippocampus, the pons, the medulla, and from around the sites of injection. Blocks were exposed to the fixative at room temperature for an additional 1 hour, postfixed for 1 hour in 1% osmic acid, dehydrated, then embedded in Epon. Thick sections were screened and suitable blocks were selected. Thin sections on grids were double stained with uranyl acetate and lead citrate before examination with a Hitachi HU-12 electron microscope.

By electron microscopy, myelinated axons in the cerebral white matter were seen to contain paracrystal-like masses. These paracrystal-like masses had two similar configurations related to the plane of section. When cut longitudinally, the paracrystals appear as parallel rows. In cross sections, taken 5 hours after intracerebral administration of vinblastine, the paracrystals appear as a closely packed array of circular profiles in a honeycomb-like structure (Figs. 12-9, 12-10, and 12-11). Paracrystal formations

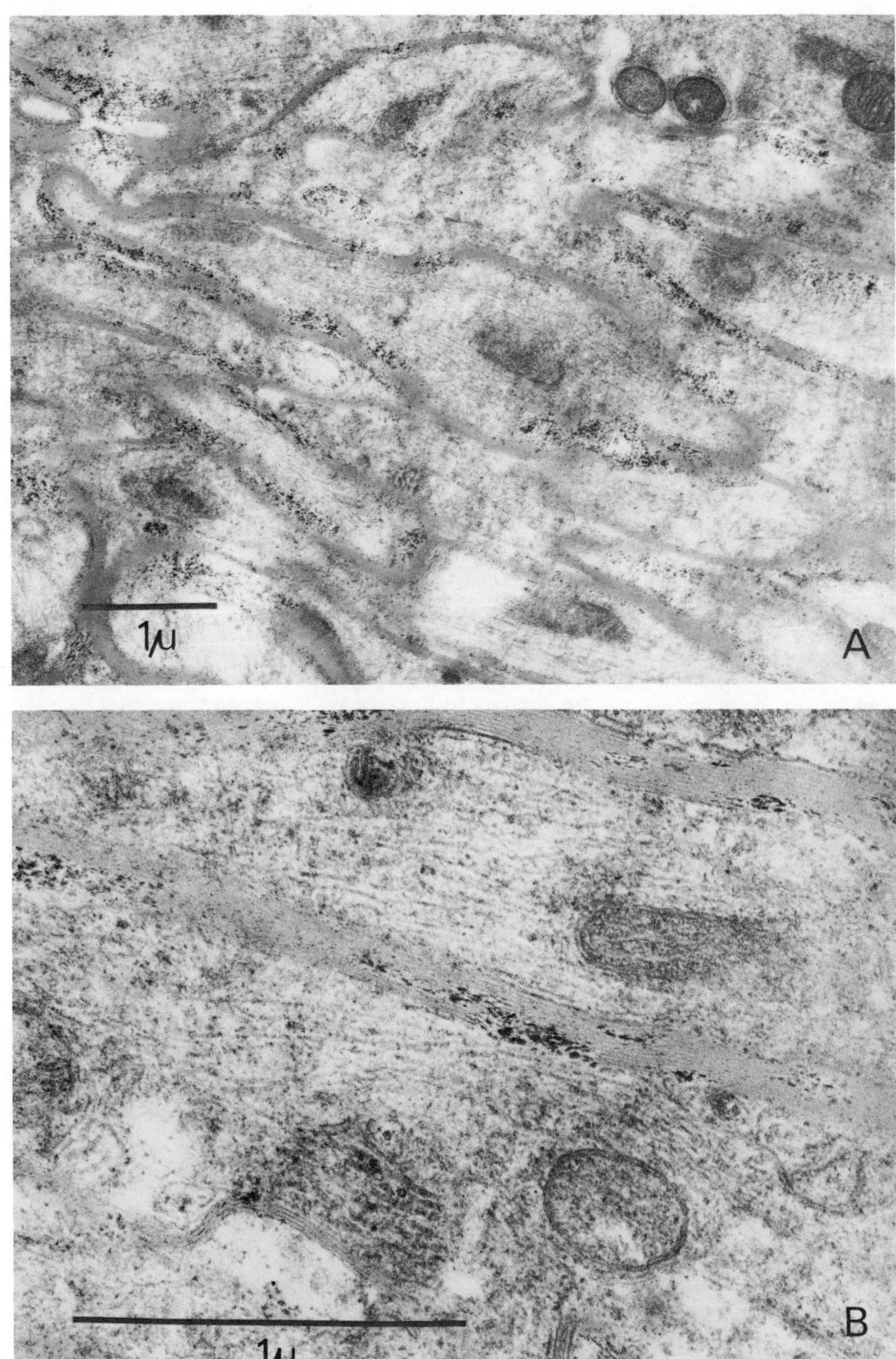

Figure 12-9. (*A*) Longitudinal section of a normal myelinated axon in cerebral white matter. The axon contains many fibrous structures. (*B*) An area similar to that illustrated in (*A*). Many microtubules are visible.

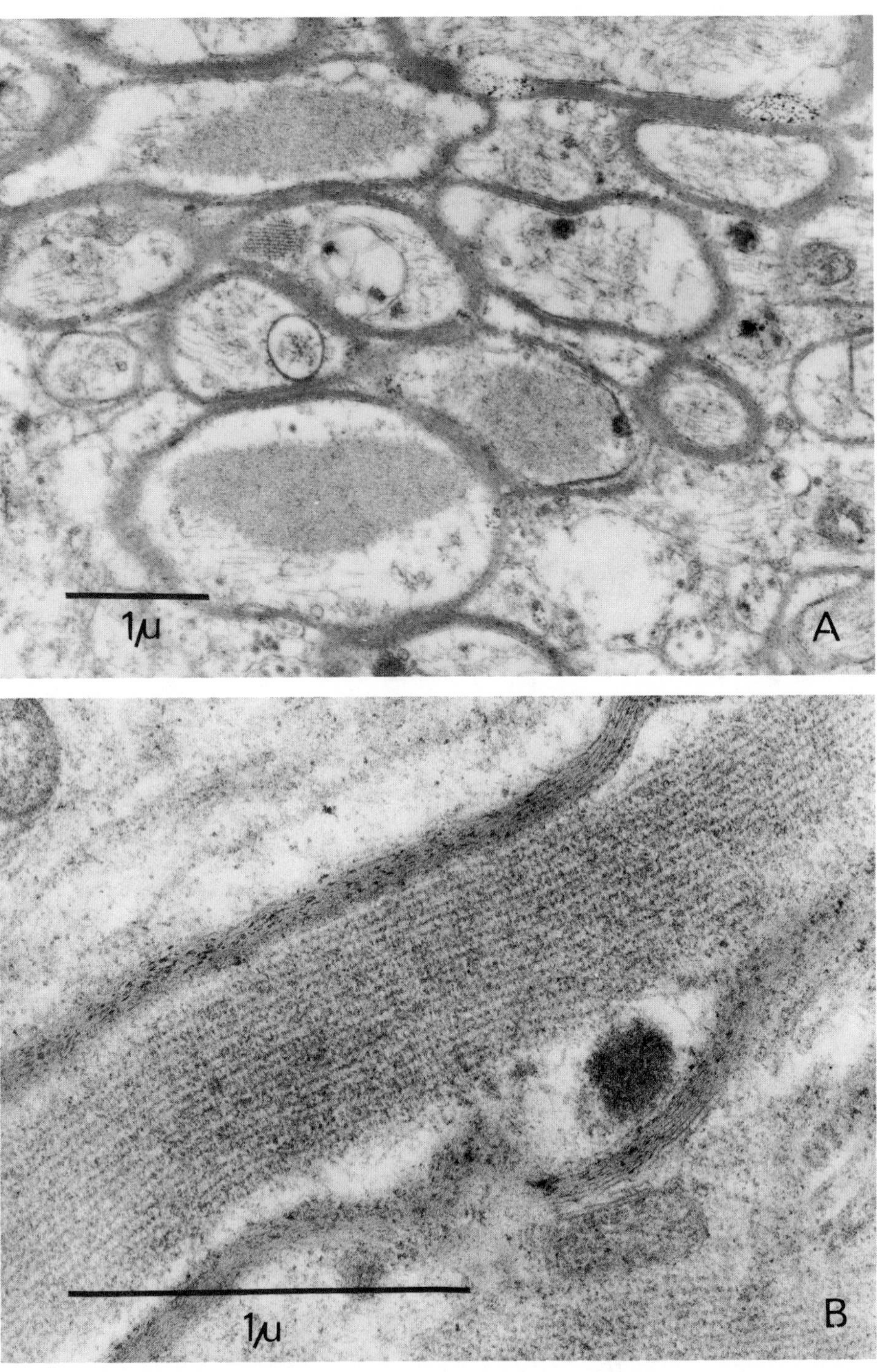

Figure 12-10. (*A*) Longitudinal section of a myelinated axon in the hippocampus of a mouse 5 hours after vinblastine implantation Paracrystals within a myelinated axon are visible. (*B*) High magnification of a portion of (*A*).

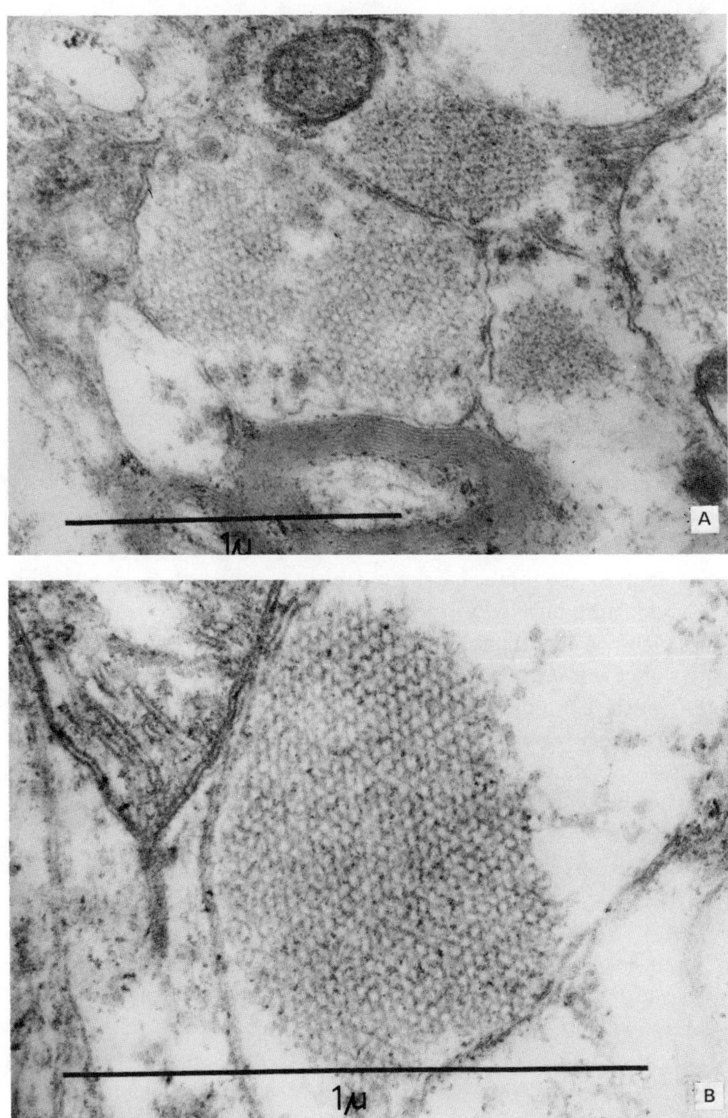

Figure 12-11. (*A*) Transverse section of a myelinated axon in the pons paracrystals appear as an array of circular profiles resembling a honeycomb. Microtubules around the paracrystals have virtually disappeared. (*B*) High magnification of a portion of (*A*).

were also present in the pons and the hippocampus and involved both myelinated and unmyelinated axons. In some areas near the sites of injection, almost all of the neuronal processes contained paracrystals. When paracrystals were present, microtubules were virtually absent.

Extensive paracrystal formation was still present 24 hours and 1 week after the injections of vinblastine.

DISCUSSION AND SUMMARY

Microtubules are a major fibrous system revealed by electron microscopy and have been found in all eukaryotic cells so far studied. Numerous reports and reviews of various aspects of microtubules have appeared recently (24–27). Vinblastine, a mitotic inhibitor, causes disruption of microtubules and induces the formation of tubulin paracrystals in the brain (15–17,28,29). These structural changes are known to affect other cellular functions. Blockage of axoplasmic transport (3,4,7–10,12,19,20), increase in miniature end-plate potential frequency, and the induction of giant potentials (2,23,30,32) have all been described.

Moreover, for many years, behavioral scientists have suggested that neurological changes occur during the acquisition and retention of learning. These changes could represent memory.

In autoradiography, 1 hour after stereotaxic infusion of ^{3}H-vinblastine into the frontal lobes, the label was dispersed throughout the entire brain. Grain density was highest over brain tissue immediately surrounding the lateral ventricle, third ventricle, aqueductus cerebri, and fourth ventricle. Proceeding radially from the ventricle system along its entire length, the level of grain density decreased progressively. High concentrations of label were found in the limbic system, which is adjacent to the third ventricle. Moreover, ^{3}H-vinblastine injected intraperitoneally was incorporated in the ependymal zone of the ventricles in less than 1 hour. Grain density was relatively low compared with the profiles after intracerebral administration. These differences in the distribution of the label may affect learning ability and memory retention. In both cases label was still present in peripheral regions of the ventricle 1 week after administration.

Electron microscopy showed that 5 hours after intracerebral administration, many paracrystal masses were present in the myelinated axons of the cerebral white matter and in both myelinated and unmyelinated axons of the limbic system. There was little paracrystal formation in the brain after intraperitoneal administration. These differences were reflected in differences in both acquisition and retention of avoidance training.

In recent years, a number of investigations have indicated the role played by macromolecules in higher brain function. Alterations in brain RNA and protein metabolism in response to a variety of stimulations were reported, and differences in macromolecular metabolism were observed in a number of training situations (1,6,11,14,18,31). Antibiotics were useful in the analysis of macromolecular metabolism during training experiments. Vinblastine was different because it disrupts the structure of microtubules, which causes blockage of axoplasmic transport and macromolecular metabolism.

Disruption of microtubules is known to inhibit both axonal transport and the fast transport of materials from the cell body into dendrites. These processes may be important in either the maintenance of synaptic viability, or in the mediation of local changes in membrane structure during the formation and modification of synapses. The disruption of microtubules, therefore, might interfere with memory formation. Experiments on this have been reported by Cronly-Dillon (5) and Murakami (21,22).

The present results show that intraperitoneal injection of vinblastine interfered slightly with both acquisition and retention of avoidance training. However, it did not produce any loss of memory that had been previously acquired. Intracerebral administration of vinblastine interfered significantly with the acquisition and retention of avoidance training and produced a profound loss of memory that had been previously acquired. These findings suggest that microtubules are significantly involved in the processes of memory formation and retention.

ACKNOWLEDGMENT

I would like to express my gratitude to Professor Isamu Nisida for his helpful comments in the preparation of the manuscript. Thanks are also due to Professors Nobuaki Sawada and Osamu Ochi, Ehime University, to whom I owe much for the preparation of the electron micrographs.

REFERENCES

1. Agranoff BW: Memory and protein synthesis. *Scientific American* 216:115–122, 1967.
2. Albuquerque EX, Warnick JE, Tasse JR, et al: Effects of vinblastine and colchicine on neural regulation of the fast and slow skeletal muscle of the rat. *Exp Neurol* 37:607–634, 1972.
3. Banks P, Mayor D, Mitchell M, et al: Studies on the translocation of noradrenaline-containing vesicles in post-ganglionic sympathetic neurones *in vitro*. Inhibition of movement by colchicine and vinblastine and evidence for the involvement of axonal microtubules. *J Physiol* 216:625–639, 1971.
4. Bund AH, Lund RD: Vinblastine-induced blockage of orthograde and retrograde axonal transport of protein in retinal ganglion cells. *Exp Neurol* 45:288–297, 1974.
5. Cronly-Dillon J: The effect of colchicine on memory. *J Physiol* 243:104P–105P, 1973.
6. Eichenbaum H, Quenon BA, Heacock A, et al: Differential behavioral and biochemical effects of regional injection of cycloheximide into mouse brain. *Brain Res* 101:171–176, 1976.
7. Edström A, Mattsson H: Fast axonal transport *in vitro* in the sciatic system of the frog. *J Neurochem* 19:205–211, 1972.
8. England JM, Kadin ME, Goldstein MN: The effect of vincristine sulphate on the axoplasmic flow of proteins in cultured sympathetic neurons. *J Cell Sci* 12:549–565, 1973.
9. Fernandez HL, Burton PR, Samson FE: Axoplasmic transport in the crayfish nerve cord. The role of fibrillar constituents of neurons. *J Cell Biol* 51:176–192, 1971.
10. Friede RL, Ho K-C: The relation of axonal transport of mitochondria with microtubules and other axoplasmic organelles. *J Physiol* 256:507–519, 1977.
11. Glassman E: The biochemistry of learning: An evaluation of the role of RNA and protein. *Ann Rev Biochem* 38:605–646, 1969.
12. Hammond GR, Smith RS: Inhibition of the rapid movement of optically detectable axonal particles by colchicine and vinblastine. *Brain Res* 128:227–242, 1977.
13. Hara T: Genetic improvement of mouse through the avoidance learning. *Okayama Igakkai Zasshi* 89:1549–1560, 1977 (in Japanese).
14. Hayakawa M: The effect of cycloheximide on mouse learning. *Acta Med Okayama* 31:161–175, 1977.
15. Hirano A, Zimmerman HM: Some effect of vinblastine implantation in the cerebral white matter. *Lab Invest* 23:358–367, 1970.
16. Hirano A, Zimmerman HM: Glial filaments in the myelin sheath after vinblastine implantation. *J Neuropathol Exp Neurol* 30:63–67, 1971.
17. Hirano A: The pathology of the central myelinated axon, in Bourne GH (ed): *The Structure and Function of Nervous Tissue,* vol 5. New York, Academic Press, 1972, pp 73–162.
18. Jakoubek B: *Brain Function and Macromolecular Synthesis.* Bristol, England, JW Arrowsmith 1974.
19. Komiya Y, Kurokawa M: Axoplasmic transport. *Protein, Nucleic Acid and Enzyme* 22:545–553, 1977 (in Japanese).

20. Lundberg D: Effect of colchicine, vinblastine and vincristine on degeneration transmitter release after sympathetic denervation studies in the conscious rat. *Acta Physiol Scand* 85:91–98, 1972.

21. Murakami TH: Microtubule and memory. *Igakuno Ayumi* 93:306–307, 1975 (in Japanese).

22. Murakami TH: Effect of destruction of microtubules upon the memory function of mice. in Ito M (eds): *Integrative Control Functions of the Brain.* Tokyo, Kodansha, 1978, vol 1, pp 428–430.

23. Pécot-Dechavassine M: Action of vinblastine on the spontaneous release of acetylcholine at the frog neuromuscular junction. *J Physiol* 261–31–48, 1976.

24. Peters A, Palay SL, Webster H. deF: *The Fine Structure of the Nervous System: The Neurons and Supporting Cells.* Philadelphia, WB Saunders, 1976.

25. Roberts K: Cytoplasmic microtubules and their functions. *Progress in Biophysics and Molecular Biology* 28:373–420, 1974.

26. Sakai T: Filamentous proteins in the brain. *Protein, Nuceic Acid and Enzyme* 22:647–660, 1977 (in Japanese).

27. Schmitt FO: Fibrous proteins. Neuronal organelles. *Proc Nat Acad Sci USA* 60:1092–1101, 1968.

28. Schochet SS Jr, Lampert PW, Earle KM: Neuronal changes induced by intrathecal vincristine sulfate. *J Neuropathol Exp Neurol* 27:645–658, 1968.

29. Schochet SS Jr, Lampert PW, Earle KM: Oligodendroglia changes induced by intrathecal vincristine sulfate. *Exp Neurol* 23:113–119, 1969.

30. Sellin LC, McArdle JJ: Colchicine blocks neurotrophic regulation of resting membrane potential in reinnervating skeletal muscle. *Exp Neurol* 55:383–492, 1977.

31. Shashoua VE: RNA metabolism in the brain. *Internat Rev Neurobiol* 16:183–231, 1974.

32. Turkanis SA: Some effects of vinblastine and colchicine on neuromuscular transmission. *Brain Res* 54:324–329, 1973.

33. Zemp JW, Wilson JE, Schlesinger K, et al: Brain function and macromolecules. I. Incorporation of uridine into RNA of mouse brain during short-term training experience. *Proc Nat Acad Sci USA* 55:1423–1431, 1966.

13 Neurochemical Correlates of Early Learning in the Chick

Steven P. R. Rose

In this chapter, I propose to review experiments from our laboratory and those of some collaborators on the neurochemical correlates of two types of early learning in the chick—imprinting and one-trial learning of a passive avoidance response. The experiments on imprinting are the outcome of more than a decade of collaboration with Dr. P. P. G. Bateson and Professor G. Horn of the University of Cambridge and with Drs. J. Hambley, J. Haywood, and A. Longstaff in the Brain Research Group Laboratory at the Open University; the passive avoidance experiments have involved a collaboration with Drs. J. Hambley and M. Gibbs of the Australian National University, Canberra, and La Trobe University, Melbourne, respectively.

In our experiments, we have been concerned with two types of questions, the first behavioral, the second biochemical. We take it as axiomatic that a consequence of learning must be the laying down within the brain of a specific trace, a structural or physiological correlate of the learning phenomenon that can later participate in the process of recall. At the behavioral level, the problems that concern us are that for an animal to learn, certain things are necessary: it must be able to perceive and to discriminate stimuli; it must be sufficiently motivated to attend to and to relate diverse stimuli. If it is learning an experimenter-imposed task, the experimenter will only be able to register that learning has occurred if the animal is constrained to respond in some way to the stimulus, by approaching or avoiding it. Hence, some motivational factors and stress are also likely to be of importance. Some of this multitude of processes may be necessary precursors or concomitants of learning; others may be more or less fortuitously associated phenomena. Hence, the behavioral question becomes one of distinguishing those brain processes and changes that are the necessary, sufficient, and exclusive correlates of learning from those that are fortuitous concomitants. This is the case regardless of whether the brain processes being studied in association with the learning are physiological, biochemical, or morphological.

Further behavioral questions follow: If a brain process is identified as the necessary, sufficient, and exclusive correlate of a particular piece or type of learning, is it safe to assume that the observation can be generalized to cover all types of learning, or are there as many different types of storage systems as there are types of learning, or of transmitters, or of neurons? Learning itself is a time-dependent process, and the memory trace(s) appear to be of several behaviorally distinct types; there is both a short-term and long-term memory process, and the brain correlates of each are probably distinct. If labile memory—to use Gibbs' and Ng's (10) term—is to be included, a third brain process must be added, and doubtless as analysis of the events immediately following the arrival and decoding of sensory inputs in the brain proceeds, further short-term aspects of storage such as comparator, novelty, and importance functions will also be demonstrated. Are the brain processes underlying learning of a constant type or do they change as an animal matures, so that early learning, which occurs in a period of considerable general brain plasticity, involves fundamentally different mechanisms from adult learning?

We do not really know the answer to any of these questions, and our work, like that of others in the field, makes use of a number of simplifying, heuristic assumptions. Until it is shown otherwise, we assume (*a*) that the brain phenomena underlying learning all involve similar cellular processes, (*b*) that learning depends on the modulation of cellular connectivity, and (*c*) that the scale and specificity is conferred by the number and addresses of the cells whose connectivity is being modulated. There is a further useful assumption to be made: learning is only one aspect of the plasticity of the brain, especially during early development. For example, general environmental enrichment or impoverishment produces changes in brain morphology, biochemistry, and physiology and in neuronal connectivity in the young mammal. These lasting responses can be seen as cruder analogues, involving many cell systems, of learning.

What of the biochemical issues? The major problem is to identify those biochemical processes involved in the encoding process, to specify the brain and cellular loci of the coding, and to show how these changes can form the brain code for learning by demonstrating their involvement in the events of recall. To do this it is necessary to redefine at the biochemical level the terms "necessary," "sufficient," and "exclusive" used previously with respect to the behavioral questions. To take an example, if enhanced protein synthesis underlies learning, there is likely to be an associated increase in cellular energy metabolism, glucose, oxygen, and amino acid uptake, and hence in localized cerebral blood flow. We can measure such changes, which may be necessarily associated with the learning; but they are neither sufficient nor exclusive correlates, anymore than is the fact that enhanced cerebral blood flow may increase the flux across the cell membrane of precursors other than those involved in the learning-associated changes. We must therefore distinguish between mobilization for particular biochemical responses and the side effects of those responses. Similarly, we must distinguish between biochemical responses underlying short-term phases of memory and its pre-processes and those underlying long-term memory.

Furthermore, biochemical processes involved in a response to learning may be of three general types. First, during the learning experience itself there are likely to be a number of changes in localized metabolic rates, precursor utilization and modulations of transcription-translation events, ion fluxes, internal cell messengers such as cAMP and enzyme activities associated with both nuclear mobilization of RNA synthesis and synaptic transmission. These changes are transient however, and within a time course of minutes to hours will tend to revert to some "ground-state" level once more. I have elsewhere referred to these changes as exemplars of "thermolabile" plasticity (21–24).

Lasting biochemical changes may themselves be of two types: localized alterations in the absolute amounts of particular molecules—for example, of enzymes or membrane constituents subserving connectivity—and changes in the metabolic rate and turnover times of these or other substances. These lasting changes I have called "thermostable" plasticity. In our experiments, some of which I am going to describe, we have examples of all these types of biochemical responses to learning and sensory/environmental stimulation.

I turn now to a discussion of the first of the experimental models for learning we have been using, that of imprinting—the process whereby young birds learn to recognize and to demonstrate a preference for a prominent moving object, an analogue of the bird's mother in the natural environment.

The merits of imprinting, which may be regarded as a special case of learning (1) are not merely that it clearly represents a very important experience for the young bird, substantially influencing its subsequent behavior, but that many aspects of the experience can be controlled and manipulated. The exposure and test situations enable a battery of behavioral measures to be made, including approach latency, running activity, distress, and contentment calls, as well as the direct measure of preference for the familiar object, that is, the degree of learning.

Our strategy in the chick studies has been first to define a relatively large anatomical region in which biochemical changes occur during learning; second, to attempt to show that such changes are specific correlates of the learning; and third, (the stage we are now entering) to focus more precisely on the exact sequence of biochemical events and on their more precise anatomical localization.

The chicks are hatched and maintained in the dark until a little before the optimal period for imprinting, some 18 to 24 hours after hatching. The chicks are then removed to individual pens or wheels, either facing the imprinting stimulus, a colored, flashing light, or in the dark. After appropriate periods of exposure and rest they are tested for their preference for the familiar object (2,3). Before, during, or after training or testing, radioactive precursors may be given by injection into the heart region. Samples are taken from several different brain regions: the midbrain, containing the optic tectum and most of the thalamic nuclei; the base of the forebrain, containing predominantly neo-, ecto-, and palaeostriatum; the posterior forebrain roof, containing hippocampus; and the anterior forebrain roof, containing hyperstriatum. The samples are then assayed for radioactivity or enzyme content.

Early experiments (reviewed in ref. 16) showed an enhanced incorporation of radioactive precursors into protein and RNA during or just after exposure to the imprinting stimulus in one brain region, the anterior forebrain roof. Such changes could be associated with many aspects of the bird's response to the situation in which it finds itself while learning the characteristics of the imprinting stimulus, as discussed in general terms above: motor or stress activity, sensory input, arousal, attention, and so forth. Three control experiments will be described briefly all using the single biochemical measure of uracil incorporation into RNA; all have helped clarify the nature of this response. (see also ref. 21).

The first (17) takes advantage of the complete decussation of the optic tract, which makes possible a "split-brain" preparation. In this experiment, the supraoptic commissures of 12 chicks were divided shortly after hatching, and after recovery from the operation, one eye of each chick was covered with a patch. The animal was exposed to the stimulus for 1 hour and then was tested, first with the trained eye and then with the untrained eye. No transfer of learning between the hemispheres took place, and there were no differences in free radioactivity between the trained and untrained sides of the brain (ruling out assymetric blood flow). However, incorporation of uracil into the RNA in the forebrain roof (but in no other region) in the trained side was significantly elevated when compared with the control side. Hence, it is unlikely that the changed incorporation results from general hormonal response to stress, nonvisual sensory input, or differences in motor activity.

However, trained and untrained halves of the brain differ in the amount of visual input they receive. To test this as a possible cause of the biochemical changes the effects of duration of learning before precursor incorporation were examined (4). Birds were exposed to the stimulus for 20, 60, 120, or 240 minutes on the first day after hatching. On the second day, they were injected with ^{3}H-uracil, and all were exposed to the stimulus for 60 minutes. None of the groups differed from the others in activity during training during the second (60-minute) exposure, but the incorporation into the anterior part of the forebrain roof was negatively correlated with the duration of exposure on day 1. That is, those birds with the least exposure on day 1—and therefore, we reason, the most to learn on day 2—showed the highest incorporation in the anterior forebrain roof. This was not due to a "carry-over" effect from the first day's treatment, because the incorporation of precursors into birds kept in the dark on day 2 was identical regardless of their treatment on day 1. This experiment would tend to rule out sensory stimulation per se as a trigger for the biochemical effects. In addition the results run counter to any "vigilance" interpretation of the biochemical effect, as the birds' activity did not differ on day 2 between the groups exposed for varying periods on day 1. However, it might be argued that the onset of visual stimulation on day 1 had initiated a process of neuronal differentiation which, in the case of short-exposure birds, was not complete by day 2, and that this process was not necessarily related to memory or learning; this possibility is not ruled out by the experiment.

The last of this series of experiments (5) used only trained birds. There is great variability among birds from the same hatch in their behavior toward the imprinting stimulus: some respond very early in the exposure period and others much later; some develop a weak and others a strong preference for the familiar stimulus. A large number of measures of the birds' behavior, during both exposure and testing, were recorded, and we examined their degree of correlation with the extent of incorporation in four brain regions. There were precursor incorporation effects (depressions) in the whole brain, which correlated with the latency of response to the stimulus, and a just-significant correlation between specific radioactivity in the anterior forebrain roof and preference for the familiar, the measure of learning used in these experiments. When the depressions were accounted for by relating the incorporation in the two portions of the forebrain roof to that in the forebrain base and midbrain, there remained only one significant correlation, namely, between the incorporation in the anterior forebrain roof and the bird's preference for the familiar as opposed to a novel stimulus. To put it simply, the more the birds learned, the more uracil they incorporated into RNA in the anterior forebrain roof. No other behavioral measure among those we made could be related to an elevation in incorporation.

These behavioral controls are not, of course, exhaustive. For example, it could be argued that both the bird's propensity to learn and to incorporate uracil into RNA are consequences of a separate, earlier effect, for example, ontogenetic or other differences in "attention" or "motivation." And of course the fact that one of our biochemical measures (uracil incorporation) shows *no* correlation except with learning does not logically allow the inference that the same is true for all the others, whether the protein incorporation or the enzyme changes (see below).

We do however claim that, taken together, our imprinting experiments have brought us to the point where we can embark on the next phase of our strategic approach—the identification of the precise sequence of biochemical changes and their anatomical localization, which represent the necessary, sufficient, and exclusive correlates of imprinting. It is thishas occupied us over the last few years. First, my collaborators, Horn and Bateson, have been able to improve greatly on our anatomical localization of the site of the biochemical changes. In experiments in which the imprinting exposure period was spread over 2 days, as in the second of the control experiments referred to above, they could, on day 2, select pairs of overtrained and undertrained birds, matched for overall motor activity. ^{14}C-uracil was injected before exposure on day 2, and after exposure serial coronal sections of the forebrain were cut in a cryostat. Alternate sections were stained with cresyl violet for histological examination and prepared for autoradiography. The optical density of the autoradiograph was measured in a microdensitometer as an index of radioactivity in the section. On this basis an increase in incorporation of radioactivity was found to occur only in the medial part of the hyperstriatum ventrale (MHV) (a difference significant at the 0.001 level), which lies in the anterior forebrain roof region of our earlier dissection (18). This suggests a more circumscribed locus for study of biochemical and physiological responses. Preliminary experiments by the Cambridge group indicate that lesions placed in this "hot spot" area impair the acquisition of the imprinting response in naive birds, and its recall in trained birds, while quantitative measurements of the number of dendritic spines per unit length of dendrite in the MHV after Golgi staining indicate that there is an increase in dendritic length after exposure to the imprinting stimulus (personal communication, G. Horn)

Turning now to the biochemical data, which have been the focus of work of the group at the Open University, our initial endeavors were directed at identifying the temporal sequence of biochemical changes from the onset of exposure to the imprinting stimulus. In this work we have tended to simplify the behavioral comparisons, for instance, to contrasting trained vs. dark-maintained birds or those exposed to constant overhead illumination, so we cannot be certain that all the biochemical changes we observe could stand up to the rigorous exclusion of the fortuitous concomitants of learning that we have achieved using uracil incorporation as a marker. Indeed, we may be sure that some do not, since they are widely distributed across brain regions rather than confined to the anterior forebrain roof. These we take as general biochemical mobilizing responses—for instance, there is an elevated uptake (approximately 20%) of precursors, such as lysine or fucose, into all brain regions during an hour's exposure to the stimulus conditions. Nonmetabolizable analogues of amino acid precursors such as 2-amino-isobutyrate also show an elevated uptake. However, only certain brain regions show changes in incorporation into macromolecules, suggesting that precursor uptake is not rate limiting for such modulations. In addition, we can detect handling effects—transient fluctuations in pool sizes and levels of such sensitive indicators as cAMP merely as a result of shifting birds from a communal dark-maintained brooder into individual dark pens. And all the changes we observe are superimposed on the rapid developmental alterations in levels of metabolites and enzymes that occur over this period. Some of these transient fluctuations have been described in earlier papers (e.g., refs. 11, 13); others remain part of laboratory lore that we have not committed to print. Tables 13-1 and 13-2 encapsulate most of

Table 13-1. Changes in Metabolite Levels and Enzyme Activities in Chick Brain After Exposure to an Imprinting Stimulus[a]

System	*Stimulus Onset (Offset) to Killing (Min)*	*Brain Region*	*100 I/D*	*Reference*
cAMP	15	Roof	35	12
	15	Midbrain	160	12
RNA polymerase	30	Roof	134	14
Adenyl cyclase	30	Midbrain	78	11
	60	Roof	150	11
Choline acetyltransferase	60	Midbrain	110	15
Acetylcholinesterase	120 (60)	Roof	111	15
	420 (360)	Roof	113	15
	420 (360)	Base	112	15
	420 (360)	Midbrain	110	15
	780 (720)	Midbrain	87	15

[a] From Rose (21). Enzyme activities were determined in brain regions from day-old chicks at varying times after exposure to imprinting stimulus. Maximum length of stimulus exposure, 60 minutes. Data are expressed as (activity in imprinted/dark control) × 100, and only significant elevations or depressions are shown ($P < 0.05$ or better; n is 12 or more for each condition).

our salient earlier data on changes in enzymes, activities in metabolite levels, and in the incorporation of precursors after onset of exposure to the imprinting stimulus.

The interesting observation for the present is the temporal sequence that the changes follow. Thus, after 15 minutes of exposure there is a profound lowering of cAMP levels in the forebrain roof—an effect that vanishes after 30 minutes (11)—although this is *not* matched by comparable changes in adenylate cyclase activity at that time. Adenylate cyclase activity does, however, show a slower response to the exposure situation. It would be of interest, although we have not done the experiment, to see if there is a reciprocal elevation in cGMP matching the decline in cAMP. After 30 minutes of exposure there is a 34% elevation in nuclear RNA polymerase in the anterior forebrain roof—an effect that has disappeared within an hour (15). The region-specific elevation in uracil incorporation into RNA follows after an hour of exposure, and that in incorporation of ^{3}H-lysine into protein within 2 hours. (Longer exposure times generalize the RNA response to other brain regions as well.) It is of interest that the elevation in incorporation of ^{3}H-lysine into protein may be obtained even if exposure to the imprinting stimulus is terminated at an hour and the birds are returned to the dark before the radioactive precursor is administered. That is, the increased incorporation is a response to recent past experience but does not require current exposure for it to take place (13). Other sequelae of exposure, which can be detected within hours of returning the bird to the dark, are all transient. For example, we have detected changes in the activities of the enzymes choline acetyltransferase, acetylcholinesterase, and adenylate cyclase.

What do such changes signify? It may be that transient modifications in the activity or amounts of enzymes associated with transmitter systems and intracellular modulators of metabolism like cAMP are part of the cellular mechanisms associated with Gibbs' and Ng's short-term and labile memory phases, while the ordered mobilization of protein synthesis may be concerned with the production of new (although not unique) macromolecules involved in the longer term remolding of the synaptic connections. It should be noted that Haywood, Hambley, Bateson, and I, in unpublished experiments, have found that cycloheximide administered at the time of training, while without effect on approach behavior examined immediately after the training, does inhibit its expression when the birds are tested on a subsequent day; so, too, does colchicine (Bateson and Rose, unpublished), an antimitotic agent that inhibits axonal flow without significantly impairing overall brain protein synthesis (25). However, in neither of these cases could we be sure that the only effect of the drug was on the recall process, since the overall approach activity of the birds was lowered. In any event, if the protein incorporation changes *are* associated with synaptic modification, we should be able to ask sensible biochemical questions about the types of protein concerned and about their biological role in the cell.

We have not carried identification of these modifiable protein fractions as far as in the case of our parallel studies in the rat visual system, where we have identified a role for a small number of (glyco) protein fractions synthesized in the neuronal perikaryon and transported thence, possibly to the synapses; for certain glycoproteins of the synaptic membranes, for tubulin, and for the muscarinic acetylcholine receptor protein (for reviews see refs. 21, 22). However, we have shown that at least a proportion of the increased incorporation of lysine is into the 100,000-g supernatant fraction (13), and by analogy with our observation on the effects of visual experience on the tubulin concentration and turnover in the rat (27,30), Mr. Longstaff and I have been examining the effects of the imprinting procedure on incorporation of ^{14}C-leucine into the acidic (tubulin-enriched) proteins (absorbed on DEAE cellulose filter disks) using a training protocol spread over 2 days as described above. Birds that showed learning on day 2 also demonstrated a 25% increase in ^{14}C-leucine incorporation into acidic proteins of the anterior forebrain roof compared with birds that did not show learning. In this brain

Table 13-2. Changes in Uptake and Incorporation Rates of Precursors in Chick Brain During and After Exposure to an Imprinting Stimulus[a]

System	*Stimulus Onset (Offset) to Killing (Minutes)*	*Incorporation Time (Minutes)*	*Brain Region*	*100 I/D*
^{3}H-uracil into RNA	76	150	Roof	120
	150	150	All regions	~125
^{3}H-lysine into protein	150	90	Roof	117
^{14}C-lysine into protein	80 (20)	20	Anterior roof	125
^{14}C-lysine into pool	80 (20)	20	All regions	~121
^{14}C-2-amino-isobutyrate into pool	80 (20)	20	All regions	~122

[a] From Rose (21). Incorporation, as disintegrations per minute per mg protein, either in acid-insoluble (RNA and protein) or acid-soluble (pool) fractions from the studied brain regions from day-old chicks, is expressed as that into (imprinted/dark controls) × 100. Only differences that are significant are shown ($P < 0.05$ or better); n is 15 or more for each condition. No significant differences occur at other times or regions.
In the ^{3}H precursor experiments incorporation took place during exposure; in the ^{14}C precursor experiments it took place immediately following exposure. ^{14}C-2-amino-isobutyrate is a nonmetabolizable amino acid used as a marker for uptake (and hence probably blood flow) changes. Data are calculated from Bateson et al (3) and Hambley et al (13).

region, but in no other, there is a weak positive correlation between the measure of learning (preference for the familiar) and the specific radioactivity of the acidic proteins ($P < 0.05$). Experiments to assess whether there is also an effect on the total amount of colchicine-binding protein in these brain regions are still in progress, and we therefore cannot yet say with confidence that there is a lasting change, either in the metabolism or in the quantity of specific proteins, as opposed to the transients we have recorded as a consequence of imprinting.

Our imprinting experiments show an anatomically localized biochemical sequence of events that occur during, and consequent to, exposure to the learning situation and that are apparently associated with an aspect of the storage of new information. It is sometimes argued that imprinting, being a developmentally programmed event, is not comparable with other forms of learning but must be seen as a special case. While we would not accept that imprinting is sui generis but would argue it is merely one form of early learning (see refs. 1, 16), it remains of interest to see whether the biochemical sequence and/or the anatomical area localized in the imprinting experiments may be implicated in other forms of early learning in the chick. Also, a training procedure that is of some duration and therefore one in which the effects of training per se are likely to be confounded with those of acquisition in its early phases is not the most appropriate for a study of the transient phenomena associated with short-term learning. I have therefore been studying the biochemical correlates of an alternative form of early learning in the chick, a one-trial passive avoidance response. This response, in which the bird learns from a single trial not to peck at a bead coated with the aversive substance methylanthranilate, has been the subject of considerable study by Gibbs and her colleagues (10,20). They have shown that, after a single exposure to the bead coated with methylanthranilate, the birds will not peck subsequently at a similar but uncoated bead.

The time course of consolidation of this response has been followed by examining the effects of intracerebral injections of agents such as lithium, glutamate, ethacrynic acid, ouabain, anisomycin, or cycloheximide at varying times before and just after training, and it is on the basis of the time course of the amnestic effects of these agents, that Gibbs and Ng have postulated a three-phase model for consolidation with a period of several minutes preceding a labile phase of half an hour, followed by the long-term retention, which is disrupted by protein-synthesis inhibitors, such as cycloheximide. Although further experiments seemed likely to add to the complexity of such a model, the learning situation itself seemed an appropriate one to explore with correlative biochemical techniques.

In our initial experiments we have been examining responses in two biochemical markers: the incorporation of precursors into protein and the activity of the acetylcholine transmitter system. The choice of the latter follows from the observations that the chick brain is particularly rich in the enzymes of the acetylcholine system, and that in the rat, first exposure to visual stimulation resulted in a transient increase in the activities, not merely of the enzymes of acetylcholine metabolism, cholineacetyltransferase and acetylcholinesterase, but also in the amount of the muscarinic acetylcholine receptor in the visual cortex, as measured by its capacity to bind the radioactive ligand ^{3}H-quinuclidinyl benzilate (QNB) (26).

In the experiments, the results of which I present here, 1-to 2-day-old chicks, reared communally and exposed to normal laboratory illumination for some hours before training, were subjected to a training schedule that consisted of housing the birds in pairs in small pens and pretraining them to peck at a water-wet bead. Birds were then (in some experiments) given an intraperitoneal injection with ^{3}H-lysine and 5 to 10 minutes later were presented for 10 seconds with *either* a water-wet bead or one that had been coated with methylanthranilate. Birds that tasted the methylanthranilate responded with a characteristic backing away from the bead, a vigorous shaking of the head, and sometimes attempts to wipe the beak. Birds were killed at 10, 30, or 180 minutes after the trial. In some experiments immediately before killing they were again presented with a bead, identical in appearance to that of the training bead but now dry, and pecks during a 10-second trial were recorded. More than 85% of the birds trained on methylanthranilate refrained from pecking in the trial, whereas all the control birds pecked. The birds were then killed, and the optic lobes and forebrain were homogenized and assayed for ^{3}H-QNB binding by the method of Yamamura and Snyder (31) as described by Rose and Stewart (26). AChE activity was measured by an automated version of the method of Ellman et al (8), and additional samples of homogentates were taken for protein and radioactivity determination.

Table 13-3 shows the results of these experiments in terms of QNB binding in the forebrain, collated from experiments performed both in Australia (Canberra and La Trobe) and at the Open University by Dr. Gibbs, Dr. Hambley, and myself. At 30 minutes, but not at 10 minutes or 3 hours after training, there is a 21% increase in the QNB-binding capacity of the tissue. In younger (1 day) animals the elevation was even greater and somewhat more prolonged. There was no change in QNB binding in the optic lobes under the conditions of these experiments, nor was there any change in AChE activity after training (unlike the situation in the rat where the increases in QNB binding and AChE activity follow a similar time course).

Preliminary results suggest an elevation of incorporation of ^{3}H-lysine into TCA-precipitable material over the 30 minutes from training to testing and killing.

An obvious possible behavioral explanation of these results would be that the aversive taste of the methylanthranilate was responsible for a modulation of the QNB binding; however, merely introducing the methylanthranilate into the beak does not result in any change in QNB binding (Table 13-4). Also, ouabain or cycloheximide injected intracranially at 0.02 mg/kg and 1.0 mg/kg, respectively, immediately before training, produced a time-dependent amnesia for the avoidance response, and both agents abolished the training-induced rise in QNB binding.

There are two interpretations of such an observation. On the one hand, if memory fixation was contingent on a transient increase in the levels of the muscarinic cholinergic receptor, and the process of fixation was abolished by the cycloheximide, the consequent

Table 13-3. One-Trial Passive Avoidance and QNB-Binding in Chick Forebrain[a]

Time After Training (Minutes)	*pmol QNB Bound/mg Protein*				
	Untrained	*Trained*	*% T/U*	*t*	*P*
10	0.308 ± 0.013 (55)	0.339 ± 0.016 (57)	110	1.47	ns
30	0.307 ± 0.013 (71)	0.372 ± 0.013 (85)	121	3.53	<0.001
180	0.305 ± 0.011 (52)	0.308 ± 0.012 (52)	101	0.18	ns

[a] From Rose et al (28). One- and 2-day-old chicks were trained on passive avoidance of methylanthranilate-coated beads, and QNB-binding were determined varying times after training. Means ± SEM of number of birds shown in parentheses.

rise in QNB binding would also be abolished. On the other hand, cycloheximide could inhibit two distinct processes, the one leading to memory fixation and the other to the increased de novo synthesis of muscarinic acetylcholine receptor protein; the rise in QNB binding would thus, although occurring in parallel with, be distinct from the process underlying memory. At any event, the passive avoidance learning model is one that is worthy of further investigation, and we are currently studying among other biochemical processes the effects of the procedure on glycoprotein and on tubulin synthesis (both of which have been implicated in the rat first exposure situation) as well as the more precise anatomical localization of the changes we have found.

If we are to interpret our results beyond the present data, they are compatible with a model for the modulation of synaptic properties and cell connectivity in which short-term recall (of the order of minutes to hours) is maintained by transient changes in transmitter responsiveness, controlled by a regulation of the activity of the number of postsynaptic receptor sites. (We have no reason to believe, of course, that the muscarinic cholinergic system is the only transmitter system to be involved in such modulation, it is merely the one we have, perhaps fortunately, chosen to measure.) Such a transient enhanced postsynaptic receptivity either could be the signal for or could merely hold the learning steady while a more permanent modification of the synaptic properties of both presynaptic and postsynaptic cells occurred. This modulation could involve the production of increased amounts of or different types of membrane constituents. However, to date in our experiments in both chick and rat, we have biochemical evidence not so much for increased quantities of particular substances but for an increased rate of metabolism. Thus, in the rat, first visual experience doubles the rate of incorporation of precursors into a tubulin-enriched fraction, but there is only a transient elevation in total polymerizable tubulin as measured by a colchicine-binding technique (27,30). In preliminary experiments with Dr. R. Mileusnic we have evidence for a similar increase both in ^{14}C-leucine incorporation into tubulin and in colchicine binding in the anterior forebrain roof 30 minutes after methylanthranilate training. In parallel experiments, Dr. Robert Sukumar and I have found a 29% increase in incorporation of ^{3}H-fucose into particulate glycoprotein in the anterior region of the forebrain roof (Table 13-5). Hence, a similar regional specificity to that in the case of imprinting is becoming apparent. The changes in dendritic spine number reported above imply that there must be a permanent change in the quantity of at least some membrane components. If, as I have proposed

Table 13-4. Effect of Taste of Methylanthranilate (MeA) on QNB-Binding in Chick Brain[a]

Region	*Age (Days)*	*pmol QNB Bound/mg Protein*		*%MeA/H₂O*	*P*
		H_2O	*MeA*		
Forebrain	1	0.215 ± 0.019	0.205 ± 0.021	95	ns
	2	0.400 ± 0.019	0.374 ± 0.027	94	ns
Optic lobe	1	0.262 ± 0.011	0.215 ± 0.027	82	ns
	2	0.253 ± 0.024	0.260 ± 0.022	103	ns

[a] From Rose et al (28). QNB binding was determined in 1- and 2-day-old chick forebrain and optic lobes 30 minutes after bird had tasted either water (H_2O) or methylanthranilate (MeA). Means ± SEM of 10 birds in each group.

Table 13-5. Methylanthranilate (MeA) Learning: Protein and Glycoprotein Incorporation and Tubulin Levels[a]

Measure	*Region*	*%MeA/H_2O*	*P*
^{3}H-fucose →	Anterior roof	129 (22)	<0.01
particulate	Posterior roof	117 (22)	ns
glycoprotein	Base	101 (22)	ns
	Optic lobe	96 (22)	ns
^{14}C-leucine →	Roof	120 (26)	<0.01
protein	Base	92 (26)	ns
^{14}C-leucine →	Roof	131 (26)	<0.001
tubulin	Base	92 (26)	ns
Colchicine-	Roof	125 (26)	<0.01
binding capacity	Base	97 (26)	ns

[a] Data derived from R. Mileusnic, R. Sukumar, and S.P.R. Rose (20a). For incorporation studies, isotope (^{3}H-fucose or ^{14}C-leucine) was injected 5 minutes before starting the training, and birds were killed immediately after testing and 30 minutes after training. Results are %trained/untrained with numbers of experiments in parentheses; *P* values were calculated by the *t* test. Elevations in incorporation into glycoprotein are confined to the particulate fraction; for ^{14}C-leucine they are apparent in both a particulate and a postmitochondrial supernatant fraction.

elsewhere (21–24), the developmental plasticity of the nervous system (for example, in the response to sensory stimulation and deprivation or to environmental enrichment and impoverishment) serves as a model for learning, then by analogy with the large changes in dendritic dimensions and branching found under such conditions (for a recent account see ref. 7) we should also expect to find such changes. Neither we, nor others working in the field of the biochemistry of learning, have yet found them. The development of new immunological and other techniques for the detection of brain-specific membrane proteins points to the direction in which this endeavor must proceed in the next few years.

In the mid 1960s, the field of the biochemistry of learning was for a time a fashionable "bandwagon" area. Many hopes were raised by sensational reports of experimental results that subsequently turned out to be either incapable of replication or poorly controlled, at either the biochemical or the behavioral level, and hence impossible to interpret. As a consequence, perhaps, there was a period in the early 1970s when the field fell into some disrepute, and those people who had been attracted to it earlier because of the likelihood of immediate breakthroughs moved on elsewhere (9). It has been one of my intentions in this chapter to show that there is now a sounder framework for both biochemical and other neurobiological work in this potentially enormously exciting field. The basis is there, I believe, for significant further progress to be made.

ACKNOWLEDGMENTS

I should like to thank my colleagues Pat Bateson, Marie Gibbs, John Hambley, Gabriel Horn, Alan Longstaff, Radmila Mileusnic, and Robert Sukumar for permission to quote from unpublished experiments, and Pat Bateson, Marie Gibbs, Jeff Haywood, and Gabriel Horn for comments on an earlier draft of this manuscript. Some of the experiments described were conducted during a sabbatical period at the Australian National University, Canberra, and I am grateful to Professor Richard Mark for laboratory facilities during this period; during some of the experiments described, Dr. Gibbs was a sabbatical visitor at the Open University.

REFERENCES

1. Bateson PPG: Characteristics and context of imprinting. *Biol Rev* 41:177–220, 1966.
2. Bateson PPG, Jaeckel JB: Imprinting: correlations between activities of chicks during training and testing. *Anim Behav* 22:899–906, 1974.
3. Bateson PPG, Wainwright AAP: The effects of prior exposure to light on the imprinting process in domestic chicks. *Behaviour* 42:279–290, 1972.
4. Bateson PPG, Rose SPR, Horn G: Imprinting: lasting effects on uracil incorporation into chick brain. *Science* 181:576–578, 1973.
5. Bateson PPG, Horn G, Rose SPR: Imprinting: correlations between behavior and incorporation of [^{14}C] uracil into chick brain. *Brain Res* 84:207–220, 1975.
6. Bateson PPG, Horn G, McCabe B: Imprinting and incorporation of uracil in chick brain—autoradiographic study. *J Physiol* 275:70p, 1978.
7. Borges S, Berry M: The effects of dark rearing on the development of the visual cortex of the rat. *J Comp Neurol* 180:277–300, 1978.
8. Ellman GL, Courtney KD, Andres V et al: A new and rapid colorimetric determination of acetycholinesterase activity. *Biochem Pharmacol* 7:88–95, 1961.
9. Gaito J: Molecular psychobiology of memory: its appearance, contributions, and decline. *Physiol Psychol* 4:476–484, 1976.
10. Gibbs ME, Ng KT: Psychobiology of memory—towards a model of memory formation. *Biobehav Rev* 1:113–136, 1977.
11. Hambley J, Rose SPR: Effects of an imprinting stimulus on adenylate cyclase and adenosine 3′:5′-phosphate in neonatal chick brain. *Neuroscience* 2:1115–1120, 1977.
12. Hambley J, Rose SPR, Bateson PPG: Effects of early visual experiences on the metabolism of adenosine 3′:5′-cyclic monophosphate in chick brain. *Biochem J* 127:90p, 1972.
13. Hambley J, Haywood J, Rose SPR, et al: Effects of imprinting on lysine uptake and incorporation into protein in chick brain. *J Neurobiol* 8:109–118, 1977.
14. Haywood J, Rose SPR, Bateson PPG: Effects of an imprinting procedure on RNA polymerase activity in the chick brain. *Nature* 228:373–374, 1970.
15. Haywood J, Hambley J, Rose SPR: Effects of exposure to an imprinting stimulus on the activity of enzymes involved in acetylcholine metabolism in chick brain. *Brain Res* 92:219–225, 1975.
16. Horn G, Rose SPR, Bateson PPG: Experience and plasticity in the central nervous system. *Science* 181:506–514, 1973.
17. Horn G, Rose SPR, Bateson PPG: Monocular imprinting and regional incorporation of tritiated uracil into the brains of intact and 'split-brain' chicks. *Brain Res* 56:227–237, 1973.
18. Horn G, McCabe BJ, Bateson PPG: An autoradiographic study of the chick brain after imprinting. *Brain Res* 168:361–373, 1979.
19. Longstaff A, Rose SPR: (to be published).
20. Mark RF, Watts ME: Drug inhibition of memory formation in chickens: I: long-term memory. *Proc Roy Soc B* 178:439–454, 1971.

20a. Mileusnic R, Rose SPR, Tillson P: *J Neurochem* (in press).

21. Rose SPR: Early visual experience, learning, and neurochemical plasticity in rat and chick. *Phil Trans Roy Soc B* 278:307–318, 1977.

22. Rose SPR: In Roberts S, Lajtha A, Gispen W (eds): Are experience and learning regulators of protein synthesis in the cerebral cortex? *Mechanisms, Regulation and Special Functions of Protein Synthesis in the Brain*. Elsevier North Holland 1977, pp 307–318.

23. Rose SPR: Macromolecular mechanisms and long-term changes in behaviour. *Trans Biochem Soc* 6:844–848, 1978.

24. Rose SPR: In Brazier M (ed): *Brain Mechanisms in Memory and Learning*. Raven Press, New York, 1979, pp 165–178.

25. Rose SPR, Sinha AK: Rapidly labelling and exported neuronal protein; [^{3}H]fucose as a precursor, and effects of cycloheximide and colchicine. *J Neurochem* 27:963–966, 1976.

26. Rose SPR, Stewart M: Transient increase in muscarinic acetylcholine receptor and acetylcholine sterase in visual cortex on first exposure of dark-reared rats to light. *Nature* 271:169–170, 1978.

27. Rose SPR, Sinha AK, Jones-Lecointe A: Synthesis of tubulin-enriched fraction in rat visual cortex is modulated by dark-rearing and light-exposure. *FEBS Letters* 65:135–139, 1976.

28. Rose SPR, Gibbs ME, Hambley J: *Neurosci* (in press).

29. Sinha AK, Rose SPR: Dark rearing and visual stimulation in the rat: effect on brain enzymes. *J Neurochem* 27:921–926, 1976.

30. Stewart M, Rose SPR: Increased binding of [^{3}H]colchicine to visual cortex proteins of dark-reared rats on first exposure to light. *J Neurochem* 30:595–599, 1978.

30a. Sukumar R, Rose SPR, Burgoyne RD: *J Neurochem* (in press).

31. Yamamura MF, Snyder SH: Muscarinic cholinergic binding in rat brain. *Proc Nat Acad Sci (US)* 71:1725–1727, 1974.

14
Genetic and Environmental Factors in Relation to Behavioral Rigidity and Plasticity

Alberto Oliverio

BEHAVIORAL RIGIDITY AND PLASTICITY: A COMPARATIVE APPROACH

Memory and learning have been studied in their simplest forms in monocellular organisms and in invertebrates. However, a number of neurophysiological and psychobiological studies have pointed out the differences existing between the behavioral systems of invertebrates and of vertebrates, indicating that it is rather difficult to generalize about the mechanisms and strategies characterizing a paramecium, an insect, or an octopus. In this regard Altman (3) has indicated that a phylogenetic approach to learning must consider the structure of the nervous system, and that different mechanisms characterize the spinomedullary level typical of the protochordates like the amphioxus, the paleoencephalic level typical of the protovertebrates like amphibia, and the mesencephalic level typical of protomammalian behavior.

The mammalian nervous system may be subdivided into three functional components: the spinomedullary, the paleoencephalic, and the neencephalic, three structures that, in agreement with Altman (3) and McLean (30), control three separate classes of behavioral functions. This tripartite organization of the different animative activities is distributed within a continuum ranging from stereotyped innate activities to personal and acquired behaviors. The spinomedullary activities control a number of neuromuscular functions that are dependent on morphogenetic processes; that is, the activities are innate reflex capacities that are resistant to modification by experience. The paleoencephalic nuclei, through the mesencephalon, the diencephalon, and the limbic system, control a major class of activities that have been defined as recurrent catering or servicing activities; these include a number of appetitive, consummatory, agonistic, and affiliative behaviors and the control of circadian energy-deployment processes. The ends of these activities—which may be defined as instinctive—are set by inborn needs and dispositions; however, their mode of execution is guided and may be altered through interaction with the environment. Finally, the neencephalic functions consist of novel, variable, and highly adaptive behaviors that individuals display in response to unique situations or to new problems raised by the environment; these activities cannot be directly programmed by inborn mechanisms but are developed by the individual within a given environment. In other words, they are acquired capacities. The structural subdivision of the mammalian brain corresponds to a functional subdivision that is responsible for classes of behavioral activities ranging from the mostly innate and stereotyped to the acquired and unique strategies; starting from the species-specific behaviors we arrive at the individual-specific behaviors.

This short evolutionary foreword points out that the behavioral abilities of different species may be determined in more rigid or more plastic terms depending on their level of encephalization. At the lowest level, protochordates such as the amphioxus are characterized by a spinomedullary nervous system and by "reflex" activities; at the intermediate level, protovertebrates such as amphibia or reptiles depend on paleocephalic mechanisms and on "instinctive" processes; and at the highest level, protomammals and mammals are endowed with neencephalic structures and respond with individual "intelligent" behaviors. However, among mammals the role of "instinctive" or of "intelligent" processes may be more or less relevant depending on the importance played by paleoencephalic or by neencephalic mechanisms: there are species that are characterized by fixed-action patterns and species that are more plastic and rely on flexible strategies. At one extreme, the nervous structure and the behavior that it allows confine the *specialist* animal to a relatively narrow niche. At the other end of the continuum, the structure and behavior are more flexible and versatile and allow the animal to exploit a greater array of environmental situations. These broad-niched animals are known as *generalists.* What are the advantages of these two conditions? In a slowly changing environment of low variability, behavioral specialization may represent an advantage for the specialist. However, there is the evolutionary risk that the environment might deviate too rapidly for the individual to adapt. On the other hand, the generalist organism, with a reduced number of behaviors that are organized with a minimum of personal experience, spends his entire life solving problems that the specialist's genetic background has solved for it. While specialist species rely on fixed-action patterns and on other behaviors that are more structurally determined, generalist species are more flexible, depend on individual experience for acquiring useful behaviors, and are able to temporarily link diverse responses in new ways to solve new problems (38,49).

The distinction between specialist and generalist species has been based not only on cerebral evolutionary correlates but also on the different mechanisms that may produce response variability. In addition to their brain development, the security from predators or living in a nonagonistic social framework—defined as a hedonic mode by Chance (14)— is conducive to the generation of variable behaviors. Other mechanisms that have been related to the production of behavioral variability are (*1*) living under relaxed motivational pressures (49), (*2*) play behavior, and (*3*) paradoxical sleep. The last mechanism has been related to the evolutionary level of different species, and it has been indicated that paradoxical sleep plays a more important role in the most evolved mammals (24,54). Of course the possession of a diverse behavioral repertoire must not be passively connected with the level of adaptive behavior or intelligence, but that repertoire (and behavioral plasticity) represents the necessary starting point.

BRAIN MATURITY AT BIRTH AND BEHAVIORAL ADAPTATION

In addition to their relationships with the level of encephalization, behavioral rigidity or plasticity (specialization or generalization) may be considered from the point of view of the maturity of mammals at birth. In the precocial species (such as guinea pigs or ruminants), sensory and motor maturation at birth allows immediate identification with the mother and the establishment of social and mother-offspring relationships resembling imprinting in birds (58,61). However, in nonprecocial (altricial) mammals, which form a heterogeneous group ranging from other species of rodents to carnivores and primates, including humans, the immediate postnatal period is characterized by great maternal dependency, by a later onset of primary and social relationships, and by immaturity of sensory and motor abilities.

From an evolutionary point of view, precocity at birth may be equated, for given aspects, to behavioral specialization, and immaturity at birth, to behavioral plasticity and generalization. The precocial species have the advantage that the ontogeny of the CNS is realized during the fetal period and that the newborn organism is practically mature enough for independent life soon after birth. The behavioral adaptation of a precocial species is set, in large part, through innate mechanisms (59). The immaturity of behavioral functions in the altricial neonate, at birth and during the first days—or months and even years—of postnatal life, is compensated by parental behavior. The immature brain passes through critical developmental periods under different influences of the external environment, which may have positive (or negative) effects on the process of brain and behavioral maturation. In other words, while precocial species have the advantages of the "specialist" and rely to a greater extent on innate patterns, altricial species have the advantages of the "generalist," that is, they are more flexible and open to the effects of the environment.

These different points are summarized in a tentative model in Figure 14-1, where the various mechanisms leading to behavioral rigidity or plasticity are considered in relation to infancy and adulthood. Different maturational and behavioral patterns during infancy lead to specific interactions with the environment; similarly, the stimulating or detrimental effects of the environment have a more pronounced effect on those species that reach maturity at a later age. Whether an adult animal is a specialist or a generalist depends on these early mechanisms and behavioral categories, on the type of interaction with the environment, and, finally, on the evolutionary genetic mechanisms that set the types of species-specific or individual cerebral and behavioral organization.

A GENETIC APPROACH TO BEHAVIORAL ADAPTATION

The existence of species or individual differences in relation to learning and memory is not a negative point and must be considered. These differences indicate the presence of intraspecific individual variability or of species-specific mechanisms that have their roots in the genetic and environmental mechanisms that modulate these complex abilities. A second research strategy may find its roots in the existence of this variability, and the question: What are the psychological and neurochemical correlates of learning and memory? may be turned into another question: What are the neurophysiological and neurochemical bases of behavioral individuality? This problem rests on the early work

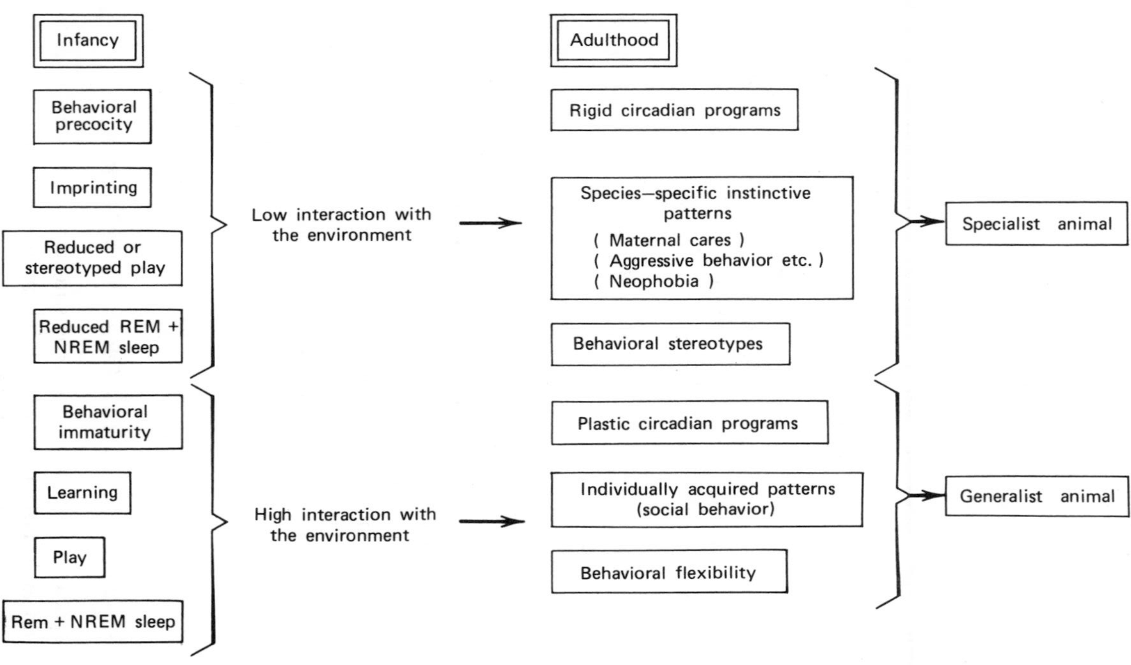

Figure 14-1. Behavioral rigidity (specialization) or plasticity (generalization) in relation to a number of factors acting during infancy or adulthood.

in the field of behavior genetics, which is based on artificial selection experiments: since the first experiments on the maze-learning abilities of the mouse at the beginning of this century, a great number of behavioral abilities have been determined for rodents.

Research on the genetic determinants of individual differences, based on a comparative approach, is justified by the similarity of many neurophysiological processes among mammals. In particular, many learning mechanisms, such as short-term or long-term memory, consolidation processes, and different learning abilities, show a number of interspecific similarities. It is therefore possible that a comparative behavioral genetic study might be a fruitful approach to investigating the organic foundations of behavioral individuality, individual learning abilities, and a number of conditions resulting in mental retardation.

A number of programmatic studies of the phylogeny of learning have been conducted, using different procedures that vary the conditions under which the different species try to solve specific problems (7,8). However, these types of investigations only indicate the existence of species-related differences in specific learning tasks, and it is difficult to equate the experimental procedures or to correlate behavioral differences to specific brain characteristics. To understand the mechanisms of behavioral evolution, within-species comparisons seem more fruitful than the interspecific approach, since, as pointed out by Schneirla (57), the existence of outstanding individual differences within the same species must be regarded as a powerful tool for these studies. Such differences among individuals or lines of the same species do, in fact, exist; consider such mechanisms as precocity or immaturity at birth, behavioral rigidity or plasticity, and specialization or generalization.

Within the framework of a theoretical behavioral genetic approach to the problem of rigidity and plasticity, it is important to work with a species characterized by (*1*) clear phenotypic differences at the brain and behavioral level, (*2*) differences in relation to precocity and maturity at birth, and (*3*) behavioral rigidity or plasticity in relation to a number of paleoencephalic (instinctive) or neencephalic (adaptative) patterns. From an analysis of the data available from the literature, the mouse seems to represent "a prototype" (27,40) for any behavior genetic analysis, and some inbred lines characterized by different patterns of behavioral plasticity or rigidity may represent a useful model in this type of analysis. It is worthwhile to examine some of the empirical data available today to outline a tentative model.

BRAIN AND BEHAVIOR AS A PHENOTYPE

A very large number of strains of mice is available today (22,39,64), their genetic homozygosity resulting from a number of studies based on different immunological methods. Thirty-nine strains have also been characterized for their alleles for as many as 16 polymorphic loci. The variability among these strains is at least as great as in any single feral population, a large group of inbred strains with unique alleles and no overlapping pedigrees being available as the best group to screen for a hoped-for variant (53). The existence of clear intraspecific phenotypic differences at the level of the peripheral or central nervous system has also been assessed.

A search of the literature up to 1978 produced a total of 107 reports, 71 dealing with a number of biochemical or enzymatic differences at the peripheral level (nerves, ganglia, and organs) and 36 with differences at the brain level. It is important to note that, on the one hand, most the estimates at the brain level deal with four strains: 55 biochemical estimates have been conducted in C57BL/6 mice, 55 in DBA/2 mice, 20 in BALB/c mice, and 14 in the SEC 1/Re/J strain. On the other hand, there are only 40 estimates dealing with 11 other strains. These figures are not trivial, since they indicate that (*1*) there are strains in which a number of biochemical estimates have been (or are being made because of their interesting behavioral patterns, and that (*2*) it is worthwhile concentrating on these strains from a behavioral or biochemical genetic point of view to increase the number of findings already available.

If we consider in detail the field of learning, one basic step in the behavioral experiments was to demonstrate that while individual mice belonging to random-bred populations attain disparate learning levels, inbred strains are characterized by homogenous performances within each strain. In a large number of learning situations ranging from positively rewarded maze learning to negatively rewarded active avoidance, different strains of mice were ranked for their high, intermediate, and low learning patterns (9). For example, by comparing the overall performance attained by nine strains of mice, Bovet et al (9) were able to show that their strains were very poor in avoidance performance in the shuttle box, and that in Lashley III maze situations, two other strains (DBA/2J and C57Br/cdJ) attained a very high level of performance, while other strains showed intermediate values. These behavioral differences were also demonstrated to be qualitative, since the study of distributed versus massed practice in avoidance and maze learning showed that under the same training conditions some strains were characterized by good short-term performance, while other strains were characterized by more efficient memory storage mechanisms. A number of behavioral measures have been assessed in some of the strains that have been used in diallel studies and that have been intercrossed until the F_2 and F_3 generations to assess genetic correlations (44). For example, the high-avoiding strains SEC/1ReJ and DBA/2J mice, which are also good maze learners, are characterized by low levels of exploratory behavior and running activity, while the C57BL/6J strain shows poor avoidance performance and maze learning but is very active (44). By using different strains it has also been shown that the mode of inheritance of a given behavioral measure depends on the crosses considered: crossing the C57 strain with the SEC strain resulted in SEC-like progeny, while crossing DBA with C57 yielded an offspring similar to the C57 genotype. A similar behavioral pattern was evident for avoidance and maze learning.

A number of findings are available today on these three strains (C57BL/6, DBA/2, and SEC/1Re); their biochemical differences at the brain level are reported in Table 14-1. A number of estimates dealing with the GABAminergic, noradrenergic, dopaminergic, and cholinergic systems or with amino acids and protein synthesis were considered; due to the different technical procedures used by various authors, the differences evident between these strains were expressed by using a ranking procedure. The results indicate that the three strains clearly differ in their brain biochemistry—which is rather obvious—but also that a number of possible behavioral-biochemistry correlates are evident, a point that will be discussed later.

At the present time it is important to point out that the reason for assessing these biochemical estimates was related to the amount of behavioral data indicating that these strains are different and represent a useful behavioral model. Some behavioral findings are also summarized in Table 15-1; however, for the sake of clarity it is worth remembering the main characteristics of these strains.

Table 14-1. Biochemical and Behavioral Differences Between Three Inbred Strains of Mice[a]

	Strains		
Biochemicals	*C57/BL/6*	*DBA/2*	*SEC/1Re*
Glutamic acid decarboxylase	II 51,67,69; I 76	I II	
GABA transaminase	II 76	I	
GABA	I 60	II	III
Monoamine oxidase	I 31,69; II 50,51	II I	
Catechol-O-methyl transferase	I, 69	II	
Tyrosine hydroxilase	II 15; I 16	I II	
Tyrosine hydroxilase – pons + medulla	I 68	II	
Tyrosine hydroxilase – hypothalamus	II 68	I	
Cyclic AMP	III 55	I	II
Noradrenaline – pons + medulla	I 25	III	II
Noradrenaline – hypothalamus	I 25	II	III
Noradrenaline – cortex	II 25	I	III
Noradrenaline – amygdala	II 75	I	
Noradrenaline – frontal cortex	II 75	I	
Noradrenaline – hypothalamus	II 75	I	
Noradrenaline – hippocampus	I 75	II	
Dopamine	II 25	I	III
Serotonin	I 25	III	II
Aromatic-L-amino acid decarboxilase	III 50,51	I	II
Choline acetylase	II 69	I	
Choline acetylase – frontal	II 18,36,37,43	I	III
Choline acetylase – temporal	III 18,36,37,43	I	II
Acetylcholine esterase – total	III 18,36,37,43,51,69	I	II
Acetylcholine esterase – frontal	II 18,36,37,43	I	III
Acetylcholine esterase – temporal	III 18,36,37,43	I	II
Choline esterase	I 50,51	II	
Na^+ K^+ ATIase	II 65	I	
Taurine, aspartine, glutamic acid	I 60	III	II
GABA	I 60	II	III
Serine, arginine	III 60	II	I
Histidine	II 60	III	I
Polyribosome/ribosome	I 29	II	
Synaptic membranes	I 23	II	
Hypoxanthine-guanine phospo ribosil transferase	II 66	I	
S100 protein	II 35	I	
Behavior			
Exploratory activity	I 44, 71	II	III
Aggressive behavior	I 23,27,52,62	II	
Active avoidance	III 9,13,44,51	II	I
NREM sleep	II 70	I	
Wheel running activity	I 34,42,44,47	II	III
Circadian rhythmicity	I 42,47	II	III
Maternal behavior	I 17		II
Brain weight	III 53	I	II
Cortical thickness	II 21		I

[a] The roman numerals refer to the ranking order between the three strains (ranking I indicates the highest observed value for a given characteristic); the arabic numbers, to the references.

C57 mice are characterized by lower brain weight (53) and lower thickness of brain cortex and corpus callosum (21) than SEC or DBA mice, by higher amounts of maternal care (17) or of aggressive behavior (52,62), by higher exploratory locomotor and wheel-running activity (34,42,44,71), by more pronounced circadian wheel running and sleep rhythmicity (34), and by lower levels of passive or active avoidance and maze learning (9,44,63) than DBA or SEC mice. Finally, the time spent in non-REM and REM sleep is lower in the C57 strain than in the other two strains (70).

It is obviously difficult to summarize in a limited space the large number of findings available. However, it is possible to indicate two main points: (*1*) The three strains considered are characterized by sharp phenotypic differences at the brain and behavioral levels, and (*2*) within the framework of the classification proposed by Altman (3), it is possible, in a general way, to indicate that the behavioral patterns of C57 mice are characterized to a large extent by the role of paleoencephalic or instinctive processes (circadian patterns, locomotor activity, maternal behavior, emotional and aggressive behavior), while the behavioral patterns of SEC (or DBA or BALB/c) mice are characterized by a more relevant role of the neencephalic processes or individual adaptation (escape and avoidance behavior, visual discrimination, maze learning, etc.). These behavioral data have been fitted into a tentative theoretical model in which the two strains are considered in terms of innate contributions or of learning (Fig. 14-2).

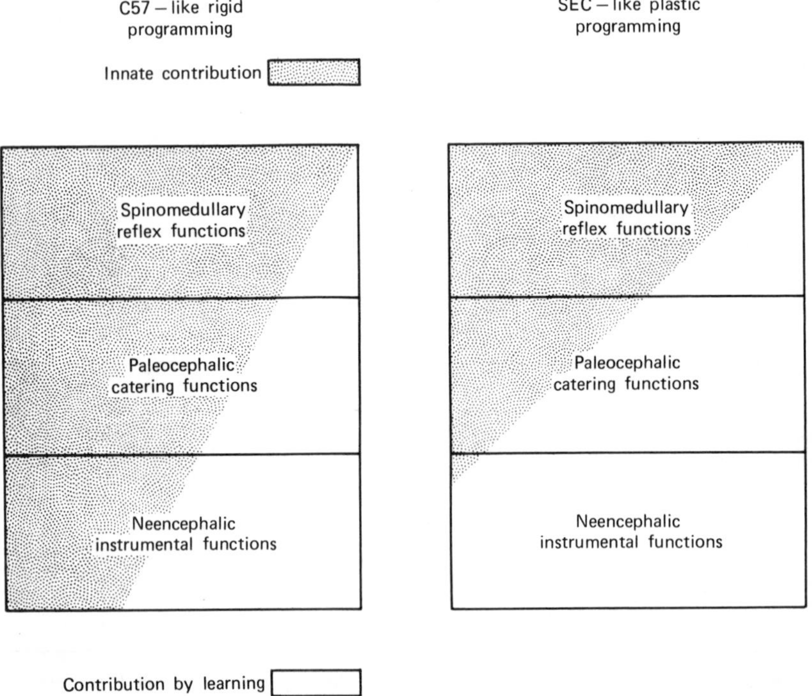

Figure 14-2. A theoretical model for the role of innate contribution or of learning in the reflex, catering, and instrumental functions in two strains of mice (C57BL/6 and SEC/1Re).

A GENETIC APPROACH TO MATURITY AT BIRTH AND BEHAVIOR ONTOGENY

A second approach deserves consideration, that is, the study of behavioral ontogeny. For example, a number of studies have demonstrated that capacity for long-term memory increases during postnatal development: a variety of mechanisms, both behavioral and neurological, may account for the increase in memory and learning during ontogenesis, as is evident in a comprehensive review by Campbell and Spear (12).

The psychogenetic, and also the ontogenetic, approach to behavioral adaptation may be based on a less direct strategy: instead of looking for the direct correlates of specific memorization a study of the neurological and neurochemical ontogeny, which parallels memory and learning development, may be very fruitful. In addition to a number of behavioral changes taking place during development (reflex activities, locomotor activities, mother-offspring relationships, memory, and a number of complex adaptive behaviors), there are a number of changes in the central nervous system that result in behavioral maturity: myelinization, cell differentiation, development of electrical activity, neural transmission, nucleic acid content, protein synthesis, and metabolic rate are just a few examples of these complex developmental changes.

This type of approach may also be based on an analysis of the role exerted by the genetic and environmental factors on behavioral ontogenesis. The importance of the gestational and early postnatal environments in human infants has been stressed by Soviet psychologists, chiefly by Luria (28), who suggest that a heterogeneous number of gestational and perinatal factors may result in mental retardation. Similarly, the interest in the early determinants of behavior has increased as a result of a number of studies that indicate that infants react to environmental differences from the first days or weeks of life (48,56,73). This approach has resulted in the development of a number of scales, measures, and physiological tests that may be applied from the first days of life. While Soviet psychologists are more inclined toward the use of electrophysiological measures, which may be assessed in the newborn, the trend in the United States is oriented more toward the use of different scales in which a number of reflex activities and of behavioral postures are quantified (6,10,11).

It is worth stressing that the experiments conducted on animal models may represent a useful step toward a better knowledge of the role of the environment on behavioral ontogenesis.

It was previously noted that maturity at birth in mammals represents an important point in evolutionary terms, since the behavior of precocial species must be related in part to innate mechanisms, while altricial species, in which brain and behavioral maturation occurs later, are more plastic and are modifiable to a greater extent by the environment. The strains of mice previously considered are also different in their patterns of postnatal neurological and behavioral development. If we consider the electrocorticographic activity, which was shown to parallel the different stages of maturation of the cortex (26), there are strains such as C57 that are more mature at birth and strains such as SEC that are less mature: at 8 days of age the electrical activity of the cortex of SEC mice was similar to that evident in the C57 strain on day 1 of postnatal life (45). Similar developmental differences were also evident when a number of reflex activities were considered. Reflexes such as cliff aversion, righting, placing, grasping, or the startle response appeared at an earlier age (3 to 4 days sooner) in the C57 strain (46). These findings indicate that there are clear genetic differences in the intraspecific patterns of postnatal maturation, which suggests that the individual genetic makeup may also set the limits within which the environment is able to affect the patterns of postnatal maturation.

It may well be that a strain that is more precocial at birth is less reactive to environmental differences (*1*) because its behavior is more "rigidly" determined and (*2*) because a more precocial brain maturation leaves less room for the stimulating or detrimental effects of environmental situations (see Fig. 14-1). Independent of the mechanisms implicated, it was shown that the effects connected with an early impoverished or enriched environment were less evident in the C57 strain than in the SEC strain. In fact, SEC mice reared postnatally in an enriched or impoverished environment attained, when adults, a higher or lower performance, respectively, in different learning tasks. However, the effects of the two environmental situations were less evident in the C57 strain (41).

Thus, a number of biochemical and morphological differences at the brain level characterize strains that also differ in their pattern of postnatal development and that present clear-cut behavioral differences in the adult. Other findings indicate that the strains considered not only are different in their developmental rhythms or are characterized to a larger extent by "instinctive" processes or by patterns of individual adaptation respectively but are also characterized by behavioral rigidity or plasticity in different environmental situations.

BEHAVIORAL RIGIDITY OR PLASTICITY

As previously noted, the paleoencephalic activities control a number of circadian energy-deployment processes. As for the strains considered in our theoretical model, it was shown that C57 mice are characterized by clear-cut differences between the circadian patterns of sleep, while no sharp differences are evident in the SEC strain (70). Recent data on these strains of mice also indicate that free-running rhythms of sleep and activity may be plastic or rigid, depending on the genetic factors involved in the expression of circadian rhythmicity. Under 12–12 hour light-dark (L-D) schedules it was shown that the external synchronizer induces well-defined activity phases at night and lower levels during the hours of light in C57 and SEC mice. However, when the running activity of the strains was assessed under constant light (L-L) or darkness, it was shown that C57 mice (and other strains) maintain a pronounced circadian rhythm in the absence of external synchronizers, while SEC mice (and other strains such as BALB/c) do not show a clear-cut circadian rhythm (33,41).

A clearer demonstration of the importance of the genetic factors in modulating the plasticity or rigidity of those two (and others) strains was evident by studying wheel running and sleep under L-D schedules shorter than 12-12 hours. The effects of 12–12-hour, 6–6-hour, 3–3-hour, and 1–1-hour L-D cycles and of constant light (L-L) were studied in C57 and SEC mice (47). Wheel-running activity and sleep were inhibited by light and were enhanced by darkness; however, in the C57 strain the L-D induced changes were less pronounced and were superimposed on a clear circadian rhythm. Under the subsequent L-L schedule, clear patterns of daily rhythmicity were evident in the C57 strain but not in the SEC strain (Fig. 14-3). A second finding was rather interesting: SEC mice shifted from a short L-D schedule to a condition of constant light retain for a short time the experience of their previous rhythmic performance, that is, they show a rhythmic behavior similar to that induced by the previous L-D schedule, which might indicate that a pacemaker is able to "memorize" a rhythm determined by environmental cues. This finding and the absence of rhythmicity of SEC mice under constant light indicate that there are nonspecific structures that may assume a transient pacemaker function when the circadian rhythms are not rigidly programmed. Therefore, it seems likely that some strains are more plastic and are influenced by the environment not only for a number of acquired "neencephalic" behavioral activities but also for such instinctive paleoencephalic behavioral processes as sleep or locomotor activity.

Do these findings mean that these patterns of circadian rhythmicity respond essentially to inborn mechanisms, and that we must consider that the C57-type of circadian rigidity is determined by an inborn mechanism? Generally it is assumed that a number of circadian functions respond to strict inborn mechanisms; however, it may be that for some individuals or species these mechanisms may be modulated by early experience as well. The rhythms of animals have been studied for generations under constant conditions and also under unusual day-light schedules to ascertain whether behavioral rhythms are learned early in life or whether they respond to inborn mechanisms (4). The problem is rather difficult since, under conditions of constant light, mammals could bequeath circadian rhythms to their young by rhythms of maternal activity. These rhythms may be transmitted to the young mammals through successive generations despite constant or anomalous environmental conditions. Since C57 mice are more mature at birth than SEC mice, this fact may play an important role in a number of precocious interactions with the environment: it might also be that in an altricial species such as *Mus musculus* imprinting-like phenomena play an important role, and that this role is more evident in those strains that are more mature at birth. As a matter of fact, the relationships between early experience and sexual preferences in the mouse were assessed by Mainardi et al (32) and recently were discussed by Bateson (5).

The experiments on circadian rhythmicity support the existence of imprinting-like mechanisms and indicate that rearing in constant light or imprinting to 12–12-hour L-D cycles can affect wheel-running activity. As was previously noted, a clear circadian rhythm is characteristic of C57 mice reared under 12–12-h L-D cycles when their activity rhythm is allowed to free run in continuous light, while no evidence of circadian rhythmicity is evident in the SEC mice. On the contrary, C57 and SEC mice reared under constant light do not show a clear pattern of daily rhythmicity under continuous light. C57 mice imprinted to 12–12-h L-D cycles during days 15 to 18 show a clear circadian pattern under constant light. As expected no evidence for the imprinting-life phenomenon was evident in the SEC mice (33).

In subsequent experiments it was also shown that synchronizers other than light may play a role in entraining activity rhythms when the animals are subject to these synchronizers early in life (1). Similarly, it was also shown that in strains such as C57—but not in those such as SEC—imprinting-like phenomena also play an important role in sexual behavior (2) (Fig. 14-5).

In general the findings reported in this section emphasize the existence of rigid or plastic behavioral mechanisms within the same species and also in relation to paleoencephalic mechanisms, which should be strictly set by the genetic makeup. Again, the possibility that cerebral precocity or maturity at birth influences behavioral specialization or generalization cannot be ignored.

At this point it is perhaps possible to link together all the findings presented within

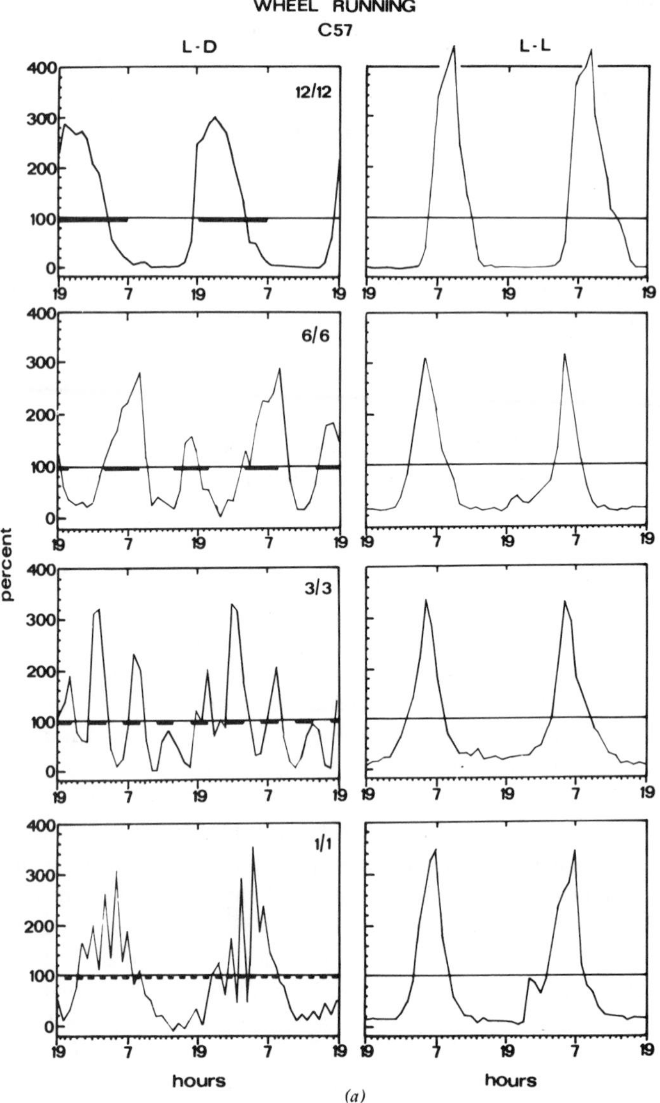

(a)

Figure 14-3. Wheel-running behavior of different groups of C57 (*a*) and SEC mice (*b*) subjected to different L-D schedules (12–12, 6–6, 3–3 and 1–1 hours; left) and subsequently to a L-L schedule (right). The parameters are plotted as mean percent deviations from the average 24-hour activity (100% level) for successive 1-hour periods (e.g., the value plotted at 7 applies to the period from 6 to 7). The black bars superimposed on the 100% performance line indicate the dark periods. The L-D graphs refer to the performance of different groups of 8 mice during days 19 and 20. The graphs on the right (L-L schedule) refer to the performance of each group of mice on days 21 and 22. (From Oliverio and Malorni, ref. 47.)

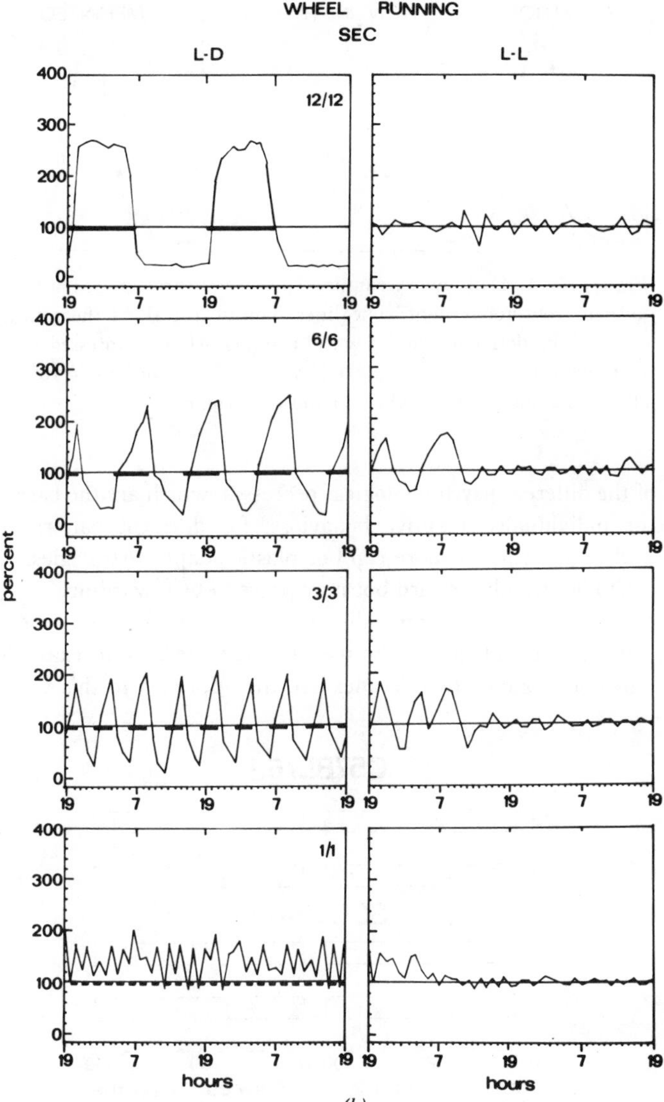

(b)

Figure 14-3. (Continued)

the framework of this genetic model and to look at its possible implications. The advantages of a genetic approach to the problem of behavioral adaptation—ranging from simple habituation to complex learning and adaptive strategies—are not only connected to the crude application of simple or complex biometric techniques: tracing gene-behavior pathways may represent a direct approach but, apart from indicating a major or minor genetic involvement, it is questionable whether this approach might be helpful in solving through artificial selection or other quantitative genetic techniques the problem of the psychobiological-neurochemical and neurophysiological correlates of the adaptive mechanisms. On the contrary, behavior genetics may offer an indirect approach

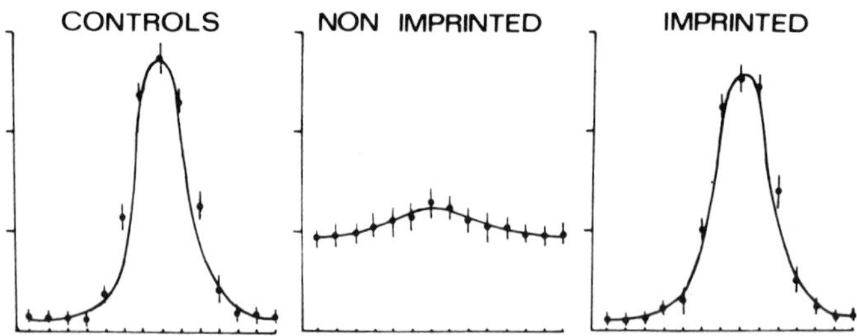

Figure 14-4. Daily wheel-running rhythms of three groups of C57 mice in continuous light. The lines indicate the fitted theoretical curves. The dots indicate the wheel-running activity expressed as a percentage (± SEM) of daily mean level. Scale: ordinates 100%, abscissas 2 hours. (From Malorni and Oliverio, ref. 33.)

to the study of the different psychobiological processes, which are the bases for a number of instictive or individually adaptive behaviors, for different patterns of behavioral ontogenesis, and in general, for more rigid or plastic adaptive strategies. This approach may not appear to be straightforward but may prove to be rewarding.

To consider the advantages of an indirect, more comprehensive genetic model, and before going into it in detail, it may be useful to consider, as an example, the field of learning and memory: one or two decades ago the approach to this field aimed at the

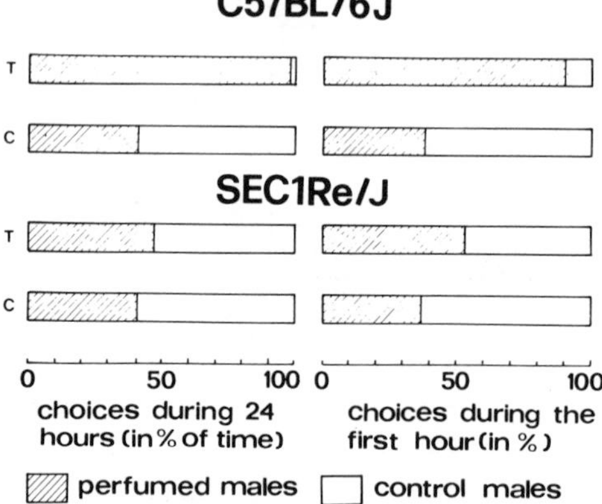

Figure 14-5. Choices during 24 hours (in percentage of time spent with males, left) and choices during the first hour (in percentage of choices between the two compartments homing a control or a perfumed male, right). Data plotted on the right graph were obtained by dividing the first hour of the test in 10 blocks of 6 minutes each, for example, for a given 6-minute block a score of 100% was assigned to a female who spent more than 50% of her time with one of the two males. The columns express the mean scores of a group of females during the 10 blocks.

study of simple animal models, different types of learning being studied in their simplest forms in monocellular organisms or in invertebrates with the purpose of finding the general laws of this behavior. From a biochemical point of view the approach to learning and memory was also rather straightforward and was based on the analysis of macromolecular storage, chemical transfer, and neurotransmitters and on the effects produced by a number of chemical or physical agents interfering with learning or memory consolidation. This large array of studies and the number of findings reported in the literature indicate that the problem is really complex, and that there are a number of systems or subsystems to be investigated: this also is indicated by a recent review by Will (74) in which he analyzes the main correlational studies between learning and neurochemistry. Many findings indicate possible correlations with the cholinergic system or with adrenergic, serotoninergic, or dopaminergic mechanisms. Other studies analyze the role of proteins and nucleic acids (Table 14-2). These were the "main" correlative studies up to 1977, but today there is a body of research dealing with naturally occurring peptides, which no doubt play a role in a number of adaptive mechanisms.

It is difficult to state whether all the neurochemical systems and chemicals listed in Table 14-2 play a primary or a secondary role in these behavioral states, whether a given biochemical response is related to stimulation, acquisition, or experience. Certainly, this direct correlational approach is extremely complex, as indicated in a comprehensive review by Entingh et al (19), and seems to justify an indirect approach based on a neurophysiological and neurochemical analysis of behavioral individuality. In this regard the existence of strains that present a number of phenotypic differences at the brain level, that are behaviorally more precocial or less precocial at birth, and that are more rigid or plastic in relation to a number of environmental situations, seems to offer a powerful model. Let us then start from this point of view, that the existence of large individual (or strain) differences at the brain level represents the necessary condition for different adaptive behavioral mechanisms. A major role of some paleoencephalic

Table 14-2. Correlational Studies Between Learning and Neurochemistry[a]

Parameter	*Number of Studies*[b]
Cholinergic system	29
"Enzymes"	28
Serotoninergic system	10
Noradrenergic system	8
Proteins and nucleic acids	8
Dopaminergic system	5

[a] Summarized from Will (74).

[b] Total number of studies on inbred mice: 12.

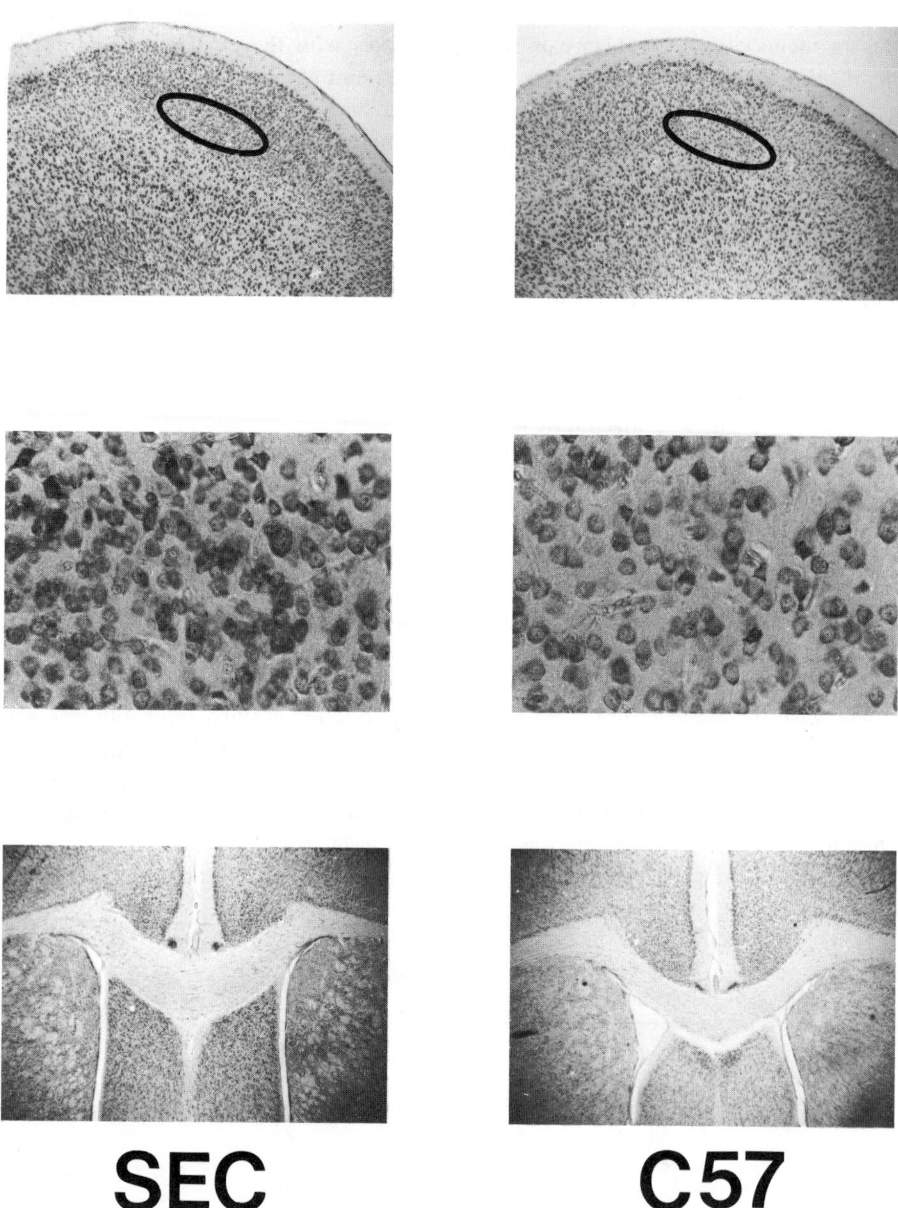

Figure 14-6. Photomicrographs of sections of cerebral cortex (top and middle) and corpus callosum (bottom) of SEC (left) and C57 (right) strains. The circled areas, which correspond to the fourth layer, are enlarged in the middle pictures (toluidine blue staining). (From Gozzo et al, ref. 21.)

or neencephalic nuclei (see Wahlsten, ref. 72, for a review), a higher amount or turnover of a neurotransmitter on a specific structure produce (and reflect) differences in the levels of arousal, in stereotyped or variable activities, in behavioral rigidity or flexibility. Independent of whether this biochemical diversity represents the starting point for a behavioral diversity or whether it depends on a selective pressure that exploits some "useful" behavioral differences there are outstanding regional differences for the levels and the turnover of some key mediators between different strains of mice.

When we consider the genetic model proposed in this chapter it is possible to observe, as was suggested by Mandel and his coworkers (18,25,36,37), that the strains that are more behaviorally aroused and that present more "stereotyped" exploratory activities (such as C57 mice) are characterized by more active noradrenergic mechanisms at the level of the pons and medulla or by lower levels of serotonin. On the contrary, the cholinergic turnover is higher at the level of the temporal cortex (which is associated with memory processes) in the SEC or DBA strain. Similarly, some estimates of protein synthesis indicate a lower activity in the C57 strain, which is characterized by poor performance in a number of learning tasks. These are just some indications that there are a number of biochemical differences that may justify the behavioral findings.

It is worth noting that differences in cholinergic activity or in protein synthesis may also be connected to the dramatic morphological differences evident between the brains of C57 and SEC mice; Figure 14-6 in the latter strain the second, third, and fifth layers of the temporal cortex and of the corpus callosum are thicker and the gray-cell coefficients in the frontal region are higher (21). The lower neuronal density in the cortex of C57 mice results in a reduced number of synaptic connections within each hemisphere and between the two hemispheres, as suggested by the decreased thickness of the corpus callosum when compared with the SEC strain. The higher neuronal density in the cortex of SEC mice seems to be a possible interesting morphological correlate for their behavioral flexibility. A second factor that leads to behavioral plasticity or rigidity is related to the patterns of postnatal maturation; these patterns are different in various inbred strains, which are more or less mature at birth from a neurological and behavioral point of view. It is possible that the genetic "programs" that lead to maturational differences also involve differences in the role of the instinctive or of the individual adaptation processes. In other words, as previously suggested, there are strains that are similar to precocial species and strains that are similar to altricial species. However, it is obvious that those strains that are characterized by slower maturational patterns are more sensitive to the effects of the environment and have more opportunities (and needs) to work up individual adaptive strategies.

This model, shown in Figure 14-7, indicates that species, strains, or individuals are different not for a single aspect of their behavior but for a number of behavioral

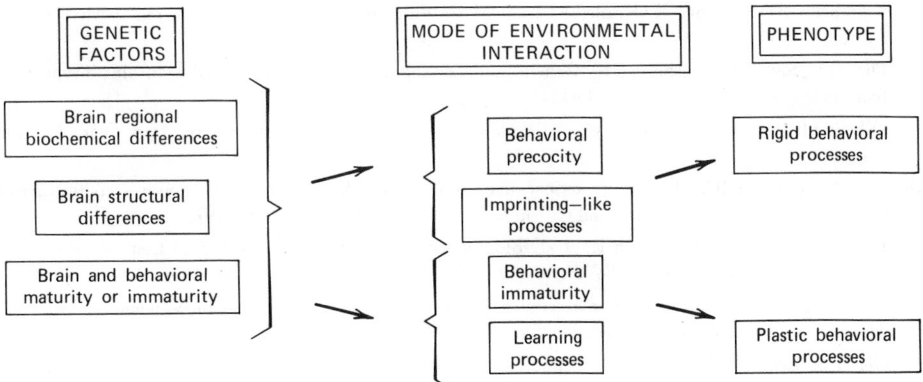

Figure 14-7. A theoretical model for the role of genetic and environmental factors related to behavioral rigidity or plasticity.

strategies and neurophysiological and maturational process that also set the mode of their interaction with the environment. Within the same species, strategies such as instinctive processes, early experience, or learning may represent different mechanisms of survival and adaptation. The analysis of a number of behavioral patterns such as sleep, early experience, play, aggression, reactions to new stimuli, neophobia, perseverance, or response variability and of their possible psychobiological correlates should allow in the future a better understanding of the different environmental and behavioral situations that produce new responses and therefore the passage from behavioral specialization and rigidity to generalization and plasticity.

REFERENCES

1. Alleva E, Renzi P, Oliverio A: Rearing in presence of acoustic rhythms affects circadian locomotor rhythmicity of adult mice. *Neuroscience* (submitted).
2. Alleva E, D'Udine B, Oliverio A: Early experience and sexual preferences in the females of two strains of mice. *Behavioral Processes* (submitted).
3. Altman J: *Organic Foundations of Animal Behavior.* New York, Holt Rinehart and Winston, 1966.
4. Aschoff J: Exogenous and endogenous components in circadian rhythms. *Symp Quant Biol (Cold Springs Harbor)* 25:11–27, 1960.
5. Bateson PPG: Early experience and sexual preferences, in Hutchison JB (ed): *Biological Determinants of Sexual Behaviour.* London, Wiley, pp 29–53.
6. Bailey N: *Manual for the Bailey scales of infants.* New York, Psychological Corporation, 1969.
7. Beritashvilii IS: *Vertebrate Memory. Characteristics and Origin.* New York, Plenum Press, 1971.
8. Bitterman ME: Phyletic differences in learning. *Am Psychol* 20:396–410, 1965.
9. Bovet D, Bovet-Nitti F, Oliverio A: Genetic aspects of learning and memory in mice. *Science* 163:139–149, 1969.
10. Brazelton TB: *Neonatal Behavioral Assessment Scale.* London, Heinemann Medical Books, 1973.
11. Broman SH, Nichols PL, Gennedy WA: *Preschool IQ. Prenatal and Early Developmental Correlates.* Hillsdale, NY, Lawrence Earlbaum Associates, 1975.
12. Campbell BA, Spear NE: Ontogeny of memory. *Psychol Rev* 79:215–236, 1972.
13. Caspari E: Genetic basis of behavior, in Roe A, Simpson GG (eds): *Behavior and Evolution.* New Haven, Conn, Yale University Press, 1958.
14. Chance MRA: Social cohesion and the structure of attention, in Fox R (ed): *Biosocial Anthropology.* New York, Wiley, 1975.
15. Ciaranello RD, Barchas R, Kessler S, et al: Strain differences in biosynthetic enzyme activity in mice. *Life Sci* 11:565–572, 1972.
16. Diez JA, Sze PY, Ginsburg BE: Genetic and developmental variation in mouse brain. Tryptophan hydroxylase activity. *Brain Res* 109:413–417, 1976.
17. D'Udine B: Behavioral differences in maternal care in two different strains of mice. *Anim Behav* (submitted).
18. Ebel A, Hermetet JC, Mandel P: Comparative study of acetylcholinesterase and choline acetyltransferase enzyme activity in brain of DBA and C57 mice. *Nature-New Biol* 242:56–57, 1973.
19. Entingh D, Dunn A, Glassman E, et al: Biochemical approaches to the biological basis of memory, in Gazzaniga HS, Blakemore C (eds): *Handbook of Psychobiology.* New York, Academic Press, 1975.
20. Fuller JL: Suggestions from animal studies for human behavior genetics, in Vandenberg SG (ed): *Methods and Goals in Human Behavior Genetics.* New York, Academic Press, 1965.
21. Gozzo S, Renzi P, D'Udine B: Morphological differences in cerebral cortex and corpus callosum are genetically determined in two different strains of mice. *Int J Neurosci* 9:91–96, 1979.
22. Green EL: *Biology of the Laboratory Mouse,* ed 2. New York, McGraw-Hill, 1966.

23. Gurd RS, Mahler HR, Moore WJ: Differences in protein patterns on polyacrylamide-gel electrophoresis of neuronal membranes from mice of different strains. *J Neurochem* 19:553–556, 1972.

24. Jouvet M: *L'histoire naturelle du rêe.* Paris, Institut de France, 1976.

25. Kempf E, Greilsamer J, Mack G, et al: Correlation of behavioural differences in three strains of mice with differences in brain amines. *Nature* 247:483–485, 1974.

26. Kobayashi T, Inman O, Buno W, et al: A multidisciplinary study of changes in mouse brain with age. *Recent Adv Biol Psychiat* 5:293–308, 1963.

27. Lindzey G, Thiessen DD: *Contributions to Behavior—Genetic Analysis. The Mouse as a Prototype.* New York, Appleton-Century-Crofts, 1970.

28. Luria AR: *L'enfant retardé mental.* Paris, Privat, 1972.

29. MacInnes JW, Schlesinger K: Effects of excess phenylalanine on in vitro and in vivo RNA and protein synthesis and polyribosome levels in brains of mice. *Brain Res* 29:101–110, 1971.

30. MacLean PD: The imitative-creative interplay of our three mentalities, in Harris H (ed): *Astride the Two Cultures.* London, Hutchinson, 1975, pp 187–213.

31. MacPike AD, Meier H: Genotype dependence of monoamine oxidase in inbred strains of mice. *Experientia* 32:979–980, 1976.

32. Mainardi D, Marsan M, Pasquali A: Causation of sexual preferences of the house mouse. The behavior of mice reared by parents whose odour was artificially altered. *Atti Soc It Sc Nat* 104:325–338, 1965.

33. Malorni W, Oliverio A: Imprinting to light-dark cycle or rearing in constant light affect circadian locomotor rhythm of mice. *Neuroscience Letters* 9:93–96, 1978.

34. Malorni W, Oliverio A, Bovet D: Analyse génétique d'activité circadienne chez la souris. *CR Acad Sci Paris* 281:1479–1484, 1975.

35. Malup TK, Sviridov SM: Neurospecific S-100 protein content in brains of different mouse strains. *Brain Res* 142:97–103, 1978.

36. Mandel P, Ayad G, Hermetet JC, et al: Correlation between choline acetyltransferase activity and learning ability in different mice strains and their offspring. *Brain Res* 72:65–70, 1974.

37. Mandel P, Ebel A, Hermetet JC, et al: Etudes des Enzymes du système cholinergique chez les hybrides F1 des souris se distinguant par leur aptitude au conditionnement. *CR Hebd Séanc Acad Sci Paris* 276:395–398, 1973.

38. Mayr E: Behavior programs and evolutionary strategies. *Amer Scient* 62:650:650–659, 1974.

39. Medvedev NN: On the breeding of the laboratory strain mice. *Biulletini Moskoskogo Obestva Ispitateki Prirodvi* 63:117–133, 1958.

40. Oliverio A: *Genetics, Environment and Intelligence.* Amsterdam, Elsevier/North-Holland, 1977.

41. Oliverio A: La maturation de l'EEG et du sommeil: Facteurs génétiques et du milieu. *Rev EEG Neurophysiol* 7:263–268, 1977.

42. Oliverio A, Catellano C: Postnatal brain maturation and learning in the mouse, in Oliverio A (ed): *Genetics, Environment and Intelligence* Amsterdam, Elsevier/North-Holland, 1977, pp 117–131.

43. Oliverio A, Catellano C, Ebel A, et al: A genetic analysis of behavior: a neurochemical approach, in Costa E, Gessa GL, Sandler M (eds): *Advances in Biochemistry and Psychopharmacology*: Serotonin New Vistas, vol 11. New York, Raven Press, 1974, pp 411–418.

44. Oliverio A, Catellano C, Messeri P: A genetic analysis of avoidance, maze and wheel running behaviors in the mouse. *J Comp Physiol Psychol* 79:459–473, 1972.

45. Oliverio A, Catellano C, Renzi P: Genotype or prenatal drug experience affect brain maturation in the mouse. *Brain Res* 90:357–360, 1975.

46. Oliverio A, Catellano C, Puglisi-Allegra S: Effects of genetic and nutritional factors on post-natal reflex and behavioral development in the mouse. *Exp Ag Res* 1:41–56, 1975.

47. Oliverio A, Malorni W: Wheel running and sleep in two strains of mice: plasticity and rigidity in the expression of circadian rhythmicity. *Brain Res* 63:121–133, 1979.

48. Papoušek H: Conditioning during early postnatal development, in Brackbill Y, Thompson J (eds): *Behavior in Infancy and Early Childhood.* New York, The Free Press, 1967.

49. Parker CE: Behavioral diversity in ten species of non human primates. *J Comp Physiol Psychol* 87:930–937, 1974.

50. Pryor GT: Postnatal development of cholinesterase, acetylcholinesterase, aromatic L-amino acid decarboxylase and monoamine axidase in C57BL/6 and DBA/2 mice. *Life Sci* 7:867–874, 1968.
51. Pryor GT, Schlesinger K, Calhoun WH: Differences in brain enzymes among five inbred strains of mice. *Life Sci* 5:2105–2111, 1966.
52. Puglisi-Allegra S: Unpublished results.
53. Roderick TH, Ruddle FH, Chapman VM, et al: Biochemical polymorphisms in feral and inbred mice, *Mus musculus*. *Biochem Genet* 5:457–466, 1971.
54. Rojas-Ramirez JA, Drucker-Colin RD: Phylogenetic correlations between sleep and memory, in Drucker-Colin RR, Mc-Gaugh JL (eds) New York, Academic Press, 1977.
55. Sattin A: Cyclic amp accumulation in cerebral cortex tissue from inbred strains of mice. *Life Sci* 16:903–913, 1975.
56. Scarr-Samapatek S, Williams ML: The effect of early stimulation on low-birth-weight infants. *Child Dev* 44:94–101, 1973.
57. Schneirla TC: Behavioral development and comparative psychology. *Q Rev Biol* 41:283–302, 1966.
58. Scott JP: *Animal Behavior*. Chicago, University of Chicago Press, 1958.
59. Sedlacek J: The significance of the perinatal period in the neural and behavioral development of precocial mammals, in Gottlieb G (ed) *Aspects of Neurogenesis*. New York, Academic Press, 1974, pp 245–273.
60. Simler S, Randrianarisoa H, Koehl C, et al: Pool des acides animés libres du cerveau de souris de lignées consanguines présentant des différences d'aptitude à l'apprentissage. *CR Soc Biol Paris* 171:942–946, 1977.
61. Slucking W: *Imprinting and Early Learning*. Chicago, Aldine, 1965.
62. Southwick CH, Clark LH: Aggressive behavior and exploratory activity in fourteen mouse strains. *Amer Zool* 6:559, 1966.
63. Sprott RL: Inheritance of avoidance learning. *The Jackson Laboratory's Annual Report* 42:78, 1971.
64. Staats JL: Standard nomenclature for inbred strains of mice: fifth listing. *Cancer Res* 32:1609–1646, 1972.
65. Stefanovic V, Ebel A, Hermetet JC, et al: Na^+-K^+-aptase activity in brain regions of C57 and DBA Mice, *J Neurochem* 22:1139–1141, 1974.
66. Suran AA: Hypoxanthine-guanine phosphoribosyl transferase in brains of mice. Regional distribution in seven inbred mouse strains. *Life Sci* 13:1779–1788, 1973.
67. Sze PY: Genetic variation in brain L-glutamate decarboxylase activity from two inbred strains of mice. *Brain Res* 122:56–69, 1977.
68. Tiplady B, Killian JJ, Mandel P: Tyrosine hydroxylase in various brain regions of three strains of mice defering in spontaneous activity, learning ability and emotionality. *Life Sci* 18:1065–1070, 1976.
69. Tunnicliff G, Wimer CC, Wimer RE: Relationships between neurotransmitter metabolism and behaviour in seven inbred strains of mice. *Brain Res* 61:428–434, 1973.
70. Valatx JL, Bugat R, Jouvet M: Genetic studies of sleep in mice. *Nature* 238:226–227, 1972.
71. van Abeelen JHF: Effects of genotype on mouse behavior. *Anim Behav* 14:218–225, 1966.
72. Wahlsten D: Heredity and brain structure, in Oliverio A (ed): *Genetics, Environment and Intelligence*. Amsterdam, Elsevier/North-Holland, 1977, 93–116.
73. White BL: *Human Infants, Experience and Psychological Development*. Cambridge, Mass, Harvard University Press, 1971.
74. Will BE: Neurochemical correlates of individual differences in animal learning capacity. *Behav Biol* 19:143–171, 1977.
75. Wimer RE, Norman R, Eleftheriou BE: Serotonin levels in hippocampus, striking variations associated with mouse strain and treatment. *Brain Res* 63:397–401, 1973.
76. Wong E, Schousboe A, Saito K, Immunochemical studies of brain glutamate decarboxylase and GABA-transaminase of six inbred strains of mice. *Brain Res* 68:133–142, 1974.

15 Methodological Problems in Observing Learning and Memory by Operant Conditioning in Rats

Hisashi Kuribara
Tetsu Hayashi
Kyoichi Ohashi
Sakutaro Tadokoro

INTRODUCTION

In recent years, various problems of learning and memory have attracted attention in the fields of neurophysiology and psychology. The elucidation of their basic mechanisms is considered one of the most important objectives of scientific study. Not only have such basic studies become part of the fields of pharmacology, toxicology, and endocrinology but so too has the application of findings on learning and memory processes. For example, the development of irreversible damage to the central nervous system produced by a drug or a chemical may be detected as a behavioral disorder or as a deficit in learning. On the other hand, if a dysfunction is produced by a certain drug at a particular brain site, as well as the retardation of learning, one may be able to find a key for the elucidation of the mechanisms of learning and memory. Regardless of the object of the experiment on the animal level, it is important to establish a method by which learning and memory processes can be observed easily, reliably, quantitatively, and objectively.

In this chapter we wish to discuss, on the basis of operant behavior experiments in rats obtained from our laboratory, the following problems: first, what kinds of reinforcement schedules are suitable to observe the learning and memory processes and second, what kinds of factors affect these processes.

MATERIALS AND METHODS

Experimental Animals

Adult male albino rats of the Wistar, Sprague-Dawley, and Holtzman strains were used. They were all supplied by the breeding colony of the School of Medicine, Gunma

University. The Wistar rats have been maintained by brother-sister mating for about 25 years. Groups of three to four animals were kept in wire mesh cages, 38 (D) × 25 (W) × 19 (H) cm, and fed a solid diet MF (Oriental Yeast Co., Tokyo) and tap water ad libitum. The temperature of the breeding room was kept at 25 ± 2°C throughout the experimental period. Humidity was not controlled. At the start of training, the animals were 10 weeks of age and weighed about 250 gm. For the rats used in the avoidance tests, breeding conditions were not altered even during the training period, and all animals were allowed to take food and water freely in their home cages except during the time of training. However, the animals used in the positive reinforcement schedule were reduced in body weight by food deprivation to about 80% of those free feeding. Water was given freely.

Reinforcement Schedules

Figure 15-1 schematically shows an operant conditioning chamber and its attachments. With this apparatus, three schedules were used to observe the acquisition process in rats: free-operant avoidance schedule; discriminated avoidance schedule; and multiple fixed-ratio 1 extinction of food reinforcement schedule (MULT FR 1 EXT).

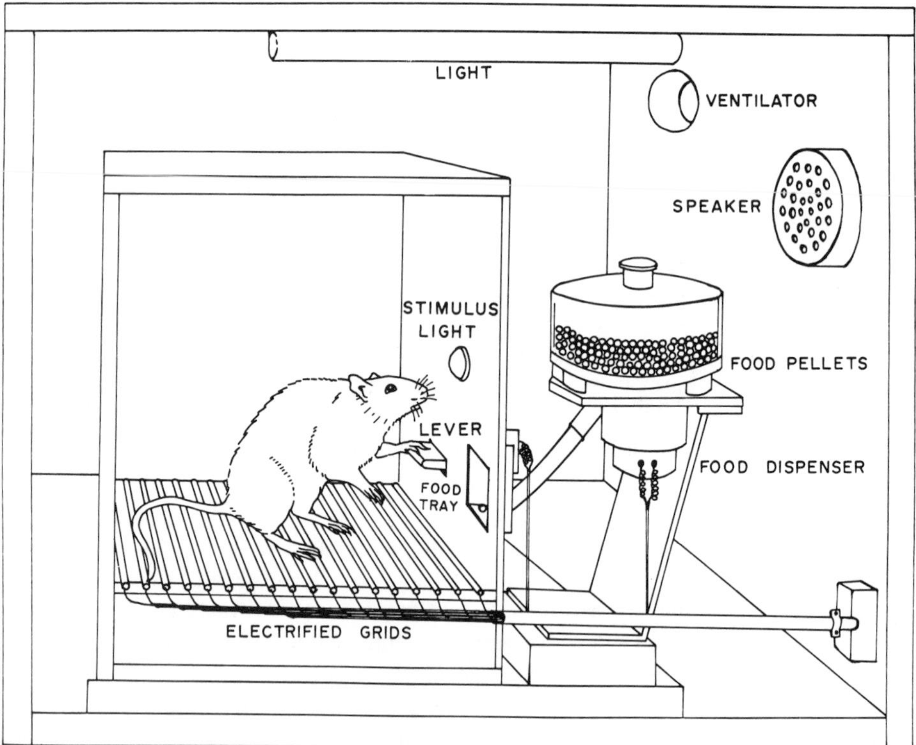

Figure 15-1. Drawing of a lever-press operant conditioning chamber and attachments for the rat. The chamber is made of acrylfiber and aluminium plates. The floor is a grid of stainless steel rods that are wired to pass an electric current for shock presentation. A food dispenser, which delivers a 40-mg food pellet to the rat, is set on the right, outside the chamber. The chamber is placed in a wooden sound-attenuating box to limit the effects of an external noise. Visual and auditory stimuli can be presented as shown. Fresh air is introduced throughout the experimental period.

Free-operant Avoidance Schedule (1,2)
This schedule consisted of two independent temporal factors. One was the shock-shock (S-S) interval, at which a brief shock was repeatedly delivered to a rat by passing an electric current (150 V, 0.5 mA, 50 Hz AC) for 0.5 second through the floor grid. When, however, the rat pressed the lever with a force of more than 15 gm, the delivery of shock was postponed for a certain time; this is the response-shock (R-S) interval. In this schedule, neither a visual nor an auditory stimulus, which would predict the delivery of the shock, is presented. Instead, all lever-pressings (responses) are effective in postponing shock delivery. Thus, if the rat responds at intervals less than the R-S interval, shock would always be avoided. Lever holding is ineffective for shock avoidance. As the indices of behavior, response rate and number of shocks delivered were recorded. Since the avoidance behavior often displayed a warm-up effect in the early period of each training session, the data during the first 30 minutes after the start of the session were excluded from the data collection. A session lasted for 1 to 2 hours and was held every other day.

Discriminated Avoidance Schedule (3–5)
This schedule is the same as the free-operant avoidance one in that electric shocks can be avoided by a response. Under this schedule, however, the effective response for postponing shock delivery is limited. Thus, the warning stimulus (visual and auditory), which predicts the succeeding delivery of a shock, is presented to the rat at a definite interval (intertrial interval ITI) for a certain time (warning duration). When the rat presses the lever during the warning period with a force of more than 8 gm, the warning stimulus terminates immediately, and the shock-delivery schedule returns to the starting point. All other responses are ineffective in altering the shock schedule. Lever holding is also ineffective in the avoidance of shock.

The discriminated avoidance schedule can be divided into two types according to the programmed pattern of shock delivery. In the first, the duration of shock delivery is always 0.5 second (5), while in the second, the duration is 5 seconds at the longest, but escape is possible (3,4). Thus, even after shock onset, the warning stimulus and the shock are terminated immediately after a lever press. When no response is emitted within the 5 seconds, the warning stimulus and the shock are automatically terminated, and the schedule is returned to the starting point. One of these two schedules was selected according to the purpose of the experiment. The shock intensity was of the same magnitude as that of the free-operant avoidance schedule. As the indices of the behavior, the response rate and the avoidance rate (number of successful responses/total number of warning presentations) were recorded. A warm-up effect was also observed with the avoidance behavior, and the data during the first 30 minutes after the start of each training session were excluded in the calculation of the mean values. Sessions lasted for 2 hours (the former method) or 1 hour (the latter method) per day and were held at 2- to 3-day intervals.

Multiple Fixed Ratio 1 Extinction of Food Reinforcement Schedule (***MULT FR 1 EXT***) (6)
This is a positive reinforcement schedule with the same temporal factors as the discriminated avoidance schedule. Thus, visual and auditory stimuli are presented to the rat to indicate the availability of a 40-mg food pellet at a definite interval (ITI) and for a certain time (stimulus duration). The rat receives the pellet only when it presses the

lever with a force of more than 15 gm during the period of stimulus presentation. Responses emitted during the ITI, as well as lever holding, are ineffective. As already indicated, rats were food deprived and magazine trained before the start of the conditioning. As the indices of the behavior, response rate and food intake rate (number of successful responses/total number of stimulus presentations) were recorded. Under this schedule, the warm-up effect was not evident, and consequently all the data during each session were included in the calculation of the mean values. A session consisted of 1 hour of training a day and was held every other day.

RESULTS AND DISCUSSION

Standard Acquisition Processes of Operant Behaviors in Rats

In this section, the standard acquisition processes of rats under the three operant schedules, that is, free-operant avoidance, discriminated avoidance, and MULT FR 1 EXT, are shown.

Figure 15-2 presents the acquisition process for male Wistar rats under the free-operant avoidance schedule (R-S = 30 seconds, S-S = 5 seconds, one session = 1 hour). In the early stage of the training, the rat received many shocks, but it soon began to hold the lever and started to avoid shocks. With continued training, the rat tended to emit the response at a relatively stable rate, and finally the mean number of shocks delivered and response rate were 0.3/min and 6.5/min, respectively. Five to 10 sessions were required to achieve this result. Previously we pointed out that the acquisition of the free-operant avoidance response in Wistar rats was established after about six sessions of training and was independent of the R-S interval, the duration of the training session (7), and the intervals between sessions (8). These findings suggest that the free-operant avoidance procedure can be used for the study of learning processes in rats. Under the schedule of R-S = S-S intervals, however, the acquisition was often insufficient, and sometimes drop-out animals were found (6). It is therefore considered an inadequate condition for studying the learning process in rats.

Figure 15-3 presents the acquisition process of male Wistar rats under the discriminated avoidance schedule without an escape contingency (9) (ITI = 25 seconds, warning duration = 5 seconds, and one session = 2 hours). In the early stage of the training, rats received many shocks and showed freezing or jumping behaviors during the warning periods and/or immediately after the exposure to shock. But once the animal found that the shock could be avoided by lever pressing, the avoidance rapidly increased, attaining 90–95% of the avoidance rate after 15 to 20 sessions. Thereafter the performance was stabilized. The response rate became stable at about 8.5/min after 15 training sessions. The acquisition of the discriminated avoidance response in Wistar rats was established almost independently of the ITI and the session intervals (9,10). These results suggest that the discriminated avoidance procedure can be used for the study of rat learning processes. The difficulty with this schedule is, however, that one session of training requires more than 2 hours. Moreover, many repetitions of training are required. It is assumed that the acquisition of the behavior may be rather difficult for the rat. But for this reason it can be expected that fine differences in learning ability may be detected so much better.

When the escape contingency is introduced into the discriminated avoidance schedule, the establishment of the avoidance response becomes smoother (6,11). Figure 15-4

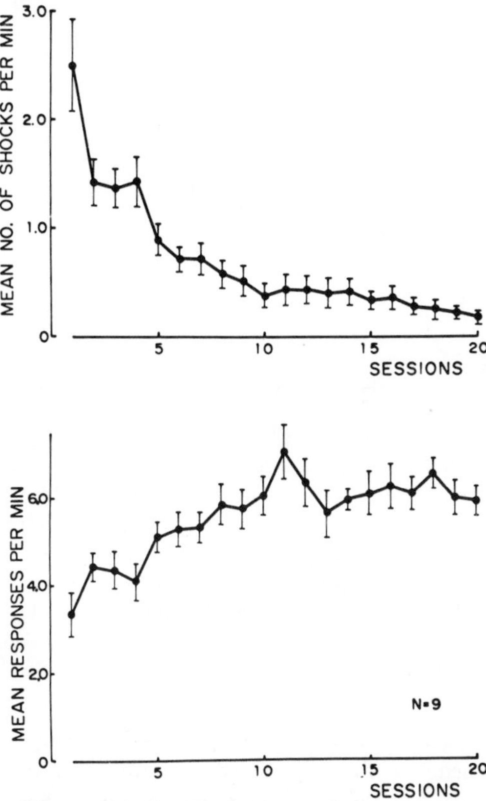

Figure 15-2. A standard acquisition process for male Wistar rats under the free-operant avoidance schedule (R-S interval = 30 seconds, S-S interval = 5 seconds, and the duration of the training session = 1 hour). Ordinate denotes mean number of shocks delivered (upper panel) or mean response rate (lower panel); abscissa, the number of the training session. The data during the first 30 minutes after the start of the each session were not included in data collection to exclude warm-up effects.

shows the acquisition process for male Wistar rats under the schedule (ITI = 25 seconds, warning duration = 5 seconds, shock duration = 5 seconds, and one session = 1 hour). Since the rat was placed in a more severe condition than that in the previous schedule, the rat held the lever from an early stage of the training and emitted escape responses. After about 10 sessions, all the animals showed a high and stable avoidance rate of more than 95%. The mean response rate was about 2.5/min and was maintained thereafter without marked change. Moreover, drop-out cases hardly ever occurred under this schedule. This procedure, then, would appear to be well suited to the study of the acquisition process in rats.

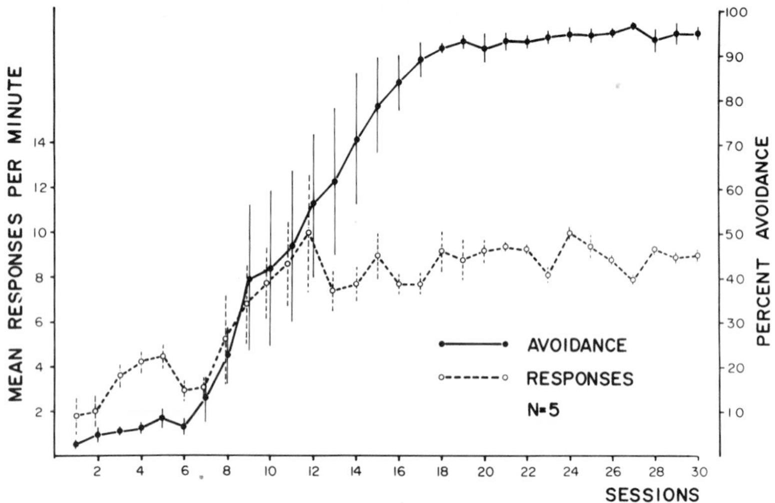

Figure 15-3. A standard acquisition process for male Wistar rats under the discriminated avoidance schedule without escape contingency (ITI = 25 seconds, duration of the warning stimulus presentation = 5 seconds, and duration of the training session = 2 hours). The duration of the shock delivery is fixed at 0.5 seconds. Ordinate denotes mean avoidance and response rates; abscissa the number of the training session. The data during the first 30 minutes after the start of the each session were excluded from the data collection.

Figure 15-4 also presents the acquisition process for male Wistar rats under the MULT FR 1 EXT schedule (ITI = 25 seconds, stimulus duration = 5 seconds, and one session = 1 hour), which has the same temporal factors as those of the discriminated avoidance schedule. In the upper panel, the ordinate indicates the food intake rate, instead of the avoidance rate as in the previous schedule. The rats subjected to magazine training were quite active in the experimental chamber and began lever pressing during the first session. After about five sessions, all rats showed nearly 100% of the possible food intake. The mean response rate was about 10.0/min, which was notably higher than that under the avoidance schedule.

It may be difficult to compare the avoidance rate with the food intake rate in regard to speed of acquisition. But from the viewpoint of the establishment of behavioral baselines, that is, stabilized response rate and high rate of the avoidance or food intake, food intake can be said to demonstrate higher speed. It may be that the food pellet is a more direct reinforcer than shock avoidance and consequently elicits a more rapid speed of acquisition. This view may be also supported by the duration of the warm-up effect. Thus, under the avoidance schedule, the motivation for the shock avoidance is gradually elevated during the repetition of the trials, and the warm-up effect persists for a long period. There is a report (12) that neurophysiologically the neural pathway differs according to whether the behavior is governed by a rewarding or noxious stimulus. On the other hand, Tadokoro (8) reported that free-operant and discriminated avoidance behaviors were memorized for a whole lifetime, and even after the discontinuation of the training for more than a year, they were revived within 30 minutes of retraining. In the case of positive reinforcement, it was difficult to maintain a constant level of food deprivation, and an alteration in the condition elicited a change in behavior. Because of this variability, the positive reinforcement schedule is somewhat limited as a retention test. These experimental results indicate that the behaviors maintained by the positive reinforcer are more susceptible than the avoidance schedule to the effects of various nonlearning factors. Therefore, the negative reinforcement procedure is considered to be more suitable than the positive one for the study of learning processes in rats.

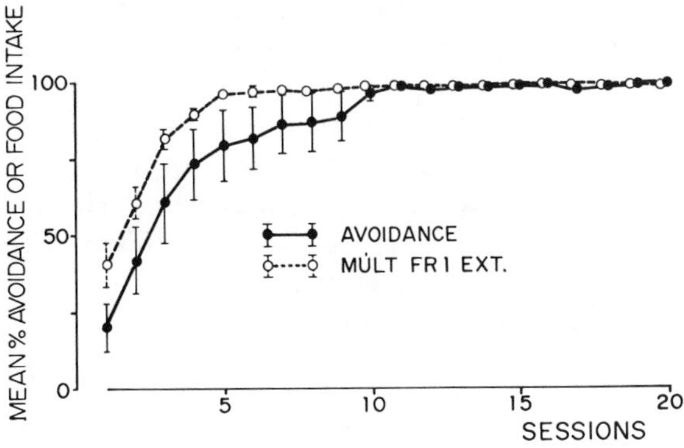

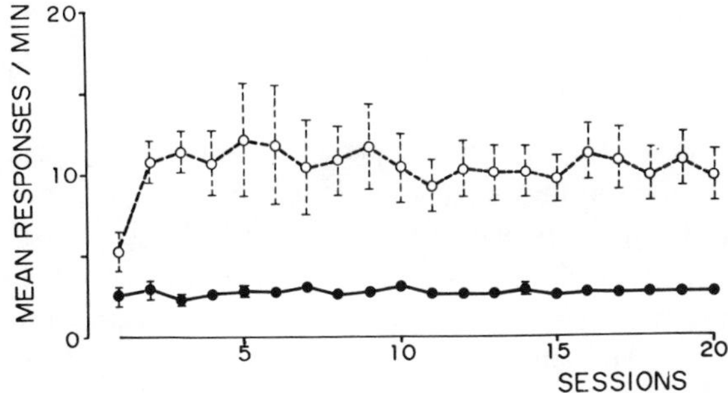

Figure 15-4. Standard acquisition processes for male Wistar rats under the discriminated avoidance schedule with escape contingency (ITI = 25 seconds, duration of the warning stimulus presentation = 5 seconds, the maximum duration of the shock presentation = 5 seconds, and duration of the training session = 1 hour) and the multiple fixed-ratio 1 extinction of food reinforcement schedule (ITI = 25 seconds, duration of the stimulus presentation = 5 seconds, and duration of the training session = 1 hour). Ordinate denotes mean avoidance rate or mean food intake rate (upper panel) or mean response rates (lower panel); abscissa, the number of the training session. The data during the first 30 minutes after the start of the each session were excluded from the data collection in the avoidance schedule but not in the food reinforcement schedule. N = 9 and N = 11, respectively.

Rat Strain Differences in the Acquisition of the Avoidance Responses

It has been reported by many workers that, even in the same animal species, the physiological and biochemical characteristics (13,14), as well as behavioral phenomenon such as emotionality, motor activity, and/or pattern of the conditioned behavior (5,13–20), vary depending on the genetic background. On this account, it is important to know the specific traits of the strain. This section provides information on the marked differences among Wistar, Sprague-Dawley, and Holtzman strains of rats in acquisition processes under the free-operant and discriminated avoidance schedules.

Figure 15-5 compares the acquisition processes under the free-operant avoidance schedule (R-S = 20 seconds, S-S = 5 seconds, and one session = 2 hours) among the three strains of rats. The mean response rate was higher in the order of Holtzman > Sprague-Dawley > Wistar until the third session, but in the fourth and later sessions there was no difference among the strains. The number of shocks delivered was conversely higher in the order of Wistar > Sprague-Dawley > Holtzman until the second session. For the Wistar strain, however, the number of shocks delivered was abruptly decreased with each repetition of the training, with the order becoming Wistar ≑ Sprague-Dawley > Holtzman in the third session, Sprague-Dawley > Holtzman ≑ Wistar in the sixth session. The last order remained thereafter. Any of the three strains showed stable response rates and number of shocks delivered after about 6 sessions of training. This result suggests that the free-operant avoidance behavior is established after about six sessions regardless of the strain, but there are marked strain differences in the acquisition process and in performance. The Wistar strain is superior to the other two, and Sprague-Dawley is inferior. The persistence of the warm-up effects was longer in the order of Sprague-Dawley > Holtzman > Wistar, which also indicates the same ordering of performance.

Figure 15-6 compares the acquisition processes under the discriminated avoidance schedule without escape contingency (ITI = 15 seconds, warning duration = 5 seconds, and one session = 2 hours) among the three strains of rats. Long-term training was needed for the acquisition of the avoidance response, but nevertheless the result was similar to that of the free-operant avoidance procedure. Thus, the order in response rate was Sprague-Dawley ≑ Holtzman > Wistar until the tenth session, with exception of the first, but thereafter there was no difference among the strains. Also, with regard to the avoidance rate, nearly the same order of Sprague-Dawley ≑ Holtzman > Wistar lasted until the eighth session, but the rate for Wistar increased abruptly after several sessions and attained 95% and above at about the twentieth session and after. The Holtzman strain showed about an 80% avoidance rate by the twenty-fifth session, but this was the final limit, and no further improvement was observed with continued training. The result for the Sprague-Dawley strain was evidently inferior to those of the other strains, and despite the repetition of the training, the avoidance rate remained at 60–70% and moreover was unstable. The order of persistence of the warm-up effect was Sprague-Dawley > Holtzman > Wistar. For the Sprague-Dawley strain, the effect was observed for as long as 2 hours.

According to these results, there were marked differences among strains of rats in the aquisition processes under the two avoidance schedules. The Wistar strain result was inferior to that of either of the other two strains in the early training stage under these two schedules. But this fact can hardly be considered to reflect directly the learning ability of rats. It is quite likely that animals of a strain with a high level of activity

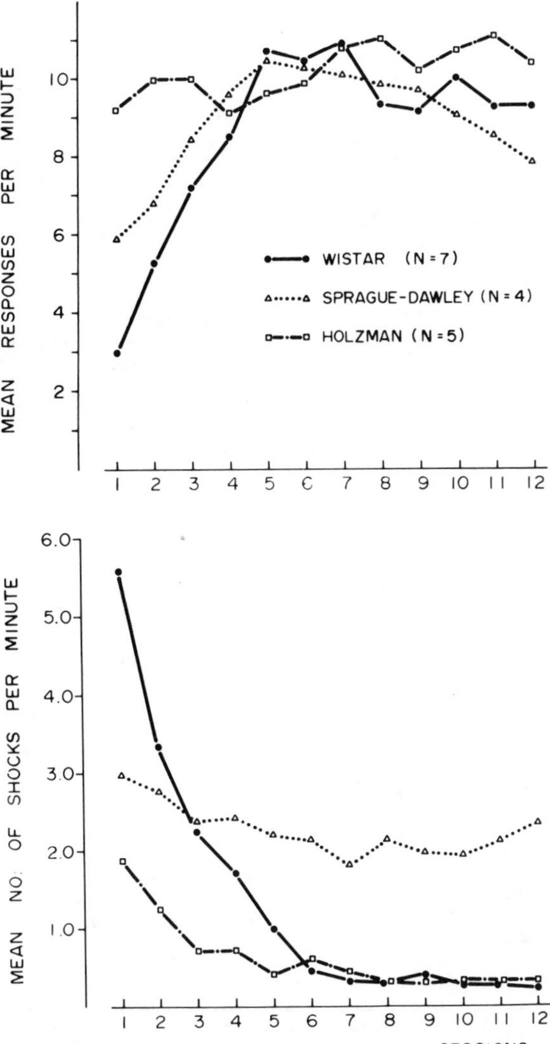

Figure 15-5. Acquisition processes in Wistar, Sprague-Dawley, and Holtzman rats under the free-operant avoidance schedule (R-S interval = 20 seconds, S-S interval = 5 seconds, and duration of the training session = 2 hours). The data collected during the first 30 minutes after the start of the each training session were excluded from the data collection. Upper panel: mean response rates, lower panel: mean number of shocks delivered.

DISCRIMINATED AVOIDANCE

(ITI = 15 sec, WARNING = 5 sec)

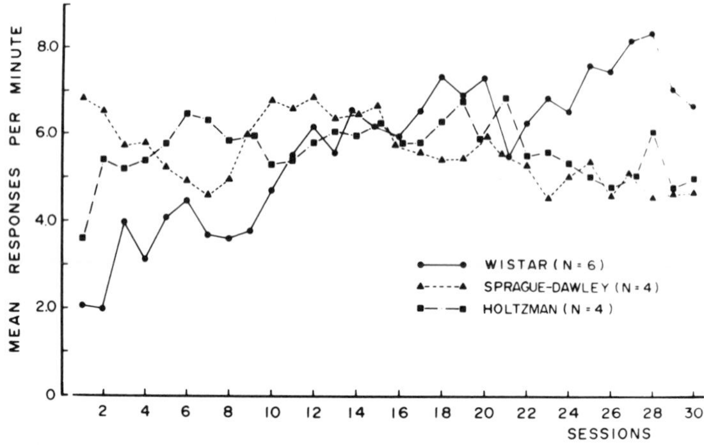

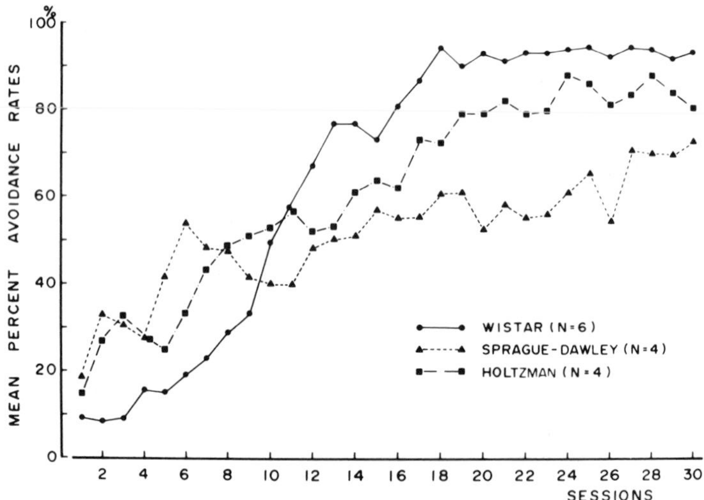

Figure 15-6. Acquisition processes in Wistar, Sprague-Dawley, and Holtzman rats under the discriminated avoidance schedule without escape contingency (ITI = 15 seconds, duration of the warning stimulus presentation = 5 seconds, and duration of the training session = 2 hours). The data during the first 30 minutes after the start of the each session were excluded from the data collection. Upper panel: mean response rates, lower panel: Mean avoidance rates.

simply display a higher probability of lever pressing. Actually, according to gross observation, the Sprague-Dawley rats displayed a higher activity than the Wistar rats. On the other hand, the result was better, after sufficient training, in the order of Wistar > Holtzman > Sprague-Dawley, while the warm-up effect persisted conversely in the order of Sprague-Dawley > Holtzman > Wistar. These results indicate that the Wistar rats displayed adaptation to the experimental condition, and that Sprague-Dawley rats were evidently less fitted. If the avoidance rate or number of shocks delivered can be taken as an index of the learning ability or of the dexterity of the rat, Wistar rats may be the highest and Sprague-Dawley rats the lowest in learning ability. There is, however, a report (19) that the Sprague-Dawley strain exceeds the Wistar strain in the acquisition of an avoidance conditioning. Moreover, under the differential reinforcement of low rate schedule, which requires more training sessions than other operant conditioning schedules, there was no report evaluating Sprague-Dawley as inferior to any other strains (21). Therefore, we cannot definitely conclude that the Sprague-Dawley rat is always lower in learning ability than the other strains. But since according to the present results, there were differences of the same trend among the strains under two different schedules, the presence of the strain differences in the acquisition processes under these schedules is assumed to be highly reliable. Besides strain differences, colony differences are also noticed frequently, and it seems important, therefore, to take this factor into consideration.

Effects of Hypophysectomy on the Acquisition of Operant Responses

The anterior pituitary gland, which controls the function of many endocrine glands, is assumed to play an important role in learning and memory. There are many reports that not only the pituitary-thyroidal pathway but also the pituitary-adrenocortical pathway, affect the learning process (22,23), and that adrenocorticotropic hormone (ACTH) exerts its effect on the process (24–27). For these reasons, the investigation of the learning process in hypophysectomized rats is of considerable interest. This section describes the effect of hypophysectomy on operant response acquisition processes in rats hypophysectomized in adulthood.

Hypophysectomy

Hypophysectomy was performed on 13-week-old Wistar rats under ether anesthesia by the transtracheal method. Training for the conditioning was started post operatively after 1 month only for those rats in which the absence of weight gain and the intraperitoneal latent presence of the testis were confirmed.

Figure 15-7 presents the acquisition curves of hypophysectomized and intact rats under the free-operant avoidance schedule (R-S = 30 seconds, S-S = 5 seconds, and one session = 1 hour). The number of shocks delivered was markedly higher for the hypophysectomized rats than for the intact ones in all sessions, and the response rate was also lower in the former. From these results, it would appear that a severe learning impairment had been induced in the hypophysectomized rats.

In the next phase of the study, ACTH, 2.0 IU/kg × 2/day for 21 days, or hydrocortisone, 2.0 mg/kg × 2/day for 10 days, was given sc to the rats to examine any replacement effect relating to the pituitary adrenocortical pathway, but the impairment-remitting effect was not observed to any degree.

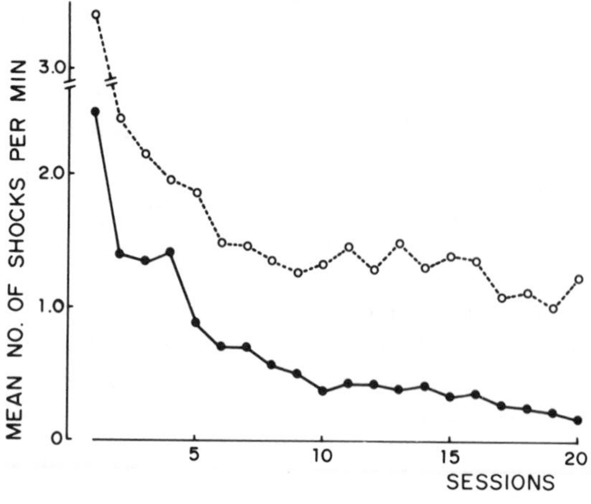

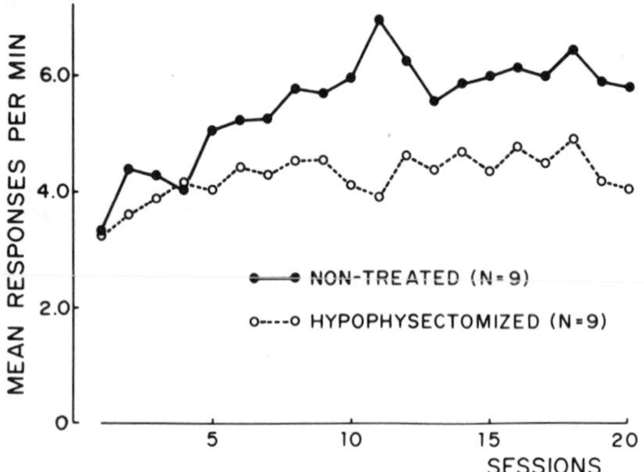

Figure 15-7. Acquisition processes in hypophysectomized and nontreated rats under the free-operant avoidance schedule. Methods of training and the data presentation are the same as those in Figure 15-2.

Figure 15-8 represents the acquisition processes of hypophysectomized and the intact rats under the discriminated avoidance schedule with an escape contingency (ITI = 25 seconds, warning duration = 5 seconds, shock duration = 5 seconds, and one session = 1 hour). The result was almost the same as under the free-operant avoidance schedule. The low rate of avoidance and response were manifested in spite of continued training sessions.

Figure 15-9 shows the acquisition processes of hypophysectomized and the intact rats under the MULT FR 1 EXT schedule (ITI = 25 seconds, stimulus duration = 5 seconds, and one session = 1 hour). Before the start of training, both groups of animals were subjected to food deprivation to maintain body weight at 80% of normal. The performance of the hypophysectomized rats was inferior to that of the intact ones in all sessions. Behavior was also less stable. The mean food intake rate for hypophysectomized rats rarely attained a level higher than 40%, and response rate was also low, thus showing an impairment in performance.

In the present experiments, hypophysectomized rats displayed a learning ability inferior to that of intact rats under all three schedules. Under the two avoidance schedules, similar results were anticipated since they have the common negative reinforcement content. However, the behavior under the MULT FR 1 EXT schedule, where the response was maintained by food reinforcement, is essentially different in nature from the avoidance behaviors. Therefore, it seemed highly plausible that hypophysectomy could produce such significant functional disorders of the central nervous systems as to retard learning. However, there still remained a problem as to the possibility that hypophysectomy might have decreased general activity only, and therefore, these animals would have been only apparently inferior. To solve this question spontaneous motor activity of hypophysectomized and intact rats was compared.

The hypophysectomized or the intact rat was transferred individually from the home cage to a chamber of 25 (D) × 45 (W) × 60 (H) cm, made of acrylfiber board, and the activity of each animal was measured with ANIMEX DS (AB Farad, Sweden) for 1 hour. The results are shown in Figure 15-10. The activity of the intact rats was high immediately after the start of the observation and thereafter decreased steadily over the time course of the observation period. The activity of the hypophysectomized rats was

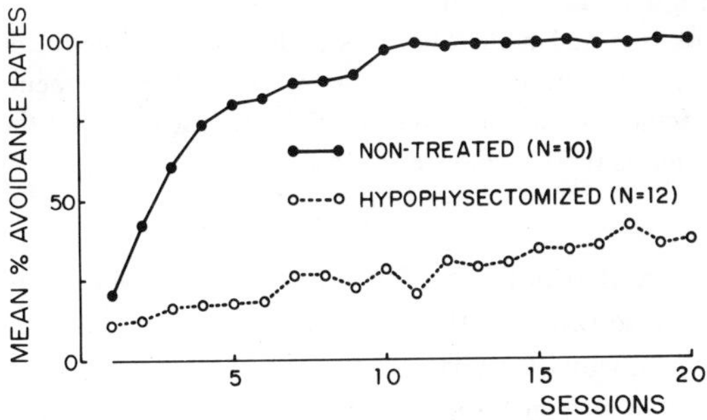

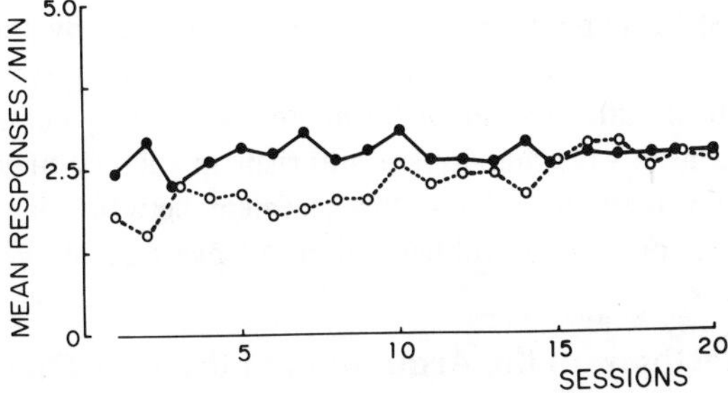

Figure 15-8. Acquisition processes in hypophysectomized and nontreated rats under the discriminated avoidance schedule with escape contingency. Methods of training and the data presentation are the same as those in Figure 15-4.

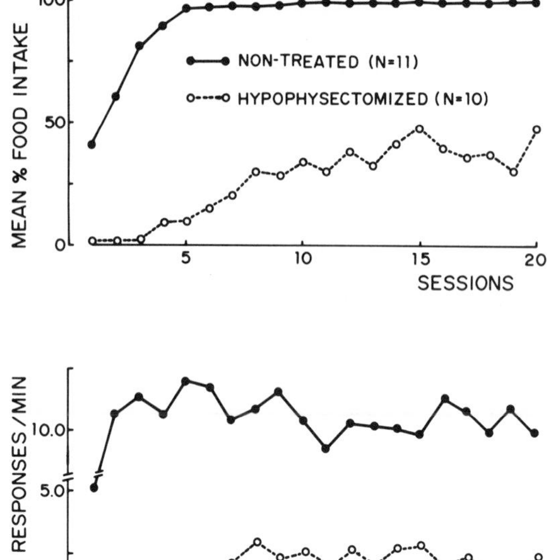

Figure 15-9. Acquisition processes in hypophysectomized and nontreated rats under the multiple fixed-ratio 1 extinction schedule of food reinforcement. Methods of training and the data presentation are the same as those in Figure 15-4.

sluggish from the beginning and after 40 minutes was lower. It is therefore probable that low operant response rates for the hypophysectomized rats may, at least partly, be attributed to low spontaneous activity. In the case of learning under the positive reinforcement schedule, it may also be necessary to ascertain any altered intensity in food consummatory behavior.

The present experiment differs from previous reports (22,23,25) in that the learning-retardation produced by hypophysectomy was not improved by the administration of ACTH or hydrocortisone. This suggests the possibility that factors other than the pituitary-adrenocortical pathway and/or hormone systems may be involved in the cause. Furthermore, it has been said that hypopituitarism in infancy may result in pituitary dwarfism without low intelligence. The disagreement between the present results and those of other researchers raises a problem still to be investigated.

Effects of Thyroidectomy on the Acquisition of the Free-Operant Avoidance Response

It has been known that hypothyroidism in infancy produces cretinism, dwarfism with a low intelligence. This indicates that thyroid hormones such as thyroxine (T_4) and triiodothyronine (T_3) play an important role in the growth of both the physique and the brain. This section describes the effects of thyroidectomy and the replacement effects of

T_4 on the acquisition process of the free-operant avoidance responding in rats as obtained by Tadokoro and Ohashi (28) of our department.

Thyroidectomy

Hypothyroidism was developed in Wistar rats by the following procedure: at the age of 1 to 2 weeks, the rats were given methymazole, 1.0 mg/kg sc, once a day to keep them in a state of hypothyroidism, and at the age of 3 weeks, thyroidectomy was performed bilaterally by microsurgery. The rats were divided into five groups according to treatment with T_4 (10–20 μg/kg/day sc) after the hypothyroidism: group 1 (nonreplaced rats)—no T_4 was given for the entire experimental period; group 2 (early T_4 administered rats)—T_4 was given only during the period of 1 to 4 weeks of age; group 3 (later T_4 administered rats)—T_4 was given from 10 weeks of age to the termination of the experiment; group 4 (full T_4-administered rats)—T_4 was given from 1 week of age through the entire experimental period; and group 5 (control rats)—saline was administered instead of methymazole and a sham-operation was performed instead of thyroidectomy. The training was started at the age of 13 weeks in all cases.

In group 1, growth was markedly retarded, displaying depilation and skin cornification. Activity was sluggish. In group 2, there was some remission of these symptoms. In group 3, the remission became more clear. In group 4, the general condition was no different in appearance from that of the control rats (group 5). At 18 weeks of age, the order of the body weight was group 5, group 4, group 3, group 2, and group 1. The mean body weight for the nontreated rats (group 1) was about 40% of that for the control rats (group 5).

Figure 15-11 presents the free-operant avoidance schedule (R-S = 30 seconds, S-S = 5 seconds, and one session = 1 hour) acquisition for thyroidectomized rats. The control rats showed a predominantly high level of response, attaining a rate of about 8.5/min after 10 sessions of the training, which thereafter remained stable. Against this, the non-

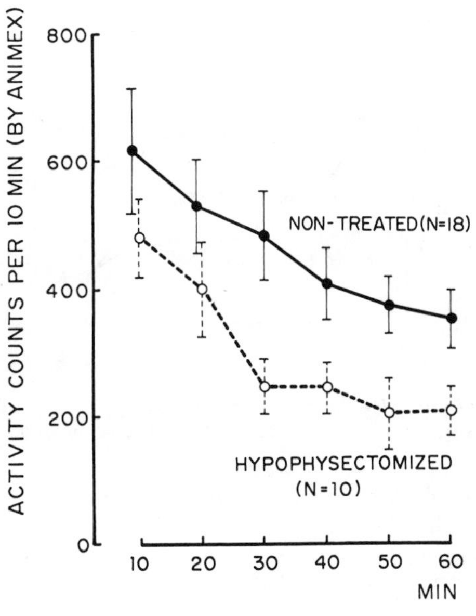

Figure 15-10. Temporal changes in locomotor activity measured by ANIMEX DS in hypophysectomized and nontreated rats. Ordinate denotes the mean activity counts per 10 minutes; the abscissa, the time scale.

replaced rats showed an extremely low level, which remained at 3.0/min in spite of continued training. The response rates for the T_4-administered rats were higher than those for the nontreated ones but were not restored to the level of the control group. The number of shocks delivered for the control rats decreased up to the tenth session and thereafter showed a low and stable rate. On the other hand, the nonreplaced rats showed an extremely high level of shock delivery, demonstrating scarcely any advance in acquisition. The rate for the full T_4-administered rats nearly equaled that for the control after the tenth session. In both of the imperfectly T_4-administered rats, the results were only slightly better than that for the nontreated rats.

In mature thyroidectomized rats (12 weeks of age), the response rate was slightly, but not significantly, lower than that for the sham-operated ones, and no difference was observed in the number of shocks delivered.

The present results suggest that there may be some differences by the time of hypothyroidism in the learning ability of the free-operant avoidance response. These results are in agreement with previous reports (29–36). The present results, however, demonstrated that the behavioral disorder derived from hypothyroidism, especially learning impairment, was not completely abated by T_4 administration, although physical symptoms could be removed by it. To correct this impairment as far as possible, it is possible that T_4 must be administered not only in the infant or adult stage but throughout life.

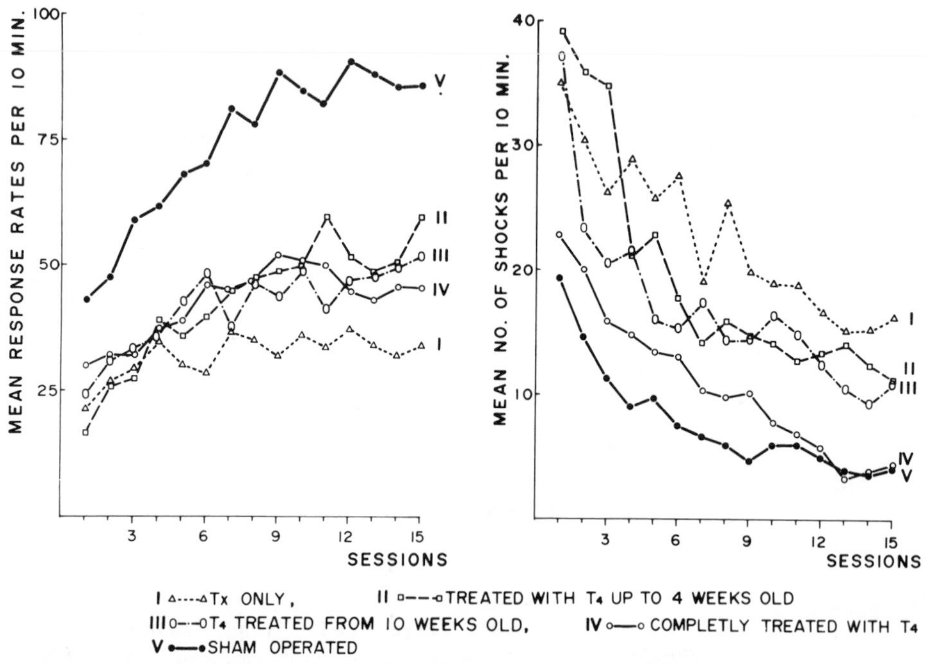

Figure 15-11. Acquisition processes in hypothyroidism rats under the free-operant avoidance schedule. The training method is the same as in Figure 15-2. The replacement-effects of thyroxine (T_4, 10–20 μg/kg/day sc) on the process are also shown in this figure. Left panel: mean response rates per 10 minutes, Right panel: mean number of shocks delivered per 10 minutes.

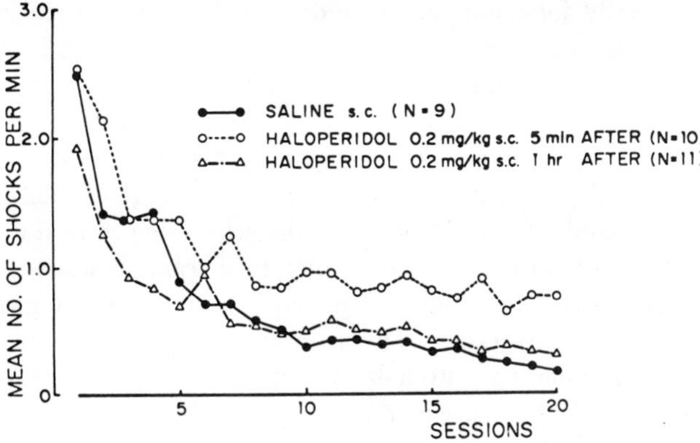

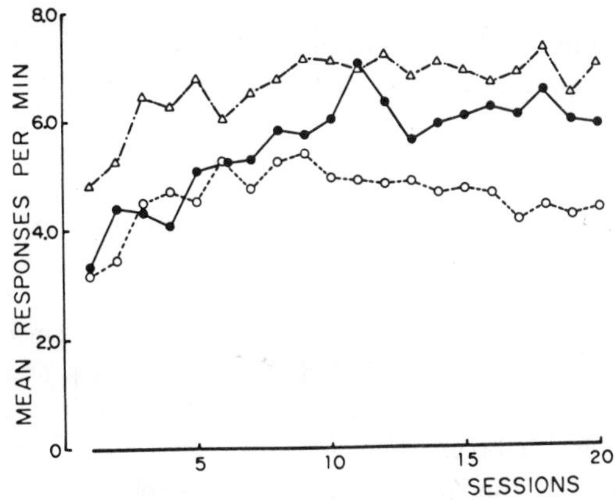

Figure 15-12. Acquisition processes in rats given haloperidol, 0.2 mg/kg sc, within 5 minutes or after 1 hour after the termination of each training session under the free-operant avoidance schedule. Methods of training and the data presentation are the same as those in Figures 15-2 and 15-7.

Effects of Haloperidol Given After the Training Session on the Acquisition of Avoidance Responding

Recently pharmacological techniqes have been applied to elucidate the mechanisms of learning and memory. The effects on the retention process of CNS-acting drugs given either before or after training has been investigated. The study described in this section concerns the effect of haloperidol (Cerenace Inj., Dainippon), 0.2 mg/kg sc, given to male Wistar rats on the course of acquisition under the free-operant avoidance schedule (R-S = 30 seconds, S-S = 5 seconds, and one session = 1 hour) and under the discriminated avoidance schedule with escape contingency (ITI = 25 seconds, warning duration = 5 seconds, shock duration = 5 seconds, and one session = 1 hour). Haloperidol, a strong and representative neuroleptic drug, has a blocking effect on the catecholaminergic, especially dopaminergic, receptor (37). In previous experiments (38), 0.2 mg/kg sc of this drug completely inhibited the avoidance response in rats for several hours. The drug was given within 5 minutes or after 1 hour after the termination of each training session, and the intervals between sessions were at least 2 days to eliminate the direct depressive effect of the drug on the performance.

Figure 15-12 shows the acquisition processes of rats given haloperidol, under the free-operant avoidance schedule. It can be seen that the acquisition seemed to be retarded in the group given the drug within 5 minutes after each training session, but not in the group given the drug after 1 hour. Thus, haloperidol-induced learning retardation was time dependent on the administration. This is in agreement with a previous report (12) and supports the assumption that catecholamine, inclusive of dopamine, may play a role in the memory process. In fact, it was reported that chlorpromazine (39) and various other CNS-depressants (40), administered immediately after the training period, induced impairment of learning.

Under the discriminated avoidance schedule, however, haloperidol did not show the learning-impairment effect.

Because of this difference in the effects between the two avoidance schedules, it is hard to confirm the impairment-inducing effect of haloperidol to learning. If at all, the effect is estimated to be weak.

SUMMARY

In the present study, we did not intend to investigate the mechanism of learning and memory but rather looked into the properties of the acquisition processes of operant behaviors in rats that could be applied to medical studies, especially in the fields of pharmacology and toxicology. It becomes evident in the present studies that there are various nonspecific factors affecting performance that are not based on learning or memory processes. When impairment of operant conditioning is observed, learning and memory cannot be assumed to be the only processes involved. However, operant procedures have many advantages in that behavior can be used to estimate the process of acquisition quantitatively, objectively, continuously, and automatically. In particular, responding by lever pressing requires little energy output by the rat, so the effect of somatic damage resulting from an operation or drug administration may be minimal. However, since it is risky to draw any conclusion from an experimental result detected by a single schedule, multiple investigations should be carried out using a number of schedules. Conclusions can be formed about an effect on learning and memory processes only when similar changes in their behaviors have been confirmed collectively.

From the results of the present experiments, the following conclusions can be drawn:

1. The establishment of appropriate observation methods can produce reliable results not only in physiological and psychological studies of the mechanism of learning and memory but also in more extensive and collective studies.
2. In the selection of operant conditioning procedures, the negative reinforcement schedules, and thus the avoidance schedules, are found more appropriate than positive reinforcement ones with respect to ease and simplicity in the experimental arrangements and results.

3. For the free-operant and the discriminated avoidance schedules, R-S > S-S and inclusion of an escape contingency, respectively, appear useful.
4. Finally, it must be added that since learning speed varied according to the strain of rats used, genetic factors might also be involved in determining behavior.

ACKNOWLEDGMENT

The authors thank Professor John L. Falk for his comments on the manuscript.

REFERENCES

1. Sidman M: Avoidance conditioning with brief shock and no extroceptive warning signal. *Science* 118:157–158, 1953.
2. Sidman M: Avoidance behavior, in Honig WK (ed): *Operant Behavior: Areas of Research and Application*. New York, Appleton-Century-Crofts, 1966, pp 448–498.
3. Hoffman HS, Fleshler M, Chorny H: Discriminated bar press avoidance. *J Exp Anal Behav* 4:309–316, 1961.
4. Hoffman HS: The analysis of discriminated avoidance, in Honig WK (ed): *Operant Behavior: Areas of Research and Application*. New York, Appleton-Century-Crofts, 1966, pp 499–530.
5. Kuribara H, Ohashi K, Tadokoro S: Rat strain differences in the acquisition of conditioned avoidance responses and in the effects of diazepam. *Jap J Pharmac* 26:725–735, 1976.
6. Kuribara H, Hayashi T: Observation of acquisition using operant conditioning in rats. *Jap J Pharmac* 28(suppl):32 P, 1978.
7. Kuribara H, Okuizumi K, Tadokoro S: Analytical study of acquisition on free-operant avoidance response for evaluation of psychotropic drugs in rats. *Jap J Pharmac* 25:541–548, 1975.
8. Tadokoro S: Studies on various factors influencing upon acquisition of conditioned continuous avoidance and discriminated avoidance, and effects of methamphetamine on the way of learning process. *Folia Pharmac Japon* 67:135p–136p, 1971 (in Japanese).
9. Tadokoro S, Okuizumi K, Kuribara H, et al: Varieties of drug-actions' intensities according to learning skillfulness of conditioned avoidance responses in rats. Effects of chlorpromazine and methamphetamine. *Folia Pharmac Japon* 70:67p, 1974 (in Japanese).
10. Tadokoro S, Ogawa H: Behavioral pharmacological tests—especially about operant behavior—I. Actual methods of the training and data analysis of the operant behaviors. *Basic Pharmacol Ther* 2:1189–1204, 1974 (in Japanese).
11. Hayashi T, Kuribara H, Tadokoro S: Methods for observation of acquisition processes using operant conditioning procedures in rats. *Seibutsu Kagaku* 30:159–167, 1978 (in Japanese).
12. Squire LR: Pharmacology of learning and memory, in Glick SD, Goldfarb J (eds): *Behavioral Pharmacology*. Saint Louis, CV Mosby, 1976, pp 258–282.
13. Broadhurst PL: The Maudsley reactive and nonreactive strains of rats: a survey. *Behav Gen* 5:299–319, 1975.
14. Coyle JT Jr, Wenden P, Lipsky A: Avoidance conditioning in different strains of rats: neurochemical correlations. *Psychopharmacol* 31:25–34, 1973.
15. Nakamura CY, Anderson NH: Avoidance behavior differences within and between strains of rats. *J Comp Physiol Psychol* 55:740–747, 1962.
16. Broadhurst PL: Determination of emotionality in the rat. III. Strain differences. *J Comp Physiol Psychol* 51:55–59, 1958.
17. Wilcock J, Broadhurst PL: Strain differences in emotionality: open-field and conditioned avoidance behavior in the rat. *J Comp Physiol Psychol* 63:335–338, 1967.

18. Schaefer VH: Differences between strains of rats in avoidance conditioning without an explicit warning stimulus. *J comp Physiol Psychol* 52:120–122, 1959.

19. Myers AK: Avoidance learning as a function of several training conditions and strain differences in rats. *J Comp Physiol Psychol* 52:381–386, 1959.

20. Bignami G: Selection for high rates and low rates of avoidance conditioning in the rat. *Animal Behav* 13:221–227, 1965.

21. Ando K: Profile of drug effects on temporally spaced responding in rats. *Pharmac Biochem Behav* 3:837–841, 1975.

22. De Wied D: Effect of peptide hormones on behavior, in Ganong WF, Martini L (eds): *Frontiers in Neuroendocrinology*. New York, Oxford University Press, 1969, pp 97–140.

23. Lande S, Witter A, De Wied D: Pituitary peptides. *J Biol Chem* 246:2058–2062, 1971.

24. De Wied D, Pirié G: The inhibitory effect of ACTH 1-10 on extinction of a conditioned avoidance response: its independence of thyroid function. *Physiol Behav* 3:355–358, 1968.

25. Dunn AJ, Gispen WH: How ACTH acts on the brain. *Biobehav Rev* 1:15–23, 1977.

26. Bohus B: Central nervous structures and the effect of ACTH and corticosteroids on avoidance behavior: a study with intracerebral inplantation of corticosteroids in the rat, in De Wied D, Weijnen JAWM (eds): *Progress in Brain Research: Pituitary, Adrenal and the Brain,* vol 32. Amsterdam, Elsevier, 1970, pp 171–184.

27. Gispen WH, Schotman P: Effects of hypophysectomy and conditioned avoidance behavior on macromolecule metabolism in the brain stem of the rat. In De Wied D, Weijnen JAWM (eds): *Progress in Brain Research: Pituitary, Adrenal and the Brain,* vol 32. Amsterdam, Elsevier, 1970, pp 236–244.

28. Tadokoro S, Ohashi K: Thyroid gland and learning behavior in rat. *Saishin Igaku* 32:1784–1787, 1977 (in Japanese).

29. Denenberg VH, Myers RD: Learning and hormone activity: I. Effects of thyroid levels upon the acquisition and extinction of an operant response. *J Comp Physiol Psychol* 51:213–219, 1958.

30. Denenberg VH, Myers RD: Learning and hormone activity: II. Effects of thyroid levels upon retention of an operant response and upon performance under starvation. *J Comp Physiol Psychol* 51:311–314, 1958.

31. Eayers JT: Age as a factor determining severity and reversibility of the effects of thyroid deprivation in the rat. *J Endocrinol* 22:409–419, 1961.

32. Davenport JW: Cretinism in rats: enduring behavioral deficit induced by tricyanoaminopropane. *Science* 167:1007–1009, 1969.

33. Davenport JW, Dorcey TP: Hypothyroidism: learning deficit induced in rats by early exposure to thiouracil. *Hormones and Behavior* 3:97–112, 1972.

34. Eayers JT, Levine S: Influence of thyroidectomy and subsequent replacement therapy upon conditioned avoidance learning in the rat. *J Endocrinol* 25:505–513, 1963.

35. Tsukada Y: Change of substances mediating the learning behavior. *Scientific American* (Japanese edition) 5:90–103, 1975 (in Japanese).

36. Hamburgh M, Lynn E, Weiss EP: Analysis of the influence of thyroid hormone of prenatal and postnatal maturation of the rat. *Amat Rec* 150:147–159, 1964.

37. Janssen PAJ: The pharmacology of haloperidol. *Int J Neuropsychiat* 3:s10–s18, 1967.

38. Kuribara H, Okuizumi K, Shirota M, et al: Effects of penfluridol, a psychotropic agent, on operant behavior in rats. *Folia Pharmac Japon* 71:491–503, 1975 (in Japanese).

39. Johnson FN: The effects of chlorpromazine on the decay and consolidation of short-term memory traces in mice. *Psychopharmacol* 16:105–114, 1969.

40. McGaugh JL, Petrinovich LF: Effects of drugs on learning and memory. *Int J Neurobiol* 8:139–196, 1965.

16
Visual Discrimination Studies in Pigeons

Shigeru Watanabe

It has been shown that a split-brain animal was able to learn a discrimination task with one eye and a reverse discrimination task with the other eye (9,17,19). In other words, the animal accomplished the conflicting discrimination with each eye. The ability to learn conflict discrimination with each eye suggests lack of interocular transfer of learning. It is claimed that a contradictory memory is formed independently in each hemisphere. However, intact pigeons and fish exhibited interocular transfer of learning (5,7,8,12,21,23) and also showed successful learning of conflict discrimination with each eye (2–4,6,15). Sheridan (16) also reported accomplishment of conflict discrimination in albino rats in which crossing of the optic chiasm was nearly complete. Cats with sectioned optic chiasm showed interocular transfer of learning and could learn conflict discrimination (11). These findings suggest that formation of the conflict discrimination is based on separate visual input for each hemisphere. However, restriction of visual input to each hemisphere is not necessary for learning conflict discrimination, because Myers (11) sectioned the right visual tract of cats so that only the crossed system for the right eye and the uncrossed system for the left eye projected to the left hemisphere and found successful learning of conflict discrimination with each eye in these cats.

There is another explanation for conflict discrimination. That is, conflict discrimination with each eye can be considered to be a conditional discrimination in which the eye used for training determines which stimulus is associated with the reinforcement. In other words, an animal can use its viewing condition as a cue for a conditional discrimination. This explanation does not predict a failure of interocular transfer of learning. The experiments discussed in this chapter examine such conditional discrimination with pigeons.

Two different training methods have been used in conflict discrimination. One is successive reversal training used by Myers (10,11), Sperry (17,18), and Sheridan (16). In this method, subjects were trained on one discrimination with one eye until they accomplished this task. Then they were trained on a reverse discrimination with the other eye. After they accomplished the reverse discrimination, they were trained on the first discrimination with the first eye again. This procedure was repeated until the subjects accomplish both discrimination tasks. Formation of conflict discrimination with this method may be influenced by formation of a reversal learning set in which the presence of reinforcement is a cue for discriminative behavior.

Another method is parallel training in two tasks (2–4,6,15). Subjects were trained in alternate sessions on one discrimination with the right eye and on the reverse discrimination with the left eye. The two trainings continued alternatively until the subject accomplished both tasks. This method is preferable because it minimizes the factor of a reversal learning set.

Figure 16-1 summarizes the general plan of the present experiments. In the first experiment, each eye was trained independently in a contradictory task. Acquisition of

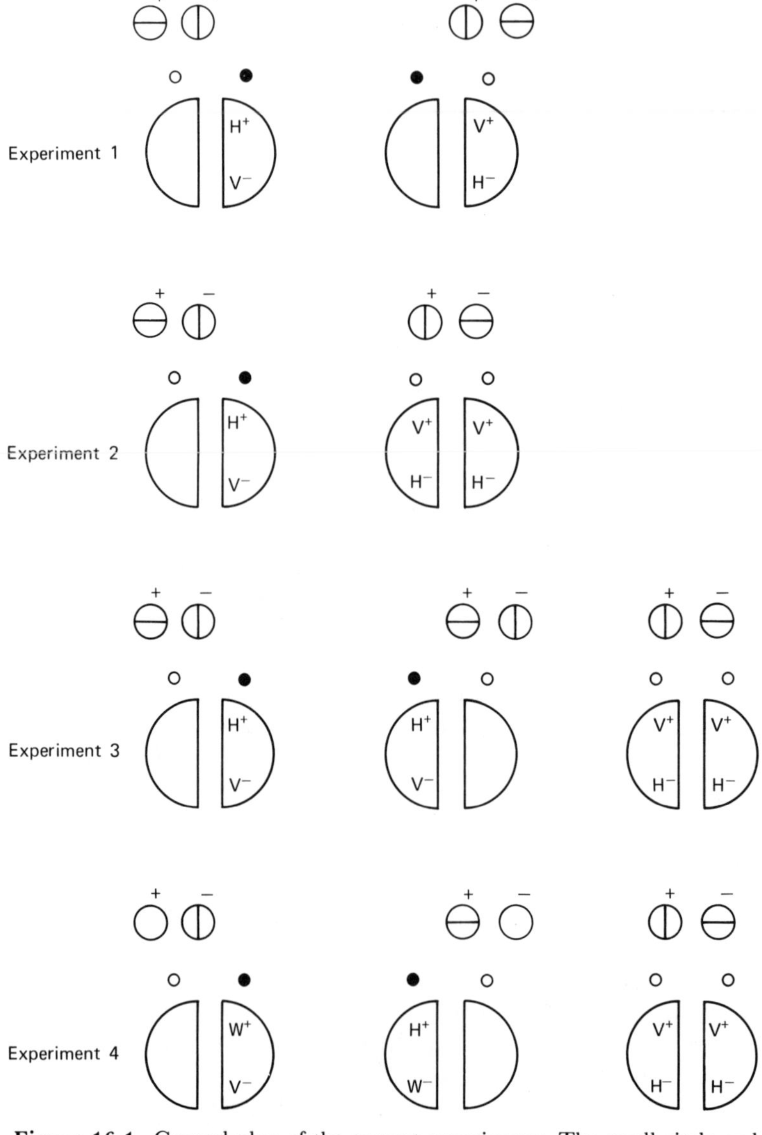

Figure 16-1. General plan of the present experiments. The small circle and the half circle represent the eye and the hemisphere, respectively. Closed circle indicates the eye covered; open circle, the eye uncovered. The vertical and the horizontal line in the top circle in each experiment represent the stimulus to be discriminated. Explanation is given in the text.

these tasks can be explained either by formation of conditional discrimination or by independent formation of memory in each hemisphere. In the second experiment, the subject were trained binocularly on one task and on the reverse task with the left eye. Memories are incompatible with each other in the right hemisphere. In the third experiment, the subject was trained binocularly on one task and on the reverse task with each eye monocularly. Assumption of independent formation of memory predicts failure of learning of these tasks, because memories are incompatible with each other in each hemisphere. In the last experiment, each task is a partially reversed task of other tasks. The subjects must discriminate the three different eye conditions for successful learning of these tasks.

GENERAL METHOD

Experimentally naive pigeons (*Columba livia*) were used. They were maintained at about 80% of their free-feeding weights throughout the experimental period.

The experimental chamber was an operant chamber (16 × 31 × 24 cm) with a single pecking key (diameter, 30 mm). Minimum pressure for the key was about 15 gm. A grain feeder for reinforcement was attached 15 cm below the key. A reinforcement was a 4-second presentation of the feeder. A 2-mm-wide line stimulus, illuminated by white light on a dark background, or color stimulus, was displayed on the key by a microprojector. Presentation of the stimulus and the schedule of reinforcement were controlled by a microcomputer system (UP-8). The number of responses for they key and reinforcement was counted by this system.

Each subject was trained to peck the key illuminated by white light by the method of successive approximation. Then plastic goggles were placed over both eyes of the subjects with collodion. The outer and inner diameters of the goggles were 18 mm and 12 mm, respectively, and their shape was similar to those developed by Catania (1) to limit the pigeon's vision to the anterior field. One side of the goggles was covered during monocular training. Following 30 continuous reinforcements, the subjects received two sessions of variable interval (VI) 25-second training with each eye, respectively. One session consisted of 10 presentations of white light each lasting 25 seconds and separated by a 5-second blackout period.

In each experiment, discriminative training was carried out with mult VI25"-EXT, that is, response for a positive stimulus (S^D) was reinforced on VI25", but response for a negative stimulus (S^Δ) was extinguished. One daily session consisted of 10 presentations each of S^D and S^Δ. One presentation period was 25 seconds followed by a 5-second blackout period. S^D and S^Δ were presented in accordance with the Gellerman series.

After the discriminative training, the subjects received a stimulus control test in which S^D and S^Δ were presented in the same order and duration as those in the daily training session but no reinforcement was given. Maintenance of discriminative behavior under this condition means that the discriminative behavior was not based on a reversal learning set.

EXPERIMENT 1

In this experiment, pigeons were trained in discrimination with one eye and in the reverse discrimination with the other eye.

Method

Ten pigeons were used in this experiment. They were trained to respond to a horizontal line but not to a vertical line on the days when they were trained with the left eye, and to respond to the vertical line but not to the horizontal line on the days when they were trained with the right eye. Training was performed once every day with only one eye. The eye used for daily training was alternated in accordance with the Gellerman series. The discriminative training continued until the subject reached 90% of the correct response ratio, calculated by dividing the number of responses for S^D by the sum of responses for S^D and S^Δ, for each eye. Then a stimulus control test with S^D and S^Δ was carried out for each eye.

Result and Discussion

All subjects were able to learn the discrimination tasks with each eye. Table 16-1 summarizes the number of sessions required to attain the criterion with each eye. There is no significant difference between the sessions with the right eye and those with the left eye. The results of the stimulus control test are also represented in Table 16-1. Although the subjects showed individual differences in rate of responding, all demonstrated clear discriminative behavior under extinction. This means that the subjects learned the conflict discrimination with each eye and did not form a reversal learning set.

Figure 16-2 shows representative examples of discriminative learning curves. The curves differ from the usual learning curve, which shows a gradual increment. The curves in the present experiment show a zigzag pattern and cross each other. Seven of the 10 subjects exhibited similar learning curves. When pigeons were trained on a horizontal-vertical discrimination with one eye and on a 45°-135° discrimination with the other eye, the learning curves of each task showed a smooth increment (25). Although

Table 16-1. Number of Sessions Required to Reach the Criterion and Results of the Stimulus Control Test in the First Experiment

				Stimulus Control Test[a]					
	Sessions to Criterion			*Right Eye*			*Left Eye*		
Subjects	*Right*	*Left*	*Total*	*V*	*H*	*V/V+H*	*H*	*V*	*H/H+V*
74006	8	10	18	107	3	0.97	450	46	0.91
74009	19	20	39	167	12	0.93	129	9	0.93
74902	12	7	19	116	39	0.75	86	2	0.98
74065	9	10	19	583	39	0.94	553	55	0.91
74922	6	8	14	378	51	0.88	300	29	0.91
74917	9	7	16	306	9	0.97	562	21	0.96
75032	8	8	16	235	5	0.98	339	24	0.93
75093	9	8	17	228	1	1.00	223	33	0.87
75084	8	9	17	532	77	0.87	321	11	0.97
75071	8	7	15	422	29	0.94	582	22	0.96
Mean	9.7	9.4	19.0	307.4	26.5	0.923	354.5	25.2	0.933

[a] V and H indicate, respectively, the number of responses emitted for the vertical line and for the horizontal line in the test session.

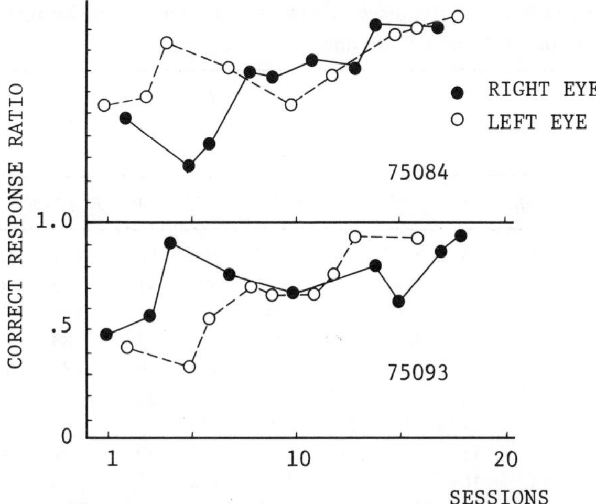

Figure 16-2. Discriminative learning curves in the first experiment. Closed circles represent performance with the right eye; open circles, performance with the left eye.

the present learning curves indicate mutual disturbance of the two contradictory learnings, all subjects finally overcame the disturbing interaction of the two learnings.

When the line stimulus was presented on a red key in the training with the left eye and on a green key in the training with the right eye, no disturbing interaction could be observed in most of the subjects (26). In this case, the colored background was irrelevant to the horizontal-vertical discrimination but gave the pigeons a signal for conditional discrimination. Therefore, the conditional discrimination based on external cue did not cause mutual disturbance of learning.

EXPERIMENT 2

In this experiment, pigeons were trained on a discrimination binocularly and on the reverse discrimination with the left eye.

Method

Ten pigeons were used in this experiment. They received binocular vertical-horizontal discrimination training in which the vertical line was S^D and the reverse horizontal-vertical discrimination training with the left eye. The eye condition for the daily training was alternated in accordance with the Gellerman series. The training continued until the subject reached 90% of the correct response ratio with each eye condition. After the training, the subjects received the stimulus control test with S^D and S^Δ with the left eye, with the right eye, and with both eyes.

Results and Discussion

Table 16-2 represents the number of sessions required to attain the criterion under each eye condition. All subjects reached the criterion more rapidly with both eyes than with

Table 16-2. Number of Sessions Required to Reach the Criterion and Results of the Stimulus Control Test in the Second Experiment

	Sessions to Criterion			*Stimulus Control Test*[a]								
				Binocular			*Left Eye*			*Right Eye*		
Subjects	*Binocular*	*Left*	*Total*	*V*	*H*	*V/V+H*	*H*	*V*	*H/H+V*	*V*	*H*	*V/V+H*
74914	7	18	25	409	13	0.97	130	54	0.71	160	97	0.62
74021	7	10	17	544	5	0.99	592	41	0.94	68	7	0.91
74023	6	7	13	530	76	0.87	402	7	0.98	176	38	0.82
74901	11	11	22	565	182	0.76	434	92	0.83	355	41	0.90
74916	6	20	26	634	3	1.00	423	99	0.81	610	48	0.93
74927	8	10	18	411	23	0.95	595	26	0.96	528	47	0.92
75009	3	11	14	337	27	0.93	40	0	1.00	95	0	1.00
75030	7	8	15	770	36	0.96	317	30	0.91	202	9	0.95
75078	4	14	18	46	0	1.00	122	0	1.00	124	3	0.98
75097	4	10	14	359	37	0.91	278	65	0.81	132	29	0.82
Mean	6.3	11.9	18.2	460.5	40.2	0.934	333.3	41.4	0.895	245.0	31.9	0.885

[a] V and H indicate, respectively, the number of responses emitted for the vertical line and for the horizontal line in the test session.

the left eye. Statistical analysis reveals a significant difference between the sessions with both eyes and those with the left eye ($P < 0.005$, Sign test). The results of the stimulus control test are also summarized in Table 16-2. Seven subjects emitted more responses in the binocular test than in the monocular tests. All subjects demonstrated clear discriminative behavior in each stimulus control test. One interesting finding is the result with the right eye. All subjects preferred the vertical line, which had been S^D in the binocular training. That is, they responded as if they were tested binocularly. This suggests that memory of the binocular discrimination was confined within the left hemisphere, because the memory was incompatible with memory for the left eye discrimination in the right hemisphere. Research on spreading depression suggests another explanation. Schneider (14) claimed that interhemispheric transfer could be considered as a stimulus generalization along the dimension of the state of the organism. According to him, the difference between one hemisphere depressed state and the other hemisphere depressed state is greater than the difference between one hemisphere depressed state and both hemispheres intact state. In the present experiment, the discriminative behavior with the right eye can be explained in terms of generalization from the binocular condition to the right eye condition.

Figure 16-3 shows representative examples of discriminative learning curves. Both subjects exhibited dominant progress of binocular learning over monocular learning. Eight of the 10 subjects showed a similar process of learning. The remaining two subjects showed interaction of two learnings such as that oberved in the first experiment. In another experiment, 10 pigeons were trained on a binocular vertical-horizontal discrimination in which the line stimulus was displayed on a green background and on the reverse horizontal-vertical discrimination with the left eye in which the line stimulus was displayed on a red background, and dominant learning of the binocular task was observed in the majority of the subjects (26). Thus, an added external cue for the conditional discrimination did not affect the dominance of the binocular learning.

EXPERIMENT 3

In this experiment, pigeons were trained binocularly on a discrimination, and on the reverse discrimination with the right eye and also with the left eye.

Method

Ten pigeons were used in this experiment. Five of them were trained binocularly on a vertical-horizontal discrimination with the vertical line S^D and monocularly on the reversed horizontal-vertical discrimination with each eye. The remaining five pigeons received binocular green-red discrimination training with green S^D and the reverse red-green discrimination training with the left eye and with the right eye. One daily training session was carried out with only one of the three eye conditions, and the eye condition for the daily training was quasirandomly alternated, that is, one eye condition never continued for 3 days. The criterion of discrimination was 90% of the correct response ratio in the session after the session on the different discrimination task. The training continued until the subject attained the criterion or until 60 sessions of training were completed. Then the subjects received the stimulus control test under the three eye conditions.

Results and Discussion

Table 16-3 summarizes the number of sessions required to reach the criterion. Although pigeons 75923 and 76901 failed to attain the criterion with the left eye, the correct response ratio in the last session with the left eye was 85% in both subjects. The other eight subjects were able to learn the tasks. Thus, they showed establishment of a conditional discrimination in which the binocular or monocular eye condition determined the polarity of discrimination.

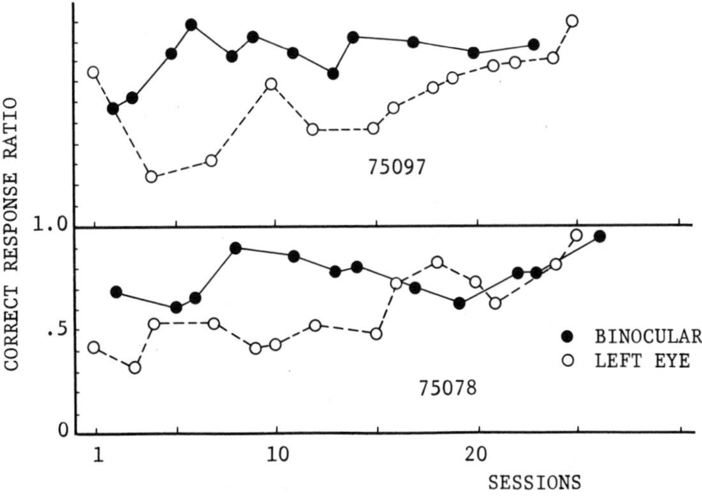

Figure 16-3. Discriminative learning curves in the second experiment. Closed circles represent performance with both eyes; open circles, performance with the left eye.

Table 16-3. Number of Sessions Required to Reach the Criterion and Results of the Stimulus Control Test in the Third Experiment[a]

	Sessions to Criterion[a]				Stimulus Control Test[b]								
					Binocular			*Left Eye*			*Right Eye*		
Subjects	*Binocular*	*Left Eye*	*Right Eye*	*Total*	*V*	*H*	*V/V+H*	*H*	*V*	*H/H+V*	*H*	*V*	*H/H+V*
75920	12 (7)	16 (16)	14 (14)	42 (37)	171	1	0.99	235	9	0.96	162	7	0.96
75923	12 (11)	20 (20)	17 (16)	49 (47)	381	14	0.96	173	13	0.93	282	9	0.97
75926	13 (9)	10 (9)	6 (4)	29 (22)	709	84	0.89	306	15	0.95	101	3	0.97
75901	19 (19)	20 (20)	18 (9)	57 (48)	129	1	0.99	264	89	0.75	432	65	0.87
76906	16 (10)	12 (9)	12 (12)	40 (31)	114	4	0.97	147	5	0.97	262	3	0.99
					G	*R*	*G/G+R*	*R*	*G*	*R/R+G*	*R*	*G*	*R/G+R*
75934	10 (10)	10 (7)	10 (7)	30 (24)	422	6	0.99	670	24	0.97	382	3	0.99
76903	7 (3)	10 (7)	7 (6)	24 (16)	352	14	0.96	118	0	1.00	97	0	1.00
76904	18 (16)	10 (3)	19 (15)	47 (34)	495	70	0.88	78	39	0.67	140	117	0.54
76907	12 (8)	20 (10)	11 (9)	43 (27)	390	27	0.94	265	16	0.94	177	4	0.98
76908	15 (15)	15 (2)	8 (8)	38 (25)	150	19	0.89	58	16	0.78	20	5	0.80
Mean	13.4 (12.1)	13.0 (7.9)	12.2 (10.0)	39.9 (31.1)	331.3	24.0	0.946	231.4	22.6	0.892	205.5	21.6	0.907

[a] The criterion was a 90% correct response ratio after the session on the different task. The number in ( ) indicates the sessions in which the 90% correct response ratio was first reached.

[b] V, H, G, and R indicate the number of responses emitted for the vertical line, for the horizontal line, for the green key, and for the red key, respectively.

There is no significant difference between the binocular condition and each monocular condition in the number of sessions required to reach the criterion. However, because the subjects were trained on the monocular horizontal-vertical discrimination with the right eye and with the left eye, the number of sessions required to learn the monocular horizontal-vertical discrimination was about twice the number of sessions required to learn the binocular vertical-horizontal discrimination. Therefore, a quantitative difference of acquisition of discrimination with both or separate eyes was obtained. A similar quantitative difference of performance with both hemispheres or with one hemisphere was reported with split-brain cats but not with intact cats (13,20).

Table 16-3 also represents the results of the stimulus control test. All subjects, except for pigeon 76904 in the test with the right eye, demonstrated clear discriminative behavior in each test. The two subjects that failed to attain the criterion also showed clear discrimination. The difference in rate of responding using both eyes or one eye could be observed in six subjects.

Representative examples of discriminative learning curves are illustrated in Figure 16-4. Mutual disturbance of learning of two tasks, described in the first experiment, can be observed between the binocular and the monocular learnings. In the case of a similar training with an external cue for conditional discrimination, mutual disturbance was not observed in most of the subjects (26).

EXPERIMENT 4

In this experiment, pigeons were trained on an intradimensional discrimination binocularly, on an excitatory interdimensional discrimination with the right eye, and on an inhibitory interdimensional discrimination with the left eye.

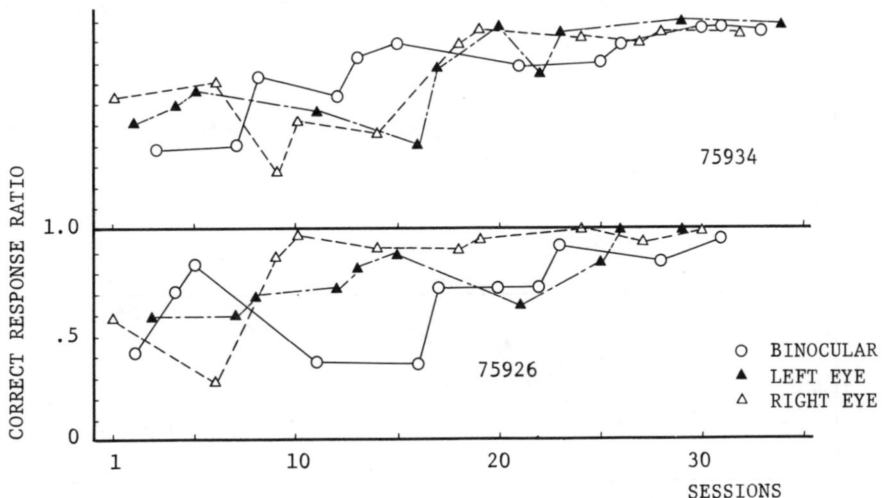

Figure 16-4. Discriminative learning curves in the third experiment. Open circles indicate performance with both eyes, closed triangles that with the left eye, and open triangles that with the right eye.

Method

Ten pigeons were used in this experiment. Five were binocularly trained on a vertical-horizontal discrimination in which the vertical line on the dark key was S^D, on a white-vertical discrimination with the left eye in which the key illuminated with plain white light was S^D, and on a horizontal-white discrimination with the left eye in which the horizontal line on the dark key was S^D. The remaining five pigeons were trained on a green-red discrimination binocularly, on a vertical-green discrimination with the left eye, and on a red-vertical discrimination with the right eye. In each case, the line stimulus was presented on a dark background.

The eye condition for daily training was alternated in the same manner as in the third experiment. The criterion of discrimination was identical to that in the third experiment. After the training, the subjects received a stimulus control test with S^D and S^Δ.

Results and Discussion

Table 16-4 represents the number of sessions required to reach the criterion. Nine subjects showed slower acquisition of the task for the left eye. There is a significant difference between the number of sessions with both eyes and that with the left eye and between the number of sessions with the right eye and with the left eye ($P < 0.05$, Sign test). Accomplishment of the tasks in the present experiment means that the pigeons discriminated the three viewing conditions and established their discriminative behavior based on that discrimination.

The results of the stimulus control test are also represented in Table 16-4. All subjects showed clear discriminative behavior for each task. A difference in rate of responding between the binocular condition and the monocular condition could not be observed in this experiment.

Examples of discriminative learning curves are represented in Figure 16-5. Most the subjects showed parallel progress of three learnings, as represented by pigeons 75928

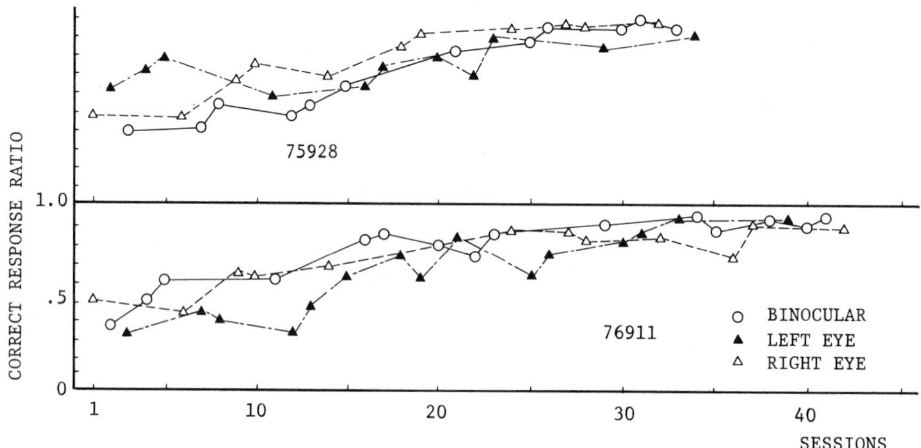

Figure 16-5. Discriminative learning curves in the fourth experiment. Open circles represent performance with both eyes, closed triangles that with the left eye, and open triangles that with the right eye.

Table 16-4. Number of Sessions Required to Reach the Criterion and Results of the Stimulus Control Test in the Fourth Experiment

	Sessions to Criterion[a]				Stimulus Control Test[b]								
					Binocular			Left Eye			Right Eye		
Subjects	*Binocular*	*Left Eye*	*Right Eye*	*Total*	*V*	*H*	*V/V+H*	*W*	*V*	*W/W+V*	*H*	*W*	*H/H+W*
75927	12 (12)	19 (19)	8 (8)	39 (39)	319	119	0.73	348	59	0.86	418	8	0.98
75928	10 (9)	10 (8)	8 (7)	28 (24)	456	3	0.99	365	150	0.71	566	26	0.96
75929	7 (7)	7 (7)	7 (7)	21 (21)	676	70	0.91	780	232	0.77	503	19	0.96
75925	5 (4)	6 (6)	5 (3)	16 (13)	443	86	0.84	395	17	0.96	636	8	0.99
76913	13 (13)	16 (16)	4 (4)	33 (33)	219	28	0.94	601	30	0.95	436	23	0.95
					G	*R*	*R/R+G*	*V*	*G*	*V/V+G*	*R*	*V*	*R/R+V*
76911	10 (10)	14 (14)	12 (11)	36 (35)	342	20	0.94	363	9	0.98	354	11	0.97
76910	13 (13)	18 (18)	13 (13)	44 (44)	123	3	0.98	140	24	0.85	223	17	0.93
76905	13 (4)	13 (11)	13 (13)	39 (28)	141	14	0.91	195	5	0.98	85	3	0.97
76909	7 (7)	20 (20)	19 (19)	46 (46)	340	3	0.99	263	29	0.90	339	32	0.91
76912	19 (11)	17 (4)	20 (20)	56 (35)	603	21	0.97	132	12	0.92	649	17	0.97
Mean	10.9 (10.3)	13.3 (11.4)	9.9 (9.4)	35.8 (31.8)	366.2	36.7	0.920	358.2	56.7	0.888	420.9	16.4	0.959

[a] The number in ( ) indicates the number of sessions.

[b] V, H, G, R, and W indicate the number of responses for the vertical line, for the horizontal line, for the green key, for the red key, and for the white key, respectively.

and 76911. Dominant learning of the task for the binocular condition was observed in one subject, and dominant learning with the right eye was observed in another.

SUPPLEMENTARY EXPERIMENT

In this experiment, learning of conflict discrimination without the cue of the eye condition was examined. That is, pigeons were trained on discrimination tasks identical to those in the previous experiments with fixed-eye condition.

Method

Eight pigeons were divided into two groups described below. Table 16-5 gives the discrimination tasks for each subject. In the first group, the subjects were trained on two discriminations alternatively in accordance with the Gellerman series. This group is a control group for experiments 1 to 3. The subjects in the second group were trained on three discriminations alternatively in the same manner as in the fourth experiment. This group is a control group for the fourth experiment. Training was conducted for 40 or 60 sessions. Then the subjects received a stimulus control test with S^D and S^Δ. Because the two tasks in the first group differed with respect to the order of stimulus presentation during the training, the test was carried out twice with the reversed order of stimulus presentation.

Table 16-5. Discrimination Tasks in the Supplementary Experiment[a]

		Task 1		*Task 2*		*Task 3*	
Subjects	*Eye*	S^D	S^Δ	S^D	S^Δ	S^D	S^Δ
1st							
74916	R(40)	V	H	H	V		
76829	B(60)	V	H	H	V		
76999	L(60)	G	R	R	G		
76927	B(60)	G	R	R	G		
2nd							
76926	L(60)	V	H	H	W	W	V
76929	B(60)	V	H	H	W	W	V
76821	L(60)	G	R	R	V	V	G
76920	B(60)	G	R	R	V	V	G

[a] R, L, and B in the *Eye* column indicate the right eye, the left eye, and the binocular conditions, respectively. The number in ( ) represents the number of sessions. V, H, G, R, and W in the *Task* column represent the vertical line, the horizontal line, the green key, the red key, and the white key, respectively.

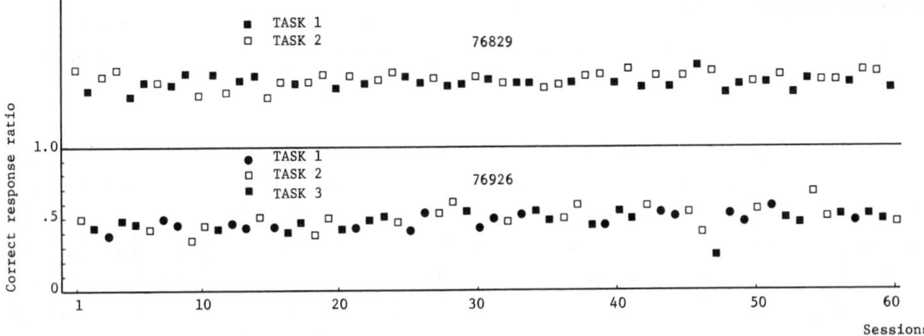

Figure 16-6. Daily performance in the supplementary experiment. Pigeon 76829 received conflicting vertical-horizontal discrimination training; and pigeon 76926 received vertical-horizontal discrimination training, horizontal-white discrimination training, and white-vertical discrimination training.

Results and Discussion

All subjects were unable to accomplish the conflict discrimination. Figure 16-6 demonstrates the representative examples of daily correct response ratio. No improvement was observed.

Table 16-6 shows the results of the stimulus control test. The subjects in the first group showed change level performance, but pigeons 76920 and 76929 in the second group showed correct response ratios above chance level in one or two tasks. However, no subjects showed high correct response ratios in all three tasks. These results support the conclusion that the discriminative behavior obtained in the previous experiments was based on the eye condition.

Table 16-6. Results of the Stimulus Control Test in the Supplementary Experiment[a]

	Task 1			*Task 2*			*Task 3*		
Subjects	S^D	S^Δ	%	S^D	S^Δ	%	S^D	S^Δ	%
1st									
74016	136	205	40	251	424	37			
76829	242	299	45	359	263	58			
76999	207	126	62	86	67	56			
76927	258	247	51	182	187	49			
2nd									
76926	415	276	60	169	141	55	181	198	48
76929	205	45	82	252	59	81	282	213	57
76821	80	126	39	192	72	73	88	62	59
76920	187	301	38	245	288	46	264	36	88

[a] S^D and S^Δ, respectively, indicate the number of responses emitted for S^D and S^Δ in the test session.

CONCLUSION

Because an assumption of separate formation of memory in each hemisphere cannot be applied to the case in the third and the fourth experiments, I conclude that the pigeons can learn the conditional discrimination in which the eye condition is a cue. However, the nature of the cue is not clear. Pigeons have a narrow binocular visual field (15°), so discriminative behavior found in the first experiment may be based on discrimination between the right and the left monocular visual fields. But in the third experiment, the pigeons received equivalent training with the right eye and with the left eye and contradictory training with both eyes. Thus, they could not use the difference of the left or the right monocular visual field as a cue for conditional discrimination. However, they might attend to stimulus in the monocular visual field regardless of its side during the monocular training and to stimulus in the binocular visual field during the binocular training. But these explanations are only speculative; in fact, the manipulation of the pigeons' viewing condition provides the pigeons sufficient information to control their discriminative behavior.

In the other experiments, I found that manipulation of the viewing condition had effects similar to change of stimulus outside the subject on operant behavior. Watanabe (22) trained pigeons on a monocular fixed interval (FI) schedule. After the subjects attained a steady state of performance, the eye used for the training was changed to the naive side. The postreinforcement pause of responding, which is a feature of FI-controlled behavior, disappeared in the transition state with the untrained eye. A similar effect could be obtained by change of color displayed on the pecking key.

In another experiment, I trained pigeons monocularly on a reaction time task and obtained a skewed distribution of reaction times similar to a Gamma distribution. Change of the eye used in the training or change of the stimulus displayed on the key flattened the distribution of reaction times.

Both the experiments described above support the formation of conditional discrimination with eye condition as the cue.

REFERENCES

1. Catania AC: Techniques for the control of monocular and binocular viewing in the pigeon. *J Exp Anal Behav* 6:627–629, 1963.
2. Catania AC: Interocular transfer of discrimination in the pigeon. *J Exp Anal Behav* 8:147–155, 1965.
3. Ingle D: Interocular integration of visual learning by goldfish. *Brain Behav Evol* 1:58–85.
4. Konnerman VG: Monokulare Dressur von Hausgäsen, z.T. mit gegengesettzer Merkmalsbedeutung für beide Augen. *Z Tierpsychol* 23:553–580, 1966.
5. Lee-Teng E: Visual discrimination versus visuo-motor learning in interocular transfer in fish. *Psychon Sci* 5:209–210, 1966.
6. Levine J: Studies in the interrelations of central nervous structures in binocular vision. *J Gen Psychol* 67:105–142, 1945.
7. MacClearly RA, Longfellow LA: Interocular transfer of pattern discrimination without prior binocular experience. *Science* 134:1418–1419, 1961.
8. Mello N, Frevin FR, Stanley C: Intertectal integration of visual information in pigeons. *Bol Inst Estud Biol Mex* 21:519–533, 1963.
9. Myers RE: Function of corpus callosum in interocular transfer *Brain* 79:358–363, 1956.

10. Myers RE: Interhemispheric communication through corpus callosum: limitation under condition of conflict. *J Comp Physiol Psychol* 52:6–9, 1959.

11. Myers RE: Transmission of visual information within and between the hemispheres: A behavioral study, in Mountcastle (ed): *Interhemispheric Relations and Cerebral Dominance.* Baltimore, Johns Hopkins Press, 1962.

12. Ogawa T: Interocular generalization on color stimuli in pigeons. *Ann Anim Psychol* 16:87–102, 1966.

13. Robinson JS, Voneida TJ: Quantitative differences in performance on abstract discrimination using one or both hemispheres. *Exp Neurol* 26:72–83, 1970.

14. Schneider AM: Control of memory by spreading cortical depression. *Psychol Rev* 74:201–215, 1967.

15. Shapiro SM: Interocular transfer of pattern discrimination in the goldfish. *Amer J Psychol* 78:21–38, 1965.

16. Sheridan CL: Interocular interaction of conflicting discrimination habits in the albino rats: a preliminary report. *Psychon Sci* 3:303–304, 1965.

17. Sperry RW: Corpus callosum and interhemispheric transfer in the monkey. *Anat Rec* 131:297, 1958.

18. Sperry RW: Some development in brain lesion studies of learning. *Fed Proc* 20:609–616, 1961.

19. Trevarthen CB: Double visual learning in split-brain monkeys. *Science* 136:258–259, 1962.

20. Voneida TJ, Robinson JS: Effect of brain bisection on capacity for cross comparison of patterned visual input. *Exp Neurol* 26:60–71, 1970.

21. Watanabe S: Interocular transfer of stimulus control in pigeons. *Ann Anim Psychol* 24:1–14, 1974.

22. Watanabe S: Interocular transfer of learning in pigeons: an analysis with FI schedule. *Proc. 38th Ann Congr JPA*, 1974, 1216–1217 (in Japanese).

23. Watanabe S: Interocular transfer of generalization along line-tilt dimension in pigeons.*Jap Psychol Res* 17:113–140, 1975.

24. Watanabe S: Interocular transfer of learning in pigeons: An analysis of reaction time, in: *Collection of Papers Dedicated to Keizo Hayashi.* 1977, pp 69–77.

25. Watanabe S: The mirror image discrimination with each eye in pigeons. *Physiol Behav* 22:331–337, 1979.

26. Watanabe, S: Conditional discrimination both with the external cue and the viewing condition cue in pigeons. *Behav Brain Res* 1 (in press).

AUTHOR INDEX

Note: Numbers in parentheses are reference numbers and indicate that the author's work is referred to although his name is not mentioned in the text. Numbers in *italics* show the pages on which the complete references are listed.

SUBJECT INDEX